Karolinum Press

Martin C. Putna
Rus – Ukraine – Russia
Scenes from the Cultural History of Russian Religiosity

VÁCLAV HAVEL SERIES

Martin C. Putna

Rus
Ukraine
Russia

Scenes from the Cultural
History of Russian Religiosity

KAROLINUM PRESS

KAROLINUM PRESS
Karolinum Press is a publishing department of Charles University
Ovocný trh 560/5, 116 36 Prague 1, Czech Republic
www.karolinum.cz

Originally published in Czech as *Obrazy z kulturních dějin ruské religiozity*,
Prague: Vyšehrad, 2015
Czech edition reviewed by Vratislav Doubek (Department of Political Science,
Faculty of Arts, Charles University, Prague), Alena Machoninová (Department
of Slavic Languages and Cultures, Lomonosov Moscow State University)

Cover and graphic design by /3.dílna/
Frontispiece photo author's archive
Set and printed in the Czech Republic by Karolinum Press
First English edition

Cataloging-in-Publication Data is available from the National Library
of the Czech Republic

ISBN 978-80-246-3580-4
ISBN 978-80-246-3581-1 (pdf)
ISBN 978-80-246-4739-5 (epub)
ISBN 978-80-246-4738-8 (mobi)

CONTENTS

INTRODUCTION

Czech Perspectives on the Cultural and Spiritual Roots of Russia

This book is being written at a time when the Czechs' relationship to Russia has again become a question, one that concerns the country's internal norms and its place in Europe. It is being written as Russia vigorously asserts its claims in Ukraine and, no less vigorously thought by different means, reasserts its influence in Central Europe and thus in the Czech lands as well. One part of Czech society expresses shock at these developments, the other part trivializes Russia's actions or even supports them as part of a desirable process that is historically and morally justified. Both sides appeal in their arguments to historical experience, referring to Russian mentality and its roots as well as to the history of Russian-Czech relations. While this Czech book about Russia avoids direct engagement with contemporary politics, it does seek to provide a more systematic interpretation of those historical experiences and to describe the spiritual and cultural roots from which the present situation has arisen.

In the long history of Czech thinking about Russia's spiritual roots, there have been several different traditions. First among them is romantic Russophilism. It arises from the idea of a genetic and historically fatalistic bond connecting all those nations which speak Slavic languages. Russophiles admire the power of the Russian state and the hierarchical structure of Russian society; they desire as strong a Russian influence as possible in the Czech lands, even direct annexation of their country by Russia. This tradition was born of European romanticism in the early nineteenth century and its spirit pervaded the scientific and artistic creations of that era.

The canonical expression of early Czech Russophilism in this sense was provided by Jan Kollár's epic poem, *The Daughter of*

Sláva (*Slávy dcera*). In typically romantic fashion, Kollár considered himself no less a scientist than a poet, expressing in verse the same truths revealed in his etymological and archaeological studies.[1]

Kollár's ideas contributed to the development of the Czech National Revival during the early nineteenth century. His ideas were picked up in literature by many writers not normally considered particularly Slavophile: one might for example consider the many Russian motifs in the work of Julius Zeyer.[2] Slavic scholars of greater caliber than Kollár developed his ideas further.[3] In the twentieth century Kollár's thinking was adopted in cultural and political writings by authors of a national-conservative persuasion: texts by Josef Holeček emphasizing the supposed moral purity of the Russian people,[4] Karel Kramář's project of "neo-Slavism" with its vision of a Slavic federation headed by Russia,[5] Rudolf Medek and his experiences as a Russian legionnaire,[6] or Karel VI Schwarzenberg's references to the genealogical and heraldic ties between the ruling dynasties of Bohemia and Russia.[7] This tradition retreated to the background during the communist era and survived on the margins in exile—only to emerge more recently on the extreme right-wing of the political spectrum.[8]

A second tradition was born of Czech liberal-democratic orientation and observed Russia with equally great interest, but did in a way

1   Cf. Jan Kollár, *Slávy dcera: Báseň lyricko-epická v pěti zpěvích*, with commentary by Martin C. Putna (Prague: Academia, 2014).

2   Cf. Janina Viskovatá, *Ruské motivy v tvorbě Julia Zeyera* (Prague: Slovanský ústav, 1932).

3   Cf. Milan Kudělka, *O pojetí slavistiky: Vývoj představ o jejím předmětu a podstatě* (Prague: Academia, 1984).

4   Cf. Josef Holeček, *Rusko-české kapitoly* (Prague: privately printed, 1891).

5   Cf. Ljobov Běloševská and Zdeněk Sládek, eds., *Karel Kramář: Studie a dokumenty* (Prague: Slovanský ústav, 2003).

6   Cf. Katya Kocourek, *Čechoslovakista Rudolf Medek: Politický životopis* (Prague: Mladá fronta, 2011).

7   Cf. Martin C. Putna, ed., *Karel VI Schwarzenberg: Torzo díla* (Prague: Torst, 2007).

8   Cf. *Proti Proud: Kontrarevoluční magazín Petra Hájka*, protiproud.parlamentnilisty.cz, accessed June 9, 2015.

that was critical and analytical. A "forerunner" of this perspective was the first modern author from Bohemia to spend time in Russia, Count Joachim von Sternberg, who had experienced life there while traveling with priest and linguist Josef Dobrovský. In his narrative of the journey, *Bemerkungen über Russland* (Remarks about Russia, 1794), the author wrote of his shock at the inhumane treatment of the Russian people.[9] But it was not until Karel Havlíček penned his Pictures from Russia (*Obrazy z Rus*), published serially in the 1840s, that the "realistic" Czech approach to Russia received its foundational text. Based on the author's long sojourn in Russia among the Slavophiles of Moscow, Havlíček clearly demonstrated that neither the tsarist regime nor Russian mentality could provide a model for Czechs to follow at home. The greater part of Czech society, with Palacký at its head, arrived at a similar conclusion after witnessing tsarist armies crush "the springtime of peoples" in Europe.[10]

Havlíček toyed with the idea of writing an original history of Russia in Czech, but he never found time for more than a collection of essayistic observations. What Havlíček originally intended, T.G. Masaryk brought to completion with his work *Rusko a Evropa* (1913–1919, originally published in German as *Russland und Europa*, in English as *The Spirit of Russia*), a systematic, scholarly and in-depth analysis grounded above all in Russian literature and religious (as well as anti-religious) philosophy. While many of the details found in Masaryk's study have since become outdated, the work's enduring value consists in its distinction between two currents in Russian mentality: the nationalistic-theocratic-autocratic and the liberal-critical-democratic. However, when considering present events these currents can no longer be categorized according to

9   Cf. Vladimir Andrejevič Francev, *Cesta J. Dobrovského a hraběte J. Šternberka do Ruska v letech 1792–1793* (Prague: Unie, 1923).

10   Cf. František Stellner and Radek Soběhart, "Rusko jako hrozba? Vytváření negativního obrazu Ruska u české veřejnosti v letech 1848–1849" in *19. století v nás: Modely, instituce a reprezentace, které přetrvaly*, ed. Milan Řepa (Prague: Historický ústav, 2008), 554–566.

Masaryk's original labels "Muscovite" and "Saint Petersburgian." Those Czechs familiar with the literature considered the work by the Russian historian and liberal politician Pavel Milyukov, Studies in the history of Russian culture (*Ocherki po istorii russkoi kultury*, translated into Czech as *Obrazy z dějin ruské vzdělanosti* between 1902 and 1910), to be a Russian parallel to Masaryk's analysis.

Many Czech historians and publicists continued to develop Masaryk's line of thought, most notably Jan Slavík. One result of Masaryk's attention to democratic currents in Russia was the Russian Action, an extensive relief operation to support exiles who left the country following the Bolshevik coup of 1917.[11] The literary scholar Václav Černý provided a distinctive postscript to Masaryk's volume with his study *Vývoj a zločiny panslavismu* (The development and crimes of pan-Slavism). Černý wrote the work at the beginning of the 1950s, though it would not be published until 1993, after the author's death. Composed in the early days of Czech vassalage to the USSR, the work bears the mark of passionate indignation.[12] According to Černý's dark vision, a direct path leads from naively romantic pan-Slavism, which arose in Russia as a response to German and Czech influences (Herder and Kollár),[13] right up to the ideological justifications of the Soviet Union's incursion.

The third tradition concerns the culture of Czech Catholicism. In this instance, too, one can identify a "forerunner": baroque Slavism, or the interest taken by seventeenth-century Catholic (but also Protestant) scholars in Bohemia, Poland, and Hungary in the historical ties between Slavic-speaking peoples, and above all their interest in Russia. Many looked to Russia for deliverance from the

---

11 Cf. Václav Veber, ed., *Ruská a ukrajinská emigrace v ČSR v letech 1918–1945* (Prague: Karolinum, 1996).

12 The study was first published by the journal *Střední Evropa* in 1993, as a book in 1995 and again in 2011. See Václav Černý, *Vývoj a zločiny panslavismu* (Prague: Václav Havel Library, 2011).

13 Though Russian pan-Slavism with its vision of the powerful state as the carrier of a spiritual message can also be traced back to the thinking of Hegel.

Turkish menace—and a possible destination for Catholic (and Protestant) missionaries.[14] In the nineteenth century Catholic Unionism followed in the footsteps of baroque Slavism. It was a movement that adopted as its proximate goal the study of Russian religious traditions. Its aim was to unite the Roman Catholic and Orthodox Churches (Scene 14). In the Czech lands, Unionism flourished more than anywhere else in Moravia among revivalist circles gathered around the person of František Sušil. Its symbolic center was Velehrad, once the seat of the mission of Sts Cyril and Methodius, whom Unionism understood as models for a Slavic-speaking church not yet divided into antagonistic Eastern and Western parts.[15]

While it is true that Unionism did not arouse mass sympathy for Catholicism among Russians, it did engender a large quantity of scientific and cultural material in the fields of Russian, Slavic, and Byzantine studies. In the form of translations and commentaries, Unionism introduced an abundance of texts from Kievan and Muscovite Orthodox culture (or their echoes in modern culture), texts with which the representatives of liberal trends, such as Havlíček and Masaryk, had little patience. The philologist and Catholic priest Josef Vašica was the prime mover of this cultural transfer. Thanks to him, Russian spiritual texts became a dominant feature of Josef Florian's Catholic publishing program in Stará Říše.[16] One of them, the publishing house of Ladislav Kuncíř, released a book in 1930 titled *Duch ruské církve* (The spirit of the Russian church), a first attempt at the comprehensive treatment of Russia's older spiritual history. Written in Czech and adopting a Unionist standpoint, the work emphasized those personalities and currents of thought that

14   Cf. Rudo Brtáň, *Barokový slavizmus: Porovnávacia štúdia z dejín slovanskej slovesnosti* (Liptovský Sv. Mikuláš: Tranoscius, 1939).
15   Cf. Michal Altrichter, *Velehrad: filologoi versus filosofoi* (Olomouc: Refugium Velehrad-Roma, 2005).
16   Cf. Libuše Heczková, "Rozanov a ti druzí: Rozhovor s Andrejem Stankovičem," *Volné sdružení českých rusistů* 8 (1992): 65–67.

aimed to unite the Eastern and Western Churches. Its author was a Russian exile, the publicist Valerij Vilinskij. Although his later fate caused some controversy,[17] Vilinskij's work played a role for sympathizers of the Czech-Catholic take on Russia not unlike that played by Milyukov in liberal circles.

Needless to say, these views were removed from public sight along with the rest of Catholic culture after the communist seizure of power in 1948. From the 1960s, however, they began to appear again, at least marginally, in the tolerated "gray zone." Scholars of Church Slavonic or Byzantium, for example, were permitted to have their work published by Vyšehrad, a publisher that released series of translations of medieval legends and other mainly religious texts of eastern Christendom.[18] Other scholars chose exile. At least two, both of them Catholic priests, won renown abroad for propagating the understanding of Russian religious culture and eastern Christianity more generally: the Byzantine scholar František Dvorník[19] and the popularizer of eastern, especially monastic, spirituality, Tomáš Špidlík.[20] The latter was a close acquaintance of Pope Karol Wojtyła. Špidlík's appointment to Cardinal in 2003 was intended to demonstrate the church's official interest in the spiritual traditions of Orthodoxy. It was by way of Špidlík and Wojtyła that sympathy for Orthodoxy arrived to the Czech lands, where it has exerted a considerable influence since the 1990s.

The fourth tradition is that of the Czech left, which began looking with hope to Russia in 1917, the year of the Bolshevik take-over. This tradition found cultural expression in emphatic odes to Lenin and the revolution penned by first-rate authors like J. Wolker,

---

[17] Cf. Anne Hultsch, *Ein Russe in der Tschechoslowakei: Leben und Werk des Publizisten Valerij S. Vilinskij, 1901–1955* (Köln: Böhlau, 2011).

[18] Cf. Pravomil Novák et al., *Sborník 70 let nakladatelství Vyšehrad* (Prague: Vyšehrad, 2004).

[19] Cf. Ludvík Němec, *Francis Dvorník: Mistr historické syntézy* (Olomouc: Refugium Velehrad-Roma, 2013).

[20] Cf. Tomáš Špidlík, *Spiritualita křesťanského Východu* (Olomouc: Refugium Velehrad-Roma, 2002).

V. Nezval, F. Halas, and V. Holan, or in uncritical accounts of "building socialism" in the USSR, the tone for which was set by Julius Fučík's book *O zemi, kde zítra již znamená včera* (In the land where tomorrow is already yesterday). In scholarship, the tradition found expression in the obedient acceptance of theses put forward by official "Soviet science" in the USSR about the political and cultural history or Russia and the Czech lands. Political and artistic attitudes that before 1948 had been counted as private matters after 1948 became tests of loyalty to the regime in power, entry tickets into public life. The great paradox is that however much this new culture and science wished to emphasized its novel break with the traditions of pre-revolutionary Russia (tsarism, religiosity, reaction, and backwardness), it was in fact permeated by the tradition of Russophilia. Its exponents emphasized the superiority of Russian history, Russian culture, and the Russian nation. But "Soviet science" could never obscure the fact that it was, in truth, the heir of romantic-era "Slavic science."

The fifth tradition emerged from polemics with the fourth, developing as it were within the womb of the latter. Some members of the interwar left reconsidered their enthusiasm for Soviet Russia after confronting its underside. An example of this waning enthusiasm are the novels written by Jiří Weil, whose books *Moskva-hranice* (Moscow-border, 1937) and *Dřevěná lžíce* (The wooden spoon, published posthumously in 1992) offer a literary depiction of Stalinist terror. During the communist era in Czechoslovakia, Russian studies were elevated to the status of a privileged scholarly and cultural discipline that drew many Czech intellectuals into its orbit, albeit not always voluntarily. In other words, there were among the Russianists some who engaged with their subject in a "subterraneous" manner: scholars who resuscitated marginalized, forgotten, or repressed authors; who recovered lost intellectual trends and values, presenting them to the public under the guise of disseminating "fraternal Russian culture." They did so as much as was permitted by the cultural politics of the regime. When this sort of subterfuge proved unworkable, finished texts were set aside for publication as samizdat.

With regard to this tendency, mention should be made of Jan Zábrana, a poet who was allowed to work as a translator in the "gray zone"—but who at the same time helped translate Solzhenitsyn's *Gulag Archipelago* into Czech for samizdat, noting with bitterness in his diary how revolting he found "Byzantine Asiaticism, characteristic not only of Stalin, but of Russian mentality generally—Chaadaev knew that about his compatriots already."[21] Mention must also be made of Karel Štindl, who by contrast directly joined the dissidents and translated the works of Russian religious authors. One should mention Miluše Zadražilová, who translated and composed epilogues together with her husband Ladislav Zadražil, although her name was no longer permitted to appear in print after 1968. Zadražilová simultaneously maintained secret contact with Russian dissidents inside the USSR and in exile (Scene 19).

After the fall of the communist regime in 1989, Zadražilová and her husband, Karel Štindl and other Russianists of the "gray zone" or dissident circles arrived—or returned—as instructors in the department of Russian Studies at Prague's Philosophical Faculty. Once there, they began to foster a new conception of Czech Russian studies: the Czech Russianist should not be one who loves, admires, and propagates all things Russian. Above all, he should not be a supporter of Russian or Soviet imperialism. The Czech Russianist should be intimately familiar with the Russian cultural context and, as a consequence, be able to evaluate it critically. The Czech Russianist should support those people and values in Russia that stand on the side of individual freedom against the regime, against state terror, against hollow institutions, against the repression of freedom of conscience and expression. It was of secondary importance whether these individuals and their values hailed from the liberal

---

21 Jan Zábrana, *Celý život: Výbor z deníků 1948–1984* (Prague: Torst, 2001), 440.

tradition (in the spirit of Havlíček or Masaryk), from the religious tradition (in the spirit of Vašica or Špidlík), from the tradition of leftwing social criticism, or whether they maintained an ironic, postmodern distance from all preceding values.

I passed through this school myself and, like many others, I initially found myself having become an "involuntary" Russianist. From the mid-1990s, when I began to turn my attention to topics beyond the field of Russian studies, I repeatedly ran up against the problem of Czech perceptions of Russia: in my work on the history of Czech Catholic literature and the Unionist tradition of Sušil and Vašica; in my study about Václav Havel's reception of the liberal-critical tradition of Masaryk and Černý; when working through the legacy of Karel VI Schwarzenberg and also upon composing a commentary to Kollár's *Slávy dcera* about the tradition of romantic Russophilism. Thus instructed, I now return by way of detour, motivated by the intention to address one of Czech society's urgent needs as well as by a feeling of gratitude to my former teachers and the desire to repay old debts by means of the present book.

✕✕✕

This Czech book about Russia is titled "scenes from the cultural history of Russian religiosity." The title is meant to recall Havlíček's *Pictures from Russia* and Milyukov's *Studies in the History of Russian Culture*. But above all, it follows my earlier book, *Obrazy z kulturních dějin americké religiozity* (Scenes from the cultural history of American religiosity).22 As in that volume, this book arranges vast and complicated material—material which might have threatened to become too unwieldy or to take on the proportions of Masaryk's *Spirit of Russia*—into a collection of "scenes." Each "scene" represents a chosen moment, a point in Russian history when an event of fundamental significance occurred within some spiritual current

---

22 Martin C. Putna, *Obrazy z kulturních dějin americké religiozity* (Prague: Vyšehrad, 2010).

or movement, an event directly or indirectly reflected in some particular cultural object, an object which itself in turn shaped the further development of Russian spirituality.

The crucial importance of literary works for the comprehension of developments in Russia has been demonstrated many times over. In Russia, where beyond a few brief epochs and happy exceptions an open and free public life has never existed, let alone an open and free political life, literature played an even more important role as medium for social reflection than it did in Central or Western Europe, to say nothing of America. For that matter, Masaryk's *Russia and Europe* also considered Russian literature as the key to understanding Russian spiritual life. As with Masaryk, the objective here is not so much to offer an aesthetic analysis of Russian literary works and artistic creations (there are plenty of those already) as it is to examine how these works document spiritual trends. The concern is with the scenes chosen and the works selected; some classic authors will be addressed only marginally, others not at all, while in some scenes the more "marginal" works will prove the most illustrative.

As a method, this approach to "setting the scene" comes with certain risks. Many important personalities, works, and events are of necessity left out (this book is not and does not want to be a substitute for a history of Russian literature or of the church in Russia). Nor does the method necessarily prevent one from drowning in the material—it is enough to recall Alexander Solzhenitsyn suffocating in his attempt to structure the history of the Russian Revolution into similar historical "junctures" in his voluminous, and never completed, cycle *The Red Wheel* (1984–1991, see Conclusion). Solzhenitsyn's attempt should thus serve as a warning and admonishment to single out that which, from the perspective of the book's conception, represents—put biblically—the *unum necessarium.*

But what is the *unum necessarium,* the "one thing necessary?" Five basic thoughts run through the individual "scenes" which comprise this book, scenes that I consider necessary for understanding

Russia's spiritual past and, by means of them, understanding Russia's present, politics included.

The first three are "negative"—they consist of reversing the ideological trinity of Russian imperialism, a motto formulated in 1833 by the tsar's minister of education, Count Sergei Uvarov (Scene 15): autocracy, orthodoxy, and nationality. The motto is clear and intelligible as a political program—formulated in full awareness that it was to force into its image a reality to which it did not at all correspond.

First: a single Russia with a single, immutable identity has never existed. Rather there existed several distinct formations, each one with a separate regional center and cultural trajectory: Kievan Rus, Novgorodian Rus, Lithuanian Rus, Muscovite Rus, Ukrainian Rus and Belarus, and the exile "Russia beyond Russia." The word "Russian" itself contains multiple, mutually exclusive meanings. It is usually identified with the Muscovite state and its imperial successors right up through the USSR and the empire of Vladimir Putin. But such an association is an "Uvarovian" simplification. One can only understand the ambiguity and contradictions of that which we call "Russianness" after recognizing the many and varied traditions of Rus.

Second: never in its history has "Russianness" been identical with Orthodoxy. On the one hand, Orthodoxy itself was never so unchanging in its cultural forms (Scene 4). On the other hand, there were contacts with Roman Catholicism and Protestantism, Uniatism or Greek Catholicism. There were individual attempts to combine confessional identities, as in various forms of domestic "heterodoxy" from the ultra-Slav Old Believers to radical "sectarians", or as in Judaism and esoteric beliefs. These all belong to the cultural history of Russia. The dynamism of Russian culture does not arise from some single, permanent Orthodoxy—to the contrary, it comes from religious plurality.

Third: never in its history has Russian culture been ethnically homogenous. The Scandinavian Rurikid dynasty, Finnish shamanism, Byzantine Orthodoxy, Bulgarian apocrypha, Mongolian military and administrative forms and families of Tatars intermarrying with families of Russian boyars, German intellectuals and officers from the conquered Baltics and from Germany itself, Polish intellectuals and officers from "tripartite" Poland, and of course Jews—these all contributed to the making of Russian culture. Moreover, Ukrainians and Belarusians—the former more vociferously than the latter—assert a claim to no small part of that history which the ordinary Russian simply assumes to have been ethnically Russian. The unity of all this is real only on the level of Russian as a shared language of culture, one that forms a discrete sphere of civilization. And even with that caveat, one must remain aware that up to the era of Petrine reforms the cultural language of this civilization was a slightly modified form of Church Slavonic, of which we can regard Russia as an heir. There were also periods in which other languages predominated, above all French.

The fourth basic thought is "culturally comparative." It consists in recognizing the uneven cultural development of Russia, on the one hand, and Western and Central Europe, on the other. If in Europe one can identify a "pendulum of artistic movements"[23] according to which artistic creation and thinking developed along the arch "Romanesque art—Gothic—Renaissance—Mannerism—Baroque—Classicism—Romanticism—Realism" etc., then in Russia, and above all in Muscovite Russia after centuries of isolation from the West, this sequence cannot not be applied. Historians of art and literature have resorted to various criteria to discern something one might label a Russian Gothic, Russian Renaissance, or a Russian Baroque (in fact, only with the rise of Classicism in the eighteenth century does one finds any true correspondence, Scene 11). They find parallels in slightly delayed echoes of Western influences (influence that of course were present in Lithuanian Rus, but by no means

23 Cf. Jiří Kroupa, *Školy dějin umění: Metodologie dějin umění* (Brno: Masarykova univerzita, 2007).

in Muscovite Rus),[24] or they find them in much belated cultural effects, which allegedly play roles analogical to phenomena which in the West occurred several centuries earlier (hence the literature of Pushkin's era is sometimes referred to as the "Russian Renaissance"[25]). Or they do not find them at all—and consider this absence not a sign of Russian cultural backwardness, but instead evidence of Russia's cultural autonomy and singularity.[26] This book stands neither with the first nor with the second of these theses, but rather with a third. It seeks to show that this ambiguity in the definition of cultural epochs, this alteration of voluntary and involuntary isolations and belated "Renaissances" taken together lent unique form to the dynamic of Russian culture.

The fifth basic thought, which might be called "religiously comparative," concerns modern Russian culture roughly from the end of the eighteenth century—that is, from the time when Russia "caught up" with the culture of Western Europe. Under the impact of the radical reforms of Peter the Great, Russian society also underwent the process that had transformed Europe—secularization, edging the church out of public life and especially out of the cultural horizon of intellectuals. A specifically Catholic culture emerged in Europe as a reaction to this secularization, one that can be represented by the three points of a conceptual triangle: Catholic reformism, Catholic restoration, and Catholic romanticism. In the West, nineteenth and early twentieth-century Russian literature and religious thought are considered the most valuable and original contributions

---

24   Cf. Evgeny Vasil'evich Anichkov, *Zapadnyye literatury i slavyanstvo* (Prague: Plamya, 1926); Cf. Dmitrij Lichačov, *Člověk v literatuře staré Rusi* (Prague: Odeon, 1974).

25   Or they at least speak of the Pushkin era as a "golden age." See Radegast Parolek and Jiří Honzík, *Ruská klasická literatura* (Prague: Svoboda, 1977), 57ff.

26   Consider the extreme notion of the theologian Ioann Ekonomtsev that "Russian Renaissance" is actually Hesychasm and that a further wave of the Renaissance is the return to patristics in the restorationist spirituality of the 19th century. Ioann Ekonomtsev, "Isikhazm i vozrozhdenie (Isikhazm i problema tvorchestva)," in *Pravoslavie, Vizantiya, Rossiya,* vol. 2 (Lewiston, NY: Edwin Mellen Press, 1999), 177–206.

Russia has made to the world. The fifth thought does not deny this. It does however insist that the entire gallery of geniuses, writers such as Gogol, Tolstoy, or Dostoevsky; religious thinkers the likes of Rozanov, Berdyaev or Sergei Bulgakov, must *also* be understood contextually in analogy to the modern Catholic culture of Western Europe. It is possible, even necessary, to speak of an "Orthodox reformism," "Orthodox restauration," and "Orthodox romanticism" as well as of those wider streams of thought which the above-named authors met and contended with in their works.

The first four thoughst may be found in various formulations in the works of historians and interpreters of Russian culture, Russian and Western. Should we wish to do so, we can place this book into the context of contemporary historiographical trends such as postcolonial history, penetrating below the surface of imperial interpretations of history; area studies, penetrating below the surface of national interpretations of history; or *histoire croisée*, aiming to establish connections between previously antagonistic imperial and national approaches to history.[27] The fifth thought behind this book, the one pointing to the analogous development of modern Russian Orthodoxy and European Catholic culture, represents the most recent contribution to my method of interpretive spiritual history which I have developed over the last quarter century on topics ranging from Czech Catholic culture, the culture of late antiquity, American religious culture etc. This fifth idea I take the liberty of calling my own, regarding it as this Czech book's original contribution to the history of Russia.

---

27 Cf. Michael Werner and Bénédicte Zimmermann, "Beyond Comparison: Histoire Croisée and the Challenge of Reflexivity," *History and Theory* 45, no. 1 (February 2006): 30–50.

Russia before Russia:
Antique Cultures
along the Black Sea Coast

YEAR:
422 B.C.

PLACE:
Crimea

EVENT:
Founding of the Greek colony Tauric Chersonesus

WORKS:
The Histories by Herodotus (before 425 BC);
Iphigenia in Tauris by Euripides, Goethe, and Gluck
(412 BC, 1779, 1787); "Who Knows the Land?"
by Alexander Pushkin (1821); *The Sun of the Dead*
by Ivan Shmelev (1926); *The Island of Crimea*
by Vasily Aksenov (1981)

Narratives about the cultural history of Russia typically begin with Kievan Rus. But to comprehend the modern Russian, Ukrainian and, indirectly, Belarusian senses of identity and understand their historical place on the map of European civilization (or their absence from it), one must penetrate more deeply into the past. One must take account of Russia's "prehistory," of the ancient cultures which shaped a region critical to Russian and Ukrainian self-understandings—the area along the northern Black Sea coast and the territory of Crimea.

The Greeks sailed as far as the Black Sea in their massive effort to colonize every favorable piece of coastline—favorable, that is, because it possessed something of a Mediterranean climate and reminded the explorers of their Greek fatherland. A chain of Greek settlements emerged along the Black Sea coast as early as the seventh and sixth century before Christ: from Olbia near modern-day Odessa to Tanais near what is now Rostov-on-Don. One of the last settlements was founded in 422 BC, just as the great wave of colonization began to subside. It would go on to play a crucial role in the future Russia and Ukraine—as Tauric Chersonesus on the southern tip of the Crimean Peninsula.[28]

Neither here nor elsewhere did the Greeks set out to subjugate the "barbarian" peoples of the interior. It sufficed to turn them into objects of intellectual inquiry and thereby draw them into the Greek mental orbit. Herodotus performed this sort of intellectual subjugation in the fourth book of his *Histories* (before 425 BC), where he describes in detail the territory and inhabitants of the northern Black Sea region: the Scythians and their predecessors, the Cimmerians in present-day Ukraine, the Tauri of the Crimea, the Sauromatae (Sarmatians) along the Don.

In certain passages, Herodotus trades the role of historian for that of natural geographer, as when he describes the physical landscape

28   Cf. Jan Bouzek and Radislav Hošek, *Antické Černomoří* (Prague: Svoboda, 1978).

of northeastern Europe, what would become Russia and Ukraine (the first author to do so). He calls attention to the landscape's characteristic features: the open steppe, rivers teaming with fish (most remarkable are the sturgeon), and winters full of snow. Apparently confused by second-hand reports, Herodotus supposes snow to be made of feathers, which is not entirely incomprehensible since something of the sort could hardly have been imaginable to a blissful inhabitant of the Mediterranean: "It is said to be impossible to travel through the region which lies further north, or even to see it, because of falling feathers—both earth and air are thick with them and they shut out the view."[29]

Herodotus elsewhere changes into a cultural anthropologist, describing the manners and habits of the peoples who inhabit the region. From the perspective of a Greek, these were clearly the customs of barbarians. The Scythians and others blind their slaves, use the skulls of their enemies as goblets, fashion handkerchiefs and overcoats from the flayed skin of humans, they drink mares' milk and human blood. They don't know civilization. On the other hand, they honor the same gods as the Greeks. Despite the bizarre details, Herodotus' description all the while remains objective, detached, and free of prejudice or offense. What's more, he integrates these northerly peoples into the Greek system of mythology. The Scythians, reports the historian, descend from Heracles. When the latter led the oxen of Geryon by a rather circuitous route from Spain to Greece via the Black Sea, he lay with the local viper-maiden and begot a son, Skythes. The Sauromatae, for their part, resulted from the union of local men with Amazons.

Other ancient authors relate other legends drawn from Greek mythology taking place along the Black Sea. Prometheus was chained to a rock in the Caucasus. The Argonauts sailed to Colchis, or Georgia, in their quest for the Golden Fleece. Thetis carried the ashes of

29 Herodotus, *The Histories* 4.7.

her son Achilles to the island of Leuke, today the Ukrainian island Zmiinyi near the Danube delta, thereby founding an enduring local cult of Achilles. The Crimean Peninsula, or Tauris, provided the setting for Euripides' play, *Iphigenia in Tauris* (412 BC), which more than any other work is responsible for associating Greece with the Black Sea. Iphigenia was to be sacrificed for the benefit of the Trojan expedition, but Artemis intervened and swept her off to Tauris. She was found there by her brother, Orestes, and brought back to Greece along with a sacred statue of Artemis. They stopped in Attica, at the sanctuary Brauron, where Iphigenia was made priestess of the "Crimean" cult of Artemis (and where today one finds remarkable evidence of the veneration of Artemis as patron of childbirth and traces of local female initiation ceremonies). Athens and Crimea thus hosted the same cult, for, as related again by Herodotus, "the Tauri themselves claim that the goddess to whom these offerings are made is Agamemnon's daughter, Iphigenia."[30]

There is thus a local dimension to Euripides' play, as it relates the origin of one of the most important cults in Athens. The play also features an existential dimension, describing the ordeal of siblings lost in the wide world, afflicted by an indifferent fate, offering a meditation on the human condition. It isn't surprising that the story provided material for many later adaptions, including the opera by Christoph Willibald Gluck, *Iphigenia in Tauris* (1779), and a play of the same name by Johann Wolfgang Goethe (1779–1787). There is also an intercultural dimension to the play: confrontation between Greeks and barbarians, the latter represented by the Thoas, king of the Tauri. None of these variations—neither in Euripides, nor in Gluck, nor in Goethe—would satisfy adherents of Edward Said[31] who define as "Orientalism" Western perceptions of the East as inferior, populated by barbarians and cruel, unmanly cowards.

---

30 Ibid. 4.103.
31 Cf. Edward Said, *Orientalism* (New York: Vintage Books, 1994).

Thoas is an adversary—but a noble adversary who in the end releases Iphigenia and her brother, along with the sacred statue, and allows them to go in peace. He does so, according to Euripides and Gluck, in order to submit piously to the will of Artemis. In Goethe's version, he acts out of pure benevolence.

The life of the Greek cities along the Black Sea coast drew from more than references to "creation myths." The Greek-speaking Bosporan Kingdom arose in Crimea and parts of the adjacent mainland. It was controlled first by Athens then fell under the sway of various Hellenic empires until finally coming under the authority of Rome. The fourth century saw the migration of peoples, decline of the Bosporan Kingdom, and alternating dominance of various "barbarian nations" (Goths, Huns, Khazars). A small strip of land on the southern Crimean coast around the city of Chersonesus, however, survived the period's upheavals and remained in the possession of the Byzantium, the "second Rome" or "Christian Greece."

Christianity arrived to Crimea during the Roman period—and gave rise to new "creation myths." The fate of three early Christian heroes is associated with the region. The first church historian, Eusebius, reported that when "the holy apostles and disciples of our Savior were scattered over the whole world" Andrew was chosen for Scythia.[32] Tradition has it that the pagan emperor Traianus banished the fourth Bishop of Rome, Clement (or Pope Clement, to use his later title), to Crimea, where he was then drowned in the Black Sea. One of his successors, Martin I, was banished to the same location in the seventh century, but this time by the Christian Byzantine emperor, Constans II.

These early Christian heroes provided models for the early Christian martyrs among eastern Slavs more generally. Cyril and Methodius allegedly found the remains of Clement in Crimea while

32 Eusebius, *The History of the Church from Christ to Constantine*, trans. G.A. Williamson (New York: Penguin Books, 1965) 3.1.

undertaking their political and religious mission to the Khazar Khanate in 860, which at the time stretched along the territory of the earlier Scythians. The remains served them as the "armor of God" during subsequent journeys to Greater Moravia and Rome (where Clement's remains rest today in the Basilica of San Clement, known for its splendid collection of twelfth-century mosaics and the tomb of Saint Cyril). When the Kievan prince Vladimir had himself baptized in 988, he did so precisely in Crimean Chersonesus, which still belonged to the Byzantines. And when the chronicler Nestor assembled his collection of ancient chronicles in the beginning of the twelfth century, he dated the beginning of Kievan Christianity from the blessing given to the region by the apostle Andrew.

That, then, is the "Greece" from which Kievan and Muscovite Rus arose. Not the Greece of the Amazons and Iphigenia—but instead the Greece of Andrew the apostle, of the Crimean martyr Clement, of the missionaries Cyril and Methodius, and of St. Prince Vladimir "Equal of the Apostles." The Greece of which a small, peripheral part comes fatefully into contact with the boundary of Kievan Rus in Crimea and along the Dnieper Delta.

The northern Black Sea became part of the Crimean Khanate and an outpost of the Muslim world for several long centuries following the "barbarian" waves which swept across Kievan Rus in the thirteenth century, particularly the Mongolian raids (Scene 5). At the close of the eighteenth century, Catherine II and her favorite consort, Gregory Potemkin, succeeded in defeating the Khanate. Having conquered it, they adjoined it to the Russian Empire, doubtless a key moment in the political and diplomatic game of empire building (Scene 11). After the first war Catherine sought merely to "neutralize" the Crimean state and initially refused to incorporate the territory officially as a part of Russia: "It is not at all Our intention to have the peninsula and the Tatar hordes that belong to it in Our servitude. We wish only to see it torn away from Turkish subjugation and remain forever independent."[33] It was the allegedly intolerable domestic conditions on the peninsula that, in the end, moved Catherine to annex the Crimean state to Russia in 1783.

Of course, the annexation of Crimea was outfitted with a specific ideological interpretation. What Catherine and Potemkin had in fact accomplished was Russia's return to a land over which it had historically held sovereignty: "Russian" Greece. But watch out! It was not Christian or Byzantine Greece that Catherine and Potemkin had in mind—but rather classical Greece, Greece of the Amazons and Iphigenia! A wave of Philhellenism swept across Europe at a time when cities were being reconstructed in the neoclassical spirit, Greek monuments unearthed by archaeologists, and writers turning to classical Greek materials and motifs.[34] The period when Catherine and Potemkin incorporated Crimea was also the time of Gluck and Goethe's *Iphigenia in Tauris*!

The annexed territories received the name "Taurida," in antique fashion, and Potemkin was granted the agnomen "Taurian." The former Potemkin Palace in Petersburg, a gem of Russian neoclassicism, became the "Tauride Palace." Catherine stylized herself as queen of the Amazons, sitting at the head of her female entourage during festivities. Newly founded cities along the Black Sea were given Greek names and older Tatar settlements were renamed after antique localities or outfitted with Greek neologisms. Hence today one finds on the map of Crimea and the adjacent mainland names such as Sevastopol ("city of the venerable ruler"), Simferopol ("city of the common good"), Melitopol ("city of the bees"), Eupatoria ("city of the good father"), or Odessa (after a mistaken identification

---

33 Cited in Marina E. Lupanova, *Krymskaya problema v politike Ekateriny II* (Riazan: RVAI, 2006), 75. The citation of Catherine's rescript in this work is explicitly formulated so as to celebrate a brilliant diplomat sitting upon the Russian throne.

34 Cf. Terence Spencer, *Fair Greece, Sad Relic: Literary Philhellenism from Shakespeare to Byron* (Athens: Denise Harvey & Company (1986); Cf. Martin C. Putna, *Řecké nebe nad námi a antický košík: Studie ke druhému životu antiky v evropské kultuře* (Prague: Academy, 2006).

with the Greek village of Odysseus, which in fact lies in present-day Bulgaria.)[35]

Naturally, the formal Hellenization of Crimea—a process, it should be mentioned, in which the surviving Black Sea Greek minority played no role whatsoever[36]—involved interests other than those of politically detached philhellenes among Europe's elite. Catherine planned, in a further move, to take Constantinople from the Turks and thereby renew the Byzantine Empire—with Russian oversight, to be sure. In what appeared a grand production of *Iphigenia in Tauris,* Russia's annexation of Crimea reflected the wider ambition to create a "Byzantine" axis stretching from Kiev to Chersonesus to Constantinople.

Two other ideas, each central to modern Russian history, were involved in the annexation of Crimea and the Black Sea coast. The first is the concept of New Russia. This term was introduced as a designation for the region along the Black Sea, a territory larger than Taurida itself, the entire southern half of modern Ukraine and territory farther to the East in the direction of the Caspian Sea and the Caucasus. In distinction to the historicizing label "Taurida," the notion of New Russia held purely colonial connotations, something similar to New England in America, New Brunswick in Canada, or New Zealand. Contrary to most of these other "New" territories, however, New Russia was not separated from old Russia by the sea. And so today, unlike those others, New Russia is not regarded by its rulers as part of a *former* colonial empire, but is instead seen as an integral part of Russia. This applies not only to New Russia on the Black Sea, but also to other parts of the Russian colonial empire.[37]

35 Cf. Gwendolyn Sasse, *The Crimea Question: Identity, Transition, and Conflict* (Cambridge: Harvard University Press, 2007).

36 Cf. Yu. D. Pryakhin, *Greki v istorii Rossii, XVIII–XIX vekov: Istoricheskie ocherki* (Sankt-Peterburg: Aleteyya, 2008).

37 Alexander Etkind, *Internal Colonization: Russia's Imperial Experience* (Cambridge, UK: Polity Press, 2011).

The second idea is that of the Potemkin village. In 1787 Catherine undertook a famous journey to the newly conquered territory, for which occasion Potemkin prepared his famous villages, duplicitous facades before which new Russian settlers enacted a happy existence. Some historians consider the story about Potemkin villages to be an exaggeration (arguing that the prince merely ordered the villages to be decorated prior to Catherine's arrival), or even hold it to be a malicious fabrication.[38] Whatever the veracity of Potemkin's villages, their relevance as a constantly recurring theme in Russian imperial culture cannot be denied. One need only recall the "Potemkin villages" presented to western intellectuals in Stalin's Russia, which artfully covered up the true condition of a terrorized society.[39]

The staging of Crimea and Taurida as "Greece in Russia," of course, did not remain an ideological construct. Eager visitors arrived from Russia and the West to take in this unexpected Arcadia with its nearly Mediterranean climate and recently unearthed ancient monuments, a place so unlike the "old," proverbially cold and inhospitable Russia. Alexander Pushkin (Scene 11) wrote enthusiastically of his visit to Crimea in 1821:

Who knows the land where finest show of nature
Inspirits oaken groves and meadows nigh,
Where waters run and sparkle in their rapture
Caressing peaceful banks as they pass by,
Where on hills the laurels by their stature
Forbid the gloomy snows to fall and lie?[40]

38   See the overview provided by Lupanova in the work cited above. Lupanova of course labels western historians who accept the reports about Potemkin villages as Russophobes. Lupanova, *Krymskaya problema*, 26.
39   Cf. Michael David-Fox, *Showcasing the Great Experiment: Cultural Diplomacy and Western Visitors to the Soviet Union, 1921–1941* (Oxford: Oxford University Press, 2012).
40   Alexander Pushkin, "Who Knows the Land?" trans. Adrian Room, in *The Complete Works of Alexander Pushkin*, vol. 2, *Lyric Poems: 1820–1826* (Norfolk: Milner, 2000), 57.

The educated European reader of the time would have recognized Pushkin's verse to be (just like the Czech national anthem!) a variation of Goethe's "Mignon," the heraldic poem of longing for Italy as a country of the South, an idyll, and symbol of antiquity:

> Know'st thou the land where lemon-trees do bloom,
> And oranges like gold in leafy gloom;
> A gentle wind from deep blue heaven blows,
> The myrtle thick, and high the laurel grows?
> Know'st thou it, then?
> 'Tis there! 'tis there,
> O my belov'd one, I with thee would go![41]

The philosopher Peter Chaadaev numbered among those Russian intellectuals who worried over Russia's status in relation to European civilization (Scene 14). Amidst their worriment, many of these intellectuals turned to the theme of a "pre-Russian" Black Sea. Their musings were often ambivalent. Which ancient inhabitants of the land should they appeal to? To the Greeks—or to the local "barbarians," the Cimmerians, Scythians, and Tauri? To Iphigenia—or to King Thoas? In these moments of doubt, one discerns that question so central to modern Russian identity: Is Russia (or better, does Russia want to be) more "European" or "Asian"?

In 1918, as the Bolsheviks seized power, the symbolist poet Alexander Blok (1880–1921) composed his poem titled "Scythians." He expressed in the poem what he felt was the insurmountable and fatal analogy with the barbarians who stand between Europe and Asia and are called upon to destroy the delicate blossom of culture so long as the "old world" will not submit:

---

41 Johann Wolfgang von Goethe, *Wilhelm Meister's Apprenticeship and Travels,* trans. by Thomas Carlyle (London: Chapman and Hall, 1907), 124.

Try us in combat—let us see who dies!
Yea, we are Scythians! Yea, Asia gave us birth—
Gave us our slanted and our greed-filled eyes!
[…]
Between the Mongols and Europe's clans
For long we served as but a battered shield.
[…]
For the last time, Old World, think ere you cease!
Come to our feast as brethren; share our fire!
For the last time, to share our toil and peace
We summon you with our barbaric lyre!**42**

Another symbolist, the poet and painter Maximilian Voloshin (1877–1932) who had spent his life in Koktebel on the Crimean coast, also made frequent reference to one of the ancient and mysterious inhabitants of the region—the Cimmerians. His poetic texts include "Cimmerian Twilight" and "Cimmerian Spring" as well as a number of culturological-esoteric essays on the spiritual history of Crimea (Voloshin had studied the science of anthroposophy with Rudolf Steiner in Swiss Dornach). The "Greek" and the "barbarian," in his view, by no means stood opposed to one another. Voloshin claimed it was the task of Russians, as heirs to Crimea, to join both together in a spirit of reconciliation, to fertilize and cultivate the barbarian by means of the Greek. The poet pursued his purpose in writings as well as in his own rather extravagant personal appearance—the poet wandering about Crimea dressed in pseudo-classical garb.**43**

Around the same time, Ukrainians also began to appeal to the antique traditions of Crimea and the Black Sea region. In the course of

---

42 Alexander Blok, "The Scythians," trans. Guilbert Guerney, in *An Anthology of Russian Literature in the Soviet Period: From Gorki to Pasternak* (New York: Random House, 1960), 27–29.

43 Cf. Maximilian Voloshin, *Istoriia moei dushi* (Moscow: Agraf, 1999).

(re)constructing their own historical identity, Ukrainians presented themselves as an autochthonous people and therefore more legitimate heirs to ancient traditions than were the "northern" Russians. It is by no means a coincidence that Kotlyarevsky's *Eneyida* (1798), a humorous Ukrainian take on Virgil's classical epic (Scene 12), became the foundational work of modern Ukrainian literature. Nor is it coincidental that the Ukrainian exile poet Evhen Malanyuk (1897–1968) spoke of his country as the "Hellados of the Steppe."[44] The Ukrainian conception lacks the ambivalence characteristic of the Russians. Ukrainians wish to see themselves as a people close to the Greeks and as far away as possible from the barbarian (i.e. Russian) North.

Of course, the nineteenth and twentieth century saw the rise of new myths centered on Crimea—by now these myths were explicitly political. There is the myth about the Russian defense of Sevastopol, first against marauders from the West during the Crimean War (1854–1855) and later during the Second World War (1941–1942). This myth functions as a heroic monument binding Crimea forever to Russia. And then there is the myth of the "white Crimea." Crimea held out as the last preserve following the Bolshevik coup, as the war between "reds" and "whites" led to the gradual diminution of "white Russian" territory. The final act of this "white drama" played out in the fall of 1920 as General Wrangel evacuated his massive army and thousands upon thousands of refugees from across Russia poured into Crimea before moving on to Constantinople and finally Europe where they founded the exile "Russia beyond Russia."[45] The red terror then arrived to Crimea.

---

44 Jevhen Malanjuk, "Varjažská balada," in *Děti stepní Hellady: Pražská škola ukrajinských emigrantských básníků,* edited by Alena Morávková (Prague: Česká koordinační rada Společnosti přátel národů východu, 2001), 38.
45 Cf. Martin C. Putna and Miluše Zadražilová, *Rusko mimo Rusko: Dějiny a kultura ruské emigrace 1917–1991,* 2 vols (Brno: Petrov, 1993–1994).

The fate of "white Crimea" has been immortalized in numerous literary works, two of which deserve special attention here. The first is an autobiographical novel by Ivan Shmelev (Scene 16), *Sun of the Dead* (1926), which became famous in Europe and earned the respect of literary celebrities such as Thomas Mann. Shmelev stayed behind in Crimea even after its fall and experienced Béla Kun's bloody reign of terror during which his only son was executed. Shmelev, broken and exhausted, was permitted to leave for Paris in 1922. His immediate concern was to bear witness to his experiences—to the destruction of Crimea, the daily bouts with hunger, the friends who had perished, and to the "dead sun" which scorched everything left alive in that once bright, "antique" Crimean landscape. Memory stood in absolute contrast to the present devastation. Shmelev's reporting gives way to the author's passionate indictment of everything held to be responsible for the ruin—not just the cruelty and stupidity of Bolsheviks, whose heads were clouded by a handful of confused phrases, but also the indifference of Europe that had allowed Crimea to fall.

The second work is a novel by Vasily Aksenov (1932–2009), *The Island of Crimea* (1981). The idea behind Aksenov's work is counterfactual; what would have happened had Crimea been an island rather than peninsula, if instead of falling into the hands of the Bolsheviks it had survived as an enclave of freedom near the Russian mainland, something similar to Taiwan off mainland China. An exile himself, Aksenov ironically describes how this "European" Russia on the utopian island of Crimea—free, democratic, and prosperous—fails to value its freedom, allowing itself to be devoured from within by Bolshevik agitators. Having sufficiently corroded the spirit of freedom among the Russians there, the Bolsheviks finally launch a naval invasion and occupy the island.

Miluše Zadražilová said of the work in 1994: "Reading the novel today is more tantalizing than ever—who knows whether Aksenov's fictional wordplay might not somewhere be taken up as one of the possible solutions to problems currently facing Crimea?"[46] Twenty years later, the situation corresponds to her words exactly: Crimea, since 1954 part of Ukraine and inhabited by three nationalities (Russians, Ukrainians, and Tatars), has been occupied by the Russian military and annexed to Russia—the official explanation being that this is the people's wish, that the land has been Russian since time immemorial.

The military occupation of Crimea and its ideological justification were prepared long in advance. Since the beginning of the 1990s when Ukraine became an independent state, Russian propaganda has churned out dozens of studies about Crimea, about "Taurida" and "New Russia"—historical studies, works of archeology, ethnography and even esoteric literature—purporting to show that the entire area, the whole of southern Ukraine belongs by historical right to Russia.[47] If one were to follow this line of thinking to its logical conclusion, then Crimea and the entire northern Black Sea would have to belong, "by historical right," to Greece. Or perhaps rather to the Scythians and Cimmerians?

---

46 Ibid. 2:230.
47 T.M. Fadeeva, *Krym v sakral'nom prostranstve: Istorija, simvoly, legendy* (Simferopol': Biznes-Inform, 2000); A.G. Makarov and S.E. Makarova, eds., *Malorossija, Novorossija, Krym: Istoricheskij i etnograficheskij ocherk* (Moscow: Airo-XXI, 2006); G.T. Chupin, *Predystoriya i istoriya Kievskoy Rusi, Ukrainy i Kryma* (Kharkov: Litera Nova, 2010).

Viking Rus
and Germanic Culture

YEAR:
862

PLACE:
Novgorod and Kiev

EVENT:
The Viking Hrœrikr conquers both

WORKS:
The Russian Primary Chronicle by Nestor (1113);
Oblomov by Ivan Goncharov and Nikita Mikhalkov
(1859, 1979); "An Iron Will" by Nikolai Leskov
(1876); *The Brothers Karamazov* by Fyodor
Dostoevsky (1880)

The cultural history of the eastern Slavic peoples begins with that formation called Rus with its center in Kiev. However, it was a non-Slav social elite who shaped this formation into a state—the Germanic Vikings, referred to in Slavic sources as "Varangians" and in later scholarly discussions (inaccurately) as Normans. Between the eighth and eleventh centuries, the Vikings circumnavigated Europe from northern Britannia to southern Italy. Their ships even navigated upstream deep into the continent's interior—mostly to plunder; only rarely did they create permanent settlements in these parts.[48] Thus the report of Nestor the Chronicler (Scene 4) seems almost unbelievably idyllic when he describes how the inhabitants of the eastern European plains themselves invited the Vikings, telling them: "Our land is great and rich, but there is no order in it. Come to rule and reign over us."[49] Among the first generation of Viking rulers is supposed to have been a certain Rurik (probably originally *Hrœrikr*), from whose line stems the Rurikid dynasty that governed Russia up to the beginning of the seventeenth century.

From the tribal name of these Vikings came the name of the state and nation: "These particular Varangians were known as Russes, just as some are called Swedes, and others Normans, English, and Gotlanders. [...] And on account of these Varangians, the district of Novgorod became known as the land of Rus."[50] Russia thus received its name from the Germanic Russes, rulers from a foreign land, just as Normandy was named after the Normans, France after the Franks, Andalusia after the Vandals, or Lombardy after the Langobards. The name, however, was mediated by a third group, the Finns, who at the time were spread broadly among the Germans and Slavs. The term *Rus* is not Germanic, but Finnic: *Ruotsi* is the Finnish designation for Swedes.

---

48   Cf. Angus Konstam, *The Historical Atlas of the Viking World* (New York: Checkmark Books, 2002).
49   Nestor, *The Russian Primary Chronicle*, Laurentian text, trans. and ed. Samuel H. Cross and Olgerd P. Sherbowitz-Wetzor (Cambridge, MA: The Mediaeval Academy of America, 1953), 59.
50   Nestor, *The Russian Primary Chronicle*, 59–60.

The analogy extends further, for just as the Franks and Lango-bards underwent a gradual process of Romanization, so the Vi-king-Russian princes in Kiev, Novgorod, and other cities quickly became Slavicized. The first princes and their entourages, according to Nestor, held names that were recognizably Germanic: Askold, Sveneld, Igor (Ingvar), or Olga (Helga). Igor and Olga's son, how-ever, was already named Sviatoslav. The ninth-century sieges of Constantinople by the rulers Olga and Sviatoslav, as recounted by Nestor, thus represent the final episode in the European-wide cam-paign of Viking expansion.

A temporary period of "re-Germanization" occurred under Svia-toslav's grandson, prince Yaroslav the Wise (governed 1016–1054), related by marriage to the ruling houses of the North. Yaroslav kept a large entourage of Scandinavians in his Kievan court, including two singers of skaldic poetry. The liberal-mindedness and, naturally, irritability of individual princes can be attributed to the Norman pattern of "warrior democracy" rather than the autocratic ideal of the Byzantine Empire.

By contrast, rather few direct influences from the North were preserved in the culture of the Kievan period. There was no "Slavic Edda," but merely "ancient Kievan legends" in Nestor's chronicle, stories about the oldest generations of Kievan princes—Oleg, Igor, Olga, and Sviatoslav. These stories in some ways resemble northern Sagas, both stylistically (speaking in riddles, the use of alliteration) and thematically (prince Oleg's death from his own horse, torches tethered to birds, the motif of sitting on sleighs as a metaphor of death and so on). Instances of cultural misunderstanding occur, but are rare: for example, as when the Slavs supposedly failed to under-stand that the Viking prince had just declared a blood vengeance against them.[51] In the version related by Nestor, Kievan history does

---

51   Dmitrij Tschiževskij, *Geschichte der altrussischen Literatur: Kiever Epoche* (Frankfurt a.M.: V. Klostermann, 1948).

not feature any principled conflict of interest between Germans and Slavs. Nor do the Byzantine chroniclers, describing the same history from a contemporary point of view (Constantine Porphyrogenitus, in particular), differentiate in any significant way between the Viking and Slavic inhabitants of Rus.[52]

The coexistence of Scandinavians and Slavs in Kievan Rus itself seems, given the roughness of the times, almost idyllic. But then modern interpretations present the era as one of violent struggle. Ethnic difference was not central to the self-perception of Kievan Rus. For the self-perception of the modern Russian Empire, however, it was. The Germanic origin of the Russian state began to be felt as somehow degrading. Attempts to "de-Germanize" Russian history took place even before the nineteenth-century waves of nationalism and Slavophilism. Think of the Northern War, which Tsar Peter I waged against Charles XII, king of Sweden and descendent of the Vikings, at the beginning of the eighteenth century. It is therefore no surprise that the first "anti-Viking" interpretations came from the pen of amateur historian Vasily Tatishchev (1686–1750), a close collaborator of Peter the Great. Starting with Tatishchev, nationally-minded Russian historians came up with increasingly sophisticated arguments to demonstrate that the Varangians were not Scandinavian Germani, that the name *Rus* has nothing to do with the Varangians. The first scholarly edition of Nestor's chronicles was prepared by the German historian August Ludwig von Schlözer, who used it as a basis for refuting Tatishchev's theories. Schlözer spent several years as a professor in Saint Petersburg and became the true "father of Russian history"—although this title has traditionally been accorded to the enthusiastic patriot Tatishchev. Schlözer was granted an aristocratic title by Alexander I for his efforts to expand the knowledge of ancient Russian history. The Czech poet Jan Kollár provided him

---

[52] Cf. František Dvorník, ed., *Konstantinos Porfyrogennetos: "De Administrando imperio"* (London: Athlone Press, 1962).

a place in the "Slavic heaven" described in *Slávy dcera* (The Daughter of Slava); in the poem's 499th sonnet, Schlözer found himself in the company of J.G. Herder, Jacob Grimm, and other "Germanic" historians and philologists who "having joined us in spirit,/ thus deserve of this revelry."[53]

Curiously enough, Kollár showed himself to be less virulent in his pan-Slavism and Germanophobia than later Russian historians and publicists. The latter accused Schlözer of pro-German bias and first formulated the truly perfidious notion of a "Norman theory"— as if it were a complicated matter to demonstrate that Viking-Varangian-Normans were Germani and that they founded the Russian state, and not the other way around! The Varangians were declared to be Slavs, or at least Finns, since in the nineteenth century Finland belonged to the Russian Empire and it seemed somewhat more appropriate that a nation now subordinate to the Russians should stand at the beginning of the Russian state.[54] Historians sought alternative accounts for the origin of the name *Rus* (in the name of the river Ros, for example, a tributary of the Dneiper), searching above all in materials that predated the Vikings (even pointing to a king named Rhos mentioned in the Greek Old Testament, the *Septuagint*).[55] In the effort to come up with a desirable (which is to say, patriotic) solution, Russian historiography demonstrated its commitment to "romantic science," a science which confuses passionate bias with virtue.[56] In this respect, the "patriotic" historians of the imperial era differ little from their Soviet-era colleagues.[57]

The Kievan Vikings and controversy about a "Norman theory" led to a still wider phenomenon—that of uncovering "Germanic traces"

---

53 Kollár, *Slávy dcera*, 271.
54 For a summary of the discussion see Etkind, *Internal Colonization*, 45.
55 An overview of this theory is provided in František Dvorník, *Zrod střední a východní Evropy: Mezi Byzancí a Římem* (Prague: Prostor, 1999), 347–356.
56 Cf. Emanuel Rádl, *Romantická věda* (Prague: Laichter, 1918).
57 Cf. B.D. Grekov, *Kyjevská Rus* (Prague: Nakladatelství ČSAV, 1953).

in Russian cultural history. These traces begin before the Vikings and continue throughout the course of history, sometimes out in the open, sometimes streaming below the surface.

The "pre-Viking" Germanic people were the Goths—a nation that took over from the Scythians on the Black Sea and thus belong among the local "pre-Russian" cultures (Scene 1). Late antique historians of the sixth century provided detailed reports about the Goths—Jordanes, writing in Latin, in his *Gothic History* and Procopius of Caesarea, writing in Greek, in his *Wars with the Goths*.[58] Like their model Herodotus, they too sometimes changed roles from historians to geographers and ethnographers. Yet Jordanes mentions only peripherally (and Procopius not at all) the most important cultural-religious development connected to the Goths—the Gothic translation of the Bible, undertaken by the missionary Ulfilas in the fourth century. Later raids forced the Goths from their settlements and pushed them further west. In the modern period, the thesis was even introduced that the Varangians, founders of Kiev, were actually remnants of the Goths. That sort of speculation, however, must also be attributed to "romantic science," this time of a pan-German variety, every bit as passionately committed to its own biases as the pan-Slavic sort.

Among the "post-Viking" Germanic peoples, that is above all the Germans of Russia's political and cultural history, one must distinguish between "Germans without" and "Germans within." "Germans without" were adversaries engaged in a struggle over space in Eastern Europe, from the Knights of the Teutonic Order (against whom Alexander Nevsky famously did battle), to the Prussia of Frederick the Great (with which the Russian Empire became embroiled in the Seven Years War), to Germany in the First and Second World

---

58 Jordanes, *The Gothic History of Jordanes,* trans. Charles C. Mierow (Princeton: Princeton University Press, 1915); Procopius, *History of the Wars, Volume V: Books 7.36–8. (Gothic War)*, trans. H.B. Dewing, Loeb Classical Library 217 (Cambridge: Harvard University Press, 1928).

Wars. The Great Northern War between Russia and Sweden mentioned above can be added to the wider context of Russians fighting against the "Germans without." At the same time, Russians respect Germans as fierce opponents who are equal to themselves, and thus do not hesitate to form alliances whenever advantageous: from the anti-Napoleonic coalition with Prussia and Austria to the Molotov-Ribbentrop Pact, in actuality a pact between Stalin and Hitler, in 1939.

A more fundamental role in the cultural history of Russia, however, is played by the "Germans within." Germans had their own autonomous quarters in Moscow since the seventeenth century (the so-called German Sloboda) and mostly enjoyed respect as handworkers, merchants, soldiers, specialists in various trades.[59] These were people valued in a country longing "to catch up to the West." Peter the Great might have engaged in a life-or-death struggle against the Swedes—but it was he who invited large numbers of German experts to Russia. Most of them arrived from the Baltic lands, Germans who had formed the aristocratic and intellectual elite there since the medieval colonization of the Teutonic Knights. Peter acquired a part of the Baltic lands in the Northern War, the remainder fell to Russia during the occupation of Poland. The Baltic region represented "a piece of Germany in Russia." Germans entered Russia's interior from the Baltic lands, gaining positions in the court, in the military, and in academic institutions. The last duke of the Baltic Courland Duchy, Peter von Biron, set out in the other direction, to the West; his daughter, Katharina Friederike, Duchess of Sagan, would enter Czech culture as Kateřina Zaháňská, the "princess" from Božena Němcová's novel *Grandmother* (Babička).[60]

Waves of Germans also arrived to Russia from Germany's interior. Some aristocrats and intellectuals remained just a few years—Herder

59 Cf. Pavel Miljukov, *Obrazy z dějin ruské vzdělanosti III* (Prague: Laichter, 1910), 143–203.
60 Cf. Helena Sobková, *Kateřina Zaháňská* (Litomyšl and Prague: Paseka, 2007).

traveled to the Baltic, to what was still the culturally German city Riga, or the previously mentioned historian Schlözer's stay in St. Petersburg—later to return to their homelands with information about Russia and the Slavs, sometimes acting as propagators of Slavic culture. In this regard consider Herder's positive estimation of the Slavs in his *Ideen zur Philosophie der Geschichte der Menschheit* (1784–1791). Some of them assimilated (immediately or by the second generation) and became a part of Russian culture: the founder of the Russian theater, Denis Fonvizin (i.e. von Viezin); Pavel Pestel, the ideological leader of the Decembrists; or the most important liberal journalist of the nineteenth century, Alexander Herzen (Scene 18)—even the tsarina Catherine the Great (Sophie von Anhalt-Zerbst).

Catherine initiated a peaceful invasion by her compatriots—that is, German settlers who arrived at the tsarina's invitation to colonize newly acquired territories such as "New Russia" on the Black Sea and sparsely inhabited territories of the Russian interior such as the region along the Volga. Among others, communities of the German Brüdergemeinde, heirs to the Unity of the Bohemian Brethren, settled on the Volga.[61] Their main settlement, Sarepta became Tsaritsyn, then Stalingrad, then Volgograd. As the historian of Russia's inner colonization Alexander Etkind writes, "on the Volga, their towns, gardens, and fields looked like islands of prosperity and high culture."[62]

What Etkind writes about the German "Bohemian Brethren" on the Volga holds true for the archetype of the German in modern Russian culture more generally. The German normally embodies prudence, sobriety, diligence, and decency—in other words, ordinary western secular humanity. In Dostoevsky's *Brothers Karamazov* (Scene 15), one of the episodic characters is the old Dr. Herzenstube, who behaves decently toward the young and neglected

---

61 Cf. John R. Weinlick, *Hrabě Zinzendorf* (Prague: Stefanos, 2000).
62 Etkind, *Internal Colonisation*, 132.

Dmitry, eventually bearing witness in his favor at court. The hysterical Dmitry, on the other hand, represents the archetypal emotional "Russian soul"—and he breaks into tears when remembering Herzenstube's kindness: "I weep even now, German, I weep even now, thou man of God!"[63]

The same cultivated Germanness, the very contrary of Russian self-flagellation, has also been made an object of the grotesque, as in Leskov's tale "Iron Will" (1876). The story's hero, a German living in Russia, boasts of this "iron will"—when in fact this is nothing but obstinacy and pedantry leading the protagonist to ruin. To his Russian neighbors, the German is an object of derision that does not let up even above the man's coffin:

> "Who are they burying then, ducky?" [...]
> "Eh, it wasn't worth coming out to see, my love. It's the German they're carting off."
> "What German is that?"
> "You know, the one who choked on a pancake yesterday."[64]

In the cynical pose of these pious old ladies, of course, the grotesque turns back against self-satisfied and narrow-minded Russianness. Such contrast and ambivalence also forms the central theme of Ivan Goncharov's (1812–1891) *Oblomov* (1859). The title character of this novel is a good-natured Russian ne'erdowell, one who spends his life upon the divan in a conspicuously Oriental gown. His friend, the Russian-German Stolz, meanwhile is active, rational, and enterprising. He is, as his father before him, "a strict and business-like man like most Germans."[65] "Ever since a boy of eight," the young Stolz

---

63 Fyodor Dostoyevsky, *The Brothers Karamazov* (New York: Penguin Books, 2003), 848.
64 Nikolai Leskov, "An Iron Will," in *Five Tales,* trans. Michael Shotton (London: Angel Books, 1984), 184.
65 Ivan A. Goncharov, *Oblomov*, trans. David Magarshack (New York: Penguin Books, 2005), 111.

"had sat with his father over maps, spelt out the verses of Herder, Wieland, and the Bible and cast up the badly written accounts of the peasants."[66] Stolz is a Russian after his mother, speaks Russian, and his formal confession is Orthodoxy—but according to mentality he is "a German" pure and simple. The friend attempts to prevent Oblomov from rotting away in indolence and apathy. When he fails, after Oblomov's death he tries to at least save his son, whom he adopts.

At first glance, Stolz appears to be the positive hero, a favorable alternative to Oblomov and to a Russia suffering from "Oblomovism." On the other hand, the novel may also be read in a spirit more favorable to Oblomov, who after all comes across as more human than the "inhumanly" active Stolz. It was in this sense that the director Nikita Mikhalkov (*1945) reinterpreted the novel in his film *A Few Days in the Life of I.I. Oblomov* (1979, appearing in English simply as *Oblomov*). Oblomov is here above all human, vulnerable, and sensitive—whereas Stolz is made to appear ridiculous with his fanaticism for healthful nourishment, technical inventions, and workaholicism. At places, beneath the surface of the tireless assistance he provides to Oblomov, he appears as a sadistically dominant tyrant. The questions of whether "the German road" is desirable or feasible for Russia thus remains one of the central questions of Russian identity.

In the meantime, the fate of Russia's German communities has been cruelly fulfilled. They suffered in the famines in Ukraine and the Volga region during the 1920s and 1930s. After the war, the remaining communities were forcibly resettled. The last "service" was rendered to Russia's Germans by Alfred Rosenberg, himself a German from the Baltics (born in Estonian Tallin), during the Nazi occupation. In his attempt at a racialist interpretation of European history, *Der Mythus des 20. Jahrhunderts* (*The Myth of the Twentieth*

---

66 Goncharov, *Oblomov*, 141.

Century, 1930) Rosenberg wrote about mediaeval Germans forcing order onto a formless Steppe.[67] Under Nazi occupation he acted as administrator of the occupied territories and dreamed about transforming Crimea and the Black Sea into a new land of the Goths—Gotenland.

67 Cf. Alfred Rosenberg, *Der Mythus des 20. Jahrhunderts* (München: Hoheneichen Verlag, 1943), 112.

Slavic Rus and Paganism

YEAR:
980

PLACE:
Kiev

EVENT:
Prince Vladimir constructs a pagan pantheon

WORKS:
The Russian Primary Chronicle by Nestor (1113);
The Dziurdzia Family by Eliza Orzeszkowa (1885);
The Rite of Spring by Igor Stravinsky and Nicholas
Roerich (1913); *The Russian Religious Mind*
by George Fedotov (1946); *Ancient Paganism of Rus*
by Boris Rybakov (1987)

One must begin with ancient paganism if one is to say anything about the spiritual origins of Slavic Rus. The most noteworthy contemporary report on the subject again comes from the chronicler Nestor (Scene 4). According to him, "Vladimir [...] began to reign alone in Kiev, and he set up idols on the hills outside the castle with the hall: one of Perun, made of wood with a head of silver and a mustache of gold, and others of Khors, Dazh'bog, Stribog, Simar'gl, and Mokosh'. The people sacrificed to them, calling them gods, and brought their sons and their daughters to sacrifice them to these devils. They desecrated the earth with their offerings, and the land of Rus and this hill were defiled with blood. But our gracious God desires not the death of sinners, and upon this hill now stands a church dedicated to St. Basil."[68]

The "pantheon" erected by Vladimir did not last long. No more than eight years following his own conversion to Christianity, Vladimir arranged for the mass baptism of Kiev's entire population and "directed that the idols should be overthrown, and that some should be cut to pieces and others burned with fire. He thus ordered that Perun should be bound to a horse's tail and dragged down Borichev to the stream."[69] Perun ended up on the bottom of the Dnieper; Vladimir, now with the title "Equal of the Apostles," found his place in the pantheon of Christian saints.

When modern researchers turn to examine Vladimir's headlong transition from paganism to Christianity, various explanations arise as to whether the pantheon described by Nestor was just the divine sanctification of Vladimir's autocratic power or the result of a well deliberated religious position. According to the archeologist Boris

68 Nestor, *The Russian Primary Chronicle,* Laurentian text, trans. and ed. Samuel H. Cross and Olgerd P. Sherbowitz-Wetzor (Cambridge, MA: The Mediaeval Academy of America, 1953), 93–94.
69 Nestor, *The Russian Primary Chronicle,* 116.

Rybakov (1908–2001),[70] Vladimir's conversion represented an attempt to give the pagan pantheon a stronger foundation at a time when the influence of Christianity was on the rise. The more "scandalous" among the well-known Slavic deities were ignored (Volos, celebrated with orgies, and the god Rod, portrayed as a phallus) so that Christians could no longer argue against paganism's "immorality." A counterpart to the Christian Trinity was created—not that of the official Church (the Father, the Son, and the Holy Spirit), but that which was actually present in folk belief (the Father, the Son, and the Mother): the Father was identified with Stribog, the Son with Dazh'bog, and the Mother with Mokosh'. The Slavic Demeter, Mokosh', was the complement of Khors, who was likely the patron of plants. The Slavic Apollo, Dazh'boga, supplemented Simar'gl, supposed by Rybak to personify the solar disk (Rybak maintains that Nestor mistakenly divided Simar'gl into two beings, thereby inventing the non-existent deities "Sima" and "Regla"). Perun, the central figure of the group, stands for "something more"—a being without parallel in Christianity, a martial and stately god.[71] In Vladimir's conception—according to Rybak's theory—this demonstrated paganism's superiority over Christianity.

Rybakov's theory is as seductive as it is adventurous. The Czech reader is reminded of the still more seductive and adventurous theory formulated by Záviš Kalandra in his work *České pohanství* (Czech paganism, 1947). According to Kalandra, pre-Christian religiosity among the Czechs had its pantheon, too. Its characters did not, however, correspond to the deities of other Slavic tribes (Perun, Svantovit, Stribog etc.), but rather to the phases and sacred days of the cosmo-biological calendar. The pantheon can be reconstructed based on the ancient Czech legends as handed down by Nestor's contemporary, the

---

70 Cf. Boris Rybakov, *Jazychestvo drevnei Rusi* (Moscow: Nauka, 1987).
71 Reflections on the latest research about Perun may be found in Michal Téra, *Perun: Bůh hromovládce* (Červený Kostelec: Pavel Mervart, 2009).

chronicler Cosmas of Prague. The "Czech deities" were Krok and his three daughters, the prophetess Libuše and her prince Přemysl, the female belligerents of the Maidens' War, and finally St. Ludmila as the "Czech Demeter" and St. Wenceslas as the "Czech Dionysus."[72]

The ideas of Kalandra and Rybakov certainly earn the criticism laid upon them by more circumspect historians, archaeologists, religionists, and ethnologists.[73] They nonetheless hold immense value as a source of inspiration for thinking about the roots of national identities; the relation between religious systems, popular religiosity, and folklore; and for "thinking across" disciplines more generally.[74] At the same time they bear witness to themselves as artifacts: about the longing evident from romanticism through postmodernity for an "intrinsic" and "authentic" national pantheon that should as closely as possible resemble those of the bigger, older, and more developed cultures—for example, the Greeks, Hindus, or Germani.

Kalandra and Rybakov, two scholars whose fates differed (the former ended in the communist regime's gallows, the latter became a member of the Soviet Academy of Sciences) but whose ideas were very similar, are from this point of view heirs to another Russian-Czech pair of researchers who one might refer to as poets rather than scientists: Karel Jaromír Erben (1811–1870) and Alexander Afanasyev (1826–1871). The great Russian collector Afanasyev compiled the eight-volume selection *Russian Folk Tales* (1855–1863) based on his meticulous collections—tales of an "indecent," i.e. erotic, nature he left as manuscripts to be published posthumously.[75] He undertook a systematic interpretation of these materials in his work *Pozticheskie Vozzreniya Slavyan na Prirodu* (The Poetic

72 Cf. Záviš Kalandra, *České pohanství* (Prague: František Borový, 1947).

73 Cf. Zdeněk Váňa, *Svět slovanských bohů a démonů* (Prague: Panorama, 1990; cf. Martin Kindl, "Recepce díla Záviše Kalandry" (bachelors thesis, Charles University, 2011).

74 Cf. Dušan Třeštík, *Mýty kmene Čechů: Tři studie ke "starým pověstem českým"* (Prague: NLN, 2003).

75 Cf. Alexander Afanasyev, *Erotic Tales of Old Russia* (Berkeley: Berkeley Slavic Specialties, 1988).

Outlook of Slavs on Nature, 1865–1869). Karel Jaromír Erben, Afanasyev's elder contemporary, also compiled a collection of folk tales and songs, *Kytice z pověstí národních* (A Bouquet of Folk Legends, 1853), and other literary works on the basis of his activities as a collector and published a series of scholarly articles about mythology.[76] As romantic Slavophiles (Scene 16), Afanasyev and Erben both thought the comparison of Czech, Russian, south Slavic, and other Slavic materials to be a worthwhile endeavor because they believed in the existence of a common spiritual world shared by all Slavs. This is what motivated Erben to compile and publish the first Czech translation of Nestor's chronicles in 1867. As adherents to the interpretative school of the Grimm brothers, Erben and Afanasyev both hoped to find in folk tales and songs traces of the original pagan mythology beneath the layers left by Christianity.

A basic problem confronted by the researchers of these folk tradition is that "pre-romantic" reports about paganism in ancient Rus (to say nothing of ancient Bohemia, earlier and much more firmly bound to Christianity) are sparse and usually written from a disapproving point of view. The Christian-oriented writers follow the Old Testament prophets in reeling against the veneration of idols as incarnations of the devil or, according to the Latinized version of the Greek *daimōn,* as demons. According to Nestor, the convert Vladimir "appointed twelve men to beat the idol [Perun] with sticks, not because he thought the wood was sensitive, but to affront the demon who had deceived man in this guise."[77] Faith in the old gods appears surprisingly strong in *The Tale of Igor's Campaign*, though the authenticity of this text is disputed and it reveals rather more about romanticist understandings of ancient paganism than paganism as such (Scene 16). If Russian religious scholars searched for traces of

76   Cf. K.J. Erben, *Slovanské bájesloví* (Prague: Etnologický ústav a Slovanský ústav AV ČR, 2009).

77   Nestor, *The Russian Primary Chronicle,* 116.

vanished gods, then they necessarily set out to find reports about "demons" as well. Of that, there is an abundance in Russian literature and folklore.[78]

It remains a question whether the "search for gods" proved futile because the church censors so completely exorcised all recollection of the "idols," or because the archaic societies of Eastern Europe never developed anthropomorphic divinities similar to the gods of Homer, the *Edda*, or the *Rigveda*.[79] Instead of deities to parallel those of Greek or Vedic sources, the "searchers for paganism" discovered an extensive catalog of half-divine or daemonic beings, "devils" and "spirits". The majority of these were named after the locations where they were said to appear: "Domovye," protective house spirits, settle behind the stove or just below the hearth and protected the home in exchange for libations. In the oldest of times these could even take the form of human sacrifice. The feared Leshy, or woodland spirit, terrify wanderers in the forest. Vodyanoy are aquatic spirits as dreadful as Erben's water goblins. Polevoi, in contrast to the aggressive Czech field spirit found in Erben, hide quietly in the corn fields. All are but attributes of the main spirit, one whose name was rendered taboo by tradition—the devil, Chort.

The boundary separating the world of man from the world of spirits may be penetrated from both sides. For example, a young man can marry a nymph. One must, however, distinguish an ordinary nymph from a Rusalka, the water nymph who appears only during the solstice holiday Rusalnaya. A person can become a witch (*volkhv*) during his or her lifetime, perform incantations and divinations as well as influence crop yields;[80] or a lycanthrope (*vlkodlak,*

---

78   Cf. Fyodor Alekseevich Ryazanovsky, *Demonologia v drevnerusskoi literature* (Leipzig: Reprint Zentralantiquariat der DDR, 1974) (originally, Moscow: Pechatnaja A.I. Snegirevoj, 1915).
79   Cf. V.V. Ivanov and V.N. Toporov, *Slavyanskie jazykovye modeliruyushchuhe senuitucheskie sistemy* (Moscow: Nauka, 1965).
80   Contemporary studies in comparative religion speculate about connections with the archetype of the shaman, or on the contrary with the "benandanta," the "good witch," which was rediscovered by Carlo Ginsburg, cf. Michal Téra, "Staroruští volchvové a jejich souvislosti s indoevropskými

or werewolf), taking on the form of a wolf and devouring people; or a *kikimora* who, like the antique succubus or incubus, stretches beneath doorways or through keyholes in order to molest and torment the house's inhabitants; or a sorceress (*vyed'ma, striga, koldun'ya*) flying through the night sky above neighbors' houses to hold council on the peak of the Babia (Witches') or Lysá (Bald) mountain and casting spells or magical healings. Baba Yaga must be kept distinct from other witches, for she flies around in a pestle and lives in a cottage standing on chicken legs decorated with human skulls. After death, one might always become a vampire.[81]

Russian folkloric tradition also observes a cycle of festivities connected to the cosmo-biological calendar (the new-year holiday Korochun, the springtime Maslenitsa and Radonitsa, the Rusalnaya around the time of summer solstice, and others). The church tried to uproot this tradition through prohibition and persuasion. The legend of St. Niphont, translated in the twelfth century into Church Slavonic as part of the Byzantine *Izmaragd* collection, is an example: "When the blessed Niphont witnessed all this, he cried and was filled with a great sadness because of the dangers and perils set for Christians. He implored them all to abandon their devilish games and not to fall into the devil's trap, and also that they refrain from sacrificing their wealth to the perfidious Lord of Hell during the time of the pagan Rusalnaya."[82] The traditions surrounding these beings and their ceremonies nevertheless survived, melded with Christianity and its liturgical calendar (the term "double belief"), and endured into the nineteenth century when Afanasyev, driven by a romantic enthusiasm, headed to search for them in the countryside.

a eurasijskými duchovními tradicemi," in *Kulturní, duchovní a etnické kořeny Ruska: Tradice a alternativy,* (ed.) Marek Příhoda (Červený Kostelec: Pavel Mervart, 2005), 13–48.

81 Cf. Giuseppe Maiello, *Vampyrismus v kulturních dějinách Evropy* (Prague: NLN, 2004).

82 Daniela Hodrová (ed.), *Smích a běs: Staroruské hagiografické příběhy* (Prague: Odeon, 1988), 191.

Brought to the elite culture's attention during the era of romanticism, this folk paganism inspired countless cultural products in nineteenth-century Russian (or Russian-themed) literature, music, and the fine arts. These works continued in the spirit of the romantic folklore genre, as in Modest Mussorgsky's (1839–1881) two colorful and ghostly compositions *Night on Bald Mountain* (1867) and *Baba Yaga* from the piano cycle *Pictures from an Exhibition* (1874). Or, to the contrary, they inspired social-realist criticism of peasant backwardness and the persistence of superstitious beliefs, as in the novel by the Polish prose writer Eliza Orzeszkowa (1841–1910) *Dziurdziowie* (1885, published in English as *The Dziurdzia Family*). The novel is set in a Belarusian village, where the locals declare a young female healer to be a witch (*wiedźma*) and demand her hanging. The most disturbing aspect of the story is that the young woman begins to doubt herself and wonder if she is not, in fact, a witch: "'But why, Petra, did you come to that fire today?' [...] 'What do I know?' She uttered quietly, her mouth partially opened either in wonder or fright.."[83] Her doubts lead to nightmares, which she takes as evidence that she is, in fact, possessed: "Grandmother, they say the devil suffocates a person when he catches them."[84] The "witch" and her persecutors in the meantime attend church together—and they see no contradiction in doing so.

A deeper understanding of folk paganism, one moving beyond the dichotomy of romantic enchantment versus realistic criticism, was formulated early in the twentieth century by Igor Stravinsky and Nicholas Roerich in a work today regarded as the canonical expression of "Slavic paganism", *The Rite of Spring* (1913).

The Rite of Spring, in fact, came about from amidst the (neo-) romantic enthusiasm for folklore. Igor Stravinsky (1882–1971) had prepared a few dances based on Russian material for Diaghilev's

83 Eliza Orzeszkowa, *Vědma* (Prague: SNKLU, 1961), 121.
84 Ibid., 175.

ensemble of the Russian Ballet, which was then engaged in Paris. These were to become *The Firebird* (1910) and the less important piece *Petrushka* (1911).[85] From these materials rose the vision for a still more ambitious work. Stravinsky described it in his autobiography, *Chronicle of My Life* (1935): Working on *The Firebird*, he was overcome by the vision of "a solemn pagan rite: sage elders, seated in a circle, watched a young girl dance herself to death. They were sacrificing her to propitiate the god of spring."[86] Nicholas Roerich (1873–1947) composed a libretto to accompany this basic image, he also painted scenery and prepared costumes. Roerich was doubtlessly suited to the task. As a painter, he specialized in Secessionist symbolism evocative of ancient Rus. He also tried his hand in archaeology, religious studies, and cultural preservation. At the same time as he composed the text for *The Rite of Spring* and painted pictures such as *The Stone Age* or *The Ancestors of Mankind,* Roerich was also contributing articles to cultural journals arguing for the need to preserve medieval artifacts scattered throughout rural areas, to defend old churches from historicizing reconstructions, and to give more attention in research to the prehistory of Russia.[87]

No "god of spring" appears on Roerich's stage set for *The Rite of Spring,* nor does one find any other Slavic deities or daemonic beings. Man alone moves about the stage, the ancient Russian *homo religiosus*. Nor do his movements imitate any concrete ceremony documented by folklorists. The first part of the ballet, "The Adoration of the Earth," expresses the principle of primitive, natural, pagan reverence for a cosmic order directed by some inscrutable hidden force. Slavic paganism is no romantic idyll in Roerich and Stravinsky's rendition. In the performance's second part, "The Sacrifice,"

85 Cf. I. Ya. Vershinina, *Rannie balety Stravinskogo* (Moscow: Nauka, 1967).
86 Igor Stravinsky, *Chronicle of My Life* (London: V. Gollancz, 1936), 55–56.
87 Cf. Nicholas Roerich, *Vrata v budushchee: Esse, rasskazy, ocherki* (Moscow: Eksmo, 2010).

certain young women are called upon to partake in a ritual where they literally dance themselves to death.

In European cultural history, *The Rite of Spring* is known above all for the scandal which broke out upon its premier in Paris, the riotous reception of Stravinsky's outrageous, intentionally brutal neo-primitive music. The "paganism" of Roerich's libretto and stage setting, still more present in Stravinsky's musical score, apparently took hold of a Parisian public normally open to artistic experimentation. Suddenly revived, unsettling and barbaric, "pre-civilized" paganism attacked the delicate sensibility of these early-twentieth-century Europeans. It did so not by way of religious theory or journalistic declaration, but through the raw force of musical and kinetic emotion. This neopaganism, which surfaced in Europe at the time in many different forms, would just a couple of decades later be absorbed into the emotive effects and aesthetic fascination of German Nazism.[88]

Of course, all that would have taken place without Stravinsky and Roerich, whose intentions and conceptions about the future of European culture were different. It is worth noting in this regard how the two artists developed after *The Rite of Spring,* the subsequent paths of two creators who unleashed the old pagan gods without calling them by name. Stravinsky progressed from musical neoprimitivism to neoclassicism and from a foggy neopaganism back to the "clear" Christian and antique tradition of Europe, composing works inspired by biblical texts (*Symphony of Psalms*) and Greek myths (the ballet *Apollon musagète* or the oratorio *Oedipus Rex*).

Roerich, to the contrary, set out on a journey in search of deeper pagan roots, and beyond. Articles he wrote around the time of *The Rite of Spring* speculate about the connection between ancient Russia and something still older: "pre-Russian" cultures, Finnish tribes,

---

88 Cf. Peter Reichel, *Der schöne Schein des Dritten Reiches: Faszination und Gewalt des Faschismus* (Munich: Hanser, 1991).

ancient Scandinavia, and the North more generally as the common source of primitive religiosity. He later shifted his focus from the North to the East, travelling through Central Asia and Tibet to finally settle in the Himalayan village Nagar in the Kullu Valley.[89] There, he became something of a controversial celebrity, a painter, but above all a mystic who speculated on the origin of a panhuman spiritual culture, about the lost country of "Shambhala", about the "world spirit" and the lineage of Buddha–Messiah, a lineage to which, by all reports, he considered himself to belong.[90] Roerich's meditations in these later years reveal a longing for universal knowledge. At the same time, one cannot help but notice how they reflect the intellectual stereotypes of European esotericism, of an entirely concrete—and, observed from a distance, entirely "non-mystical"—form into which is incorporated the dream about a revived ancient paganism, "wiser" than the Christianity anchored in the church. Nor can one miss how all the talk about depth easily slips into nonsense. Of course, this is not a problem of Roerich alone. What makes Roerich worthy of note are not his mystical-utopian projects but his artistic works as a painter, which even in the later phase of endlessly repeated quiet Himalayan mountain scenes preserve a certain (now in a positive sense) mystical appeal. There in the middle of the Himalayas, Roerich sometimes recalled his cooperation with Stravinsky—only now did he experience that intense communion with nature which he had tried to express in *The Rite of Spring*.

Trying to extract some moral from *The Rite of Spring* and the fate of its creators, one might say that ancient Russian (and not just Russian) paganism is best comprehended not academically, but on the level of emotion and intuition. Of course, one doesn't need to accept this moral lesson. Another author who wished for a deeper

89 Nicholas Roerich, *Altai-Himalaya: A Travel Diary* (New York: Frederick A. Stokes Company, 1929).

90 Cf. L.V. Shaposhnikova (ed.), *Muzei imeni Rerikha* (Moscow: Mezhdunarodnyi Tsentr Rerikhov, 2006).

understanding of paganism than descriptive religious studies could provide was George Fedotov, but he did so by means of penetrating culturological analysis. Like his peers Stravinsky and Roerich, Fedotov spent the years after 1917 outside of Russia (Scene 17). His book, *The Russian Religious Mind* (1946), appeared in American exile.

Fedotov's reflections on the archaic phase of Russian religiosity revolve around the theme of reverence for the earth. Like others, Fedotov notes the weakness of ancient Russia's "celestial court." He then comes forward with an explanation: the "Russian heaven" was weak because the cult of the earth was strong. All the indignant testimony of church officials and the enthusiastic notes of romantic collectors about the cults of sacred groves, stones, and trees, about the custom of "confessing to the earth" (of whispering one's sins into a hole dug into the earth then filling it in)—these all represent manifestations of the central cult in Russia, the cult of being, of a force called *Mati Syra Zemlya* (literally, "damp Mother Earth). The earth is never personified, it is never revered in human form. It was probably never even named, for it was not understood as "a goddess among gods" but rather the Great Goddess above all. Mokosh is a later personification, just like the Greek Demeter was a personification of Gaia. Like Isiah's "suffering servant," Mother Earth has "no majestic bearing to catch our eye" (Isa. 53,2). "Earth is the Russian 'Eternal Womanhood,' not the celestial image of it: mother, not virgin."[91]

There is little trace of the Indo-European cult of a sacred union between heaven and earth in the Russian folk tradition. Mother Earth does not have a "celestial groom." "[The Russian Slav] was the fatherless son of the Great Mother."[92] From this ancient disposition of Russian religious sensibility Fedotov infers the archetypal

91 G.P. Fedotov, *The Russian Religious Mind*, vol. 1 (Cambridge: Harvard University Press, 1966), 13.
92 Fedotov, *The Russian Religious Mind*, 19.

characteristics of "the Russian soul": the "expansiveness" and form-lessness cursed by Dostoevsky, strong familial and generally collective sentiment, the devaluation of individual freedom and initiative, "feminine" compliancy and irrationality, a readiness to accept the rule of foreign "fathers," and to respond to exaggerated cruelty by exaggerating submissiveness to the point of self-destruction.

Kievan Rus
and Byzantine Christianity

YEAR:
988

PLACE:
Tauric Chersonesus and Kiev

EVENT:
Prince Vladimir has himself baptized, then the whole
of Kiev

WORKS:
The Russian Primary Chronicle and *Lives of Boris and
Gleb* by Nestor (1113 and after 1072); *The Conversion
of St. Vladimir* by Karel Havlíček-Borovský
(1852–1855); *The Song of the Dove Book* (written
down in the 19th century)

In 1988, the Russian Orthodox Church celebrated the millennial anniversary of the baptism of Rus (see Conclusion).[93] The anniversary commemorated the year 988, when Prince Vladimir arranged for the mass baptism of his Kievan subjects. Yet there are many other events in the early history of Rus that could also be understood as marking the beginning of Christianity among the eastern Slavs. It is as if Rus received baptism again and again, as if a single baptism did not suffice.

It has been the ambition of every Christian nation to claim for itself a direct lineage to the original apostles, those sent out into the world by Christ himself. The chronicler Nestor relates the following legend about the "baptismal preparation" of the apostle Andrew (Scene 1):

> When Andrew was teaching in Sinope and came to Kherson [...], he observed that the mouth of the Dnieper was nearby. Conceiving a desire to go to Rome, he thus journeyed to the mouth of the Dnieper. Thence he ascended the river, and by chance he halted beneath the hills upon the shore. Upon arising in the morning, he observed to the disciples who were with him, "See ye these hills? So shall the favor of God shine upon them that on this spot a great city shall arise, and God shall erect many churches therein." He drew near the hills, and having blessed them, he set up a cross. After offering his prayer to God, he descended from the hill on which Kiev was subsequently built, and continued his journey up the Dnieper."[94]

This charming legend, of course, has its barbs. It is anti-Novgorodian, for when Nestor leads Andrew to the North, to the future location

---

93 Cf. Metropolitan Philaret, *Tysyacheletiye kreshcheniya Rusi* (Moscow: Moscow Patriarchate, 1988).

94 Nestor, *The Russian Primary Chronicle,* Laurentian text, trans. and ed. Samuel H. Cross and Olgerd P. Sherbowitz-Wetzor (Cambridge, MA: The Mediaeval Academy of America, 1953), 53–54.

of Novgorod, he has him stand in uncomprehending amazement at the sight of—a Finnish sauna. It is anti-Roman, for the apostle Andrew was after all the elder brother of the apostle Peter, founder of the Roman church. Andrew's church thus becomes the equal to the church in Rome, or even stakes a claim to primacy. In this sense, ancient Russian traditions draw in part from the anti-Roman sentiment of the legend's Byzantine sources.[95] But the chronicle is also anti-Byzantine. For in drawing a direct line leading back to the apostle Andrew, it deemphasizes the mediating influence of the religious missions sent from Constantinople.

One may regard the mission of Cyril and Methodius to the Black Sea Khazars as yet another example of "baptismal preparation" (Scene 13). Although the brothers are not reported to have encountered any Slavic peoples settled north of the Khazars, the Cyrillic script that they and their followers devised for the Slavs of Moravia, Bulgaria, and Croatia would later play a crucial role in Russian cultural history.

The inhabitants of Kievan Rus adopted Christianity gradually. At first it was the members of the Viking elite who converted (Scene 2). Princess Olga, or Helga, counts among the first Viking Christians. She received baptism in Constantinople in 955. It was the Vikings, too, who became the first martyrs: in 983, according to Nestor, a father refused to hand over his son to be sacrificed to idols—and so the two were murdered together. Tradition gives these men the names Theodore the Varangian and his son John. It is surprising how little widespread was the cult of these men, both of whom after all represent "pure" martyrs to the faith. These two men sacrificed themselves without the slightest political or nationalistic motive, unlike many other martyrs who today enjoy wider followings.

---

95 Cf. František Dvorník, *The Idea of Apostolicity in Byzantium and the Legend of the Apostle Andrew* (Cambridge: Harvard University Press, 1958).

Nestor also reports on the famous "disputation of faith" which took place around 986, a religious debate between Orthodox Greeks, Judaic Khazars, Catholic Germans, and Muslim Volga-Kama Bulgars summoned by Prince Vladimir (the man who only a few years earlier had established a pagan pantheon). The scene is familiar to the Czech reader of Havlíček's biting parody, *The Conversion of St. Vladimir* (*Křest svatého Vladimíra*, 1852–1855, published posthumously in 1875). The following declaration of a cynical Russian clergyman has worked its way into popular memory:

> One God is like another;
> I'll call Him mine,
> Who best provides assistance
> keeping the peasants in line.[96]

As has the following refrain on self-presentation of individual religious organizations:

> One Church is not like any other,
> O' dearest Tsar of mine,
> The Roman (Greek, Jewish, Muslim) Church
> Is of them all the most divine![97]

Having split acrimoniously with the Catholic Church, Havlíček parodied Nestor (which had yet to be translated into Czech) to ridicule both Austrian clericalism and the romantic Russophilism of his fellow countrymen. His modern literary rendition was not all too distant in spirit from the original. Nestor's description of the event, one central to early Russian history and symbolic of the Kievan state's departure from older and stronger civilizations, is itself not

---

96   Karel Havlíček-Borovský, *Básnické dílo* (Prague: Orbis, 1951), 104.
97   Ibid., 117–118.

without elements of comedy. Vladimir might very well have decided for Islam (he found the practice of polygamy especially appealing), but he balked when it came to the prohibition on alcohol:

> One may then satisfy every desire [...] Vladimir listened to them, for he was fond of women and indulgence, regarding which he heard with pleasure. But circumcision and abstinence from pork and wine were disagreeable to him. "Drinking," said he, "is the joy of the Russes. We cannot exist without that pleasure."[98]

Catholics and Jews are barely permitted a word. The Orthodox Byzantines, on the other hand, are granted permission to describe their faith in detail, from creation to the last judgement. To be sure, the representatives of Catholicism would have offered much the same content—but Nestor, the Orthodox chronicler, knew the point he wanted to make. In the end, it was neither dogma nor learned interpretation that convinced Vladimir. It was rather the experience of beauty that moved him to accept Orthodoxy. He listened to his messenger's reports of an Orthodox service witnessed in Constantinople where "they burned incense, and the choirs sang hymns. [...] Calling their attention to the beauty of the edifice, the changing, and the pontifical services and the ministry of the deacons, while he explained to them the worship of his God. The Russes were astonished and in their wonder praised the Greek ceremonial. [...] We knew not whether we were in heaven or on earth. For on earth there is no such splendor or such beauty, and we are at a loss how to describe it."[99]

Regardless of the chronicler's many fabrications and *loci communes,* however much considerations of a more practical and political nature informed Vladimir's real-life decisions, one thing is

---

98 Nestor, *The Russian Primary Chronicle,* 97.
99 Ibid., 111.

certain—the acceptance of Christianity in its Byzantine version led to the confrontation of two cultures at vastly different stages of development. Archaic, primitive Kievan Rus at the far edge of Europe adopted the outer trappings of religion (dogmas, rites, church organization) from the more sophisticated Byzantium, an ancient culture heavy with the inheritance of Greek civilization, Roman statehood, and patristic theology, and adapted these traditions to serve its own purposes. In the framework of his cultural morphology, Oswald Spengler speaks of Russia as a "pseudomorphosis", a borrowing of older forms to fill them with content that is new.[100] From the perspective of cultural history one cannot therefore speak straightforwardly about Orthodoxy as such, but instead (at the very least) about Byzantine Orthodoxy, the Orthodoxy of Balkan nations, Russian Orthodoxy, and Orthodoxy in the Western diaspora.[101] From the perspective of the cultural history of Rus it is therefore necessary to distinguish between the original religious-cultural model, taken from Byzantium, and the transformation (or better, the transformations) of that model which took place in Rus (or better said, in the various manifestations of Rus).

Byzantine Orthodoxy itself represents a synthesis of original Christian teachings and the ancient cosmological religiosity of Neo-Platonism. To state it symbolically, it represents the union of the cross and the circle. The Byzantine worldview resembles an ingenious system of mutually interconnected sign systems—of circles and hierarchical scales that provide a comprehensive order to the life of society and the individual: the inner organization of the cathedral as a model of the cosmos and a path to salvation, from the entrance door open to all sinners right up to the most holy space of the alter; the daily cycle of services marked by morning prayers (*orthros*,

---

100 Cf. Oswald Spengler, *The Decline of the West,* trans. Charles F. Atkinson (New York: A. Knopf, 1992).

101 Cf. Ivana Noble et al., *Cesty pravoslavné teologie ve 20. století na Západ* (Brno: CDK, 2012).

or "daybreak") and those of the evening (*hesperinos*, or vespers); the annual cycle of services with rotating holidays; the hierarchy of icons and their order of appearance on the iconostasis; the typology of the icons of Christ, the Mother of God, and the saints; the celestial hierarchy of angels and saints and the terrestrial hierarchy of church officials.[102] As one of the most sophisticated Russian interpreters of Byzantine cultures, Sergei Averintsev (Scene 19), writes: the correct and pious orientation to the world consists in acknowledging one's place in the system of signs, knowing one's correct *taxis* or rank, class or status.[103]

The Russian Orthodox Church adopted this structure. But what did it actually know of its content and meaning? Cultural historians have long praised Cyril and Methodius for bestowing literature unto the Slavs, which helped them to preserve their national and cultural autonomy in a sea of foreign and more developed peoples. This is true for the Serbs and Bulgarians, who write using Cyrillic, and even more for the Latinate Croats of Dalmatia (and to an extent also the Moravians and Bohemians).[104] For the Russians, distant from the centers of culture, the gift of writing proved a mixed blessing. In the short term, at the time of the national conversion itself, the Slavic language exerted a positive influence because the liturgy could be understood. The Russian or Bulgarian could more easily identify with the stories of the Gospel and with Christian culture as a whole. In the end, however, the "Roman model" would prove the more effective route. For centuries, the barbarian peoples of western and central Europe were schooled in Latin and through it received the influence of the Latinate cultures of Christianity and

---

102 In Czech, see the dictionary of Orthodox concepts, iconography, and theology compiled by H. Hlaváčková and V. Konzal in Viktor Lazarev, *Svět Andreje Rubleva* (Prague: Vyšehrad, 1981). Among the more recent works to treat the liturgical system in detail is Hanuš Nykl, *Náboženství v ruské kultuře* (Červený Kostelec: Pavel Mervart, 2013).

103 Cf. Sergei Averintsev, *Poetika rannevizantiyskoy literatury* (Moscow: Nauka, 1977).

104 Cf. Josef Vašica, *Literární památky epochy velkomoravské* (Prague: Vyšehrad, 1996).

antiquity; after several centuries, at the peak of the Middle Ages and during the Renaissance, these peoples would bear fruit in their own national languages.

Byzantine missionaries were content with having established the foundation of the Church in Russia. It goes without saying that they themselves occupied the newly created bishop seats. They brought with them basic religious texts which in Bulgaria had been translated into a language called Church Slavonic, one easily understood in Rus (not to be confused with Old Church Slavonic, a script reserved for the works of Cyril and Methodius themselves and their direct followers).[105] Having accomplished these things, they quit. They did not concern themselves with the further education of the newly baptized nation, they did not found any schools (the first Russian schools were not developed until the seventeenth century), and for the most part they left the first Russian priests, who were barely proficient in reading Cyrillic texts, on their own. It never occurred to them that Slavic clerics should receive instruction in Greek, the key to two millennia of wisdom and beauty now under the guardianship of Byzantium. The cultural historian Sergei Ivanov maintains that this neglect fit well to the Byzantine's sense of cultural and religious exclusivity, lingering doubts as to whether "one can turn a barbarian into a Christian."[106] So what were the texts available to the Russian scholar who wished for a deeper understanding of the Christian faith and of the world more generally? The library of a medieval Russian scholar should have begun with the Bible, but Russian clerics of the time did not possess the Holy Scripture in its entirety. The New Testament had been translated and divided according to tradition into two separate books, the Synoptic Gospels and the Apostles. Of the Old Testament, however, only the Book of

---

[105] Cf. Zoe Hauptová and Věnceslava Bechyňová (eds.), *Zlatý věk bulharského písemnictví* (Prague: Vyšehrad, 1982).
[106] Cf. Sergej A. Ivanov, *Byzantské misie aneb Je možné udělat z barbara křesťana?* (Červený Kostelec: Pavel Mervart, 2012).

Psalms and Sirach were available, the latter favored as a summary of ethical teachings. The other books were known only through the succinct summaries provided in the *Paleia* (from the Greek *palaia diatheke*, or Old Testament), typically accompanied by a commentary (*tolk*) and therefore called the *tolkovaia paleia*. Rather than transcriptions of complete texts, these were "practical" collections intended to be read aloud during the liturgy: the *aprakoses, praxapostoloi,* and the Old-Testament *parimejniki*.

By contrast, many legends (called *zhitiya* in Church Slavonic) about saints of the Christian East had been translated. Most popular were the stories about martyr-warriors such as St. Georgios (Georgy or George), Theodore (or Feodor) Tiron, and Demetrius (or Dimitri) of Thessaloniki; about monks such as Anthony, founder of eremitism, known as Anthony the Hermit; about the bishops Nikolaos of Myra (or Saint Nicholas); about ascetics and holy fools (*iurodivyi*) such as Alexis, called "the man of God" (Scene 7). Reverence was even shown to a saint who had evidently been invented in Byzantium by mistake—from the word Friday, *paraskeué* in Greek (literally meaning "preparation," i.e. for the Jewish Sabbath), which in Christianity marks the Passion of Christ, there came about Paraskeva, known popularly as Praskovya. From the theological concept of the Wisdom of God and the three Christian virtues of faith, hope, and love were born the four martyrs Saint Sophia and her three daughters, Faith, Hope, and Love. Beside the "great" hagiography, there existed collections of lesser biographies arranged either according to the church calendar—the *Prolog* (the name arose by mistake, the beginning of the foreword taken to be the work's title)—or in connection to places where saintly monks resided—the *Pateriki*, Books of the Fathers: Egyptian, Jerusalem, Sinai, Roman.

The spiritual novel *Barlaam and Josephat* made its way from Byzantium to Rus in the guise of a hagiography. A father has his son, the royal prince Josaphat (Ioasaf in Russian), locked up in a magnificent palace in order to protect him from the evils of the outside world. However, following an unexpected encounter with sickness, old age, and death, the prince confronts questions of an existential nature, questions which the monk Barlaam answers for him with an interpretation of Christian teachings about sin, redemption, and eternal life. The subject matter of the novel is Indian in origin. The story made a pilgrimage across three continents and different languages and religions.[107] The problem of death and the ambition to evade the world's sufferings animated Buddhists, Christians, and Muslims alike, just as it aroused the Byzantine author John of Damascus and the Czech medieval translator Tomáš Štítný, as it moved Leo Tolstoy in the nineteenth century (Scene 17) and Hermann Hesse in the twentieth, the latter author having worked the tale into his novel *Siddhartha* (1922).

Old Russian sources preserve an astonishing catalogue of Greek names and patristic authors. Hardly any Russian monks, however, knew anything about these figures beyond the few excerpts included in collections of proverbs and sayings (the *Pandects*, *Pchela* etc.). Of works available in their entire form thanks to the mediation of translators in Bulgaria, most were of little use since the intricate Christological questions which had inspired Athanasius of Alexandria or Gregory of Nazianzus were entirely beyond the intellectual scope of old Rus. Catechisms such as the *Mystagogic Catecheses* by Cyril of Jerusalem and the *Exposition of the Orthodox Faith* by John of Damascus were more appropriate.

Of greater popularity were two preachers from the fourth century, John Chrysostom (or "golden-mouthed") and Ephrem the Syrian (or "Syriac"). Chrysostom and "the Syriac" set the tone for Russian religious ethics: the collection of Chrysostom's homilies, the *Zlatostruj*, emphasize practical ethics, Christian love for one's neighbor, and socially critical sentiments. The Syriac's collection, *Paraenesis*, calls above all else for repentance and atonement, warning of the

---

107   Cf. I.N. Lebedeva (ed.), *Povest' o Varlaame i Ioasafe* (Leningrad: Nauka, 1985).

Final Judgement which is to come. Both aspects, a stress on social sentiment and apocalyptic belief, pervade later Russian religious culture—right up to boundaries of that culture and into the secularized context of revolutionary "piety" in Bolshevik Russia (Scene 18). Rounding off the Orthodox worldview are chronicles incorporating the history of individual countries into a universal history of salvation. These include for example the *Christian Topography* by Cosmas Indicopleustes (literally, "Cosmas who sailed to India"), the symbolic interpretations of nature found in the *Hexaëmeron*, and Basil of Caesarea's account of the six days of creation (Gn 1–2).

As one can see from this reconstruction of the medieval Russian scholar's library, very little was known about Orthodoxy and its dogma in newly baptized Rus. What the new Christian wanted, what became the main "content" of his faith, was a good story. The phenomenon of storytelling, among other things, represents the intersection between ancient paganism (Scene 3) and the new faith. The Gospel as related from the temple's Ambon and illustrated by frescos and icons were the only part of the complicated liturgy that he really understood. Even if we leave aside speculation about the influence of Bulgarian dualistic "Bogomilism," this passion for telling and hearing stories, the desire to find out "how things were before" and "how they were after," is itself sufficient to explain the widespread distribution of all kinds of apocrypha, be they originally Greek and translated in Bulgaria, or originally Bulgarian.

Apocrypha present themselves as the writings of biblical figures or influential church fathers, they make use of traditional biblical genres (gospel, acts, epistles, apocalypse), patristics ("the word," i.e. sermon; the "council", i.e. exposition, disputation), or sometimes hagiography (even the *zhitiya* of a saint can be "forged").[108] How

---

108 Cf. Zdeněk Soušek (ed.), *Knihy tajemství a moudrosti: Mimobiblické židovské spisy,* 3 vols. (Prague: Vyšehrad, 1998–2013); Cf. Jan A. Dus et al. (eds.), *Novozákonní apokryfy,* 3 vols (Prague: Vyšehrad, 2001–2007).

should the poor Russian priest work his way through this tangle of stories and all their variations, each one passed down in transcribed form by someone somewhere. To transcribe it? Not to transcribe it? To destroy it? Ancient Rus thus knew of another typical translational genre: the "index," as in the index of prohibited books. Included on this list, right beside the apocrypha, are works of sorcery, prophecy, and enchantment. The first such index is found as early as the *Izbornik Sviatoslavov* (1073).

The greatest popularity was won by those apocrypha that promised the reader a glimpse of "how it was" at the world's beginning or "how it will be" at the end, apocrypha of cosmological (*Voprosy, ot skolkikh chastei sozdan byl Adam*, Questions About From How Many Parts Adam Was Created) or eschatological varieties. Among the best-known belong the *Khozhdenie bogoroditsy po mukam* (The Descent of the Virgin into Hell)—a sort of miniature *Divine Comedy* of ancient Rus in which are described punishments handed out after death for a specific sins, similar to its analogy in the Latin west, and by no means necessarily wrapped in the guise of apocrypha.[109] The thematic of the Antichrist's arrival is addressed in *Slovo Mefodia Patarskogo o tsarstvii jazyk poslednikh vremyon* (The Word of Methodius of Patarsk on the Rule of Pagans in the Last Days) and *Slovo svyatogo Ippolita ob skonchanii mira i o antikhriste* (The Word of Saint Hippolytus on the End of the World and the Antichrist).

Apocrypha, especially the eschatological variety, enjoyed enormous popularity over the centuries despite church prohibition, especially at times of apocalyptic excitement and among religious dissenters. Folk religiosity also drew from them, especially in the form of oral drama called *stikhi dukhovnye* (spiritual verses). In the era of nineteenth-century romanticism, apocrypha and spiritual verses captured the imagination of collectors, literary historians, and

---

109 Cf. Aron Gurevič, *Nebe, peklo, svět* (Jihočany: H&H, 1996).

religious scholars as extraordinarily valuable documentary evidence of how official Orthodoxy gave way to "unofficial" religiosity.[110]

It is clear from the analyses that the transformation was quite dramatic. No great distinction was made between God the Father and Christ. The Gospel and other biblical themes appear only sporadically in folk religiosity. Christ inspired fear rather than love. The actual savior of the world appears to be rather the Virgin Mary. Although the phrase "trinity" does occur, it is taken to signify a female being named Trinity. The world was created "anthropomorphically" from parts of God's body. Such is the theme handled by the most lyrical and puzzling of these spiritual verses, the *Stikh o golubinoj knige* (here *The Song of the Dove Book*, but also meaning "the book of profound mysteries"):

> I say to you, I declare it
> As I remember it, as it is written:
> The world as it first arose pure,
> It came from the Holy Spirit,
> From Christ himself, the Tsar divine,
> The beautiful sun from the face of God,
> The new moon from the bosom of God,
> The bright morning from the robe of God,
> The many stars from the eyes of God,
> Heavy rain from the mind of God,
> The exuberant sentences of the Holy Spirit,
> of Christ himself, the Tsar divine.[111]

Preserved in writing and in the form of spoken verse passed down through oral tradition, apocrypha inspired artists in the context of

110   Cf. A.N. Veselovskij, *Razyskanija v oblasti russkich duchovnych stichov,* vols I–XXIV (Saint Petersburg: Imperatorskoj Akad. Nauk, 1879–1891); Cf. George Fedotov, *Stikhi dukhovnye: Russkaia narodnaia vera po dukhovym stikham* (Paris: YMCA Press 1935).
111   "Stich o Golubiné knize," *Souvislosti* no. 1 (1994): 57–58.

"Orthodox romanticism" who desired a revival of folk spirituality in literature. The secessionist symbolist Alexei Remizov (1877–1954), author of several of stylized variations on apocryphal material, is one example. The philosopher Vladimir Solovyov is another. It was from the *Discourse of Saint Hippolytus* that Solovyov drew inspiration for his suggestive *Story of the Antichrist*—the philosopher's vision of the apocalypse (Scene 14).

Modern Russian authors draw inspiration from the ancient Russian texts just as older Russian authors of Kievan Rus let themselves be inspired by the texts of Byzantium and Bulgaria. The work of Russians writing during the Kievan era followed Byzantine models in terms of genre as well as stylistic devices.[112] Ilarion, the first Kievan metropolitan of native origin, excerpted translated works of Byzantine sermons to compile his *Sermon on Law and Grace* (1049), often considered the first significant work of ancient Russian rhetorical prose (Scene 13). Cosmas Indicopleustes's accounts of his journeys became the model for a genre known as "khozhdenie," travel literature, above all accounts of pilgrimages taken to sacred sites, the most important of them being hegumen Daniel the Pilgrim's early twelfth-century description of his journey to Palestine. *The Patericon of the Kievan Caves,* composed in the early thirteenth century on the basis of older patristic texts, describes the lives of monks at the first Russian monastery, a humorous collection often cited by literary scholars searching for the beginnings of the Russian narrative tradition.[113] Even the two relatively secular works by authors of the period, *Pouchenie* (instruction), the ideological testament prince Vladimir Monomakh (1053–1125), and the curious *Molenie*, a "petition" by the mysterious Daniel Zatochnik (12ᵗʰ century? 13ᵗʰ

---

112   See the representative selection from most of these works compiled by Emilie Bláhová, Zoe Hauptová, and Václav Konzal (eds.), *Písemnictví ruského středověku od křtu Vladimíra Velikého po Dmitrije Donského* (Prague: Vyšehrad, 1989).
113   Daniela Hodrová (ed.), *Smích a běs: Staroruské hagiografické příběhy* (Prague: Odeon, 1988).

century?), are but variations on the "sapiential" literature of Byzantium, expressions of life's wisdom in aphorisms and sayings.

In his Primary Chronicle (*Povest vremennykh let*, literally Tale of Bygone Years), the oft-quoted Nestor drew from the work of the Byzantine chronicler George Hamartolus. Another one of Nestor's books, a biography of Saint Theodosius of Kiev, is modeled after Athanasius's biography of the hermit Anthony. A third work of Nestor's also takes a foreign model, the biography of princes Boris and Gleb who were murdered by their brother Sviatopolk and later revered as saints, even though their murder was political rather than religious. Boris and Gleb were nonetheless honored as "passion bearers" (*strastoterpts*, "one who bears suffering") by the Orthodox Church, saints whose heroism consists in their literal understanding of the Gospel's non-resistance to evil. Boris prays before his death: "Glory be to you, O Lord, for you have willed it that I take this bitter death for their jealousy, that I suffer all this for the love of your Word."[114] His servant then speaks: "Our lord, dear and beloved, what goodness that for the love of Christ you do not seek to resist!"[115] The direct model for this work is not to be found in any Byzantine hagiography, but rather in the Czech legend of Saint Wenceslas (Václav), which was known in the Church Slavonic version thanks to the popular cult of Wenceslas and his grandmother Ludmila in Kievan Rus.[116] Boris himself appeals directly to Wenceslas as his model: "And he meditated on the torture and death [...] of Saint Wenceslas, for he was killed in a similar manner."[117]

If we set aside *Tale of Igor's Campaign* (which would belong to the Kievan era—if it were authentic, Scene 16), then it is Nestor who

---

114   Emilie Bláhová, Zoe Hauptová, Václav Konzal (eds.), *Písemnictví ruského středověku od křtu Vladimíra Velikého po Dmitrije Donského* (Prague: Vyšehrad, 1989), 67.
115   Ibid.
116   Cf. A.I. Rogov, Emilie Bláhová, and Václav Konzal (eds.), *Staroslověnské legendy českého původu* (Prague: Vyšehrad, 1976).
117   Bláhová, Hauptová, and Konzal (eds.), *Písemnictví ruského středověku*, 66.

is the most outstanding literary phenomenon of the Kievan era. His *Life of Theodosius of Kiev* and *The Lives of Boris and Gleb* served as the major local models for later hagiographies. Nestor's outstanding literary achievement, however, is surely *The Primary Chronicle*. Under the heading of "chronicle" we find dry descriptions giving way to drama and colorful anecdotes, troves of proverbs and folklore among which are inserted sermons and theological interpretations. Nestor may take an entirely dignified seat beside his underappreciated contemporary Cosmas, the chronicler of Bohemia's "bygone years."

To point out the dependence of Nestor and also other authors of the Kievan era on Byzantine, Bulgarian, or Czech models is by no means to imply the inferiority of Russian literature in the Kievan era. The ability to perfectly imitate older literary models is to the contrary a sign of maturity, attesting to the learnedness, cultural, and spiritual level of the author and thus of the nation to which he belonged. It is precisely through its connection in a web of relationships with the other European literatures that Kievan Rus demonstrated that it belonged to culture of European nations, a culture influenced by Christianity and, through it, antiquity.

The Kievan state, though located at the far periphery, nonetheless belonged to the Christian world. Despite undergoing a schism between the eastern and western churches in the middle of the eleventh century, a discord which left its mark in the polemics of numerous texts from the Kievan era (consider the "pro-Latinate" passages in the catechism, from which according to Nestor prince Vladimir received instruction), Kievan Rus was not regarded by the western "Latinate" states to be foreign and in principle hostile. Between Kiev and Prague, Esztergom and Gniezno, there took place not only a trade in goods, but also a trade in princesses, monks, and saints.[118]

---

118   For a summary se A.V. Florovsky, *Chekhi i vostochnie Slavyane: Ocherki po istorii cheshsko-russkikh otnoshenii (X–XVIII) vek* (Prague: Slovanský ústav, 1935).

Just as Wenceslas and Ludmila were revered in Rus, so was a cult of Boris and Gleb established at least at the Sázava monastery in central Bohemia.[119] The cult of Wenceslas and Ludmila, moreover, left an a dual impression on Kievan hagiography: on the one hand, it provided the model of a prince murdered by his brother, which influenced the biographies of the first Russian martyrs Boris and Gleb. On the other hand, the narrative of a grandmother as the teacher of Christianity and the grandson as the one to realize her teachings was transformed into the cult of Olga and her grandson prince Vladimir. Among the monks immortalized in the *The Patericon of the Kievan Caves* one finds Moses Uhrin, i.e. "the man from Hungary." According to one account, Saint Prokop founded the Sázava monastery after having received instruction in Vyshhorod near Kiev.[120] And on and on. The chaos involved in reworking the authoritative texts of Christian culture; the contention that the "objective" performance of ceremony comprises the very core of Christianity and the lack of understanding for the individual's inner-experience of faith; the construction of a pantheon of national or "dynastic" saints; the crass admixture of political interests and ecclesiastical affairs—all of this is shared by Kievan Rus and contemporary Central Europe. In terms of cultural development, Kievan Rus did not lag behind western Europe much more than did Central Europe.

Only later would it become painfully clear that the Kievan era represented the blissful childhood of the nation. The question now is, which nation? In other words, who may lay claim to the legacy of Kievan Rus (Scene 12)?

---

119 Cf. Květa Reichertová et al., *Sázava, památník staroslověnské kultury v Čechách* (Prague: Odeon, 1988).
120 Cf. Dominique Patier, "Přišel svatý Prokop z ruské kolonie u Cařihradu?" *Souvislosti*, no. 2 (2007): 178–191.

Mongolian Rus and Eurasianism

YEAR:
1380

PLACE:
Trinity Lavra of St. Sergius

EVENT:
Sergius of Radonezh blesses an attack on the Mongols

WORKS:
The Secret History of the Mongols (after 1240);
the Trinity Lavra of St. Sergius (1380); *The Life
of St. Sergius of Radonezh* by Epifanii the Wise
(1417–1418); *Andrei Rublev* by Andrei Tarkovski (1966);
Ancient Rus and the Great Steppe by Lev Gumilev
(1989)

Mongol and Tatar warriors (the two ethnic labels are often used, mistakenly, as synonyms) swept the eastern European plains in the years between 1223 and 1243. They made it as far as Central Europe, though once there they soon decided to turn back to the east. Besides devastation, they left behind them the legend of Jaroslav Sternberg and the maiden Marie Hostýnská who together sought to evade the marauder's warpath.[121] For eastern Europe, on the other hand, the consequence of Mongol invasion proved fatal. The federation of Russian princes was swept aside by the Mongols, who also leveled most of the Russian towns and murdered or carried away into slavery a large part of the population.

Was the Mongol invasion the end of Rus? It was—and wasn't. In any case, it certainly brought an end to the common development of East and West, and marked the end of Kievan Rus. Kiev was so devastated in 1239 that it would take several centuries for the city to recover. It disappeared from the Russian political and cultural scene and its legacy was claimed by several powers coming from separate directions— Moscow from the east, Novgorod and Galicia from the West (Scene 8).

Kievan Rus bore its last fruits in literature and spirituality. From the literary branch come reports of the Mongol terror, the *Povest o razorenii Ryazani Batyem* (The Tale of Batu Khan's Destruction of Ryazan) and testaments of grief such as *Slovo o pogibeli russkoi zemli* (On the Ruin of the Russian Lands). The last truly important spiritual figure was the preacher Serapion of Vladimir († 1275), hegumen of the Kievan Caves Monastery and toward the end of his life the bishop of Vladimir. His sermons dwell upon a single theme, developed through the paraphrasing of the Old Testament books of prophets and psalms: God has punished us, not for his own pleasure, but for our sins.[122]

---

121 Oldřich Králík, *Historická skutečnost a postupná mytizace mongolského vpádu na Moravu roku 1241: Příspěvek k ideologii předbřeznové Moravy* (Olomouc: Socialistická akademie, 1969).
122 Emilie Bláhová, Zoe Hauptová, Václav Konzal (eds.), *Písemnictví ruského středověku od křtu Vladimíra Velikého po Dmirtrije Donského* (Prague: Vyšehrad, 1989), 319–320.

Coincidentally, there exists a literary witness from the other side of events. The most important relic of ancient Mongolian literature, *The Secret Book of the Mongols,* was composed precisely around this time and describes these very same years. The text centers on the life of Genghis Khan, founder of the Mongolian world empire, and traces developments up to the year 1240. Through Genghis Khan appears the entire spiritual world of ancient Mongolia—the mythology of divine animals, descriptions of imperial expansion and its sophisticated organization, fragments of poetry. Ancient Mongolian poetry is archaic, full of parallels and comparisons between human society and the natural world:

> When your body, like a great old tree,
> Will fall down,
> By whom will they let govern your people
> Who are like tangled hemp?
> When your body, like the stone base of a pillar,
> Will collapse,
> By whom will they let govern your people
> Who are like a flock of birds?[123]

The "poems" found in the *Secret Book of the Mongols* often resemble the poetics of the Russian *Byliny* and other texts for which Russian literary historians try to discern medieval origins. The ancient Mongolian "Byliny," however, are reliably authentic. Though they certainly may not be included straightforwardly in the history of Russian literature, it is nonetheless instructive to compare them with it:

> For the Qa'an [Khan] I will charge forward
> So as to rend the deep water,

---

123 *The Secret History of the Mongols: A Mongolian Epic Chronicle of the Thirteenth Century,* trans. Igor de Rachewiltz, vol. 1 (Leiden and Boston: Brill's Inner Asian Library, 2004), 245.

So as to crumble the shining stone.
For him I will charge forward
So as to split the blue stone
In the place which I am told to reach,
So as to crush the black stone
At the time when I am told to attack.[124]

Standing out among these poetics are the cruelties regarded as commonplace by the Mongols. For example, the following excerpt refers to the method by which prisoners were selected for execution, "against the linchpin of a cart." The vanquished enemy was placed against the wooden wheel of a cart, the sort used by the Mongols to transport their belongings. Whoever stood taller than the wheel's linchpin was executed. Boys of up to ten years of age thus stood a moderate chance of survival:

To avenge our fathers and forefathers,
And requite the wrong, for them
We shall measure *the Tatars* against the linchpin of a cart,
And kill them to the last one,
We shall utterly slay them.
The rest we shall enslave:
Some here, some there, dividing them among ourselves![125]

A similarly laconic tone characterized reports about the conquest of Asia and of Europe's endless expanses. Among the many other nations described, mention is made of the *Orusut*—or Russian people: "I have ravaged the Orusut people and brought eleven countries and peoples duly under submission. When we turned back, pulling in the golden reins, we decided to hold a parting feast."[126]

---

124 Ibid., 147.
125 Ibid., 154.
126 Ibid., 275.

But what did "enslavement"—the "Tatar-Mongol yoke"—look like, and what was its significance for Russian culture and spirituality? The Mongols conquered giant expanses of the east European plain at lightning speed, but they never felt the need to govern it themselves. Instead, they devised a policy of ingenious simplicity: one of every dozen Russian princes was individually bound to the Khan through vassalage, responsible for collecting taxes from the territory entrusted to him and expected to periodically visit the seat of the Tatar empire. Otherwise they were left alone. "To go to the horde," most often to the capital city Sarai on the lower Volga, thus implied attaining a higher position, a more profitable fiefdom or, to the contrary, a cruel death. The Mongols, with their "oriental" inscrutability,[127] intensified the sense of dread that surrounded them. What's more, they exploited the notorious querulousness of Russian princes by situating themselves as adjudicators in the endless disputes. Chronicles of the fourteenth and fifteenth century are full of stereotyped stories about how a certain Prince A runs to the Horde with accusations directed at neighboring Prince B, whereupon the Horde sends a punitive expedition against B's principality, which it awards to Prince A. After a year, the fugitive Prince B arrives to the Horde to plead for mercy and brings with him information about a new treachery being prepared against the merciful Horde by Prince A ...

The incorporation of the major part of former Kievan Rus territory into the Mongolian world also meant separation from European civilization. This process developed rapidly during the thirteenth century. Universities, cathedrals, female mysticism, mendicant orders, scholastics, goliards, Minnesingers, and furthermore the devotio moderna, book printing, humanism, the Renaissance and the Reformation: each of these movements eventually penetrated

---

[127] We use the modifier deliberately, a fact certain to infuriate the adherents of Edward Said, see Scene 1.

Central Europe, but all of them stopped short of Russian territory under Mongol rule. It was during the Mongol era that "Russian backwardness" began, that fateful detour from the course of European development.

This is not to say that the nearly three-hundred-year reign of the Mongols represents an era of absolute cultural darkness. Culture continued to develop in the context of the Orthodox Church, the one and only civilizational institution among the Russian-speaking peoples. To be sure, even western development, from the Renaissance to the Reformation took place within the context of the Catholic Church. But there the church was an autonomous institution (or a set of autonomous institutions) in its relation to secular powers, a fact which made diversification and progress possible. The Mongols, themselves animists and, later, mostly Muslims, bid formal freedom to the church and even offered clergy members exemption from taxation—but under one condition: that they pray for the Khan. In practice, this situation meant only that the church preserved the conservative religious and cultural forms from the Kievan era and, beyond it, from the age of Byzantium and ancient Christianity. In the Mongolian era, however, these older forms played the role of a shield to guard and protect the threatened nation. Insofar as society and culture progressed, it progressed in a direction opposite the spiritual trends of contemporary Europe.

This fact can be observed in the works of the Mongol era's most prominent saintly figure, Sergius of Radonezh († 1392). The primary source about him is the *Zhitie Sergie Radonezhkego* (The Life of St. Sergius of Radonezh) recorded by the monk Epifanii the Wise between 1417–1418 in a monastery near Moscow that had been founded by Sergius and named after him as the Trinity Lavra of St. Sergius. Epifanii's text follows the typical hagiographic pattern consistent with other monastic biographies. Stress is laid on Sergius' piety, his asceticism, and the initiative he demonstrated in constructing the monastery—the western reader is reminded of Benedict of

Nursia and the Benedictine motto "ora et labora." The analogy goes further, for the Trinity Lavra of St. Sergius became a model for the founding of other monasteries in the wilderness of the northeast, in locations ever more distant from the traditional centers of culture, and of course from Mongol power as well. Sergius of Radonezh in a sense undertook in fourteenth-century Rus what Benedict had accomplished in western Europe during the sixth century—he re-settled a once-cultivated countryside devastated by a historical catastrophe. Both men also extended their monastic colonizing activities to ends of the earth which had never belonged to ancient civilization. Benedict's monks entered central and northern Europe; Sergius' monks travelled to the northeast toward the Urals and Arctic Ocean.

The Trinity Lavra of St. Sergius is a place of special significance for the arts as well; in 1422, Andrei Rublev (1360–1430) was summoned to decorate the central cathedral.[128] His icon of the *Holy Trinity*, housed today in Moscow's Tretyakov Gallery (a copy of it meanwhile hangs in the monastery's temple), took on world-wide fame during the twentieth century. It became emblematic of attempts to deepen and revive Orthodoxy on the basis of mysticism, iconography, and spirituality more generally (Scene 17). And for the West it became *the* icon of Orthodoxy, endlessly reproduced to adorn the walls of Catholic churches and homes.

In the monasteries built after the Trinity Lavra of St. Sergius spread a mystical school of thought known as hesychasm, a spiritual trend previously unknown to Russian Orthodoxy (Scene 7). There is no indication in Sergius' *Zhitie* that he himself felt any enthusiasm for this school. But for that, the *Zhitie* does emphasize one particular episode in Sergius' life considered by the Russian patriotic tradition to be a key moment in the transition from Mongolian Rus to Muscovite Rus: the blessing and prophecy Sergius offered to Prince Dmitrii Donskoi before the battle of Kulikovo Field in 1380. This

---

128 Cf. Viktor Lazarev, *Svět Andreje Rubleva* (Prague: Vyšehrad, 1981)

battle was memorialized in Russian literature by the *Zadonshchina,* a rhythmic mourning over the death of so many Russian warriors. In a second part of the text, emphasis shifted from mourning to a celebration of Russian arms and Prince Dmitrii Donskoi.[129] The *Zadonshchina* was used by romantic forgers as a source for *The Tale of Igor's Campaign,* if that work is indeed a forgery, who used an authentic medieval manuscript to produce a composition that was "more poetic" and "more medieval" according to romantic notions than the original. Or, to the contrary, the *Zadonshchina* may be a rather weak and less poetic echo of the *Tale of Igor's Campaign,* assuming the latter is not a forgery (Scene 16). In the *Zhitie* of Sergius Radonezh, the battle is unambiguously interpreted as the beginning of the liberation of Rus thanks to the exertions of the Orthodox Church and the Muscovite state:

The Grand Prince [...] thus assembled all his armies and marched on the infidel Tatars. And when he caught site of their number, he stood still in doubt, and many of his people shook with fear, wondering what they should do next. And suddenly, at that very moment, a messenger arrived with a letter from a saint in which was written: do not hesitate, but push forward. [...] And because God helped the great Dmitri to victory, the pagan Tatars were defeated and utterly destroyed. Feeling the anger and disfavor of the Divine upon them, the destitute ones gave themselves to flight. The standard with the crowd nonetheless continued in pursuit, slaughtering a countless number of them. Others, covered with wounds, fled. Others were captured alive. It was a wonderous sight and an admirable victory. Arms which had glistened were not covered in the blood of foreigners.[130]

---

129   Cf. Jan Frček, *Zádonština: Starorуský žalozpěv o boji Rusů s Tatary r. 1380: Rozprava literárně dějepisná* (Prague: Slovanský ústav-Orbis, 1948).
130   Bláhová, Hauptová, and Konzal (eds.), *Písemnictví ruského středověku,* 346.

The western reader might detect in this excerpt an echo of the crusades. Caution is in order, however, for prior to the crusading expeditions of the West into the Holy Lands there took place a "crusades before the crusades." A cult for the holy struggle against infidels was organized in Byzantium—a Byzantine "baptism" of the Islamic Jihad. Later, Dmitrii Donskoi would become the official "holy warrior" of the Russian tradition. Donskoi was canonized by the Russian Orthodox Church during the 1988 millennial celebration of the baptism of St. Vladimir (see Conclusion).

Over the centuries, the Trinity Lavra of St. Sergius became a sanctum of the Muscovite state and dynasty. The tsars made pilgrimages twice annually (on the name day of Sergius, September 25, and on Trinity Sunday) and visited the monastery before important state decisions. They also made generous use of the wealthy monastery as a bank, drawing upon it whenever they needed additional funds for military expenditures. Amid the chaos (or "Troubles") of the early seventeenth century, important events took place here involving the rise of the Romanov dynasty. Peter the Great twice sought refuge in the monastery, and each time it served as a starting point for his victorious return. The monastery was abolished during the Bolshevik era and the tomb of Sergius was ignominiously removed during an anti-religious campaign (Scene 19).[131] Now restored, it is frequently visited by pilgrims who come to kiss the remains of Sergius housed beneath a silvered gable. Visitors are greeted in front of the monastery gate by a statue of Sergius of Radonezh on the one side and—the Bolshevik leader Lenin on the other.

Although only a few artifacts in the Trinity Lavra of St. Sergius today date back to the period of transition from Mongol rule to the Moscow era, the complex itself stands as one of the great symbols of that passage.

---

131 Cf. Sergei Averintsev, *Poetika rannevizantiskoi literatury* (Moscow: Izdatelstvo Nauka, 1977).

In a different genre, the director Andrei Tarkovsky lent expression to this transition in *Andrei Rublev* (1966), a film set in the fifteenth century. One of the film's more graphic scenes depicts an "ordinary" Tatar raid on a Russian town, setting the scene for the murder of women and other defenseless victims vainly seeking refuge in a church. More horrifying than the murder itself is the sadistic grin of the Tatar chieftain as he carelessly speaks of his desire to conquer "some little town" just for fun. Another, no less brutal scene portrays the mutual animosity between Russian princes who gouge out the eyes of their rivals' servants. Other scenes feature monks, pagan rituals (Scene 3), or *iurodivye* ("holy fools," Scene 7). Rublev, being an artist, is painfully aware of the contrasts and contradictions of his surroundings—and he invests his paintings with all the suffering and hope he passionately holds for his nation's eventual revival.

It is certainly the intervention of a modern interpreter to attribute this sort of inner experience to the life of Rublev, or to read the subtext of national revival into his icons, which in truth stuck closely to traditional iconographical patterns. *Andrei Rublev* was groundbreaking in its depiction of religious settings at the time of its making (the film was directed in 1966 but released for distribution only in 1971, and that in an edited version). Despite the relative independence allowed to the director thanks to his position in the cultural "gray zone," Tarkovsky follows the accepted, national, "Muscovite" interpretation of history according to which modern Russia arose victorious over the Mongol invaders.

There is, however, a second tradition featuring an equally consistent counter-interpretation. According to this view, the Grand Duchy of Moscow reached its apogee of power and rose victorious above all the other competing Russian states precisely because it was, in a cultural sense, "Mongolian." Placed at the far periphery of Kievan Rus and surrounded by territories already occupied by Turkic-Tatar inhabitants, it was Muscovy that most consistently internalized "Mongolian instruction": cruel and without scruples in the pursuit of its interests, absolute obedience demanded by its rulers, religion subservient to worldly power. What's more, the proportion of Mongolian and Asiatic elements in society increased as Muscovy expanded further into the Asian interior. Ivan the Terrible conquered Kazan and Astrakhan, at the end of his reign he subdued the Siberian khanates as well, each time adding the corresponding epithets to his title (Scene 6). Cossack-conquerors proceeded in a Russian "Drang nach Osten" up to Kamchatka and Chukotka at the easternmost tip of Asia. In the eighteenth and nineteenth centuries, Russian rule extended into Central Asia and, for a time, the rest of Mongolia was pinched between Russian Siberia and China. The tsar in Moscow was often referred to in the languages of Siberian peoples as the "white tsar", a title originally corresponding to the Mongol khans.[132] According to this counter interpretation, Moscow is by no means the heir to Kievan Rus but instead—to the empire of Genghis Khan! Not Nestor's *Primary Chronicle,* but rather *The Secret History of the Mongols* offers the key to its prehistory!

This latter account has become a favorite among the numerous interpreters of Russian history and mentality, each in pursuit of its his own agenda. Many western observers have made use of it, from sixteenth and seventeenth-century travelers to the historian Richard Pipes in his analysis of the Russian state's divergence from the social structure of European countries.[133] Of course, journalists in search of simplified formulations also make ample use of this interpretation. Russian "westernizers" use it to express disgust at the lack of freedom in their own country. Many Ukrainian historians and publicists have turned to it to back up their own nation's claim to the traditions of Kievan Rus (Scene 20). It was utilized for example

---

132 There exist other interpretations which, in the spirit of Russian nationalism, maintain that it has to do with an originally Slavic, i.e. Muscovite, title later adopted by Siberian peoples. See V. V. Trepavlov, *"Belyi tsar": Obraz monarkha i predstavlenie o poddanstve u narodov Rossii XV–XVII veka* (Moscow: Vostochnaia literatura, 2007).
133 Cf. Richard Pipes, *Russia under the Old Regime* (New York: Scribner, 1974).

by the writer Ivan Bunin—shortly before his departure into exile—when he commented on the doings of the Bolsheviks:

> A.K. [Alexei Konstantinovich] Tolstoy once wrote, "When I recall the beauty of our history before the cursed Mongols came, I want to throw myself on the ground and roll about in despair." Yesterday Russian literature had Pushkins and Tolstoys, but now it has almost only "cursed Mongols."[134]

These commentators use the equation Moscow-equals-"Mongolia"-equals-Asia in a negative sense. However, the same equation has also been used in a positive sense by nationalistically-minded Russian historians who understand Russia's "otherness," its "non-Europeanness," and "Mongolianess" to be a source of strength, an expression of exclusivity and source of legitimacy. This approach usually goes under the name "Eurasianism," which might be taken to mean "both Europe and Asia, for Moscow's claim to power covers both," or "neither Europe nor Asia, but rather a third, autonomous civilization—Eurasia, which is the natural space for Moscow's claims to power." The distinction is irrelevant in the final analysis since both interpretations effectively back up Moscow's claim to power.

Eurasianism presents the idea of a unique "non-European" path for Russia, a sense of mission formulated by the nineteenth-century thinkers of Orthodox romanticism such as Konstantin Leontev (Scene 16). But as an organized movement, Eurasianism spread between the wars among communities of Russian emigres in Sophia and Prague. The movement's founding theses were formulated by Peter Savitsky (1895–1968), editor of the collection *Iskhod k Vostokhu* (East to the East, 1921), as well as in other publications crossing over from science (Savitsky himself was a geographer),

---

134 Ivan Bunin, *Cursed Days: A Diary of Revolution* (Chicago: Ivan R. Dee, 1998), 112–113.

to journalism and nationalist mysticism.[135] A similar balancing of different genres characterized the revival of Eurasianist thought in official Soviet science. Such was the case with the ethnologist and non-academic intellectual Lev Gumilev (1912–1992). As the son of poet Nikolai Gumilev, whom the Bolsheviks shot, and Anna Akhmatova, whom the Bolsheviks "merely" censored and humiliated, as well as an inmate of the Gulag, Lev Gumilev had little reason to feel sympathy for the communist regime. As far as his belief in Russia's unique cultural mission is concerned, however, he and the Bolshevik regime were on the same page.

Gumilev's individual works concern the ancient civilizations that shared the history and territory of eastern Slavs. His book *Discovery of Khazaria* (1966) addresses the question of what happened to the Turkic-Tatar Khazars, whose empire along the Black Sea had competed with Kievan Rus before quietly disappearing from the map (Scene 13). His answer is that the Khazars assimilated to Russian society, that they became Cossacks! His study *Searches for an Imaginary Kingdom: The Legend of the Kingdom of Prester John* (1970) deals with the question of the Mongols in a similar fashion. According to Gumilev, those Mongols who adopted Nestorian Christianity played a mediating role. There were vague reports about an "the empire of prince John" somewhere in the Far East, a legend that excited Christian society, inspired Medieval travelogues such as those of Marco Polo and Umberco Eco's novel *Baudolino*.[136] When most of the Mongols converted to Islam or Buddhism, the Christian Mongols were said to have left for Muscovite Rus. It was mainly the elite who left, warriors and Nestorian priests; and it was precisely they who contributed to the physical and intellectual dominance of Moscow over the other Russian princedoms.

---

135 Cf. Emil Voráček, *Eurasijství v ruském politickém myšlení: Osudy jednoho z porevolučních ideových směrů ruské meziválečné emigrace.* (Prague: Set out, 2004).

136 Cf. *Putování k Mongolům* (Prague: SNKLU, 1964); Umberto Eco, *Baudolino* (New York: Harcourt, Inc., 2002).

Gumilev brings these components together in a synthesis with his books *Ancient Rus and the Great Steppe* (1989) and *From Rus to Russia* (1992), fashioning a truly global theory of Russian ethnogenesis. The Russian people, according to this theory, comprise not just any old nation, but rather a "superethnos", one capable of forging an autonomous, self-contained civilization, able to assimilate other peoples and distinguished by what he calls its "pasionarita", literally its "passionateness", or put differently, by its "will to Life," a sort of exceptional biological and at the same time mystical energy. One such "superethnos" was Kievan Rus; a completely different "superethnos" is Muscovite Rus. Neither the one nor the other Rus would ever have achieved greatness had it been unable to assimilate into itself the neighboring cultures of the east, Asian civilizations erroneously underestimated by Europe.

Most mainstream anthropologists dismiss Gumilev's opinions as just so much ideological rubbish.[137] In his foreword to *Ancient Rus and the Great Steppe,* the respected literary historian Dmitry Likhachov cleverly defends Gumilev by describing him as a gifted writer. Likhachov thereby implies that Gumilev's texts are to be regarded as works of art rather than science. By contrast, the ideological cohort surrounding Vladimir Putin at the beginning of the twenty-first century are dead serious in their respect for Gumilev's thesis about a Russian "superethnos"—a necessary "scientific" legitimation of Russia's most recent campaign of imperial expansion.

---

137 Cf. *Lev Gumilev—pro et contra* (Saint Petersburg: Nauchno-obrazovatelnoe kulturologicheskoe obshchestvo, 2012); Cf. Sergei Magid, "Lev Gumilev, předposlední eurazijec" *Souvislosti* no. 2 (1994): 70–80.

Muscovite Rus and "Third Rome"

YEAR:
1523

PLACE:
Pskov

EVENT:
The monk Filofei pronounces Moscow the Third Rome

WORKS:
Correspondence by Ivan the Terrible and Andrey
Kurbsky (1564–1579); "Pan-Mongolism" by Vladimir
Solovyov (1894); *Ivan the Terrible* by Sergei
Eisenstein (1944)

In the process of subduing neighboring principalities and bringing ever greater stretches of eastern Europe under its sovereignty, Muscovy adopted all the formal markers of its new privileged status. Its ruler now called himself Grand Prince and the local bishop became the Metropolitan of all Rus. And with that began the construction of a religious-ideological justification for its claim to power.

Starting at the beginning of the fourteenth century, the Metropolitan in Moscow advanced the notion of Moscow as a "second Kiev." As such, it was called upon to unite all the lands of Kievan Rus under its scepter. Since 1440 the Moscow church regarded itself as the last stronghold, and hence guardian, of Orthodoxy worldwide. Isidor, the last Muscovite Metropolitan of Greek nationality, returned from the council of Florence that same year. There, one year earlier, the Byzantine hierarchy had concluded an ecclesiastical union with Rome. Isidor returned with a Cardinal's hat and the demand that Moscow join this union of eastern and western churches. Muscovites showed little patience for this demand. Isidor was expelled from the country and relations were broken off with a "heretical" Constantinople.

Finally, when the Turks invaded Constantinople in 1453 (Isidor, now the former metropolitan of Moscow, watched from the ramparts),[138] Moscow felt itself called upon to take on the role of global leadership. As the last Orthodox state, according to its exclusivist understanding of Orthodoxy, it was the last truly Christian state. Perhaps even the last true state at all. Nestor of Iskander's (perhaps authentic) account of Constantinople's fall was accompanied by a prophecy of Russia's succession to the legacy of Rome. "For it is written: the Rus people with the original creators shall conquer the Ishmaelites and the city upon the seven hills shall be ruled by Rus."[139]

---

138 Cf. Steven Runciman, *The Fall of Constantinople 1453* (Cambridge: Cambridge University Press, 1965).

139 Nestor Iskander, "O Cařihradu, o jeho založení a dobytí Turky v roce 1453," in *Povídky ze staré Rusi,* (ed.) Světla Mathauserová (Prague: Odeon, 1984), 154.

Moscow's claim to be the only legitimate heir to "New Rome" (Constantinople) was strengthened by Grand Prince Ivan III's (reigned 1462–1505) marriage in 1472 to Sophia Palaiologina, niece to the last emperor of Byzantium. Twenty years later, the Metropolitan Zosima would be the first to formulate the fateful thesis, one hinted at in Russian commentaries on the Union of Florence and the fall of Constantinople: Moscow had become the new Constantinople, together with all the religious and political implications of such an inheritance. The older Slavic name for Constantinople—Tsargrad, or "city of the tsar"—took on a new meaning. Moscow had become the new Tsargrad, and as such it held a claim to the old Tsargrad.

The man traditionally considered the father of the theory of Russian universal empire, a monk from Pskov named Filofei, thus in truth elaborated a thesis already widespread among the Muscovite elite of his time. In a letter to Vasily III in 1510, Filofei articulated the doctrine of Moscow as the Third Rome:

> I will say but a few words about the present Orthodox empire of our blessed and most noble Tsar, the one Christian tsar under the heavens, protector of the sacred divine alter of the holy and most blessed apostolic Church, taking the place of the Roman Church and of the Church of Constantinople, seated in Moscow, city of God's favor, in the blessed and glorious Cathedral of the Dormition, the only temple in the world more radiant than the sun. And know this, you lover of Christ and God, all the Christian empires have reached their end and joined in the one and only empire of our Tsar. Just as was revealed in the Books of the Prophets, it is the Roman Empire. For two Romes have existed already and fallen. A third now stands. And a fourth will never be. The apostle Paul mentions Rome in several of his epistles, and his commentaries say: Rome, it is the world.[140]

---

140 "Siye poslanie startsa Filofeia...," in *Tretii Rim: istoki i evoliutsiia russkoi srednevekovoi kontseptsii, XV–XVII vv*, N.V. Sinitsyna (Moscow: Izdavatelstvo Indrik, 1998), 345.

The doctrine of Moscow as the Third Rome is also rooted in official church documents of the period, specifically in the materials coming from the council of 1589 organized in Moscow by the Patriarchate, the highest order in the Orthodox hierarchy. The concept was forcefully revived at the end of the nineteenth century when the journal *Pravoslavnii sobesednik* printed a modern edition of Filofei's text in 1861. The thesis of Moscow as the Third Rome was passionately debated in politics, philosophical treatises, and works of literature by personalities like the historian Vasily Kluchevsky, the religious thinkers Vladimir Solovyov, Sergei Bulgakov and Nikolai Berdyaev, by the poets Osip Mandelstam, Georgi Ivanov, and others.

Reference to the thesis was not always celebratory. Solovyov, for example, advocated caution in his poem "Pan-Mongolianism" from 1894 (Scene 14), lest Moscow share the fate of the Romes before it:

We have no desire to learn
From fallen Byzantium's fate,
And Russia's flatterers insist:
It is you, you are the third Rome.

Let it be so! God has not yet
Emptied his wrathful hand.
A swarm of waking tribes
Prepares for new attacks.

[…]

He who neglects love's legacy,
Will be overcome by trembling fear…
And the third Rome will fall to dust,
Nor will there ever be a fourth.[141]

141 Vladimir Solovyov, "Pan-Mongolism," in *From the Ends to the Beginning: A Bilingual Anthology of Russian Verse*, ed. Ilya Kutik and Andrew Wachtel (Evanston, IL: Dept. of Slavic Languages and Literatures, viewed May 27, 2016), www.russianpoetry.net

Solovyov's apocalyptic premonitions were confirmed by the Bolshevik seizure of power. Anti-Bolshevik circles fostered the ideal of a pious Third Rome which offered a bitter contrast to the atheistic "Third International" of the communists—or, to the contrary, joined to it.[142]

To many westerners (for example, the historiosopher A.J. Toynbee), the formulation of Moscow as the Third Rome symbolizes Russian imperialism, of whatever ideological coloring. Some modern Slavophile-oriented scholars today are making efforts to rehabilitate the old monk Filofei. In reconstructing the wider social context of Filofei's work, they aim to show that his concern was not so much with the territorial expansion of Moscow as with the spiritual calling the Russian Orthodox Church. The concept of Third Rome was originally eschatological, not at all imperialistic.[143] These efforts are commendable for having revealed some historical details and certain textual modifications ("Roman tsardom" in the first version of Filofei's letter was later editions changed to "Russian tsardom"). [144] What such revision does not do, however, is refute the Muscovite church's claim to an exclusive status in global Christianity; nor the close connection, or even identification, of the Orthodox Church with the Muscovite state; nor the global ambitions of Moscow's imperialism; nor even the symbolic role played in it by the idea of Third Rome or any of its variants and transmutations.[145]

The most valuable lesson of this "rehabilitation" is the attention it brings to the European context of the Third Rome idea. Filofei's

142 Cf. Sinitsyna, "Tretii Rim v istoriografii i istoriosofii XIX–XX vv," 7–57.

143 Cf. Marek Příhoda, "Mnich Filofej a Třetí Řím: Vznik a proměny jedné ideje první poloviny 16. století," in *Kulturní duchovní a etnické kořeny Ruska,* by Pavla Gkantzios Drápelová et al. (Červený Kostelec: Pavel Mervart, 2009), 135–174.

144 Cf. Aleksandr L. Goldberg, "Tri 'poslaniia Filofeia': (opyt tekstologicheskogo analiza)," *Trudy Otdela drevnerusskoi literatury* 23 (1974), 68–97.

145 See also the dispute between Dmitry Likhachov, "de-imperializing" the idea of a Third Rome and Sergei Magid, who finds in Likhachov's arguments the typical features of Russian cultural imperialism. Dmitry Likhachov, "Mýty o Rusku" and Sergei Magid, "O nových mýtech a starých strastech," in *Volné sdružení českých rusistů* 8, (Sept. 1992): 74–84.

thesis that Moscow received its calling from Rome via Constantinople is a Russian variant of the western European theory of *translatio imperii,* or "the transfer of empire." The coronation of Charlemagne as Emperor of Rome in 800 and the later rechristening of the central European polity as the Holy Roman Empire expresses the same claim to *tranlatio imperii,* to the carrying-over of the fallen Roman Empire's spiritual and political legacy and global mission.[146] A similar motif, the "imitation of Rome," can be discerned in the activities of Charles IV, who rebuilt Prague and, by importing Roman pictures and relics, symbolically reconfigured the city as a New Rome.[147] Virtually all of the modern empires present themselves in one way or another as heirs to Rome and antique civilization in general. In this sense, New Romes include London, Paris, Vienna, and Washington D.C. Is the seat of the U.S. Congress not named, after Rome, the Capitol?[148]

Any number of empires would like to be considered the New Rome. But it also matters how this appears in practice. As written in the scriptures: "you will recognize them by their fruits" (Mt 7:20). The majority of New Romes built their imperia through militarily might and politics. When all is said and done, the model imperium of the model city, ancient Rome, arose first and foremost thanks to the achievements of the Roman army, starting from a small region in the center of Italy in its march across the ancient world. Even the domestic affairs of ancient Rome were harsh and full of intrigue and violence, the best testament to which is provided by the historian of the Augustinian age, Titus Livius, he who wished to celebrate the history of ancient Rome, not indict it.

What makes the "Romanness" of Moscow distinct from that of the Holy Roman Empire, or from that of the British and American

---

146   Cf. Jacques Le Goff, *La civilisation de l'Occident médiéval* (Paris: Grand Livre du Mois, 1964).
147   Cf. Kateřina Kubínová, *Imitatio Romae: Karel IV. a Řím* (Prague: Artefactum, 2006).
148   Cf. Andrea Giardina, André Vauchez, *Il mito di Roma: da Carlo Magno a Mussolini.* (Rome: Editori Laterza, 2000.)

empires, is not imperial ambition per se. What has distinguished Moscow from the other "Romes" is the distance which has separated its political ambitions from social and cultural reality.

In the first place, Rome, Regensburg, Vienna, London or Washington D.C. were all founded on a legal tradition and system of autonomous institutions, communities and associations, all of which together contributed to social plurality. Rome and Washington in particular emphasized the principle of freedom and the dignity of man. Second, these empires sought legitimacy not only in their appeal to spiritual and religious values, but also in their level of cultural and civilizational development. Even in its "golden age" from the fifteenth to the seventeenth century, Moscow represented an absolute contrast to western capitals. One finds there neither law nor social plurality neither respect for the freedom of the individual nor scholarly learning. There is no culture of substance. To western observers who arrived on business, diplomatic missions (the Habsburg diplomat Siegmund von Herberstein), or missions of a semi-private religious nature (the Czech Jesuit Jiří David of Zdice, Scene XIV[149]), Muscovy appeared to be a completely foreign land—barbarian, uncultivated, and hostile. Especially to those coming from the outside, Moscow appeared to be a country torn between conviction of its own superiority and a deeply seated feeling of inferiority. Even if we were to dismiss much of what these observers report as instances of what Edward Said (Scene 1) described as western prejudice toward the Orient, there would still be much that is condemning found in the texts of Muscovites themselves.

To speak of the "texts of Muscovites themselves" in the sixteenth century is to speak of journalism and polemics, mostly religious and political tracts disseminated in hand-written form since book

---

149 Cf. Jiří David ze Zdic, *Novodobý stav Velké Rusi neboli Moskevska* (Olomouc: Refugium Velehrad-Roma, 2008).

printing was still unknown.[150] A certain literary quality may be attributed to these historical or pseudo-historical "legends" which were also distributed as manuscripts. Otherwise, there existed hardly any literary fiction, poetry, artistic prose or drama, to say nothing of science and scholarship. What could be said of the Mongolian period applies to the later period of Muscovy as well—Muscovite Rus persisted in the fateful condition of backwardness relative to European development and Central European culture. The Orthodox Church represented the sole institution of culture, and even it concentrated more than anything else on the reproduction of cultural and religious patterns inherited from Kiev and Byzantium.

The trend which dominated Muscovite religious culture was Josephitism, the true Muscovite form of spirituality named after Joseph Volotsky, hegumen of the Volokolamsk monastery. The *Monastic Rule*, composed by Volotsky for the governance of his monastery, abounds in descriptions of harsh punishments meted out for the slightest of infractions. Fear was regarded as the most efficient guide to monastic life, fear of God and fear of the hegumen. Social distance between classes, normally set aside at the gates of the monastery, was to be preserved according to Volotsky's conception. Monks divided themselves into several groups according to property, each group with its own living conditions, duties, and privileges. His *Monastic Rule* demonstrated little interest in anything like an inner spirituality. The austerity of monastic life appears in Volotsky's contributions to ecclesiastical disputes as well, whether they concerned the persecution and burning of heretics (for example, the "Judaizers," Scene 8), arguments with monastic opponents of a wealthy church (Scene 7), or in his unqualified public support for tsarist autocracy.

The Muscovite alliance of throne and altar set out to organize, govern and control everything in the minutest detail. The life of the

---

150 Cf. I.U. Budovnic, *Russkaia publicistika XVI. Veka* (Moscow and Leningrad: Izdatelstvo Akademii nauk SSSR, 1947).

church—the book *Stoglavy*, a collection of commentaries on the so-bor of the same name held in 1551, similar in intent to the Catholic Council of Trent of the same period. The life of the individu-al—Ivan the Terrible's favorite, the archpriest Silvester, wrote the *Domostroi*, a name translated from the Greek *oikonomikos,* rules for the management of households, an economic and pedagogical handbook which remained a favorite of patriarchal landowners well into the nineteenth century. The life of literature—the metropolitan Macarius crammed into a single volume titled *The Great Menaion Reader* (Velikie Chetyi-Minei, literally "the great monthly reader") everything which until then had been independently circulating literature, absolutely everything (that is, everything recognized by Orthodoxy) which had ever been written down on paper from the Bible through the patristic writings up to the *Zhitie* of the most recent saints. Even the life of historical memory—Macarius and his associates assembled a universal chronicle consisting of all chroni-cles of all the principalities with only "minor" editorial intervention, i.e. rubbing out of everything hostile to the interests of Muscovy. To this "great organization of the past" also belonged the *Stepennaia kniga* (Book of Degrees), a volume presenting the uninterrupted genealogy of rulers from Vladimir the Great to Ivan the Terrible.[151]

Of course, the most striking publicist of the Muscovite era was himself the very emblem of autocracy, Ivan the Terrible (reigned 1533–1584). Ivan is the prototype of an absolutist ruler who can only be described as totalitarian, however anachronistic that word may be. He is a ruler who governed not only with great brutality, but also chaotically. One example can very well stand for the rest: Ivan first established an authoritative institution to stand proxy for the tsar, the so-called *oprichniki,* which was to assist him in liquidating the

---

151   Cf. Marija Sammut Kabanova, "Imperskiie motivy v tekste Stepennoi knigi tsarskogo radoslovia," in *Prolínání slovanských prostředí,* Marcel Černý, Kateřina Kedron, Marek Příhoda (eds.) (Červený Kostelec – Prague: Pavel Mervart, 2012), 31–39.

ancient boyar estate. After that, he had the oprichniki themselves liquidated. But as Shakespeare writes, "there's a method to his madness."[152] Ivan's reign united two principles: the tsar's will as the only law and violence as a confirmation of tsarist authority.[153]

Ivan the Terrible himself expounded upon this program in written polemics with Andrey Kurbsky, a leader of the boyar opposition who strove to maintain at least some elements of the estates system.[154] It is a cruel paradox: Muscovite Rus of the sixteenth century lacks an analogy to the western Renaissance in the arts and sciences, though by no means does it lack an analogy to that singular innovation born directly in the epicenter of the European Renaissance, in Florence: Niccolò Machiavelli's political teaching that everything is permitted the ruler in his strategic pursuits. Some of the few Muscovites who made it to the West during this period brought back home the "sensational innovation" which was Machiavellianism. The diplomat Fyodor Kurtsyn († after 1504) reworked into ancient Russian the story of Vlad the Impaler, the sadistic Moldavian count better known to the West as Count Dracula. The story is strangely ambiguous: one might read it as a warning about a domestic Russian Dracula; it is equally possible to understand as the description of an ideal ruler, one capable of establishing order in his country.[155] The adventurer and soldier of fortune for many of Europe's royal

152 *Hamlet*, act 2, scene 2.
153 In Czech one can read the well written biography from the pen of a Polish historian: Władisław Serczyk, *Ivan Hrozný: car vší Rusi a stvořitel samoděržaví* (Prague: Lidové noviny, 2004). What's all the more absurd is that the Czech historian Pavel Boček appended to the translation a postscript in which he relativizes the work of his Polish colleague, insisting that it is necessary also to understand the positive significance of Ivan the Terrible for the building of the Russian state.
154 Cf. Hana Skálová (ed.), *Listy Ivana Hrozného* (Prague: SNKLHU, 1957). Of course, there is the theory that the entire correspondence is a 17th-century forgery, cf. Edward L. Keenan, *The Kurbskii-Groznyi Apocrypha: The Seventeenth-Century genesis of the "Correspondence" Attributed to Prince A.M. Kurbskii and Tsar Ivan IV.* (Cambridge: Harvard University Press, 1971).
155 Cf. Ja. S. Lurje, *Pověsť o Drakule* (Moscow–Leningrad: Izdatelstvo Nauka, 1964); cf. Ja. S. Lurje, *Russkije sovremenniki Vozroždĕnija: Knigopisets Jefrosin i d'jak Fjodor Kuritsyn* (Leningrad: Izdatelstvo Nauka, 1988). The Czech translation with the title *O velikém caru*

houses, Ivan Peresvetov (16th century), one of the few who willingly left Lithuanian Rus for Muscovy rather than the other way around, is more unequivocal. In his letters he advises Ivan the Terrible to draw a lesson from the sultanate and supplement Orthodoxy with firm political government and programmatic cruelty "in true Turkish fashion."[156] Ivan the Terrible was happy to oblige.

As confirmed by Hannah Arendt in her analysis of one of Ivan's late admirers, Joseph Stalin, totalitarianism produces a continuous terror that, though it may lack logic, definitely has a function: it serves to terrorize the population, to rid them of every feeling of security and solidarity, to transform them into a completely subdued, perfectly defenseless mass.[157] Stalin held Ivan in such high regard that he assigned Sergei Eisenstein to produce the film *Ivan the Terrible* (1944). The purpose of the work was to depict the ruler of Russia's past in analogy with the ruler of Russia's present, both of them distinguished by their "brilliance" as statesmen and the "courage" they show in wantonly sacrificing such a large part of the population (to say nothing of other populations...) on the altar of the great national-imperial idea. One would like to add—as a sacrifice to Third Rome. In the end, however, Stalin was not satisfied with the film, and the second part would not be released for distribution until 1958.

But Ivan the Terrible did not need to wait for Eisenstein and Stalin. Ivan was already a frequent subject in the literature, painting, theater and music of nineteenth-century Russia. He appeared in multiple guises. There is Ivan leading an army. Ivan with his favorite holy fool. Ivan beside his son, whom he has just murdered,

Drakulovi is contained in Světla Mathauserová's collection *Povídky ze staré Rusi* (Prague: Odeon, 1984).
156 Cf. Marek Příhoda, "Ivan Peresvětov v kontextu ruského myšlení první poloviny 16. století," in Marek Příhoda (ed.), *Kulturní, duchovní a etnické kořeny Ruska: Tradice a alternativy,* (Červený kostelec: Pavel Mervart, 2005), 49–76.
157 Cf. Hannah Arendt, *The Origins of Totalitarianism* (New York: Harcourt, Brace & World, 1966).

devastated by the realization of what he has done. Ivan in a pose of spiritual meditation, even desiring to leave for a monastery. Usually he is a figure full of contrasts, conflicts, contradictions—yet all the while, he remains an object of admiration.[158] Almost never did he appear as he was depicted in sources of his own time, as a tyrant and human monster, a mass murderer and psychopath. Evidently, Russian historical memory has on the whole proven quite forgiving, willing to excuse all his crimes in exchange for his one accomplishment—the expansion of the Russian state. He turned Moscow into Third Rome. Because of that, all else was forgiven. Because of that, he was entitled to absolute obedience.

The historian Nikolai Karamzin celebrated not only Ivan the Terrible, he also heaped praise on Kurbsky's servant, Vasily Shibanov. It is said that Ivan became so furious upon receiving from Shibanov's hand an unpleasant letter from Kurbsky that the tsar took his staff and, with it, nailed the foot of the messenger to the floor. Without protest, Shibanov stood quietly until Ivan had finished with the letter. Shibanov demonstrated in his comportment the absolute obedience toward the tsar which his own employer, Kurbsky, so deplorably lacked. And that, according to Karamzin, but also according to poet A.K. Tolstoy's "Vasily Shibanov" (1858), represents the true Russian hero, a real "Russian soul".

This brief overview shows that Ivan's "afterlife" in Russian culture was just as terrible as was his real life. It is certainly offers a terrible and terrifying perspective on the history of Russian spirituality. Only in the most recent literature, that of dissent under the Bolsheviks and in Putin's Russia (Scene 19 and Conclusion), does a more literarily sophisticated picture emerge, one taking liberties with categories of space and time, but for all that still "realistic" as far as the substantial, archetypal, absolutely inexcusable terror of

---

158 Cf. Natalia Nikolaievna Matya, *Ivan Groznyj: Istorizm i lichnost pravitelia v otechestvennom iskusstve XIX–XX věka* (Sankt Peterburg: Aleteja, 2010).

Ivan the Terrible is concerned. The best rendered and most brutal depiction of Ivan the Terrible's legacy to date is certainly that given by the prose writer Vladimir Sorokin in his novel *Day of the Oprichnik* (see Conclusion).

There were many Muscovites of the period who held dissenting views of Ivan the Terrible and the whole ideology of Third Rome. And they began to search for alternatives, whether on the outside, across the frontier of Muscovite Rus, or from within, but beyond the official political structure of church and state.

Muscovite Spiritual Counterculture I: Nonpossessors, Orthodox Humanists, and Holy Fools

YEAR:
1518

PLACE:
Moscow

EVENT:
Maxim the Greek arrives to speak of Athos and
the Italian Renaissance

WORKS:
The Cathedral of Vasily the Blessed (1555–1588);
Boris Godunov by Alexander Pushkin (1824–1825);
Pamphalon the Entertainer by Nikolai Leskov (1887)

Critical accounts of Russia's cultural and spiritual history often place emphasis exclusively on "Muscovite spirituality," defined as the identification of the church with the state and of spiritual life with outward liturgical custom. This "Muscovite" inheritance is then carried over to the Bolshevik era, with Marxism replacing Christianity as the ideological foundation (Scene 18). Totalitarian rule founded upon the cult of an omnipotent leader venerated through a complicated system of ritual and arbitrary terror, this is often understood as a universal principle of Russian identity.

According to the opposite point of view, searching for the good and the inspirational in Russian spiritual culture, emphasis should instead fall on inwardness and depth, the emotional and mystical experience of Orthodox iconography and ecclesiastical music, the patristic wisdom of monastic elders, and the poignancy of simple believers who visit sacred icons while reciting the Jesus prayer. This idealization of "sacred Rus" is in no small measure a projection invented by Orthodox romanticism, a line of thought popularized across the world in the works of nineteenth and twentieth-century Russian artists, authors, and intellectuals such as Dostoevsky, Repin, Solovyov, Solzhenitsyn, Tarkovsky, and others. This projection, however, has its antecedents and historical roots. Its origins lie in the Muscovite period, a time when a retreat to the interior came about as a reaction to the outward violence and crudity of the state church. "Sacred Rus", in other words, born of the counterculture. And from it come all the later forms of Russian counterculture, within Christianity and outside of it. A diversity of voices, words, and gestures joined together in this quiet protest against the "Orthodoxy" of Ivan the Terrible, Joseph Volotsky, and all the other prelates and powerholders who declared obedience to authority to be Christianity's most important virtue.

The first source of spiritual counterculture was the monastic movement of the Transvolgans, also called the Nonpossessors, who brought to the Russian Orthodox Church a vision of a church turned inward, one not so concerned with ceremony and not at all with power and property. At the center of this new spiritual movement was the practice of inner prayer, hesychasm. The Greek word *hesychia* means calm, silence, and solitude. In the wider sense, all eastern monks were hesychasts, beginning with the hermits in Egypt. One speaks in a narrower sense of a hesychastic movement in late Byzantium of the thirteenth to the fifteenth centuries, above all on the sacred Mount Athos.[159]

Hesychasm had a practical aspect, a thoroughly devised psychosomatic technique called the Jesus prayer. The core of this technique, described in depth and propagated throughout the Orthodox world by St. Gregory of Sinai (1265–1346), consists in the continuous "mantric" repetition of a Greek text, Κύριε Ἰησοῦ Χριστέ, Υἱὲ τοῦ Θεοῦ, ἐλέησόν με τὸν ἁμαρτωλόν, translated into Church Slavonic, *Gospodi Isuse Christe, Syne Bozhij, pomiluj mja greshnago* (Lord Jesus Christ, son of God, have mercy upon me, a sinner). The prayer should gradually be synchronized with one's breathing to the point that it enters the subconscious mind, or, to use the more appropriate term from Orthodox mystical anthropology, until it "enters the heart." "In the heart," it becomes such a part of the monk's being that he no longer needs to think about the content of his words—the prayer is prayed by the body itself. Hesychasm also has a theoretical aspect in the teachings of Gregory Palamas (1296–1359). "Divine energies" are said to be revealed to the person in prayer, manifested through the "light of Tabor"—according to the New Testament, the light which emanated from the body of Jesus when he appeared to his apostles on Mount Tabor (Mt 17: 1–8).[160]

The reception of hesychasm in Rus was as lively as in Byzantium. The idea of a direct, "negative" or "apophatic" pathway to God (one

159 Cf. Steven Runciman, *The Fall of Constantinople 1453* (Cambridge: Cambridge University Press, 1965).

160 Cf. Basile Krivochéine, "Asketické a theologické učení sv. Řehoře Palamy," *Orthodox revue* 2 (1998): 8–47.

that turns away from all things visible) seized hold of a Russia laid waste by the Mongols and tyrannized by Ivan the Terrible, much like it had earlier enthralled a late Byzantium encircled by the Turks and in the middle of its final blossoming. Russian monks began to read Church Slavonic translations of Gregory of Sinai prepared by Bulgarian monks on the Holy Mount Athos. Some of them even made the journey to Athos themselves to receive "advanced hesychastic training." The St. Panteleimon Monastery, a Russian link in the chain of predominantly Greek monasteries of the Holy Mountain, was located here as early as the twelfth century.[161] The Jesus prayer was given the technical label *umnoye delaniye* (spiritual practice). An image of the meditative hesychast absorbed in the inwardness of prayer can be found in the angelic figures of Rublev's *Holy Trinity* (Scene 5). The enormous popularity of the Lord's Transfiguration on Mount Tabor (Metamorfósis tú Kyriú, Preobrazhenie Gospodne), one of the twelve major holy days (dodekaórton, dvunadesjatie prazdniki) which recalls the main events in the lives of Jesus and Mary, must also be sought in connection to hesychasm. The Transfiguration figures as the most direct demonstration in the life of Jesus of his divine nature.

The blossoming of Russian hesychasm occurred along a network of monasteries that were gradually built from Moscow toward the north as far as the White Sea and Arctic Ocean. The most famous of these—later transformed by the communists into a concentration camp (Scene 19)—was founded on the Solovetsky Islands in the White Sea. The region is sometimes referred to panegyrically as the Thebaid of the north (after the Thebais region in Egypt),[162] the religious movement itself, however, takes its name after the area lying "behind the Volga"—the "Transvolgans." The movement was

---

161 Cf. Sáva Chilandarec, *Kniha o Svaté hoře Athonské* (Prague: Matice česká, 1911).
162 Cf. G.P. Fedotov, *The Russian Religious Mind,* vol. 2 (Cambridge: Harvard University Press, 1966), 246, 257.

founded by the monk Nilus Sorsky (1433–1508), who had spent time on Mount Athos learning Greek. Nilus returned to Rus with a clear system of ideas. He founded a monastic dwelling (*skete*) on the Sora river not far from the St. Cyril monastery, and he soon became the primary spiritual authority and teacher of religious life. If we read Nilus' texts, above all the *The Monastic Rule* (or *Sketic Rule,* regulations for the monasteries he founded), we find the patristic tradition in its most noble form, which refrains from polemics, curses no one, and doesn't even prescribe any severe form of asceticism. Regarding the outer functioning of the monastery, Nilus says very little. The focus of the *Monastic Rule* is exclusively the spiritual life, the classification of passions and evil thoughts, introduction to the practice of mental prayer, and the (fittingly classical) advice to take "everything in moderation." The monk is supposed to engage in reflection upon each one of his actions: neither careful recitation of the sacred texts, strict fasting, nor any other aspect of outward religiosity can benefit the soul if it does not come from within, if it does emanate from the purity of the heart. Nilus developed the theme further in letters to his disciples—apparently the first letters written in the spirit of the much celebrated "council of the wise elders" (Scene 14).[163]

Not only do the teachings of Nilus Sorsky and the principles of the Transvolgans have Byzantine roots, there are also parallels in the West. Not much earlier in the Netherlands, a spiritual movement was born which quickly spread across the whole of Central Europe, the *devotio moderna* (modern devotion). Though it emerged from a different social context (the growing towns) and different intellectual background (the turn from scholasticism back to the scripture and patristic writings), it in a very similar way marked the turn from outward markers of religious devotion—from the cult

163   Gelian M. Prokhorov, "Poslaniia Nila Sorskogo," *Trudy Otdela drevnerusskoy literatury* 29 (1974), 125–143; Cf. A.I. Alexeev (ed.), *Nil Sorskyi v kulture i knizhnosti drevnei Rusi,* (St. Petersburg: Rossiyskaya natsionalnaya biblioteka, 2008).

of holy relics, liturgical refinement, and all the unruliness of the power-hungry world—to the inner experience of everyday life and the *imitatio Christi* (the imitation of Christ). Such is the title the best-known work to have emerged from the *devotio moderna*, a book of spiritual instruction written by Thomas à Kempis (1380–1471). Kempis can, cum grano salis, be regarded as the "Latinate Nilus Sorsky," or Nilus as the "Russian Kempis."[164]

Unlike the Dutch cities, the atmosphere in Muscovite Rus was inhospitable to this sort of inwardly oriented spirituality. Nilus was dragged into religious debates that eventually brought an end to his movement. He carried on a long dispute with the Josephites (the followers of Joseph of Volok) which was concerned not so much with hesychasm itself as with two other practical matters: the role of violence in religious life and the question of church property.

The first concerned a sect called the Judaizers (Scene 8). The Transvolgans did not disagree with Josephites on the question of whether to tolerate this group of heretics; tolerance in this sense was as foreign to the one side as it was to the other. Where they parted ways was in their opinions about what to do with proven heretics. The Transvolgans asked only for atonement—the Josephites demanded execution, even for those who repent. The Josephites won.

The second conflict concerned whether the church should be poor and devoted to service or, to the contrary, be rich and devoted to power—put concretely, whether monasteries should own land, villages, and "souls." The debate was at first limited to a conflict of ideas. The Transvolgans were for a poor church, and thus they received the name *nestyazhateli* (Nonpossessors). Characteristic of the Josephites in their dispute with the Nonpossessors was the claim that, should monasteries remain poor, then wealthy aristocrats wouldn't

164   Cf. Johan Huizinga, *The Autumn of the Middle Ages* (Chicago: University of Chicago Press, 1996); Martin C. Putna, afterword to *Zrcadlo prostých duší,* by Markéta Porete (Prague: Malvern, 2013).

want to join them. It would then be impossible to recruit "worthy" candidates for bishop seats. Then there was the conflict over influence. And here too, Joseph prevailed with the support of Grand Prince Vasily III. Since Joseph automatically considered his opponents to be enemies of Christ, he saw to their destruction. Nilus Sorsky died in peace, but not long after his death the Transvolgans were pursued as heretics and their monasteries were mostly closed down or demolished. The spokesman for the Transvolgans, Nilus's devoted student, the prince and monk Vassian Patrikeyev (1471–after 1531), was condemned as a heretic in 1531 and confined to the Volokolamsk Monastery (the main bastion of the Josephites), where he died after only a few months.[165]

This Josephite way of doing away with their enemies caught on in the Russian Orthodox Church. When it was decided, for whatever reason, that the condemned should not be executed, he was delivered to a monastery as if to repent, when in fact he was expected to die a quiet and "natural" death. The conditions of confinement were such that one could not be expected to live long. The person's death was not announced publicly; he simply disappeared. The communists adopted methods not altogether unlike those of the Josephites, but in a secularized form. Instead of a monastery, dissidents were sent away to a psychiatric unit—or in the case of the Solovetsky Islands, to a former monastery reconstrued as a labor camp.[166]

George P. Fedotov refers bluntly to the Transvolgans' destruction and subsequent stagnation as "the tragedy of old Russian spirituality."[167] Spiritual opposition nonetheless continued even after the suppression of the Transvolgans. Those who were unsatisfied with Orthodoxy as its existed lacked dependable leadership after Nilus's death. His place was eventually taken by a Greek monk named

165 Cf. Pavel Boček, *Stát a církev v Rusku na přelomu 15. a 16. století* (Brno: Masarykova univerzita, 1995).
166 Cf. Yuri Brodsky, *Solovki: Dvadcat' let Osobogo Naznacheniya* (Moscow: Rosspen, 2002).
167 Fedotov, *The Russian Religious Mind*, 377.

Maxim, known in Russian cultural history as Maksim Grek or Maxim the Greek (1470–1555). Originally, however, he was named Michael Trivolis. He counted among the wave of Greeks who abandoned their homeland in the aftermath of the Turkish invasion. In his youth, he journeyed to Italy and, from there, to the epicenter of the Renaissance—to Florence under the rule of Lorenzo de' Medici. He attended lectures at Italian universities and participated in the founding of Aldus Manutius's pioneering printing press. But then, under the influence of Girolamo Savonarola's sermons, Trivolis experienced a crisis of faith which led him to renounce the "pagan" Renaissance. Returning home, he entered the Vatopedi monastery on Mount Athos where he adopted the monastic name Maxim.[168] In 1516 his superiors dispatched Maxim to unfamiliar territory in the far north, a region where the church struggled with a lack of theological literature and knowledge of Greek. Thus were they moved to ask the Greeks for assistance.

Maxim, now known as "the Greek," translated manuscripts during his first two years in Moscow and he even attempted to correct some of the older liturgical texts. In doing so, however, he soon ran up against the stubbornness of Moscow, the Third Rome, which refused even to entertain the very notion that any part of the ceremony as currently performed could be in need of change. Consequently, Maxim the Greek was tried as a heretic and blasphemer. His fate was sealed when, at trial, he persisted in his efforts to persuade the ecclesiastical court of their philological ignorance, urging them to leave such learned matters up to him.[169] After a good many years in prison, he received clemency and could return to his literary work. At an advanced age, Maxim was moved to a monastery and via

---

168 Cf. N.V. Sinicyna, *Odysea Maxima Řeka* (Červený Kostelec, 2013).
169 There exists also an alternative theory according to which the real reason behind the persecution of Maxim was his criticism of the morality of Grand Prince Vasilii III and his connection to the Nonpossessors. For an overview of opinions see Boček, *Stát a církev v Rusku na přelomu 15. a 16. století*, 83–86.

facti rehabilitated. His one request was however denied: to return to Athos.

In the cell of his monastery as in prison, Maxim the Greek was constantly receiving visits by Russians eager to know about the goings-on in the world. He willingly obliged, patiently explaining a number of important issues to his Russian peers: where the apocrypha are untruthful; why they should not believe in astrology; the appearance of monasteries on Athos; the difference between Islam and Christianity; who is Savonarola, why is he a saint. It was from Maxim's letters that Russia first received word of the Egyptian pyramids and the discovery of America.[170]

Assessing the actual impact of Maxim the Greek has been the subject of much debate in cultural history. Some scholars celebrate him as a propagator of humanism and enlightenment. Others find fault with him, for though an apostle of the Renaissance, he nevertheless spoke poorly of it to the Russians, describing it in the worst possible terms as a haven of astrologists and pederasts. What he offered Russia was Savonarola, not Petrarch. Élie Denissoff captures the contours of Maxim's character best, describing him as a type of "Christian humanist" who combined humanism and the natural sciences with an unshakeable Christian faith, who rejected the ignorance and violence of Joseph Volotsky but also the neopaganism of the high Renaissance.[171]

During his life, and still more after his death, Maxim the Greek became an idol for Russian men fighting the waves of nationalism, messianism, and obscurantism that posed as the "one true Orthodox faith." Vassian Patrikeyev listened to Maxim to assemble arguments for his own struggle for a poor church. Prince Andrei Kurbsky, Ivan the Terrible's foremost opponent, declared Maxim his great

---

170 Maxim's writings have appeared in several versions, in Church Slavonic and translated into modern Russian. The collected works have appeared since 2007 under the editorship of A.F. Zamaleeva.

171 Cf. Élie Denissoff, *Maxime le Grec et l'Occident* (Paris: Université de Louvain, 1943).

instructor. Maxim gained the respect of Artemius as well, hegumen of the Holy Trinity Lavra of St. Sergius and a great admirer of Nilus. It is not at all a coincidence that Patrikeyev ended up in the gallows, Kurbsky and Artemius in exile (Scene 9). None of them intended to bring the Renaissance to Moscow, not to mention to introduce reform—what they longed for was a spiritual and intellectual deepening of Orthodoxy. One might say they desired to fashion something like an "Orthodox humanism."

A second and quite different alternative spirituality was *iurodstvo*, holy foolery. Sixteenth-century Moscow represents the major arena for performances in which men and women play themselves, reversing established religious and moral principles through feigned madness, public nudity, shouting matches, prophesy, and other improvised performances on city streets. The aura of respect (or superstition) surrounding the *iurodivyi*, the "fools for Christ" permitted behavior unthinkable for respectable Muscovites wrapped up in their warm fur coats.

The European mind associates holy foolery, the most paradoxical form of saintliness, with Russia. But its roots lie deeper. Examples of "antilogical" and intentionally disgraceful behavior, spectacular violations of social norms sanctioned by divine exemption, can be found among the prophets of the Old Testament: Hosea publicly fornicated with a prostitute (Hos. 1), Isaiah walked around naked (Isa. 20), Jeremiah wore an ox yoke (Jer. 27), Zedekiah donned horns of iron (1 Kings 22:11), and Ezekiel baked bread over excrement (Ezek. 4). One recognizes in the behavior of the Greek cynics, with Diogenes at their head, another prototype of the holy fool—the difference being that the cynic decides to live in a barrel and defecate in public based on reasoned argument and his own free will, without appealing to commandments from above.

"Classic" holy foolery emerged first in Christian Egypt and Syria between the fourth and sixth centuries, and it did so in two forms. The first is represented by an extreme and often theatrical asceticism that was practiced by the hermits in the region. These were monks who according to legend spent long years standing on top of tall poles (so-called Stylites), living in the branches of trees (Dendrites), carrying chains (Siderophores), wandering about naked (Gymnites), or covering themselves in mud (Rhypontites). The purpose of these practices was to mortify the flesh and thereby deceive the demons with which they did battle in the desert. In the hagiography of the Egyptian saint Pachomius, the quotation from Paul's first letter to the Corinthians was first used in this sense:

> We are fools for the sake of Christ, but you are wise in Christ. [...] We are poorly clothed and beaten and homeless, and we grow weary from the work of our own hands. When reviled, we bless; when persecuted, we endure; when slandered, we speak kindly. We have become like the rubbish of the world. (1 Cor. 4:10–13)

The phrase *móros dia ton Christon* (foolish for Christ) became the official label for such people, the *iurodivye*. The Greek *móros* was simply replaced by the word *salos*, an expression of unclear origins. The officially canonized *iurodivye* of Byzantium thus received the title *saloi* (fools), in Russian translation *blazhennyi*, which originally meant both "imbecile" and "blessed." Rus, given its sense for extreme corporality, developed the term *urod*, or *iurod*, which signified a person with a birth defect. The iurodivyi could thus be either a cripple or a fool. Only later did the word *urod* (cripple or freak) become semantically distinct from *iurod* (fool, *iurodivyi*).

Egypt gave rise to a second prototype of holy foolery as well—the belief in "hidden servants of the Lord." This notion follows from the idea that the entire world is full of divine energy, a holy force in search of channels through which to appear. It thus sometimes happens that divine energy pours forth through a person scorned by others, one who is otherwise perceived as lowly and sinful. Those surrounding him may not suspect it, for the saint conceals his ontological saintliness. By day he behaves as always, but at night he chooses a hidden place to pray and pours tears for his fellow citizens, sometimes even prophesizing or levitating. An eastern legend tells of an old monk who searched of someone holier than himself. To his initial consternation, an angel led him first to a prostitute, then a street conjurer, and then a lunatic. There is nothing the old monk can do but sigh together with Paul, "for the foolishness of God is wiser than human wisdom, and the weakness of God is stronger than human strength." (1 Cor. 1:25)

Modern Russian literature has reworked these religious themes carried over from an older culture. One might look to the writings of Nikolai Leskov (1831–1895) for an example. His novella *Pamphalon the Entertainer* (1875) is set in Byzantium. Leskov's depiction of Byzantium's formalized Christianity is a transparent parable about contemporary Russia. An itinerant performer turns out to be a holy and righteous man, his life a hidden counterweight to the otherwise prevalent moral evil. Though he stubbornly rejects being labeled righteous, to say nothing of being called a saint, the wanderer casually does good deeds and even performs an occasional miracle.

The life of one of the most paradoxical and most beloved saints is founded just on this principle of "hidden saintliness." This is the story of Alexis, "the man of God," well known in medieval Russia as well as in the West. According to the legend, Alexis fled the home of his wealthy and benevolent family (the Greek version places it in Constantinople, the Latin version in Rome) to wander about the world as a vagabond. He one day returned to his native city and, motivated by asceticism, lived there unrecognized as a beggar at court. He revealed himself to his parents only before death and, though they were guilty of no special offence, he caused them great pain by doing so. The meaning of this absurd legend becomes apparent once we consider the dualism of the medieval worldview: everything this-worldly is relative to that which is eternal. Alexis prays for his parents (and for his town) with all his saintly power, thereby assuring them salvation and demonstrating the highest form of love and service. To modern reader asks skeptically if it would not have been better for Alexis to have secured his family's salvation by less duplicitous means (they were not, after all, any great sinners, rather to the contrary!). The legend replies, obviously not, for inscrutable Providence sees people, things, and relations differently. Alexis's story also contains the theme of "saintly pliability," a consciously passive, kenotic or self-abating, self-vacating model of sainthood. Under the blows that fall upon the ordinary Russian from above, such an understanding of holiness represents the only weapon available to the common man, his only viable ideal. This is what Dostoevsky had in mind when he gave the name Alexei to the most congenial of characters in his novel *Brothers Karamazov*.

Alexis, the desert ascetic, and the holy prostitute carefully hide their saintliness from the crowd. The "urban iurodivyi" of the classical type, first represented by Simeon the Holy Fool (Salos) from Syrian Emesa (7th century), behaves in the opposite manner. He attacks the crowd and provokes it through the ostentatious violation of fasting, by fondling prostitutes, and throwing stones.[172] The holy fool is conceivable only in an established, outwardly Christian society. He does not permit others to continue their habitual, "civil" religiosity. His paradoxical existence overturns common assumptions about the high and the low, about virtue and sinfulness. One important fact, however, differentiates Simeon from his later followers: the contemporaries of Simeon could not have known that they were being honored by the presence of a saint. All those who succeeded him could make use of this ready-made paradigm. Whenever one came across a disheveled man spewing forth insults on the public square of Edessa or Constantinople, one had at least to stop and consider the possibility that the social deviant might in fact be a saint. Very

---

172   Text of the legend of Simeon Salos in Emilie Bláhová et al. (eds.), *Byzantské legendy* (Prague: Vyšehrad, 1980).

much for this reason, good Orthodox Christians worried over the problem of distinguishing "genuine" iurodivye from "false" iurodivye. A genuine holy fool is a saint, someone who intentionally feigns madness. A false holy fool, on the other hand, presents himself as a saint in order to enjoy the privileges of iurodstvo (absolute impunity from even the most heinous transgressions). He does so, however, without divine sanction.

For the cultural historian, iurodstvo invites interpretation. Some have found it in a form of the carnivalesque and ceremonial reversal of values;[173] others see it as a kind of service to the world, "a special mission, not by word or beneficent action but through the power of the Spirit [...] to lay bare the radical contradiction between the Christian truth and both the common sense and the moral sense of the world;"[174] or "an unconscious protest against a God who created such an imperfect world" and a sadomasochistic social therapy.[175] Others have compared it to Finnish shamanism or described it as nothing but a case for psychiatry. One can even consider further connections across cultures and understand iurodstvo in relation to such phenomena as the beatniks, hippies, and other "leftist" countercultures of the twentieth century (those who choose to live at the margins of society, rejecting traditional notions of family and social behavior); conceptual art and, within its parameters, "body art" especially (work with one's own body as an artistic artifact, sometimes bordering on self-destruction); Nietzsche or Dostoevsky's ideas about the "strong," the "initiated," those who "live beyond normal laws" (the holy fool takes the liberty of doing things not permitted to the typical Christian—and if the latter dare undertake anything similar, he faces reprimand and even punishment from the holy

173 Cf. Alexandr Pančenko, "Jurodstvo jako podívaná; Jurodství jako společenský protest," in *Smích staré Rusi*, ed. Dmitrij Lichačov and Alexandr Pančenko (Prague: Odeon, 1984), 98–168.
174 Fedotov, *The Russian Religious Mind*, 320, 322.
175 Cf. Sergey Ivanov, *Holy Fools in Byzantium and Beyond*, trans. Simon Franklin (Oxford: Oxford University Press, 2006).

fool); or ultimately Pentecostal and charismatic Christianity (ecstatic "theatrical" piety, the use of "angelic" languages).

The comprehensiveness of such associations, however, is both tempting and misleading. Iurodstvo appears to be an entirely "natural" phenomenon when perceived from within the paradigm of ancient Christian Egypt, Byzantium, or Muscovite Rus. To this model of the cosmos belongs an entire spiritual world populated by angels and daemons, full of hidden connections between words, deeds, and prayer. These are the "cosmic scales" as referred to by the French Catholic romantic Léon Bloy in his novel *La Femme pauvre,* the story of a woman who ends her days on the streets as a sort of "Catholic holy fool." The behavior of the holy fool has a specific logic in a world thus perceived. By day he undertakes to deceive the demons, at night he prays—and thus does he save souls, which is what the ancient Christian model of the world is all about. To attain this goal, salvation, one may choose from means that are good as well as extreme.

Iurodstvo had been a familiar paradigm of saintliness in Rus since the 12th century, when there first arrived a translation of the *Life of the St. Andrew Salos,* after Simeon the best known of Byzantium's holy fools (10th century). The first domestic holy fools appeared in the Kievan era. According to the Kievan Patericon, after years of asceticism and voluntary isolation, Isaac of the Cave Monastery "began to perform the foolish stunts of a iurodivyi"[176] to escape the devils who tormented him seven years long with visions of hell, spiritual torture that nearly cost him his life. For Isaac, of course, iurodstvo functioned not so much as a harsh therapy for those around him as a very personal means toward salvation. "Not wanting human glory, he began to do foolish things and to annoy people, now the abbot,

---

176 Daniela Hodrová (ed.), *Smích a běs: Staroruské hagiografické příběhy* (Prague: Odeon, 1988), 31.

now the brothers, and for this received many beatings."[177] As soon as Isaac had vanquished the demons and they gave him peace, he returned to the life of an ordinary monk.

All the holy fools after Isaac are urban and "theatrical", be they Novgorodian (especially Procopius of Ustyug, †1303, and Michael of Klop, †1456) or Muscovite (the most famous being John Bolshoy Kolpak, or Big Cap, and Basil the Blessed, or the Fool, (1469–1552)). Regarding the latter, one reads the contemporaneous account in the *Stepennaya kniga* (Book of Degrees):

> He wore no clothing but made do with that which covered his body, he owned not even a shirt as he felt no shame just like the first creation before sin. But for that he was clothed by untold kindness, which made him beautiful. […] Basil the Blessed avoided human habitation, and as if incorporeal he took frost for warmth and fire would not catch on to him. […] He secretly prayed in the divine cathedrals by night, for the church gates would by themselves open to him.[178]

In contrast to their Byzantine models, these "fools" take on a responsibility other than saving souls for eternity. Michael of Klop rendered valuable service to Moscow in its struggle with Novgorod. The holy fools of Muscovy, by contrast, made use of their immunity to openly criticize "God on earth" himself, the Tsar. Ivan the Terrible didn't concern himself all too much with anyone's opinion save a few holy fools the likes of Nicholas of Pskov or Basil the Blessed. It was allegedly out of respect for Nicholas that Ivan refrained from destroying his namesake city, Pskov, as he had earlier destroyed Novgorod. When Basil the Blessed died, a chapel was added to the cathedral on Red Square to serve as his tomb. Officially designated the Cathedral of the Intercession, the building is better known as

---

177   Ibid., 32.
178   Ibid., 196.

the Cathedral of Basil the Blessed and represents a primary visual marker of Muscovite cultural "contrariness," a total exception to European traditions in the plastic arts.

After Basil came others. Under Tsar Boris Godunov at the beginning of the seventeenth century, "an unkempt and naked man walked along the streets in a bitter frost, prophesizing calamities and openly disparaging Godunov. But Godunov remained silent, daring not to touch even a hair on his head. Perhaps because he feared the people, perhaps because he himself believed that this person was holy."[179] This was according to the enlightened historian Nikolai Karamzin. Pushkin referred to Karamzin in his drama *Boris Godunov* (1824–1825), when he has a holy fool appear before the tsar:

> SIMPLETON. Boris, Boris, the children are mean to Nikolka.
> TSAR. Give him some alms. What's he wailing about?
> SIMPLETON. The children are mean to Nikolka. Cut their throats!… the way you did the young Tsarevich.
> BOYARS. Be off, you fool! Seize the simpleton!
> TSAR. Let him be. Pray for me, poor Nikolka.
> (*He leaves.*)
> SIMPLETON. (*Calling after him*) Oh, no! No prayers for the Herod-Tsar… Our Lady won't allow it.[180]

The holy fool will go on to participate in the struggle over traditional liturgical practices in the 17th century (Scene 10). Archpriest Avvakum described one of them according to tradition: "By day he behaved as a holy fool, then all night he remained tearful and in prayer."[181] But to complicate things further, beside the holy fool-

179 Nikolai Karamzin, *Obrazy z dějin říše ruské,* vol. 2 (Prague: Odeon, 1975), 82.
180 Alexander Pushkin, *Boris Godunov and Other Dramatic Works* (Oxford: Oxford University Press, 2009), 73.
181 Bohuslav Ilek (ed.), *Život protopopa Avvakuma* (Prague: Odeon, 1975), 82.

ery of naked wanderers, Russia also knew the iurodstvo of its rulers. This was an opportunistic and unpredictable iurodstvo, a mask placed before the face at the most unexpected moments only to be removed just as unexpectedly. The Roman Emperors from Caligula and Nero to Commodus, the unworthy son of Marcus Aurelius, serve as archetypes. They were described with alarm by the period's historians Tacitus, Suetonius, and Herodian.[182] The Byzantine Michael III (9th century) enjoyed "going mad" from time to time.[183] Why then shouldn't Ivan the Terrible now and again arrange for a blasphemous liturgy with his faithful *oprichniki* at court? Why should he not occasionally sign off as "Parfeni the holy fool" or "the virginal holy fool"?[184] We even find echoes of the paradigm Tsar-as-holy fool in the absurd and bizarre behavior of Peter the Great and the cruel "pranks" of Joseph Stalin.

But as rationality and enlightenment penetrated Russia despite the country's isolation, the sacred aura surrounding iurodstvo began to diminish. As did the patience of Russia's rulers. Holy fools who sided with the Old Believers were liquidated mercilessly. The church no longer wished to know anything about them and from the beginning of the nineteenth century they began to be shut away in Russia's first asylums.

And yet iurodstvo has not disappeared. The figure of the wandering fool has continued to earn popular respect. In 1988, at the sobor marking the thousandth anniversary of the baptism of Rus, Xenia of Saint Petersburg was included among the newly canonized saints. Xenia, "fool for Christ" (†1803), a woman who decided to save the soul of her deceased husband by following the path of iurodstvo,

182 Cf. Tacitus, *The Annals of Imperial Rome* (New York: Penguin, 1956); Suetonius, *The Twelve Caesars* (New York: Penguin, 2007); Herodian, *History of the Roman Empire from the Death of Marcus Aurelius to the Accession of Gordian III.* (Berkeley: University of California Press, 1961).
183 Cf. Bohumila Zástěrová et al., *Dějiny Byzance* (Prague: Academia, 1992).
184 Cf. Dmitrij Lichačov, "Histrionství Ivana Hrozného: K otázce smíchového stylu jeho děl," in *Smích staré Rusi,* ed. Dmitrij Lichačov and Alexandr Pančenko (Prague: Odeon, 1984), 33–43.

sold all her property to wander the streets of "respectable" and "European" Saint Petersburg playing with children, prophesizing and miraculously healing the sick—and she did this while wearing her dead husband's clothes. The theme of transvestitism has accompanied iurodstvo since its beginnings in Egypt, and even when this sort of asceticism was banned by the church there remained in the hagiography a number of "holy transvestites" who fled the lechery of men by donning male attire (a certain western parallel can be found in the bearded St. Wilgefortis, or St. Starosta, of Prague's Loreta). The cult of St. Xenia of Petersburg, a female saint so unsuited to the proper manners of the Petrine era, a Russian analogy to Léon Bloy's *femme pauvre*, survived numerous regime changes to finally receive official church recognition.

The paradigm of the holy fool in the meantime has carried over to the sphere of culture. Provocative and scandalous, alternating between eccentric stunts and bursts of contrition, authors such as Nikolai Gogol, Fyodor Dostoevsky, Vasily Rozanov introduced holy foolery to the rest of the world. The latest and most thoroughgoing return of iurodstvo in its role as political protest, although perhaps not originally intended as such, was of course that represented by the band Pussy Riot and their "Punk Prayer" (see Conclusion).

Red Rus, Novgorodian Rus, and the "Window to Europe"

YEAR:
1255

PLACE:
Lviv

EVENT:
Daniel of Galicia receives the royal crown from
the pope.

WORKS:
Lviv (1256); *Legend of the Novgorodian White Cowl*
(1500); *Vadim of Novgorod* by Iakov Kniazhnin
(1789); *Martha the Mayoress* by Nikolai Karamzin
(1803)

There existed more promising, more "outward-looking" alternatives to the Muscovite state model. These alternatives included state formations whose inhabitants identified themselves as Russian, but whose societies were not characterized by totalitarian autocracy, the violent monopolization of culture, and scornful isolation from Europe. They were founded, in fact, on quite opposite qualities: estates democracy, cultural and religious plurality, and an effort to stay current with European developments from humanism and the Reformation to the Renaissance, Baroque, and Enlightenment. In the shadow of Muscovy's later metamorphosis into an expansive empire, Europe often forgets that there was not one Russia on the geographical and mental map of the fourteenth to seventeenth centuries, but several: Muscovite Rus and "the others." In terms of geography, we might label these state formations in relation to Moscow as "western" or "southern" Russia. When discussing these state formations, mention must first be made of Galicia, or Red Rus, and then Novgorodian and finally Lithuanian Rus.

The kingdom of Galicia, also called Red Rus or Red Ruthenia, represents the last political offshoot of Kiev. Galicia's Prince Daniel (1205–1255) was determined to win back the freedom of Kiev and all Rus from the Mongols, and prepared to unite with pagan Lithuanian and the Catholic West to do so. We read in the chronicle of the era, the Chronicle of Galicia and Volhynia[185], that Daniel was the first Russian ruler of European stature and with European interests since Iaroslav Osmomysl (the Wise). He fought a battle near Opava in 1252 against the army of the Přemyslid Ottokar II of Bohemia, disputing the inheritance of the Austrian Babenbergs; he urged the pope to declare a crusade against the Mongols; and in 1255 he even converted to Catholicism, receiving the royal crown from the pope and the title *rex Russiae,* King of Russia. Western promises of

---

185 Cf. Jitka Komendová, "Haličsko-volyňské knížectví a jeho letopis," in *Haličsko-volyňský letopis* (Prague: Argo, 2010), 5–37.

assistance, however, never materialized, and Daniel's forlorn campaign against the Mongols collapsed.

Daniel's efforts "merely" achieved Galicia's westward cultural orientation. At the close of the eighteenth century, this westward orientation was strengthened by Galicia's membership in the Austrian confederation. Galicia thereby found itself the only part of former Kievan Rus in the cultural space of Central Europe. As such, it also became one of the centers of the Ukrainian cultural revival (Scene 12). Galicia's capital city, Lviv, founded by Daniel, testifies to Galicia's role in the cultural revival as well as to its Central European character. Architecturally and in terms of urban layout, with its elements of the Baroque, historicism, and Secession one might easily mistake old Lviv for Brno or Zagreb. One finds in Lviv religious institutions of Orthodoxy, Greek Catholicism, Roman Catholicism as well as Judaism and even branches of the Armenian Church. In terms of literature, the authors who belonged to the city have written in Ukrainian (Olha Kobylianska, Vasyl Stefanyk), Polish (Maria Konopnicka, Stanisław Lem, Zbygniew Herbert), and German (Leopold von Sacher-Masoch), as well as Jewish authors writing in German (Joseph Roth, Martin Buber) or Yiddish (Sholem Aleichem). Among the plaques and monuments commemorating all varieties of cultural celebrities, the primacy of place still belongs an equestrian statue dedicated to "King Daniel" built in the style of the Roman monument to Marcus Aurelius. It is not only the name, Daniel, that matters to Galician self-understanding; equally important is the ruler's unambiguously European title of "King."[186]

The second formation, Veliky Novgorod, represents a distinct variation of the Kievan legacy. Thanks to its remote northern location, Novgorod had the good fortune of avoiding the Mongolian invasion. Having pushed their campaign halfway to the city, the Mongols

---

[186] Characteristic of this western orientation, Daniel receives praise primarily from Ukrainian historians like of Nikolai Kostomarov (Scene 12).

decided to turn back, Novgorod thus remained free and undamaged. While the Kievan state was founded upon the tension of two political principles, the principate and estates democracy, in Novgorod it was the second which dominated. Like Pskov and Vyatka, two other cities of Russia's north, Novgorod became something like an Orthodox republic. The highest organ was the *veche*, a free gathering of citizens. At the veche took place a competition of various "parties"—sometimes in an orderly fashion, at other times less so. The veche regularly elected the state's three highest representatives: the archbishop, who held something similar to a presidential function; the prince, nothing more than a military leader; and the *posadnik*, or, roughly, the cabinet minister. Were one of the three to fall out of favor, if he were to disrupt accepted customs and ancient freedoms, then the Novgorodians would mercilessly shove him aside.[187] This system refutes the thesis that Russian tradition is in any way necessarily tied to autocracy. Novgorod reminds one rather of Athens and the other free communities of ancient Greece, or of Venice and the medieval Italian communes. Its very name, which translates as "new town," tempts one to Hellenize Novgorod—which could so easily be translated into the Greek as Neapolis.

The analogy with Greek or Italian republics also holds for Novgorod's economic and public life which was oriented toward commerce, open to the sea and, beyond the sea, to the West. Novgorod lies on Volkhov River, which flows into Lake Ladoga and continues onward as the Neva into the Baltic. German merchants and European goods arrived along this waterway (Novgorod was an associate member of the Hanseatic League),[188] and with them the cultural and spiritual influence of the West. While Novgorod remained more or less culturally static during the Kievan era, in the

---

187 Cf. A.V. Valerov, *Novgorod i Pskov: Ocherki Politicheskoi Istorii Severo-Zapadnoi Rusi XI-XIV Vekov* (St. Petersburg: Aleteiia, 2004).
188 Elena A. Rybina, *Novgorod i Ganza* (Moscow: Rukopisnye pamjatniki Drevnej Rusi, 2009).

fourteenth century it became a cultural center with European connections. At a time when the great majority of Russian territory was isolated from the West, Novgorod served as a "window to Europe."

Themes of travel, discovery, and chance encounters play a significant role in the literature of Novgorod. A journey is attributed to the Novgorodian archbishop Ioann, who supposedly flew to Jerusalem on the back of a subdued demon. According to a text from the middle of the fourteenth century, *Poslanie Vasiliia novgorodskogo o rae* (The Letter from Vasily of Novgorod about Paradise), a certain merchant is said to have made it all the way to the Isle of Bliss during a northerly sea journey, a legend resembling that about the Irish monk Brandan or other western European travelers.[189] The originality and fantasy of these Novgorodian narratives about travel to foreign lands influenced the folklore of a later era. The most significant Novgorodian tale tells of a merchant and gusli player named Sadka who journeyed to an undersea empire—and from there to the theatrical stage as the title character of Nikolai Rimsky-Korsakov's (1844–1908) opera *Sadko* (1896). These secular, inquisitive, and amusing elements of Novgorodian literature have led literary historians to speculate about a "proto-renaissance" or something like it having taken place in Novgorod, at least a modest compensation for the absence of a Russian renaissance.[190]

As far as the history of religion is concerned, Novgorod's western character becomes visible at different levels. At its most basic, and this in keeping with the Orthodox pattern, some saints arrived—or more precisely, sailed—to the area of Novgorod from the West. Anthony of Rome came quite early as a "seeker of the true faith"; Procopius of Ustyug, a man "of Latin faith and German language," arrived as an ordinary merchant. A more sophisticated level of relations with

---

189   Cf. Magdalena Moravová (ed.), *Bájné plavby do jiných světů* (Prague: Argo, 2010).
190   Cf. Ludmila Machátová, "Cesta Jana Jeruzalémského do Jeruzaléma a zpět: K otázce protorenesance v novgorodském písemnictví," in *Prolínání slovanských prostředí*, ed. Marcel Černý, Kateřina Kedron, Marek Příhoda (Červený Kostelec and Prague: Pavel Mervart, 2012), 119–125.

the West is indicated in the *Povest' o Novgorodskom Belom Klobuke* of the late fifteenth century. This work provides a clever account of how the papal tiara worn by Roman popes ended up on the head of the archbishops of Novgorod. According to one variation, Emperor Constantin himself offered the papal tiara to Pope Silvester, and when the latter refused, Constantine had it sent to Novgorod. The plot thus represents a specific take on Russia's Roman heritage. Its emphasis is at once anti-Catholic (the line of apostolic spiritual power no longer runs through Rome) and anti-Muscovite (Russia has its center not in Moscow, but Novgorod).

The most original element in the history of Novgorod are its sects, alternative religious movements which likely arose from western influences. The *Strigolniki* of fourteenth-century Novgorod denounced clerical avarice and venality in a manner similar to the Waldensian movement in France, Italy, and Germany.[191] Like the Waldensians or the theologians of the first reformation, Wycliffe and Hus, the Strigolniks concluded that a sinful pope, one ordained for money and conferring sainthood for a price, cannot be a true pope, and that the ceremonies officiated by him are therefore invalid. The Strigolniks thus refused to participate in official services. Their obscure name, *Strigolniki*, is sometimes derived from the word *postrig*, the ritualistic cutting of hair that in Orthodoxy symbolizes entrance into a monastic order, for the Strigolniks into "the inner Church."[192]

It did not take long for the Strigolniks to be condemned and, in 1376, for their leaders to be executed according to Novgorodian tradition, tossed from a bridge into the icy-cold Volkhov River. At the close of the fifteenth century there then appeared a movement that would later be called the *Zhidovstvuyushchie*, thus something like "Judaizers." The label goes back to a Jewish merchant named

---

191 Cf. Amedeo Molnár, *Valdenští: Evropský rozměr jejich vzdoru* (Prague: Kalich, 1991).
192 Cf. Natalia Alexandrovna Kazakova and Yakov Solomonovich Lure, *Antifeodalnye ereticheskie dvizheniya na Rusi XIV-nachala XVI veka* (Moscow: Izd-vo Akademii nauk SSSR, 1955).

Skhariya who is said to have arrived in the entourage of a Lithuanian prince. The merchant supposedly convinced several Novgorodian popes of the advantages of Judaism—and then disappeared from the historical record. The entire story of the mysterious Jew Skhariya can only be the invention of clerical heresy-hunters, who characteristically attributed unorthodox attitudes to the influence of the "treacherous Jews." The possibility of Jewish influence cannot be excluded completely, however, for there certainly were many Jews in Lithuania. What little has remained of Judaizers' teachings, mostly contained in the writings of their opponents such as Joseph Volotsky (Scene 6), has more to do with the Strigolniks and their criticisms of the church oriented toward the same "protoreformation." Unlike the Strigolniks, however, Judaizers possessed that most powerful instrument of the Reformation, the complete Bible. This, too, they had apparently acquired from abroad, perhaps courtesy of their adherent Fyodor Kuritsyn, a diplomat of the Grand Prince in Moscow (Scene 20).[193]

No one can say how the spiritual environment of Novgorod would have continued to develop; it was never given the opportunity to do so. The conflict over the Judaizers took place at a time when the Novgorodian Republic struggled for its independent existence. Novgorod was conquered by the Muscovite prince Ivan III (1440–1505) in 1478. During his conquest, Ivan III experimented with methods that would later be used by Russian autocrats of all ideological stripes: he had the local elites executed or expelled to the northeastern periphery (historians speak of the "the Novgorodian purges"); he gave the property of those expelled to loyal soldiers for settlement; he saw to the destruction of relations with the Hanseatic League and the West more generally; and he replaced self-government with an administration subservient to his own

193 On the disputes over the origin and doctrine of the Judaizers, see Pavel Boček, *Stát a církev na přelomu 15. a 16. století* (Brno: Masarykova Univerzita, 1995), 7–9.

person.[194] Archbishop Gennady Gonozov (probably 1410–1505) became Novgorod's new administrator, a man who among other things completed the task of pacifying the Judaizers. It was a suitably brutal pacification, fully in keeping with the sentiments of Joseph Volotsky. Paradoxically, he also contributed something of lasting cultural value. Because the Judaizers had used the text of the Bible to back up their teachings, Gennady initiated as part of his campaign against them an "official," church-sanctioned biblical translation. This was the first complete translation of the Bible in Old Russian, the manuscript of "Gennady's Bible." Gennady's circle of translators, which included two Greeks and even one Catholic Dominican from Croatia, translated a significant portion of the Old Testament that up to then had been unavailable in Church Slavonic. Paradoxically (but for that very "Novgorodian"), it was translated from the Latin Vulgate.[195]

This period, however, marks the true end of Novgorod. Novgorod was degraded to the status of mere province, the window to Europe had been closed. Two centuries later, Novgorod would be reborn as a cultural phenomenon, further away but still on the water: Saint Petersburg, "the Russian city on the Baltic, open to Europe." The name of old Novgorod does occasionally surface in the literature of the Petersburg era as the conflict between freedom and autocracy. Katharine the Great herself initiated the revival with her drama *Istoricheskoe predstavlenie bez sokhraneniia featral'nykh obyknovennykh pravil, Iz zhizni Riurika* (A Historical Representation Without the Retention of Standard Theatrical Rules, from the Life of Riurik, 1786). The subject matter was originally of antiquity, a storyline about the Roman emperor Titus who forgives those that conspire

---

194 Cf. Marek Příhoda, "Vyprávění o pádu Novgorodu: Pojmy traduce, vláda, dědičná země" in *"Rýžoviště zlata a doly drahokamů…": Sborník pro Václava Hrnka,* ed. Věra Lendělová and Michal Řoutil (Červený Kostelec: Pavel Mervart, 2006), 317–334.
195 Cf. A.D. Sedelnikov, "Ocherki katolicheskogo vliyaniya v Novgorode v kontse XV-nachale XVI vekov," *Doklady Akademii nauk SSSR* 5, no. 1 (Leningrad: AN SSSR, 1929).

against him. In Europe, Pietro Metastasio worked through the same themes in his libretto for the opera *La clemenza di Tito* (The Clemency of Titus, 1734), a subject subsequently handled by three dozen or so composers including Mozart. In Russia, Iakov Kniazhnin (1742–1791) composed the drama *Titovo miloserdie* (The Clemency of Titus, 1785). Katherine then "Russified" the subject matter and presented the magnanimous Riurik in "Romantic" style, describing his act of forgiveness toward the conspirator Vadim of Novgorod, the latter portrayed as an opponent of "enlightened" autocracy. Kniazhnin himself, however, immediately wrote up the drama *Vadim Novgorodski* (1789), which drew inspiration from Voltaire's tragedy about the Roman tyrannicide *Brutus* (1730). In this version, Vadim is presented as not just any conspirator, but as one who fights for freedom and an opponent equal in stature to Riurik, drawing the same degree of sympathy from the audience. And it ends in the same "Romantic" style, noble suicide:

> You stand amidst your victorious armies,
> All kneel before your crown—and yet,
> What are you to one who is able to die proudly?[196]

This rendition obviously could not have met with Katharine's approval, especially not in the very year of the French Revolution! The drama was confiscated and the dramatist's career ended in disgrace. A similarly unfortunate end was met by Alexander Radishchev, who praised the freedoms of old Novgorod in his *Journey from St. Petersburg to Moscow* (1790, Scene 11). Nikolai Karamzin (1766–1826) also took on the theme in his novel *Marfa Posadnitsa ili Pokorenie Novagoroda* (Martha the Mayoress, or the Fall of Novgorod, 1803), but he did so in a cautious and ambiguous manner: the subjugation of Novgorod's "faltering" freedom by the firm hand of Moscow

---

196 Jakov Knazhnin, *Vadim Novgorodski* (Moscow: Tipografiya Mamontova, 1914), 63.

he treated as a "recognized necessity." Nevertheless, Martha, who bravely dies at the scaffold for the lost cause of Novgorod's freedom, remains a heroic and attractive figure—one anticipating the fate of heroes in subsequent Russian battles for lost freedoms.

Scene 9

Lithuanian Rus,
the Russian Reformation,
and the Russian Baroque

YEAR:
1517

PLACE:
Prague

EVENT:
Frantsishak Skaryna publishes the Bible, the first
book printed in Russian

WORKS:
Letters from Athos by Ivan Vyshensky (before 1620);
The Garden of Many Flowers by Simeon Polatsky
(1678); *Poems* by Ivan Velychkovsky (1687)

It is the third formation that most resembles Kievan Rus. This is partly because it occupied the greater part of former Kievan territory, including Kiev itself, from the fourteenth to the seventeenth century. It also concerns the state's rulers who, like the Vikings in Kiev (Scene 20), were of non-Slavic origin. They settled relatively peacefully in an "abandoned" Slavic territory but soon found themselves assimilating into the surrounding sea of Slavic-speaking people. What the rulers left was their name: Lithuania. From the small and still mostly pagan Lithuania of the fourteenth century emerged, for the most part without resistance, the Grand Duchy of Lithuania. The princely dynasty Slavicized over time, leaving the original Lithuanian population on the margins of the more important cultural developments. Its own Lithuanian revival would not occur until much later, in the nineteenth century.[197]

Lithuanian Rus thus seemed suited to claim the heritage of Kievan Rus. At least, its claim was no less legitimate than that of Muscovite Rus. The prospects of Lithuania's leaders—and their ambitions—increased in 1386 when Grand Duke Jogaila (Jagiełło) consummated his marriage to the Polish queen Jadwiga. Thereby emerged a voluntary union dubbed the Polish-Lithuanian Commonwealth, later referred to as the Rzeczpospolita ("Res publica"), Europe's most territorially expansive state. It also counted among the freest of European states. Like the old Kievan Rus, the Commonwealth combined elements of monarchism and estates democracy. And what's more, nationally and religiously it was one of the most tolerant states in Europe. Beside the Poles, Russians, and Lithuanians, the Commonwealth's principle nations, there also settled communities of Jews, Armenians and Germans. Many Greeks arrived as well after fall of Constantinople. We thus find in the early modern era not one, but two Russias: an eastern and a western, Muscovy and Lithuania.

197 Cf. Luboš Švec, Vladimír Macura, and Pavel Štol, *Dějiny pobaltských zemí* (Prague: Nakladatelství Lidové noviny, 1996).

Nor is there any uniform "Russian mentality" or "Russian society". Instead, there were two mentalities and societies facing opposite one another. Muscovy stood for the principle of autocracy and the union of church and the state; Lithuania for the principle of power-sharing between estates, municipal autonomy (the towns there operated according to Magdeburg Law), and relative religious freedom.

The culture of Lithuanian Rus in the fourteenth and fifteenth century was rather impoverished, similar to that of Muscovy. Thanks to the union with Poland, however, humanism eventually arrived to Lithuania from the West. The Reformation, Renaissance, and the Baroque soon followed. These intellectual currents arrived also thanks to eager young men from Lviv, Polotsk, and other towns in Lithuanian Rus. Their names may be found in university registries in Cracow, Bologna, Padua, or Prague, names often written with the suffixes "Rossicus," "Roxolanus," or "de Russia." Among them are the names of several relatively important Latin humanists.[198]

Without a doubt, the most important western Russian humanist to have worked in Central Europe was Frantsishak Skaryna (1490–1551), a native of Polotsk who held a doctorate in medicine from the university in Padua. Between 1517 and 1519 he oversaw the publication of the first book to be printed in an East Slavonic language, a thirty-two volume complete edition of the Old Testament. Skaryna rendered the biblical text in a living language, one close to his native dialect, and he contributed his own prefaces. For assistance he turned to the text of the Czech-language Bible (mainly the so-called Venice Bible[199]), as can be seen in the number of Bohemisms contained in his biblical Russian. Skaryna's Bible stands as one of the cornerstones of Czech-Russian spiritual and cultural relations not just because of where it was published but also due to the linguistic influence. (It

---

198 Cf. Ilya Nikolaevich Golenishchev-Kutuzov, *Gumanizm u vostochnykh slavian: Ukraina i Belorussia* (Moscow, Izdatelstvo Akademii nauk SSSR, 1963).
199 Cf. Vladimír Kyas, *Česká bible v dějinách národního písemnictví* (Prague: Vyšehrad, 1997).

also helps overcome the simplistic conception of Czech-Russian relations as being limited to relations between Prague and Moscow.) It is therefore quite appropriate that everyone who enters Clementinum (Czech National Library) on his way to the Slavonic Library passes a plaque dedicated to Skaryna's memory.

Belarusians also take pride in Skaryna and his work, regarding him as the founder of Belarusian literature. Not only does Skaryna have a monument in his native Polotsk, there is an entire museum dedicated to him and the history of Belarusian book printing. Skaryna and his work also raise a number of questions: why did he choose Prague as the setting for his pioneering efforts rather than one of the more important centers of European book printing? Was his confession Catholicism or Orthodoxy? Or should one see in him a pioneer of the Reformation who published a Bible to be read by the widest possible strata of the population at a time when Luther hung his ninety-five theses in Wittenberg? Contemporaries certainly understood Skaryna's Bible in the context of the Reformation. This is clear from the reverence shown him by reformers (Symon Budny or the Slovenian Primož Trubar) as well as from the opposition it inspired among the Orthodox, including relatively enlightened figures such as Prince Kurbsky. Prague also makes sense as a location because it was the center of Utraquism, Bohemia's moderate "proto-Reformation."

A similar moderation characterized the texts written by Skaryna himself, the prefaces he composed for the individual books of the Bible. One finds in them nothing of the early Reformation's missionary zeal. Instead, they continue in the spirit of the Christian humanism of Erasmus, recommending the biblical books as a source of general instruction:

> If you wish to know grammar, [...] then look up the psalter in the
> Bible and read it. If you would like to understand logic—it teaches the
> discernment of truth through reason and the recognition of justice from

iniquity—read the book of St. Job or the letters of the holy apostle Paul. If you intend to learn rhetoric or the art of speaking well, read the books of Solomon. If you feel like studying music or song, then in this book you will find a wealth of verses and sacred texts. If you please to know arithmetic, read the fourth book of Moses often.[200]

The "mature" Reformation in its Lutheran and Calvinist guise, however, arrived to Lithuania via Poland in the generation after Skaryna. The Reformation's main supporters comprised a number of Polish magnates, Mikołaj Radziwiłł prominent among them. But the main intellectual figures were all Lithuanian Russians, above all Symon Budny (probably 1530–1593), a preacher and author of a Catechism published in "Skaryna's" Russian at the Radziwiłł town of Nyasvizh in 1562. At the same time, Budny represented the Reformation in its most radical form: neither the Lutheran nor Calvinist Reformation, but rather an "Aryan" or Unitarian Reformation, taking the rationalistic criticism of traditional theology to the point of rejecting the dogmas of the Trinity and the divinity of Jesus. It is no coincidence that Budny was labeled a "Judaizer" by his opponents, comparing him to the "heretics" of Novgorod. Budny is rather the exception in his radical opposition to tradition. Yet overall, Lithuanian Rus had clearly moved in the direction of becoming a "Protestant" Rus by the second half of the sixteenth century. Further steps would ultimately lead in a different direction, but insofar as culture and urban conditions are concerned, the period appears in retrospect as the "golden age of Belarus."[201]

Toward the end of the sixteenth century, the wave of Reformation was succeeded by a wave of Counter-Reformation led by the Jesuits. Against the open and disruptive thinking of the Reformation, the Counter-Reformation had the advantage of discipline, unified

200 Františka Sokolová (ed.), *Francisko Skoryna v díle českých slavistů* (Prague: Národní knihovna-Slovanská knihovna, 1992), 23.
201 Cf. Stanislav Akinčyc, *Zlatý věk Běloruska* (Pardubice: Světlana Vránová, 2013).

organization and a well-developed school system. And so the process which had earlier taken place in Poland proper, in Bohemia, and in Hungary now played itself out in Lithuanian Rus: the aristocratic elite gradually turned from Protestantism to Catholicism. A process of Polonization also set in with the Counter-Reformation. Not as a conscious campaign of "denationalizing," but simply a result of the cultural dominance of Poland's more advanced culture, one connected to Catholic culture.

The successive waves of Reformation and Counter-Reformation were then confronted by those who remained true to the confession that found itself "third from behind," i.e. Orthodoxy. Fully aware that the unpopularity of Orthodoxy was partially to be attributed to its cultural inferiority, they strove to catch up with their rivals in their own domain, schooling and book production.

Initiative was taken by exiles who had fled the "Third Rome," Muscovite Rus, to save their own lives—and in doing so gave rise to a "Russia beyond Russia" (or more exactly a "Muscovy beyond Muscovy.") Artemius (dates unknown), a former hegumen of the Trinity Lavra of St. Sergius, engaged in disputes with Symon Budny. Prince Andrey Kurbsky (1528–1583), the political and cultural opponent of Ivan the Terrible and author of several accusatory epistles as well as the "White Book" which documented the crimes of the tsar, *Istoria o Velikom Knyaze Moskovskom* (History of the Grand Prince of Moscow), continued his battle from exile, and that on two fronts: against the Machiavellianism of Muscovy and the fading influence of Orthodoxy in Lithuania. In his old age, Kurbsky became a translator. Ancient theories of the state and law (which he translated from Cicero) served him as a theoretical arsenal to be used against Ivan the Terrible; translations of the patristics (John Chrysostom, Dionysius the Areopagite and others) helped him spread the spiritual message of Russian-Lithuanian Orthodoxy. The deacon and book printer Ivan Fedorov (1510–1583) produced the first printed book in the eastern Slavic lands in 1564, the *Apostolos*. He then watched as a

Josephite mob demolished his printing press, that suspicious "Latin" invention. Fedorov, to the contrary, was welcomed as a valuable helper in Lithuanian-Rus. One of the Russian-Lithuanian magnates, Prince Konstanty Ostrogski (1526–1608), acting on Kurbsky's advice, invited Ivan Fedorov to his estate in Ostrih and from 1578 he financed a permanent printing press. As Skaryna's Bible was considered heretical in Moscow and systematically destroyed, the so-called Ostrih Bible (1580) long remained the only accessible version of the holy text among Russians and provided a model for literary Russian more generally.

Orthodoxy was also defended "from below" by citizens organized into "brotherhoods." Part philanthropic institution and part mutual aid society, the brotherhoods engaged in religious activities and made efforts to raise public awareness. From 1584 on, they gradually established schools in Vilnius, Lviv, Halych, and other cities, each one organized according to the Catholic model. Lithuanian Russians distinguish carefully between Catholicism's religious influence, which they rejected, and its cultural influence, toward which they seemed to hold no prejudice. Though the brotherhoods existed to defend Orthodoxy, they nonetheless soon found themselves locked into disputes with local Orthodox bishops for having taken the liberty of expressing themselves on matters such as liturgy and official doctrines. This unheard-of attempt to involve the laity in church affairs drew strenuous resistance from the bishops.

When a group of bishops signed the Union of Brest in 1596, thereby bringing their eparchy under the papal jurisdiction of Rome and transforming part of Lithuanian Rus into a Catholic Rus (Scene 14), opposition arose precisely among that milieu of engaged laity, i.e. "from below." Prince Ostrozski in Brest organized an Orthodox counter-sobor to take place at the same time as the Uniate sobor to (though only nominally) unseat the Uniate bishops. He then undertook the impossible task of establishing a "counter-Union" aiming to bring Orthodoxy and Protestantism together in a common struggle against the papacy. When this effort foundered politically and ecclesiastically, nothing was left to the Orthodox except pen, paper, and perhaps printer's ink. Polemical texts flooded the Union. The sharpest polemicist by far and most original writer of the time was Ivan Vyshensky (probably 1545–1620), a monk residing on Mount Athos who sent one fiery epistle after the other to his homeland.

Vyshensky portrayed the condition of the Russian people and the Orthodox Church in the Polish-Lithuanian Commonwealth in the darkest possible colors, polemicizing with the Polish Jesuit Piotr Skarga, author of *Wzywanie do jednej zbawiennej wiary* (A Call for One Redeeming Faith, 1611); he also criticized the Orthodox brotherhoods for having independently engaged in the social and religious life of the Commonwealth. Vyshensky defended the thesis that the world had fallen under the sway of the Antichrist, as for example in his text *Oblichenii Diabola-Miroderzhtsa* (The Unmasking of the Devil as Ruler of the World). There exists no worldly help against the Antichrist, only by renouncing all participation in worldly affairs and hiding oneself away in a cloister—at best somewhere on Mount Athos—can one hope to escape his evil influence.[202] In his absolute pessimism, Vyshensky resembles his baroque contemporaries across confessions. But in his moral, religious, and social zeal as a preacher who held up the Gospel as a norm to be followed (in his dispute with Skarka he names poverty and persecution as the hallmarks of the true Church of Christ), Vyshensky resembles rather a proto-reformer the likes of Peter Valdes or Savonarola.

Of course, Ivan Vyshensky stood outside the mainstream of Russian-Lithuanian polemical literature, setting himself apart mainly through his open attacks on the Polish-Lithuanian state order. He rejected every form of schooling as so many temptations of the Antichrist. Vyshensky's reaction to Orthodoxy's cultural inferiority was

202   Cf. I.P. Eramin (ed.), *Ivan Vyshenskii: Sochineniia* (Moscow: Izd-vo Akademii nauk SSSR, 1955).

the same as that of the Josephites in Muscovy. We are truly uneducated, dirty, and coarse went his reply. In those things, we cannot be your equals... but those are not the things upon which salvation depends. The first Christians were spurned in just the same way, and yet they possessed the truth. With his frequent reference to the words of St. Paul, "We are fools for the sake of Christ, but you are wise in Christ" (1 Cor. 4:10), Vyshensky even drew near to the paradigm of *iurodstvo*.

However, most of the Russian-Lithuanian polemicists did not seek refuge from the world, nor did they try to present ignorance as a virtue. Quite to the contrary, they accepted the Commonwealth and attempted to win the recognition and respect of their Catholic peers. For this reason, they formulated their arguments against the Union according to the manner of scholastic dialectics. Many even went so far as to write in Polish to more effectively penetrate the enemy camp. In this sense, they considered education their most formidable weapon. During the years following the establishment of the Union, they composed not just polemical tracts but also grammars of Slavonic (Meletii Smotrytsky, Scene 12), the first Lithuanian-Russian dictionary (Lavrentii Zyzanii), compendia of pagan superstitions (which it was later necessary to censor) (Zacharias Kopystensky), they attempted to systematize Orthodox dogmas and supplement them with cosmology (Kyryl Tranquillon-Stavrovetsky).

The work of Peter Mohyla (1596–1646), the Orthodox metropolitan of Kiev (the Uniate metropolitan resided in Vilnius), represents the pinnacle of scholarly efforts. Mohyla began by reforming the memorial Kievan Cave Monastery. Then, at the Polish Sejm of 1632, he gained state recognition for the existence of the Orthodox Church in "Uniate" territory. Mohyla oversaw the publication of the first cohesive edition of liturgical books and, what's most important, he transformed the Kievan Brotherhood school into the first Russian school of higher instruction in 1633, the Kiev-Mohyla College. Instruction at the Kiev College was organized according to the Jesuit model, (at the time, the Jesuits operated an expansive system of colleges for the poor and disseminated scholarship throughout the lands of Lithuanian Rus). Mohyla sent future teachers to be trained in the West. Students learned four languages—Church Slavonic, Polish, Greek, and Latin—and received instruction in the seven liberal arts as well as scholastic theology. Of the liberal arts, the College placed strong emphasis on rhetoric and scholastic verse.

It was here, at Mohyla's Kiev College in the seventeenth century, that Russian poetry began to be cultivated as an artistic endeavor (the origin of folklore, of course, is shrouded in the mist of prehistory). It started according to the Polish example as syllabic verse and highly formalistic productions: acrostics, palindromes, epigrams, poetic riddles, but also panegyric odes to important events in the life of the church and state.[203] The College alumnus Ivan Velychkovskij (probably 1630–1700) won fame as a master of these brief, playful forms and palindromes.

Mohyla also adopted from the Jesuits the method of allegorical-historical theater as a form of instruction as well as the Catholic cult of Christmas. Students crossed the schoolyard boundary in their Christmas pageants, carrying portable puppet theaters around Kiev with which they performed various Bethlehem scenes and sang Christmas carols. Because of these unheard-of novelties, especially the fact that instruction was carried out in "diabolical" and "heretical" Latin, the College became a target of attack and earned the animosity of conservative popes. In 1635, Kievan crowds together with Cossacks attacked the College with the pious intention of destroying this nest of Latinizing heretics. The attacks were unsuccessful, for the time being. Kievan scholarship continued to catch up with the West and make up for centuries of lost time. And, as much as was

---

203 Cf. Dmitrij Tschiźewskij, *A History of Ukrainian Literature: From the 11th to the End of the 19th Century* (Littleton, Colo.: Ukrainian Academic Press, 1975).

possible, it acted as a mediator bringing humanism and the Baroque to Russia.

Among the paradoxes of Russian spiritual history belongs the fact that Kievan scholarship "matured" on the other side of the border, in Muscovy. From the second half of the seventeenth century, Moscow began to call upon Kievan intellectuals to assist in raising the prestige of the underdeveloped culture of "Third Rome." The first to be summoned was Epifanii (Yepyfanii) Slavinetsky (†1675), who was invited to assist in Patriarch Nikon's revision of the ancient liturgical books (Scene 10) and to oversee the first of Moscow's printing presses, Pechatni Dvor, where among other things Epifanii published a second edition of the Ostrih Bible.

Others followed Epifanii, the most famous of them being the monk Simeon Polatsky (1629–1680), a native of Polotsk like Skaryna before him. If Skaryna was the pioneer of humanism and perhaps even the Reformation in Russian culture, Polatsky represents the founder of the Baroque in Russian poetry and drama. The extensive collection *Vertograd Mnogotsvetnij* (The Garden of Many Flowers) is a baroque poetic encyclopedia of the world, of history of dogma and ethics in which can also be found bits of grotesque humor (jocular rebukes of drunkenness or female vanity, for example) and images of "antique" rural idylls.

Polatsky's second book of poetry, the *Rifmologion* (Book of Rhymes), is by contrast monothematic and monotonous: with the aid baroque tricks of scholastic panegyric poetry he celebrated the ruling Romanov dynasty. His *Comedy of the Parable of the Prodigal Son,* the first Russian drama, was composed after the fashion of Jesuit school dramas.[204]

Literary historians debate the existence or non-existence of a Russian Baroque. As far as formal technique is concerned—figurative

---

[204] Cf. I.P. Eramin, ed., *Simeon Polockii: Izbrannye sochinenia* (Moscow: Izd-vo Akademii nauk 1953).

poems, emblems, paradoxes and the like—something resembling the Baroque certainly did exist.[205] But if one intends to speak of a certain spiritual disposition, a reaction to the Reformation and the Renaissance, the effort to conceal the wavering of previous certainties by means of dramatic gesture, then one will find little of the baroque spirit in Simeon Polatsky and other writers of elegant verse. The exterior appropriation of technique and its tailoring to local circumstances anticipated later Russian "adoptions" and "adaptions," from the Enlightenment to German Marxism. All of which would, once on Russian soil, become something very different from their original models.

As far as Baroque as a mentality is concerned, one should speak rather of the "baroque-ness" of certain eccentric literary personalities, of excited religious imaginations such as that of Ivan Vyshensky in the literature of Lithuanian Rus or of the spokesmen of the Old Belief in Muscovite Rus, Archpriest Avvakum (Scene 10). In such cases it is rather the spontaneous disposition of thought that is concerned, expressed in a primitive and ostentatiously "unrefined" manner, but by no means a conscious literary strategy. Yet the posing of the question itself reveals sort of answer, in researching Russian cultural history, one does find something like a *longing* for the Baroque.

The departure of Kiev's most talented intellectuals for Muscovy foretold the coming decline of Lithuanian Rus. There are two causes of this decline. The first concerns the Catholicism and Polonism of the Lithuanian Grand Dukes, who in the realm of the Commonwealth also functioned as Polish kings. For though this connection opened Lithuania up to the West, it also weakened ties of identification with the Commonwealth for those who continued to practice

---

205 Cf. Andreas Angyal, *Die slawische Barockwelt* (Leipzig: E.A. Seemann, 1961); cf. Dmitrij Čiževskij, "K problemam literatury barokko u slavian" in Dmitrij Čiževskij et al., *Literárny barok* (Bratislava: Vydavateľstvo SAV, 1971), 5–59.

Orthodoxy, thereby strengthening their admiration for Moscow. The second cause is simply the fact of Muscovy's military dominance. Muscovy—thanks to its autocracy, admittedly more capable of decisive action than the estates democracy of the Commonwealth—gradually occupied Lithuanian territory from the east until finally absorbing it completely during the triple partition of Poland at the end of the eighteen century. Of the two Russias, only one was left.

The "other" Russia ceased to exist as a political entity. Its inhabitants however did not cease to exist, nor were they to merge with the inhabitants of Muscovite Rus. During the period of Lithuanian indepependence they had not given much thought to their own national identity. For they were "Russians" too, after all! At the time of the forced union of both Russias, however, the name "Russian" was claimed by the Muscovites for themselves. As a result, the Russians of Lithuania would became Ukrainians and Belarusians (Scene 12).

Muscovite Spiritual Counterculture II: The Old Believers

YEAR:
1682

PLACE:
Pustozersk on the Arctic Ocean

EVENT:
Archpriest Avvakum crosses himself with two fingers
for the last time

WORKS:
The Life of Archpriest Avvakum by Himself (1672–1675);
Boiarynia Morozova by Vasily Surikov (1887)

Muscovy's sense of divine mission rested on yet another conviction—the belief that Muscovite Orthodoxy represents the only genuine Orthodoxy, and that Orthodoxy is the only genuine Christianity. But how was the Russian monk to defend the truth of Orthodoxy when his education was limited and his understanding of theology weak? The Russian monk compensated for his subconscious lack of confidence by identifying Orthodoxy with the "one true ceremony," by insisting that liturgical texts and ceremonial gestures be observed in every detail. What else was left for him to do, after all, when he was unable to distinguish biblical texts from apocrypha, to tell the canonical mass apart from the metaphors of the hymns, to separate the essential from the inessential? Observing the history of Russian Orthodoxy from the distance of religious studies (as Pavel Milyukov was one of the first Russian intellectuals to do in his *Studies in the History of Russian Culture*, see Introduction), this form of religiosity appears strongly "magical":[206] religious ceremony, though its structure might be poorly understood, nonetheless fulfilled its magical function. Even the slightest alteration in the system might upset the balance of this magic and transform the liturgy into blasphemy, assuring church members of damnation instead of salvation.

Woe thus betide the appearance of some uncertainty or the possibility of multiple interpretations, in which case there would immediately erupt a conflict with each side accusing the other of the worst possible sorts of apostasy—to use the typical rhetoric of the place and time, accusing them of Catholicism and Judaism. In the absence of any original Greek sources and lacking knowledge of the formal methods of disputation (such as logic, dialectics, or any method of disputation whatsoever), arguments were instead hammered out according to a self-fashioned "theology," or they are endured *ad hominem*

---

206   Cf. James George Frazer, *The Golden Bough: A Study in Magic and Religion* (New York: St. Martin's Press, 1990); cf. Josef Kandert, *Náboženské systémy: Člověk náboženský a jak mu porozumět*. (Prague: Grada, 2010).

(emphasizing the moral corruption of the opponent), or even, if need be, *ad baculam* (using physical force in the place of verbal argument). The close relationship between state power and the church made the latter variety a particularly convenient argument.

This inner intellectual weakness of Muscovite Orthodoxy became particularly self-destructive in the dispute over the liturgy, a conflict that engulfed Moscow's public life during the second half of the seventeenth century. Beside the endless controversies and countless rifts within the church itself, several fascinating personalities and texts came to the forefront of the conflict. Romantics would later come to admire these individuals and hold them up as proof of the vitality and religious passion which animated pre-modern Rus. Despite such salutary "side effects," one should not forget the terror involved in these disputes, or the fact that the entire conflict resulted from a dreadful lack of theological training among the clergy of seventeenth-century Muscovy.

Foregrounding the conflicts was a paradoxical effort to revive the Russian Orthodox Church. The effort at renewal reacted to a period of turbulence, social disorganization, and strife at the beginning of the seventeenth century known as the "Time of Troubles" (*Smutnoe Vremia*), a period that involved a quick succession of tsars, claims to the throne by pseudo-tsars (three "false Dmitris" in total), Cossack and peasant rebellions, and Polish and Lithuanian-Rus intervention. Setting aside for a moment the scholarly perspective of religious studies, but still to remain within the realm of the Christian "economy of salvation," one might speak of divine retribution for the prideful boast of being the "Third Rome." One part of Muscovy's clergy understood the "troubles" as a call for penitence and change. Initiative in this came from the Trinity Lavra of St. Sergius, the center of resistance against intervention (unsuccessfully besieged 1608–1610). The local archimandrite Dionysii (1570–1633) came up with the idea of reviving the country morally and spiritually in the tradition of Maxim the Greek, and through him, in the tradition of

Savonarola, Nilus Sorsky (Scene 7), and John Chrysostom, whose works were still being read (Scene 4). Greater liturgical quality could be achieved by raising the literacy and morality of the clergy; by introducing systematic Christian education for the laity; by defending the poor against the caprice of the rich; by fighting against the remnants of paganism; and by resisting the gradually increasing tendency toward secularization. Central to all of this, however, would be the internal reform of the clerical estate itself. Everything else depended on that.[207]

The movement for a revival of the church did not emanate from a monastery, however. It centered instead around a circle of urban clergy. Ivan Neronov (1591–1670), a student of Dionysii, was appointed to the position of archpriest in Moscow's Cathedral of Basil the Blessed in 1649 (Scene 7). He gathered around himself a group of priests and engaged laity who called themselves *Bogoliubtsy* (Seekers of God), or *Revnitelei Blagochestiya* (The Zealots of Piety).[208] These men reintroduced sermons into the temple, something which had almost completely vanished during the Mongolian period, and they strove for a more dignified liturgical ceremony. The regrettable habit of *mnogoglasy*, the simultaneous chanting of multiple parts of the liturgy, had become widespread to shorten church services. The Bogoliubtsy propagated *jednoglasi* instead, the sequential recitation of one text after another. That individual texts might simply be dropped does not seem to have occurred to them, a fact characteristic of the movement. The Bogoliubtsy gained significant influence in the Orthodox Church. They oversaw the state's only printing press, Pechatni Dvor; they won the favor of the young tsar Alexis; they attained the canonization of Metropolitan Filip,

---

207   The basic work remains that of Serge Zenkovsky's *Russkoje staroobriadchestvo: Dukhovnye dvizheniia XVII veka* (Munich: Wilhelm Fink Verlag, 1970).

208   Cf. Michal Řoutil, "Kroužek horlitelů pravé zbožnosti a kulturní konflikt 17. století," in *Kulturní, duchovní a etnické kořeny Ruska: Tradice a alternativy,* ed. Marek Příhoda (Červený Kostelec: Pavel Mervart, 2005), 77–107.

a victim of Ivan the Terrible and thus a symbol of religious freedom. One was named Patriarch of Moscow in 1652.

Patriarch Nikon (1605–1681) pushed the Bogoliubtsy forward by coordinating church practices in Russia with the rest of Orthodoxy by having the liturgical books revised according to the Greek originals. Nikon acted in typical "Muscovite" fashion when the philological commission, led by the Kievan monk Epifanii Slavinetsky, began the difficult task of editing the work. Rather than wait for the commission's results, he promulgated changes to church services in 1653. The common practice of crossing oneself with two fingers was changed to a cross with three fingers; instead of reciting "alleluia" twice, it was to be recited three times; processions around the analoya (the sacramental table at the temple's center) was to go in the direction against the sun rather than with it; a two-bar rather than four-bar cross was to be imprinted upon the prosphora (ceremonial bread). Other similar adjustments were included as part of this "revolutionary" change.

Nikon's reforms called forth a fierce reaction, and that precisely among the Bogoliubtsy. Adherents of the old ceremony would sooner die a cruel death than cross themselves with three fingers. The reason for this was their ardently held magical belief in the ceremony's "functioning", a belief supported from a lack of education and an inability to distinguish between form and substance. The semiotician Boris Uspensky has attempted a more neutral description of this way of thinking: it concerns a "semiotic conflict," that is, two different ways of understanding the sacred symbology. For the Old Believers, the relationship between a sign and its divine content was considered absolute and therefore unalterable. For the representatives of the new ceremony, however, the relationship was relative and a matter of convention.[209] Uspensky's interpretation only con-

209 Boris A. Uspensky, "Schism and Cultural Conflict in the Seventeenth Century," in *Seeking God: The Recovery of Religious Identity in Orthodox Russia, Ukraine and Georgia,* ed. Stephen K.

firms, though by a different method, insights drawn from religious studies about the role of magical thought in Russian Orthodoxy.

The resistance of the Old Believers also arose from factors specific to church history. Nikon adjusted the Russian ceremony to fit the Greek model, yet by this time the Greeks were no longer revered as teachers of the faith. Since the Florentine Union they had instead been regarded as "renegades" who had been punished by God with the loss of their freedom. The occasional journeys to Rus undertaken by members of the Greek hierarchy did not give cause for a more positive evaluation: the patriarchs of Constantinople, Jerusalem, Alexandria, and Antioch all depend on the Turkish Sultan, and the primary reason for their frequent trips was "to beg for alms," to request financial support from the Muscovite church and state.[210] Sufficiently rewarded with "alms," the patriarchs would be willing to consecrate or condemn just about anyone, to declare any ceremony whatsoever to be "apostolic" or "apostasy." For those convinced of Russia's status as the Third Rome, any correction to the Russian texts could be understood as nothing other than heresy.

On the other hand, it may not have been the content of the liturgical reforms that so shocked the Bogoliubtsy, who after all belonged to the more educated of the Orthodox priests, as much as it was the way the reforms were introduced. At the very least non-canonical (according to ecclesiastical law a sobor had first to be assembled to pass the new right, something which hadn't taken place), Nikon's behavior resembled the manners of Ivan the Terrible or, even worse, of the pope. Nikon attempted to set through a sort of "papal Caesarism." He placed himself above the church as its unrestrained leader, bestowing upon himself the title *gosudar* (sovereign) with a clear pretension to leadership of the state as well. He

Batalden (DeKalb: Northern Illinois University Press, 1993), 110–127.
210 Cf. Steven Runciman, *The Great Church in Captivity: A Study of the Patriarchate of Constantinople from the Eve of the Turkish Conquest to the Greek War of Independence* (Cambridge: University of Cambridge Press, 1968).

didn't hesitate to have his opponents condemned by the church and physically liquidated. The Bogoliubtsy, motivated by a vision of the church as a community of all believers, could not but see this as a betrayal of their ideals.

As a result, the Bogoliubtsy became the most stringent opponents of Nikon's "reforms." When Ivan Neronov complained to the tsar about the patriarch in 1653, he was beaten and imprisoned by Nikon's men. Others received similar treatment, or even worse. From the boyars to the monks of the northernmost monasteries, from the Cossacks to holy fools, all of Muscovite Rus was dragged into the dispute over crossing oneself with three fingers. "Three fingers" and "two fingers" took on the significance of battle cries, or battle standards, the original sense of which was long forgotten. The dispute climaxed with the calling for a great sobor of Greek patriarchs in 1666–1667. With the patriarchs' blessing, Russian bishops condemned the unrepentant leaders of the revolt and sentenced them to cruel punishments. At the last moment, the seventy-six year-old Ivan Neronov conceded and accepted the new ceremony, and thus the leadership role and symbolism of revolt passed on to his student, the archpriest Avvakum Petrovich (1621–1682), who was soon sent into exile to Pustozersk near the coast of the Arctic Ocean. Soon after that, also with the blessing of the Greek patriarchs, Nikon himself was deposed and sent into exile. Nikon's growing ambitions had begun to irritate the tsar, who decided to rid himself of an unwelcome patron. The growing spiral of violence thus engulfed the man who had started it spinning in the first place.

The spiral of violence continued its way: The fools for Christ continued their pilgrimages from Moscow to Pustozersk and back, proselytizing the battle cry and theological interpretations of Avvakum and his fellow prisoners. Until 1670, when they were rounded up and abused. The ancient privilege of iurodstvo was abolished and the religious "estate" was destroyed. The Muscovite boyar Feodosia Morozova (1632–1675) offered refuge in her home to proponents of the

Old Belief, and in 1671 she was arrested and starved to death. The Solovetsky Monastery also rose against the new ceremony, and as a result the tsar's army captured it and executed its monks in 1676. Many tongues were torn out, many heads severed, and many pyres set ablaze. Upon the most famous of these pyres burned Archpriest Avvakum, deacon Feodor, and two other prisoners at Pustozersk on April 1, 1682. This all happened under the command of Patriarch Joachim, who once expressed his religious worldview thus: "Neither old nor new, my faith is the faith of the Tsar."

Contrary to the Stalinist maxim, "when there's no person, there's no problem," the bodies burned but the problems remained. Having suffered defeat in the field of official church politics, the question facing thousands of proponents of the Old Belief became, "what now?" The texts of the Old Belief's two main fighters, both burned to death in Pustozersk, indicated two possible directions. For all his railing against the "Nikonians" and other real or imagined traitors, Avvakum had remained optimistic to the end. Are there are no "authentic" priests, ordained according to the Old Belief? No matter, said Avvakum. Life goes on—the "Nikonian" baptism is valid, people may take turns hearing each other confess and may carry out small church services at home. Avvakum himself set the tone by refusing to respect his own suspension: "And as far as the interdiction is concerned, I throw it in the name of Christ at their feet and I will use that prohibition, put crudely, to wipe my ass."[211]

Of course, the ceremony of the "Old" Belief was in fact newer and less consistent with Orthodox tradition than that of the Nikonians. While the new Old Belief rid itself of hierarchies, temples, and saints, it preserved all the minutiae of the religious ceremony, which it elevated to the status of symbols. Above all, the "sacred" act of crossing oneself with two fingers. In truth, the Old Belief bore closer resemblance to the liturgy of the Protestant churches.

211 Bohuslav Ilek (ed.), *Život protopopa Avvakuma* (Prague: Odeon, 1975), 75.

According to Deacon Fedor († 1682), the Antichrist had already arrived with the "accursed" sobor of 1666, a year bearing the apocalyptic "number of the beast" (Rev 13.18). There was no help now that the entire world had fallen under his influence. There are no "authentic" priests and thus no genuine liturgy, there is no salvation to be had in this world. It was not Fedor's concern to found a new church based on the Old Belief. Such efforts wouldn't make sense, anyway, so near the world's end. Nonetheless, Fedor's teaching together with that of Avvakum became the cornerstone of a "schismatic" Old Belief faith, which due to the terrors of persecution had to seek refuge in the furthest reaches of the Muscovite empire. Old Believers fled north to the White Sea, east to the barrenness of Siberia, and to the southern border at the foothills of the Caucasus. They also crossed the border to the West, where adherents settled in the still religiously tolerant Lithuania, and further afield to the Danube delta, Austrian Galicia, and Bukovina. They were called Lipovans in Austria, one of the many ethnic-religious groups of the Old Monarchy and a favorite subject for ethnographical study.[212]

The same question—"What now?"—also drove the Old Believers themselves to divide into ever newer confessions and denominations (called *tolky* or *soglasiye*). The first wave of division separated the "priestly" (*popovtsy*) from the "priestless" (*bezpopovtsy*). The priestless, who were settled for the most part in Lithuania, specifically in Vietka near Gomel, employed the services of priests who had "defected" and renounced the Nikonian liturgy. The priestly, however, reflected Avvakum's historical optimism and hoped for the revival of a full-fledged hierarchy. They thus set out on a search throughout the Orthodox world for an "Orthodox" bishop. In 1846, they found a bishop from Bosnia whose belief seemed sufficiently "old," and they began to restore the church hierarchy with its seat in Bila

---

212 Cf. Hans Petschar, *Altösterreich: Menschen, Länder und Völker der Habsburger-Monarchie* (Vienna: Brandstätter, 2011), 126, 218–219.

Krynytsia in the Bukovina (in exile because the priestly church was at the time illegal in Russia). The current head of the priestly church, now seated in Moscow, still holds the title Metropolitan of Bila Krynytsia.

The priestless decided to make do without clergy at all and, as much as possible, without the interference of the Antichrist's state.[213] They formed communes resembling ancient Christian communities or the theocratic settlements of Puritans and other religious nonconformists in colonial America[214] (Lithuanian Nevel, the main seat of the Fedoseyans), or the set up monasteries (Vyg on the White Sea, the main seat of the Pomorians, where the Denisov brothers Andrej and Semion in their writings took up Avvakum and the literature of Muscovite Rus more generally). Those who held still more radical views advocated a life of endless flight from one place to another and called themselves *Stranniky* (pilgrims) or *Bieguny* (runners). The most extreme propagated suicide. One group, the "Forest Elders," considered death by starvation to be the most suitable way to go. Another, naming themselves "Filippians" after their leader, preferred to die in flames. Apostles of the "red death" wandered clear across Russia in the time of Peter the Great, a tsar many considered to be another embodiment of the Antichrist, and convinced peasants to gather their entire village into a single cottage to be set ablaze.

To complicate matters further still, a host of other groups comprised the "underground religious scene" of the eighteenth century. Not all of them originated from the conflict over the liturgical reforms; they drew from other sources as well, both foreign and domestic. Much was made of Quirinus Kuhlmann (1651–1689), a baroque mystic and poet from the German lands who was burned at the stake

---

213 Michal Siažik, "Charakteristické rysy bezpopovecké eschatologie," in "*Rýžoviště zlata a doly drahokamů…*": *Sborník pro Václava Huňáčka,* ed. Věra Lendělová and Michal Řoutil (Červený Kostelec: Pavel Mervart, 2006), 209–222.

214 Cf. Martin Putna, *Obrazy z kulturních dějin americké religiozity* (Prague: Vyšehrad, 2010).

in Moscow after a attempting to spread his doctrine about the inner illumination of the spirit.[215] At other times it was the intersection of spiritual genealogies between the Old Believers and various "sectarians" that gained attention.[216] In any case, what united all the religious dissidents was their objection to the state-backed Orthodox Church and their belief in the need of protecting genuine Christian piety from the sinfulness of civilization. These sects are normally divided into rationalists (the Dukhobortsy, Molokanye, Stundists) and mystics (the Khlysty and Skoptsy).[217] The rationalists typically rejected the outward trappings of ceremony in favor of reading the Bible (usually influenced by contact with German Protestant communities, Scene 2). On the theological side, they sometimes engaged in wild speculation. For example, one finds among them a belief in the transmigration of souls. Meanwhile, on the practical side of things, they led lives of quiet modesty. The mystics should perhaps rather be called "ecstatics," for they were characterized by their wild church services full of ecstatic displays (the Khlysty) or, what's still more eccentric, voluntary self-castration, reputedly the surest route to salvation (the Skoptsy).

To the extent that the Old Belief (or the sectarian) communities successfully preserved some stable form of organization up to 1905, the year of the first Russian revolution and the declaration of religious freedom, they could then begin to act legally in public. The period from 1905 to 1917 thus represents something of a golden age for the Old Belief, a time when the Russian public became aware that these religious dissidents numbered in the millions—and that

215 Cf. James Billington, *The Icon and the Axe: An Interpretive History of Russian Culture* (New York: Vintage Books, 1970), 174.
216 Cf. Michal Řoutil, "Kapiton Danilevskij: Příkladný asketa, nebo sveřepý heretik? K počátkům ruského sektářství nové doby," in *Kulturní, duchovní a etnické kořeny Ruska: Vlivy a souvislosti* (Červený Kostelec: Pavel Mervart, 2006), 99–114.
217 Cf. Frederick C. Conybeare, *Russian Dissenters* (Cambridge: Harvard University Press, 1921); cf. Pavel Miljukov, "Vývoj ruského sektářstvi, in *Obrazy z dějin ruské vzdělanosti*, vol. 3, ed. P.M. (Prague: Laichter, 1910), 140–214.

they represented a living inheritance of premodern Rus. Following the Bolshevik seizure of power in 1917 it was briefly thought that the Old Believers would enjoy a status superior to that of mainstream Orthodoxy (Scene 19), but they too were soon subjected to the persecution faced by all the others. Their public activities could be restored only after the fall of the communist regime when practically the entire scale of the old *tolky* surfaced once again, from the priestly to the Pomorians and Fedoseyans.[218]

In the meantime, the Old Believers had captured the attention of Russian culture. The impulse came rather paradoxically from the state and its interest in the disciplining of its subjects. By the middle of the nineteenth century the Ministry of Internal Affairs had engaged an array of intellectuals to assist in examining and describing the marginal layers of Russian society.[219] While it is true that the collaboration of literary types with the Ministry did not last long, it did bring increased awareness of several important figures from Russian literature. Old Believer characters and other sectarians are to be found, for example, in Ivan Turgenev's *A Sportsman's Sketches* (Scene 16), or *The Sealed Angel* by Nikolai Leskov (Scene 7). The latter work recounts the realistic and "unrealistic" fates of a group of Old Believer masons and transitions to an essay about iconographic symbolism and technique. Ethnographic realists devoted systematic attention to the lifestyles of the Old Believers and various sects—Pavel Melnikov-Pechersky (1818–1883) in the novelistic cycle *In the Forest* (1871–1874) and *On the Hills* (1875–1881) and Sergei Maksimov (1831–1901) in his series of studies, *Brodyachaya Rus Khrista-radi* (Rus on pilgrimage for Christ, 1877).

Subjects which made exciting material for the observation of realists became the objects of religious-apocalyptic meditation for the

---

218 For an overview of the contemporary Old Belief Church see Hanuš Nykl, *Náboženství v ruské kultuře* (Červený Kostelec: Pavel Mervart, 2013), 190–218.
219 Cf. Alexander Etkind, *Internal Colonization: Russia's Imperial Experience* (Cambridge, UK: Polity Press, 2012), 150 ff.

symbolists—strikingly so for Dmitry Merezhkovsky (Scene 17) who depicted the fanatical, suicidal advocates of the "red death" with a mix of horror and fascination in his novel *Peter and Alexis* (1904).

Other Russian intellectuals found the Old Believers and "rationalist sects" such as the Molokanye or Stundists fascinating for a different reason. What they observed in the life of these communities, whether by their own experience or through the descriptions of ethnographers, was neither passion nor prophecy, but rather diligence, quiet piety, and sobriety. This was why the Old Believers captivated Solzhenitsyn and other twentieth-century authors (Scene 19), intellectuals who envisaged a different Russia and criticized the cliché of a "deep soul"—a fondness for extremes, arrogance and extravagance, exhibitionism and sentimentality, self-abuse and chaos of every variety. They sought a middle road instead, a less affective and more dispassionate alternative lifestyle and mentality. They didn't wish to adopt this alternative straightforwardly from the West, however. It wasn't the Germanic "anti-Oblomov" Stolz (Scene 2) they looked to, but rather older domestic traditions. And surprisingly—they found it in the Old Believers. As the apocalyptic mood passed, the Old Believers adopted a more modest lifestyle on the social margins. A not insignificant part of the Russian middle class emerged from their ranks in the nineteenth century. In a sense, they played a role in Russian culture and spiritual history that might have been played by the Reformation, what Max Weber called the "ethic of capitalism."[220]

This clearly differs from the spirit of Archpriest Avvakum as revealed in his own writings, above all in his autobiography *The Life of Archpriest Avvakum by Himself,* composed during his years in exile. The old archpriest shared nothing in common with the "ethic of capitalism," nor could he be called a "Russian reformer." He possessed neither the required theological training nor the stridency

220 Cf. Billington, *The Icon and the Axe*, 193, 700.

of thought, nor did he engage critically with the problematic relationship between church, state, and society. He was no Hus, Luther, or Calvin. The latter three men fought for the chalice, opposed the worldly power of priests, or protested the sale of indulgences, Avvakum fought for the cross with two fingers. And when the archpriest did indulge in theologizing, the results were laughable (or rather, lamentable): "This Trinity, praising God, cries aloud, 'Alleluia, Alleluia, Alleluia,' by the alphabet *al* for the Father, *el* for the Son, *uia* for the Holy Ghost. [...] The Saints were agreed, both Dionysios and Basil, that they should sin aloud in triple-wise with the blessed angels of God and not in fourfold-wise according to the Roman error. It is an abomination to God to sing the fourfold song thus, Alleluia, Alleluia, Alleluia, Glory to thee, O God! And such singing He will curse."[221]

Similarly, whenever Avvakum began to discuss religious culture, he spoke as a conceited ignoramus—for example, on the topic of iconography and the names of saints: "They paint a picture of the savior Emanuel with a swollen face, red lips [...] wholly depicted as a German, fat and potbellied, only the sabre at his side is missing. And all of it is painted from the perspective of the physical, for heretics themselves have fallen in love with corpulence and have turned everything on its head. [...] Oh, oh, poor Rus, what have you taken to German manners and habits! They have even given to the wonderworker Nikolai the German name Nikolaus. [...] Among the saints there is no Nikolaus. They were the first to introduce it."[222]

Only in one respect did Avvakum resemble Hus, Luther, or Calvin: he shared their subjective religious zeal and strong personality. Avvakum was driven by the vital impulse of an Old Testament prophet or saint. Even *The Life of Archpriest Avvakum by Himself*

---

221 *The Life of the Archpriest Avvakum by Himself,* trans. Jane Harrison and Hope Mirrlees (Hamden, Conn.: Archon Books, 1963), 38–39.
222 Ibid., 127–129.

is stylized as a *zhitiye* (Life), hagiographies of saints who do battle with demons and perform miracles. It is an unusual zhitiye not only because the miracle-worker writes about himself, but also because lofty passages about suffering and wondrous deeds give way to vulgarisms, aspersions cast upon opponents, and even attacks of self-doubt: "I fought with the devils as tho' they were dogs, for three weeks for my sins [...]. I know not how it is that the days run on. I am covered about with weakness and hypocrisy and lying. I am clothed with envy of others and with self-love; I, who condemn all men, perish; I account myself as somewhat; and I, accursed one, am dung and corruption, naught but dung. [...] Thanks be to God for those powers that buried me in the earth! Tho' now I stink to myself, doing evil works, at least I am not a scandal to others."[223]

Given such eccentricities and histrionics, it is unsurprising that Avvakum referred to the words of Paul, "we fools for Christ," (1 Cor 4:10), and thus claimed the tradition (and privileges) of *iurodstvo* for himself (Scene 7). With these and other references Avvakum aimed "backwards" toward medieval and ancient Christian cultural models of the holy fools, miracle workers, and martyrs.[224] In his agitated, unbalanced, and contradictory literary style he also aimed "sideways," at the prose of the European Baroque, whose only—and, of course, unwitting!—Muscovite representative he is sometimes held to be.[225] In his obstinacy and soul-searching, however, he also aimed "forward" toward modern Russian literature, toward its mastery precisely in this discipline. Archpriest Avvakum was the first in a long line of inwardly torn, passionate, clownish, humble, and violent characters in Russian literature like those later depicted by Gogol, Leskov, or Dostoevsky. He is the first of these heroes—and

223 Ibid., 139–40.
224 Cf. Dmitrij Lichačov, "Humor protopopa Avvakuma," in *Smích staré Rusi,* ed. Alexandr Pančenko (Prague: Odeon, 1984), 69–85.
225 Cf. Světlana Mathauserová, *Cestami staletí: Systémové vztahy v dějinách ruské literatury* (Prague: Univerzita Karlova, 1988), 57–76.

at the same time the first of these authors. If Nestor's *Chronicle* is the most significant "objective" work of old Russian literature, *the* book about old Russian society—then Avvakum's *Life* is its most significant "subjective" work, *the* book about old Russian mentality. And nothing is changed by the fact that, speaking "objectively," i.e. culturally and religiously, the object of his life-long struggle was complete and utter nonsense.

Avvakum's *Life* is the most significant literary expression of the Old Belief. In the fine arts, its most significant evocation is without a doubt Vasily Surikov's (1848–1916) painting *Boiarynia Morozova* (1887). The gigantic picture measuring 3 by 6 meters, occupying an entire wall in Moscow's Tretyakov Gallery, was painted in the monumental historicist style, a style usually associated with cool skepticism. This picture, however, lacks nothing in pathos. The scene depicted by Surikov is the one described by Avvakum in his hagiographical text *Lament for the Three Martyrs:* "When the time came, Feodosia put aside feminine weakness and took up masculine wisdom. She set out for tribulations, to be tormented for the sake of Christ. Like a sly fox, the beast abducted her from her home and gave her over to the custody of the army. They dishonored her and dragged her around in chains like a fettered lion."[226] Boiarynia has her hands chained in the picture, she is set upon a sledge and carried away to the prison where she will be tortured to death. Yet she still raises her hand with two fingers extended, as if demonstrating to the crowd that has gathered in quiet horror to witness her deportation: This way! In this and no other way shall you cross yourself![227]

The absurd conflict over church ceremony once more shows itself to be a chance pretext for the universal principle of spiritual

226 Margaret Ziolkowski (ed.), *Tale of Boiarynia Morozova: A Seventeenth–Century Religious Life* (Lanham, Md.: Lexington Books), 82.
227 On Morozova's "other life" see Alexandr Pančenko, "Bojarka Morozovová: Symbol a osobnost," in *Metamorfózy ruské kultury,* ed. Alexandr Pančenko, Michal Řoutil et al. (Červený Kostelec: Pavel Mervart, 2012), 129–142.

resistance and the boyar as a living symbol of steadfastness and inner freedom. By absurd coincidence, this much-reproduced picture took on a more recent significance in the context of Czechoslovakia's normalization period under Gustáv Husák. A member of the underground church frequently subjected to police interrogations noticed a copy of Surikov's often-reproduced painting hanging above the head of his interrogator. The dissident understood this as an omen sent from above: amid the threats and intimidation of the state, the sixteenth-century religious dissident raised her fingers and admonished the man never to surrender, never to back down.

Petersburg Rus
and Russian Secularization

YEAR:
1721

PLACE:
Saint Petersburg

EVENT:
Peter the Great abolishes the patriarchate of Moscow

WORKS:
Saint Petersburg (1703); *Satires* by Antiokh Kantemir (1729–1739); "God" by Gavrila Derzhavin (1784); *A Journey from St. Petersburg to Moscow* by Alexandr Radishchev (1790); "Ode to Murr the Cat" by Vladislav Khodasevich (1934)

The reign of Peter the Great, spanning from 1689 to 1725, marks a dividing point in Russian history, separating pre-Petrine from post-Petrine Russia, or the era of Moscow from the era of Saint Petersburg. It is a paradox of the Petrine era that Peter the Great pushed through his reforms very much in the Muscovite style: brutally from above and without the least concern for the masses of unfortunates who would be crushed upon the rails of Russia's "historical mission." Thousands were sacrificed to the founding of St. Petersburg while dredging the Neva delta. Opponents, real and imagined, were tortured. There is more than a little resemblance between Peter the Great and Ivan the Terrible. Peter and his legacy thus occupy an ambiguous position in Russia's cultural memory, a fact well illustrated on historicizing canvases such as Vasily Surikov's *Morning of the Execution of the Streltsy* (1881) (Scene 20) or documented in novels like Dmitry Merezhkovsky's *Peter and Alexis* (1904).

For the cultural history of Russia, the Petrine era signaled an abrupt change in course, one that would finally connect Russia to the mainstream of European artistic developments. Whereas previously one might have doubted the existence of the Baroque in Russian outside of Lithuanian Rus, it now became clear that classicism had arrived to Russian literature and the fine arts. From the era of Peter forward, Russian culture would keep pace with Europe. In terms of spiritual history, Peter's change of course meant secularization and the exclusion of church from public life. Again, a paradox: Peter himself cared little for either art or religion.[228] He eagerly adopted any technological advance coming from Europe which might assist in building up his army or navy, but of its cultural products he adopted only fireworks (for state celebrations) and some baroque

---

228   Cf. I.Z. Serman, "Literaturno-esteticheskie interesy i literaturnaya politika Petra I.," in *Problemy literaturnogo razvitia v Rossii pervoi treti vosemnadtsatogo veka,* ed. G.P. Makogonnenko (Moscow: AN SSSR, 1974): 9–49.

symbolism (used when naming his ships).[229] He limited the power of the church not because he entertained any religious ideas of his own, but simply to prevent it from causing trouble. Peter remembered well the conflicts over church ceremony which had taken place during his childhood (Scene 10). Keeping all that in mind, the consequences of Peter's interventions were nevertheless immense. The year 1721 marks the symbolic end of Muscovite Rus, for it was in that year that Peter abolished the Moscow patriarchate and replaced it with the Most Holy Synod, an administrative body headed by an "chief procurator."

This symbolic turning point was real enough, though one must also recall the continuities stretching backward and forward in time. Looking back, Peter continued to developed trends that had been on the rise in Muscovite culture since the middle of the seventeenth century. Kievan scholars set the tone for the Moscow Academy, which was established in 1687 following the example of Kiev. A secular literature arrived to Moscow together with scholars from Kiev, or at least followed in their wake. As a rule, this literature was translated from Polish sources in Lithuania, Ovid's *Metamorphosis,* the humorous and rather indecent Renaissance text *Facetiea* by Poggio Bracciolini, even some novellas from Boccaccio's *Decameron.* And beside this there was a flood of chivalric literature, again translated or adapted from the Polish. This genre had been a favorite of Europe's burghers since the Renaissance, tales such as that of Bruncvik, Melusine, or the *Povest Vasilii Zlatovlasom, koroleviche Cheshskoi zemli* (The Legend of Vasily Zlatovlasy, Crown Prince of the Bohemian Lands).[230]

Peter's modernizing course might have appeared overly radical to many Kievan Latinists. They both, however, shared a common enemy: the proudly ignorant, isolated, devil-exorcizing Muscovite

229 Cf. A.A. Morozov, "Emblematika barokko v literature i iskusstve petrovskogo vremeni," in ibid., 184–226.

230 Cf. Světla Mathauserová, "Smysl a funkce povídky o Vasiliji Zlatovlasém," in *O Vasiliji Zlatovlasém, kralevici české země* (Prague: Vyšehrad, 1982), 67–178.

clergy following in the tradition of Joseph Volotsky and Archpriest Avvakum. For that reason alone, most of the Latinists aligned themselves with Peter, whether out of genuine enthusiasm or for more pragmatic reasons. It was precisely the Kievan Latinists who assisted Peter in his campaign to modernize the church and often served in the ecclesiastical structure itself. The most outstanding representative of this generation was the Kiev native Feofan Prokopovich, earlier a member of the Uniate Church who had received instruction in Rome. Feofan Prokopovich proselytized on behalf of Peter's modernizing reforms and was later awarded with the title Archbishop of Novgorod. Symbolically, the creation of this position presented Saint Petersburg as the "new Novgorod," a new "window into Europe" (Scene 8). Prokopovich served his office from Petersburg, where he worked out a plan for church reform, a vision that the historian of Russian theology Georges Florovsky (1893–1973) has called nothing less than a "program for a Russian reformation" (this, it goes without saying, was intended as the most damning of condemnations).[231] After the abolition of the patriarchate, Prokopovich was also named vice-president of the Most Holy Synod.[232]

Looking forward, one finds the fruit of Peter's fast-paced reforms in the arts and in spiritual life under his successors, especially under Catherine the Great. The most fitting testament to this is the magnificent political and artistic creation which is Saint Petersburg. The shifting of the city's historical significance can be traced through the evolution of the name itself. "Sankt Peterburg" of course means "the city of Saint Peter." In the appellation, one finds a reflection of Moscow's claim to a *translatio imperii,* that is, to the legacies of the first and second Rome. In the Christian tradition, Peter ("prince of the apostles") represents the spiritual ruler of the first Rome. The new capital city of the Russian Empire was named after St. Peter

---

231 Cf. George Florovsky, *Puti russkogo bogosloviya* (Paris: YMCA Press, 1988), 84.
232 Cf. Valeria Nichik, *Feofan Prokopovich* (Moscow: Mysl, 1977).

even though he had never been much esteemed in Russia. What's more, the city's name isn't even Russian, but "Germanic"—Dutch, to be precise: "Sankt Pieterburch." The original namesake was forgotten with time; instead of commemorating Peter the saint, the city became a commemoration of Peter the Great. In the same spirit, the "Sankt" and "Burg" fell away, leaving the colloquial "Piter." At the outbreak of war with Germany in 1914, the name was then completely Slavicized to "Petrograd."

This development is also reflected in the visual form of Saint Petersburg, in the buildings and monuments that shape the city's streets. Early Petersburg, the Petersburg of Peter himself, was a "gray" Petersburg as martial as it was pragmatic. This Saint Petersburg may be seen above all in the Peter and Paul Fortress, a prison which has housed many inmates from Peter's son Alexei to Radishchev and the Decembrists to several of the last members of the Romanov family after the Bolshevik seizure of power. It is to be seen in the Cathedral of Peter and Paul, in which the Romanovs were later laid to rest. The older structures of Vasilevskiy Island also date to the Petrine era. In one of his fits of enthusiastic delirium, Peter decided that the city's core should not be located on the continental coast—the elevation would have afforded security against floods—but instead on the low-lying Vasilyevsky Island. The first representative buildings were to be constructed there, structures intended to make the city a European center: rostral columns, two beacons meant to guide ships from the sea to the interior; a stock exchange located between them, the center of hoped-for trade with the west; other institutions set up after western models—an Academy of Sciences, an Academy of Art or the house of the Twelve Colleges, where all of the ministries including the Most Holy Synod were conveniently grouped together; also the Kunstkammer, Russia's first museum, where preserved human monsters and other curiosities (a fancy of Peter's) comprised the central exhibit. Further away from the city center, the Petrine era is recalled by the Alexander Nevsky Monastery, erected at the location where Alexander Nevsky was said to have defeated the Swedes (the message: we imitate the civilization of the West in order to defeat it in battle) and "little Holland," a closed-off area for Dutch craftsmen.

The Petersburg of Peter's daughter, Elizabeth (ruled 1742–1761) is by contrast a Petersburg of comfortable classicist palaces, the Winter Palace standing ahead of all the rest. Hers is a Petersburg built by Bartolomeo Rastrelli in "cheerful" hues of turquoise, white, and blue. The St. Petersburg of Catherine the Great (ruled 1762–1796) represents a magnificent collection of spiritual and cultural treasures. Catherine initiated the construction of the Hermitage Museum and Gallery. She built a "city for the citizens" along Nevsky Prospect, originally a thoroughfare leading from one "state" structure to another (from the admiralty to the monastery). Close to Nevsky Prospect, she oversaw the construction of houses of worship for the Protestant, Armenian, and Catholic confessions, some of them once again being used today (and characteristically dedicated to St. Catherine). The Petersburg of Catherine the Great is also the "Bronze Horseman," an equestrian statue of Peter the Great situated upon large boulder (read: Peter represents a rock-solid foundation). The statue itself is a gesture to the famous antique statue of the Roman emperor Marcus Aurelius (read: Peter as the emperor of the new Rome) and bears the Latin (or "Roman") inscription, *Petro Primo Catharina Secunda,* "Catherine the Second to Peter the First" (read: Catherine completes the work of Peter, Catherine the city's second founder).

A new literature came into being within the walls of Saint Petersburg, a literature which expressed the new intellectual atmosphere. Antiokh Kantemir (1798–1744) represents the first author of the Petrine era, the first secular and "western" author in Russian literature. This "first" among Russian writers was ironically not Russian at all, but Romanian. His father, a Moldavian prince named Dimitrie Cantemir (1673–1723), had joined in Peter the Great's unsuccessful bid to tear Moldavia away from the Turkish sphere of influence and place it under Russian suzerainty. The miscalculation nearly cost Cantemir his life, and he barely escaped with his family to Russia. Beside politics, Cantemir devoted himself to science and literature. Because of this, he is considered one of the founding figures of modern Romanian culture.

The work of Antiokh Kantemir, who continued the intellectual work of his father, stands at the beginning of Russian literary classicism and enlightenment.[233] A cycle of satirical verses comprises the main part of his oeuvre, which is influenced by the Roman satirical poetry of Horace and the trend-setter of French classicism, Nicolas Boileau. Kantemir's texts bear numerous traces of both Horace and Boileau as well as other antique models and French classicism. If one wishes to be contentious, one might call Kantemir a "mere" imitator and paraphraser, a writer who didn't so much produce something new (and certainly nothing groundbreaking—Kantemir's style is rigid and reveals the still rudimentary capacity of the period's literary Russian) as transfer literary models to the Russian context. He was someone who adapted the satirical invectives of France and Rome to the Russia of his day.[234]

Kantemir aimed his invectives primarily at ignoramuses, especially those who concealed their ignorance behind the guise of faith. The first satire carried the name *Na khulyashchikh uchenie* (Against the Enemies of Education). The third satire, named *O razlichii strastei chelovecheskikh* (On the Diversity of Human Passions), was dedicated to Feofan Prokopovich, whom Kantemir much admired, and contained literary caricatures of Prokopovich's conservative critics from the ranks of the Muscovite clergy. Although Kantemir was sincere in his support of Peter's reforms and he never made the tsar an object of his satire (to the contrary, he planned a heroic epic about

---

233   Cf. I.V. Shklyar, "Formirovanie mirovozzrejia Antiokha Kantemira," in *XVIII vek, sbornik 5* (Moscow and Leningrad: Izdatelstvo AN SSSR, 1962), 129–152.
234   Cf. Helmut Grasshoff, *Antioch Dmitrievič Kantemir und Westeuropa* (Berlin: Academie Verlag, 1966).

the ruler, the *Petrida,* to be modeled on the Iliad and Aeneid), he nevertheless met with incomprehension in Petrine and post-Petrine Russian society. He would not live to see his texts printed. Instead, his satires circulated as manuscripts "in the Muscovite fashion." He was sent to "honorable exile" as the ambassador to London and Paris (where he made the acquaintance of Montesquieu and Voltaire). It is understandable that the fourth satire, titled *K muze svoey* (To my Muses), reflects bitterly on the hazards of writing satire. In his sixth satire, *O istinnom blazhestve* (On True Happiness), the poet finally announces his resignation from public life (typically Horatian) and states his intention to retire to the comforts of intellectual seclusion.

Kantemir and the fate of his work testify to the speed with which the eighteenth-century Russian elite picked up on contemporary western European trends and attempted to bring what was "most modern" in them to Petersburg Rus, the Enlightenment above all. It also demonstrates the strict limits of tolerance in post-Petrine state and society. Kantemir was the first author in the modern cultural history of Russia to run up against these limits. Thankfully, he enjoyed the good fortune of living to continue his work in the West.

Other authors also contributed to the work of translation, bringing especially the works of French classicism and the Enlightenment to Russian readers.[235] Vasily Trediakovsky (1703–1768) translated Boileau's treatise, *L'art poétique* (1752), and made the first attempt to systematize the rules of Russian verse. Alexander Sumarokov (1717–1777) composed the first Russian tragedy using themes from antiquity and ancient Russian history. Denis Fonvizin (1745–1792) invented the genre of Russian sentimental comedy. Vasily Maykov (1728–1778) founded the tradition of the heroic-comical epic. Ivan

---

235 The European dimension of 18th century Russian literature is emphasized in Joachim Klein's synthesizing monography, originally written in German, *Russkaya literatura v XVIII veke* (Moscow: Indrik, 2010).

Barkov (1732–1768) won clandestine fame as the author of privately circulated erotic literature; classic examples of literary pornography and other such products are attributed to him.[236] The central genre of this sometimes halting but rapidly developing Russian secular literature was the ode—a noble, festive, antiquating poem commemorating some event or personage considered by its author to be worthy of rhetorical acclaim.

The primary benefactor of this sort of praise in the second half of the eighteenth century, of course, was the tsarina Catherine II, whom contemporary flatterers were already calling "the Great." Catherine the Great was praised in verse not just by domestic poets such as Sumarokov and Derzhavin, but also by her long-time correspondent and friend Voltaire. She was a personality who carried out the work of her predecessor Peter the Great not just in words she had carved into stone, but in her deeds as well. She was a personality who, unlike Peter, was deeply interested in cultural affairs and even penned several comedies and founded satirical journals.[237] And she was a personality firmly anchored in the European culture of her time, not least because she was not Russian at all, but German (Scene 2).

Not only do odes to Catherine the Great document the development of Russian literary style (specifically the genre of courtly flattery), they also reveal something about the self-stylization of the eighteenth-century Russian elite. Nothing remained of Orthodox terminology and symbolism. Catherine was celebrated exclusively in the symbolic language of antique mythology. She was called "the Amazon" to emphasize her masculine character (also for having conquered the Black Sea Coast, that ancient "homeland of the Amazons" as described by Herodotus, Scene 1). Voltaire was the first to lend her this title in an ode he recited at a celebration in 1766. She

236 Cf. Marcus C. Levitt (ed.), *Eros and Pornography in Russian Culture* (Moscow: Ladomir Publishers, 1999).
237 Cf. V.K. Bylinin and M.P. Odesski (eds.), *Ekaterina II. Sochinenia* (Moscow: Sovremennik, 1990).

became "Pallas Athena" and "Minerva" for having organized military campaigns to expand Russian empire. She was "Astraea," the "star of fortune," for having carried Russia into a golden age of prosperity, and the "celestial virgin" ushering in the golden age of Rome as depicted in the Fourth Eclogue of Virgil's *Pastoral Songs*, like Queen Elizabeth giving the theme a Renaissance updating. She was "Felice," the "goddess of good fortune," for having emphasized leniency during her reign; the first to call her this was Gavril Derzhavin (1743–1816) in his ode *Felitsa* (1779), a complement for which he was rewarded with the title of court poet and the sovereign's enduring friendship. She was named "Dushenka," Little Soul, the universal human spirit consecrated to the bridegroom/love/the good as in the myth of Cupid and Psyche from the Roman novel *The Golden Ass*; this she was first called by Ippolit Bogdanovich (1744–1803) in his epic *Dushenka* (1778–1783). He, too, did not walk away empty handed. And in erotic literature, concentrating on what was said to be an insatiable carnal appetite, she was always known as "Cleopatra."[238]

All this adds up to more than just classicist rhetoric, more than mere courtly play on themes from antiquity. On the one hand, Catherine's entire reign was fashioned after antiquity, returning in her own way to the idea of *translatio imperii*, Russia's claim to the legacies of ancient Greece and Rome. It is evident in her "Grecization" of conquered Crimea (Scene 1). On the other hand, much of the courtly symbolism referred to contemporary spirituality in the narrower sense. Catherine and her court poets were all officially members of the Orthodox Church, though this membership meant little in practice. In truth, they each tended in their own way toward the "Enlightenment spirituality" of western Europe, that sundry mix of an ethically understood Christianity, deism, pantheism, anticlericalism, and esoteric mysticism. There was also a pretended allegiance to

---

238 Cf. Vera Proskurina, *Mify imperii: Literatura i vlast' v epokhu Ekateriny II.* (Moscow: Novoe literaturnoe obozrenie, 2006).

Egyptian tradition, to Neoplatonism, hermetic or Rosicrucian ritual. They belonged to that spiritual admixture whose para-ecclesiastical organization was represented by Free Masonry.

„Astraea" is a masonic symbol. It was also the name of the masonic lodge in Saint Petersburg as well as daughter lodges in Moscow and Riga, and in 1815 even a grand lodge. Freemasonry arrived to Russia through the contact of Russian diplomats with their western colleagues, especially English and Prussian. It immediately captivated the Russian elite. The poets Sumarokov and Bogdanovich were Freemasons, so was the historian and prose writer Nikolai Karamzin (1766–1826), the journalist and satirist Nikolai Novikov (1744–1818), and many others.[239] Freemasons perceived in Catherine the Great a model ruler able to realize the Enlightenment ideal of a rational, tolerant, and humane government. Catherine saw in them a pillar of support—until her son, who would later become Paul I, joined the Masons in search of support for views opposed to those of his mother.

The tolerance proclaimed by Catherine had its limits. When the time came, the lodge was officially disbanded and its organizer, Novikov, was arrested. Without trail, Novikov was confined to a fortress for the remainder of Catherine's rule. Freemasonry doubtlessly played a role in Novikov's arrest, as did Catherine's fear of a Russian equivalent to the French Revolution. Novikov's journalistic activities also crossed the line beyond what Catherine considered "constructive criticism."[240]

Even through Freemasonry faced long-term repression, "masonic" spirituality represents a major element of the religious mentality of Petersburg Rus during the Catherinian era. Insofar as one discerns any religious attitude in the period's literature, it comes from the masonic form of spirituality. Two period texts serve well as

---

239 Cf. Viktor Ostretsov, *Masonstvo, kulutra i russkaia istoriia* (Moscow: Kraft, 2007); cf. Ju. V. Stennik, "Pravoslavie i masonstvo v Rossii XVIII veka," *Russkaya literatura* 1 (1995): 76–92.
240 Cf. Raffaela Faggionato, *A Rosicrucian Utopia in Eighteenth-Century Russia: The Masonic Circle of N.I. Novikov* (Dordrecht: Springer, 2005).

examples: Derzhavin's ode "God" (1784) and Radishchev's *A Journey from St. Petersburg to Moscow* (1790).

The ode to God is the first Russian poem to have made a global career, being translated into many European languages. John Bowring included it as the first text in his pioneering English anthology of Russian poetry from 1821. Russian admiral Vasily Golovnin even translated it into Japanese. The ode also inspired Czech poets as well: it was translated into Czech by František Čelakovský's collaborator Josef Václav Kamarýt, its traces are also to be found in Čelakovský's poem "Your Will be Done" as well as in the works of František Sušil and other nineteenth-century Czech authors. In sonnet 423 of his *Slávy dcera*, Jan Kollár gave a place to Derzhavin in his Slavic heaven. In sonnet 449 he also included those who popularized the poet's genius abroad, and thus celebrated the genius of Russia and the Slavs in general:

> Elysian tea and punch served in cups ornate
> to all who Rus will celebrate,
> they who Slavic genius applaud:
> who translated Derzhavin's Ode to God.[241]

What was it about Derzhavin's ode that captured the attention of the world's public across languages and confessions? He appears to have eloquently expressed that post-confessional spirituality of the age. His ode consequentially became a poetic manifesto of modern piety, a piety characterized by the classicism of the Enlightenment, by Christianity and antique culture, a moderate rationalism quietly contemplating the cosmos. One might say, a piety best characterized by freemasonry. Derzhavin begins his ode with a consideration of God as the supernatural being which transcends all categories. Only

241 Jan Kollár, *Slávy dcera: Báseň lyricko-epická v pěti zpěvích,* with an introductory essay and annotation by Martin C. Putna (Prague: Academia, 2014), 246.

a brief mention of the Trinity reminds the reader of the specifically Christian tradition:

O Thou eternal One! whose presence bright
All space doth occupy, all motion guide;
Unchanged through time's all devastating flight;
Though only God! There is no God beside!
Being above all beings! Three in One!
Whom none can comprehend and none explore;
Who fill'st existence with *Thyself* alone;
Embracing all,—supporting,—ruling o'er,—
Being whom we call God—and know no more![242]

The contemplation of God's nature gradually transforms into a meditation on man, but one that leads not a baroque contrast between divine omnipotence and the powerlessness of human beings. It expresses instead the proud "Enlightenment" assertion that God and man are similar. There is a special divinity reserved for man, though this is not to deny the frailty of his humanity:

The chain of being is complete in me;
In me is matter's last gradation lost,
And the next step is spirit—Deity!
I can command the lightning, and am dust!
A monarch, and a slave; a worm, a god![243]

In his Czech translation of the ode, the Catholic priest and "national awakener" Kamarýt toned down this verse, so central to the Russian Enlightenment, substituting the moderate *velitel já světa—*

---

242 Gavrila Derzhavin, "God," trans. John Bowring, *Specimens of the Russian Poets* (London, 1821)
243 Ibid.

otrok–červ–a duch! (I, commander of the world—slave—worm—and spirit!) for the more grandiose, "Ja tsar—ja rab—ja cherv—ja Bog!" ("I am tsar—I am a slave—I am a worm—I am God!")

One of the stops in Alexander Radishchev's (1749–1802) *A Journey from St. Petersburg to Moscow* (1790) provides a second example, another mediation on man and God from the Catherinian era. Radishchev makes several pointed observations about the less-than-salubrious side of Petersburg Rus, qualities not exactly well represented at Catherine's court celebrations. During one stop of this pilgrimage he chokes up remembering the ancient freedom of Novgorod (Scene 8); at another stop he polemicizes against censorship; in many other places, he bitterly comments on the cruel lot of the serfs or the spread of syphilis and other ailments in Catherine's Rus; at yet another stop he visits a chapel on the site of which once stood a pagan temple to the god Perun, and is moved by the experience to a sort of universal prayer:

But I cannot believe, Almighty God, that man ever addressed his soul's prayers to any other being but Thee. [...] If a mortal in his error calls Thee by strange, unbecoming, and bestial names, his worship nonetheless aspires to Thee, Ever-living Lord, and he trembles before Thy might. Jehovah, Jupiter, Brahma, God of Abraham, God of Moses, God of Confucius, God of Zoroaster, God of Socrates, God of Marcus Aurelius, God of the Christians, O my God! Though art everywhere the same, the One. [...] The atheist who denies Thee, but recognizes the immutable law of nature, thereby proclaims Thy glory, lauding Thee even more than out songs of praise. For, moved to the depths of his soul by Thy wondrous works, he stands trembling before them. Most gracious Father, Thou seekest a true heart and spotless soul; they are open everywhere for Thy coming. Descend, O Lord, and enthrone Thyself in them.[244]

244 Aleksandr Nikolaevich Radishchev, *A Journey from St. Petersburg to Moscow,* trans. Leo Wiener (Cambridge: Harvard University Press, 1958), 90–91.

Derzhavin and Radishchev thus shared a similar religious thought. One that would have unleashed a spate of fury from Archpriest Avvakum or Patriarch Nikon. At the same time, Radishchev's pilgrimage to Siberia, which led almost to the scaffold, resembled that of Avvakum before him. Namely, his pilgrimage wasn't motivated by religion but politics. There is thus a social-critical dimension to *A Journey from St. Petersburg to Moscow*.

Despite this and other examples of the strict and often inscrutable limits to Catherine's tolerance, the Catherinian era nonetheless represents a "golden age" in Russian cultural history. Catherine truly carried out a reorientation of Russian culture toward western models. Finally, a Russian tsar received the admiration of European intellectuals and fellow rulers (especially Joseph II) for something other than a fine military performance. Catherine introduced an unprecedented degree of religious tolerance into the Russian empire for Catholics, Protestants, Jews, and others.

She stimulated the advance of art and scholarship, and even if several works "didn't make the cut," the mere fact that they were produced and that their authors could reasonably hope to "pushing it through" testifies to the optimistic atmosphere of the time. Only a very few of these hopes were ever realized. For all that, many later looked back to the Catherinian era and Petersburg Rus with affection and nostalgia, as if to the "second childhood" of Rus, after the "first childhood" of Kievan Rus.

Another development that shaped culture in the era of Catherine the Great was the creation of numerous private spaces, places beyond the reach of official culture and the state where one might be culturally productive or "just" spiritually and culturally exist. Petersburg classicism consists not only in the monumental constructions of the city center. It is also to be found in the dozens and hundreds of small classicist estates spread throughout Moscow's suburbs and across Russia, "aristocratic nests" with their characteristic pastel-yellow facades, white columns and pointed gables.

Again, Derzhavin provides a literary equivalent to these columns and facades. While it is true that the poet was best known to contemporaries for his odes to the tsarina and to God, more significant for posterity was his discovery of what one could call the poetics of comfortable surroundings, a calm and modestly hedonistic rural or suburban idyll à la Horace. This is the sort of existence the poet enjoyed on his own estate in Zvanka, the so-called *zvanskaya zhizn'*, or "Zvanka life." An existence later to be glorified—but also challenged—by Alexander Pushkin (1799–1837), the last poet of the Petersburg era, someone enchanted by the Europe of the Enlightenment and its play on antiquity. Pushkin's early lyrical poetry abounds in capricious reminiscences of the classical world. It was the sort of existence that Russian culture will recollect in later, much worse, years. When the neoclassicist poet Vladislav Khodasevich (1886–1939) in Parisian exile later looks back to this "golden age" of his homeland, it is precisely Pushkin whom he recalls—and Derzhavin, too, as in the antiquating poem "Ode to Murr the Cat"—which is not only about a cat:

In play he was so wise and in his wisdom playful--
Comforting friend and my inspirer! Now
He's in those gardens, beyond the fiery river,
With Catullus and the sparrow, Derzhavin and his swallow.

O, lovely are the gardens beyond the fiery river,
Where there's no vulgar rabble, where in benefic rest
Beloved shades of poets and of beasts
Enjoy the well-earned peace of all eternity.

And when shall I depart?[245]

---

245 Vladislav Khodasevich, "On the Death of the Cat Murr," cited in "Khodasevich: Irony and Dislocation: A Poet in Exile" by Robert P. Hughes, in *The Bitter Air of Exile: Russian Writers in*

The provocatively contemptuous and impersonal reference to "vulgar rabble" calls attention to yet another aspect of Petersburg Rus. All this "catching up with Europe" and its plays on antiquity, all of the freemasonry and capricious spiritual meandering, all of the modernization and secularization—all of this affected only the uppermost strata of Russian society.[246] The broader masses continued to live on as before, shut off from society's upper classes and from its high culture, treated with irony in the texts of the post-Petrine elite (see, for example, the sarcastic "Hymn to the Beard" by the natural scientist and poet Mikhail Lomonosov). This was the old, pre-Petrine, Muscovite Rus waiting for its return.

In the meantime, of course, the tripartite division of Poland after the Napoleonic wars completely transformed old Rus, adding to it a large region of "other," "non-Russian," or more precisely, "non-Muscovite" populations. There was the population of the nationally and culturally other—the Russian-speaking population of the former Lithuanian Rus, which would go on to form new Ukrainian and Belarusian identities. Then there was the Jewish population settled in areas of Lithuanian Rus and Poland. Finally, there was the Catholic population, to which belong the Poles and Lithuanians as well as part of the Ukrainians and Belarusians. These three "counter currents," these three open questions (the Ukrainian-Belarusian question, the Jewish question, and the Catholic question) taken together comprise the spiritual world of Petersburg Rus.

the West, 1922–1972, edited by Simon Karlinsky and Alfred Appel, Jr. (Berkeley: University of California Press, 1977), 55.

246 For a modern interpretation of the theatricalization and stylization as well as of the private and public life of these newly Europeanized elites, see Yuri M. Lotman, "The Poetics of Everyday Behavior in Eighteenth-Century Russian Culture," trans. Andrea Beesing, in *The Semiotics of Everyday Russian Cultural History,* edited by Alexander D. Nakhimovsky and Alice Stone Nakhimovsky, (Ithaca, NY: Cornell University Press), 67–94.

Ukrainian Rus and White Rus

1798

Poltava

EVENT:
Ivan Kotlyarevsky launches Ukrainian literature with
a good laugh

WORKS:
Eneida by Ivan Kotlyarevsky (1798); *In Everlasting
Memory of Kotlyarevsky* by Taras Shevchenko (1838);
Minsk (after 1945); *Recreations* and "Central-East
Revisions" by Yuri Andrukhovych (1992, 2005);
Minsk: Sun City of Dreams by Artur Klinau (2006)

Over the course of the seventeenth and eighteenth centuries, Muscovy and Petersburg Rus steadily acquired the territories of Lithuanian Rus. This process of acquisition took place for the most part by the usual means: ordinary wars of conquest or politically negotiated occupation. The annexation of the Dnieper's left bank, which included the city of Kiev, proved an exception to this rule: it joined voluntarily in the middle of the seventeenth century, only a few years after having become, *de facto*, an independent state. This came about thanks to the free Cossack units, the society's social backbone which up till then had been responsible for defending the frontiers of the Commonwealth against incursions from the Crimean Khanate. But the Cossacks revolted under the leadership of Bohdan Khmelnytsky because the Commonwealth had favored Catholicism over Orthodoxy. The land of the Cossacks then became the autonomous territory within Muscovy known as "the Hetmanate."

It was at this point that the Cossacks began to use the term Ukraine (*okraïna*) to describe their territory, a word that literally means "borderland" in the sense of an interstate or intercultural frontier. However, the word has also been interpreted as derived from the Old Slavic term *kraj'*, or *ukraj*, signifying a separate country or *regio*.[247] In this case, the word *Ukraine* represents just another version of the same word from which the ancient Slavic region of Carniola took its name, once an Austrian crownland and today the core of Slovenia. A modern nation formed around the Cossacks, a nation which also called itself *Rus* or used one of its variants (including the Latin *Roxoloania*) to name its country. The people called themselves Rusyns or Ruthenians and maintained that it was they, not Muscovy, who represented the true Rus. The original Lithuanian Rus, the land of the Rusians/Rusyns/Ruthenians, had been divided into

---

247   Cf. Natalia Yakovenko, "Choice of Name versus Choice of Path: The Names of Ukrainian Territories from the Late Sixteenth to the Late Seventeenth Century," in Georgiy Kasianov and Philipp Ther (eds.), *A Laboratory of Translational History: Ukraine and Recent Ukrainian Historiography,* (Budapest: CEU Press, 2009), 117–148.

northern and southern parts already in the days of the Common-wealth, the northern part reserving for itself the name Lithuania. The southern part then gradually identified with the name Ukraine, though it was called "Little Russia" by Moscow and Petersburg. The "left over" part of the north took on the name White Russia, which in time came to be interpreted also as an ethnic label (while the label "Lithuanian," for its part, came to be identified with speakers of the Baltic language Lithuanian, whose national revival was to begin in the nineteenth century). In this way, the common heritage of Lithuanian Rus and the Russian/Rusian ethnicity developed into two separate nations, Ukrainians and Belarusians.[248]

That's not the end of complications, not by far. Belarus comprises the geographical region which, in the Middle Ages, went by the name Black Rus; Ukraine claims as part of its inheritance the region formerly called Red Rus, or Galicia (Scene 8). What's more, the eastern-Slavic-speaking peoples of Galicia and Hungarian Rus (later called Subcarpathian Ruthenia) took on the project of adopting their own collective identity, thus giving way to a fourth nation-building project in the region, neither Russian nor Ukrainian (and not Belarusian), but "Ruthenian." And that's *still* not the end of the matter, for there are also other peoples who inhabit the Polish-Ukrainian frontier, smaller groups which have quietly pursued their own, thus a fifth and a sixth, ethnic identities: the Hutsuls and Lemkos.[249]

One would like to exclaim with Jan Kollár's sonnet 337: "I cry out, Slavs scattered wide, / become one, and do not divide!"[250] Why

---

248 Czech historiography of the eastern Slavic lands seldom takes into consideration the independent identity of Ukrainians and Belarusians. A happy exception to this rule is Josef Macůrek's *Dějiny východních Slovanů,* 1–3 (Prague: Melantrich, 1947).
249 Cf. Paul Robert Magocsi, *Ukraine: A Historical Atlas* (Toronto: University of Toronto Press, 1985); Andrew Wilson, *The Ukrainians: Unexpected Nation* (New Haven: Yale University Press, 2000).
250 Jan Kollár, *Slávy dcera: Báseň lyricko-epická v pěti zpěvích,* with introduction and annotation by Martin C. Putna (Prague: Academia, 2014), 188.

suffer through the ethnonymic and ethnographic chaos, why search for its logic and sense? For the cultural historian of Russian spirituality, the heterogeneity left in the wake of Lithuanian Rus is of utmost importance. First, because it breaks apart Russian imperialism's monolithic discourse, all too eager to back up Kollár's frustrations with the unwholesome, pointless, and deleterious existence of "small" nations. Second, it calls attention to the cultural plurality of the space left by Lithuanian Rus, its multiethnicity, the interconnectedness of its cultures, Rusyns/Ruthenians, Poles, and Germans as well as Jews, Lithuanians, and others. It recalls the region's quintessential "Central European" character. Third, the culture of the two major nations that formed in the region, Ukrainians and Belarusians, communicates an important message beyond the revivalist assertion that "we are here," a message about the relationship between Russia and the Europe.

At the center of Russia's identity as an empire lies the conviction that there does not and cannot exist anything like genuinely independent, autonomous, and equally valuable Ukrainian and Belarusian identities. Russian imperial identity could not exist without the denial of these claims to independence. At least, it could not have existed in the form that it took over the course of the nineteenth century, a century of competing nationalist myths, including myths about the ancient history of the Rus lands. The Ukrainian version of this myth was born as a defensive reaction against the expansionist politics of Moscow.

A restiveness soon set in following the Cossack state's incorporation into Muscovy. The new sovereign was Orthodox but, to be sure, he was not any more liberal than had been the Commonwealth. Archbishop Lazar Baranovych (1620–1693), chancellor of the Kievan College and, after Peter Mohyla, the most important figure of the Kievan Baroque, complained in his collection of sermons, *The Spiritual Sword* (1666), about Moscow's interference in church affairs. Tsarist administrators gradually curtailed the Hetmanate's authority until they finally decided to abolish it. Cossack territory was joined together with other lands in a system of imperial governates. True to the Muscovite model, free peasants were made into serfs without rights.

To be sure, it is not that Muscovite and later Petrine Rus represented just brutal colonization. Integration into the Muscovite state appealed to a wide range of the Ukrainian political and cultural elite because it offered them the chance to act on an imperial scale. From the middle of the seventeenth century to the beginning of the nineteenth century, cultural and ecclesiastical life in the Russian empire consisted to an enormous degree of scholars trained in Kiev or Polatsk according to western models. The learning of such scholars easily surpassed that of their (half)educated peers in Muscovy. Simon Polatsky transmitted the literary Baroque to Moscow while Epifanii Slavinetsky oversaw the introduction of book printing (Scene 9). Realism was introduced to Muscovite iconography from Kiev, quite to the consternation of traditionalists (Scene 10). Dmitri Bortnyansky (1751–1825) brought to Russian ecclesiastical music Italian principles of polyphony (he was trained in Venice) and created a style often mistakenly supposed to be "typically Orthodox," whereas in fact the common church music in Muscovite Russia sounded completely different.[251] Many political and cultural figures of the Catherinian era were also of Ukrainian or Belarusian origin, such as Bogdanovich, author of the antiquizing epic poem *Dushenka* (Scene 11). To state it pointedly, one might say that the Russia of Catherine the Great appeared so European, because it was so Ukrainian and Belarusian.

This is by no means an unfamiliar pattern. It corresponds to the subjugation of Athens by Sparta, of Greece by Rome, and of Rome by Germania. Though defeated by a lesser civilization on the field

---

251 Cf. Jan Racek, *Ruská hudba od nejstarších dob po VŘSR* (Prague: SNKLHU, 1953).

of battle, the more highly developed and thus "softer" powers end up "defeating" their subjugators in the field of culture. To follow Horace, *Graecia capta ferum victorem cepit* ("Captive Greece captured her rude conqueror.")[252]

Intellectuals and artists later arrived from Ukraine to Russia, above all to St. Petersburg and Moscow, to pursue ambitions that could never have been realized at home. The nineteenth century is represented by Gogol, the twentieth century by the poet Anna Akhmatova (née Gorenk, 1889–1966). And this is to say nothing of all the Germans and Jews who arrived from Ukraine and Belarus.

There was a catch to this ambitious migration of intellects, however. Systematically abandoned by its elite, Ukrainian and Belarusian territory once more became a province, an *okrai,* but in a new sense; it became a cultural borderland of Russia. And this is why, starting at the beginning of the nineteenth century, those members of the Ukrainian elite who remained physically or mentally "at home" gave rise to an alternative myth. This myth received its first formulation in the genre of historiography, its founding text being the *Istorija Rusiv* (History of the Rus), a rather tendentious work composed in Ukrainian by an unknown author at some point early in nineteenth century (there are a number of suspects). The work circulated in manuscript form until 1846, when it was printed in Russian translation in Moscow by the Ukrainian Slavic scholar and Moscow university instructor Oleg Bodansky (1808–1878).

Istorija Rusiv builds its alternative narrative on two foundational points. First, Ukraine does not have a "short" history, one beginning with the Cossack Hetmanate, but rather a "long" history that goes back to the days of Kievan Rus. The Kievan Vladimir accordingly becomes the Ukrainian prince Volodymyr. Second, the heirs to Kievan Rus are today's Ukrainians, or "Little Russians"; today's "Great Russians" are by origin a separate nation, called "Moskals."

The *Istorija Rusiv* inspired the work of the professional histori-an Nikolay Kostomarov (1817–1885), another Ukrainian native who wrote in Russian and was active in St. Petersburg. Its influence can be seen in the scholar's many volumes about Russian history, such as the *Russkaya istoriya v zhizneopisaniyach ee glavnejshikh deyateleii* (Russian History in the Biographies of its Most Important Actors, 1873), which devotes most space to the princes of Kievan Rus and, after them, to ecclesiastical figures and scholars from Lithuanian Rus. Of greatest significance, however, is the theoretical concept formulated in his essay "Two Russian Nationalities" (1861) which asserts a fundamental dichotomy between Ruthenians, Ukrainians, and Belarusian on the one side and Moskals, Northern Russians, and Great Russians on the other. According to Kostomarov, Ukrai-nians and Belarusians are not just two regional and ethnographic variations of a common Russian theme; they are two entirely dis-tinct and equal nations.

Ukrainian national consciousness reached its peak in the work of Mykhailo Hrushevsky (1866–1934), a historian writing in his native Ukrainian language. Hrushevsky occupies a position in the cultural history of Ukraine analogous to that held by František Palacký in the history of the Czechs: a historian who becomes the political lead-er of his nation. (What's more, the Ukrainian historian maintained close contact with his Czech colleagues.[253]) His multivolume study, *The History of Ukrainian-Rus* (1898–1937), radically expanded the notion of a "long" Ukrainian history by incorporating the ancient cultures of the Black Sea coast, of the Scythians and other peoples (Scene 1). Hrushevsky's conception of Ukrainian history in this way represents a union of indisputably scholarly erudition and (post)ro-mantic nationalism, a combination whose extreme form was real-ized a century earlier in Bohemia by the scholar-poet Jan Kollár in

---

253 Cf. Bohdan Zilynskyj, "Mychajlo Hruševsky and His Relations to Bohemia and to the Czech Scholarship," *Acta Universitatis Carolinae—Studia Territorialia* 1, no. 2 (2001): 185–200.

his *Staroitalia Slavjanská* (Ancient Slavic Italy, 1853). Hrushevsky underscores the characteristic "essentialism" of his ethnic claim to the entirety of Ukrainian history by using the hyphenated name for his land and people, Ukraine-Rus. Though a condensed expression of Ukrainian national ambitions, Hrushevsky's label is a more fitting designation for the territory and its nation than any of the other names proposed before or since.[254]

Belarusians stand, as it were, "third in line" in this Russian-Ukrainian contest over a common history. Not only are Belarusians, in the Great Russian scheme of things, reduced to the status of a local minority, from the Ukrainian perspective they are also often regarded as little more than useful allies in the fight against Great Russian dominance, as the weaker branch of a common Ruthenian/South Russian identity. Given their smaller numbers and (relatively) smaller territory, Belarusians have never asserted claims equal in ambition to those forwarded by Ukrainians. They have "merely" sought to call Russia's and Europe's attention to the fact of their existence. The history of Lithuanian Rus buttressed this effort, it being a state with a Lithuanian dynasty but Russian (read: Belarusian) as its language of culture and a Russian (read: Belarusian) ethnic majority. That which later arose from the territory of the old Lithuanian Rus, specifically from its northern parts, was later reinterpreted as Belarusian and its history reconstructed as Belarusian in proper revivalist fashion. Francisk Skoryna and Simeon Polotsky play the role of founding fathers in this nationalized narrative—where they are called Frantsishak Skaryna and Symeon Polatsky.[255]

254 For criticism of this sort of "essentialism" see Georgiy Kasianov and Philipp Ther (eds.), *A Laboratory of Transnational History: Ukraine and Recent Ukrainian Historiography* (Budapest: CEU Press, 2009).
255 Cf. Alena Ivanova and Jan Tuček (eds.), *Cesty k národnímu obrození: Běloruský a český model* (Prague: UK FHS, 2006); Cf. Stanislav Akinčyc, *Zlatý věk Běloruska* (Pardubice: Světlana Vránová, 2013).

The Ukrainian and Belarusian revivals, furthermore, treated certain markers as signs common to both national identities. This dual understanding of nationhood received the backing of two outside sources. Outside, but not completely. Historically and geographically, Ukrainians and Belarusians have been wedged between Poles and Russians, a fact which itself could serve as a foundation of identity. They were influenced and scrutinized from both directions, understood by both neighbors as a (dual) nation which was not truly "foreign." Both the Polish and Russian points of view regard the region as a borderland and cultural periphery. Poles and Russians entertain their own visions of "Ukrainianness" and "Belarusianness." For better or for worse, these neighborly visions affect the self-perception of Ukrainians and Belarusians themselves.

The Polish side always supported Ukrainian and Belarusian claims to national specificity. They did so, in part, as a form of "revenge" against Moscow for having destroyed the Commonwealth. Romantic Polish intellectuals began studying Ukrainian and Belarusian folklore at the beginning of the nineteenth century, composing poetry after the fashion of Ukrainian or Belarusian folk sagas, even going so far as to stylize themselves as Ukrainian and Belarusian peasants, appearing at their aristocratic soirées in folk dress, a sort of counter-cultural escapade and escaping into an idealized past of the Polish-Ruthenian Commonwealth.[256] This was also true of the fine arts: the national gallery in Lviv exhibits as part of its nineteenth-century collection a number of canvases depicting folkloristic or historisizing scenes: Cossacks venerating icons on the Steppe, Jews in synagogue, Hutsuls in the forests. The names of the artists, meanwhile, are all Polish or (Austrian) German.

---

256 Volodomir Okariňskij, "Formuvaňňa polskogo narodoljubnogo ukrainofilstva, jak nonkonformistskoj sociokulturnoi tečii," in *Slovanský svět: Známý či neznámý?* Kateřina Kedroň and Marek Příhoda (eds.) (Červený Kostelec: Pavel Mervart, 2013), 157–166.

The impact of the Polish view is stronger in Belarus than in Ukraine. The actors of Belarusian cultural renewal were bilingual literati from the circle surrounding Poland's national poet Adam Mickiewicz (Scene 14), who himself appealed to the provincial patriotism of Lithuania. For Polish Romantics such as these, "Ukraine" and "Belarus" add up to so many projections of a bygone folk culture, plebian, agrarian, picturesque, and archaic, a preserve for an age long passed and a happiness lying beyond the current of modern history.

The Russian point of view—insofar as it even recognizes Ukrainian and Belarusian culture—sometimes shares in this idyllic, folkloristic vision. But they often give it a different accent. Ukraine, the country of fiercely independent Cossacks, symbolizes a land of freedom in the Russian mind, a counterpoint to the absolutist state of Great Russia in which the individual is powerless, the ruler and his machinery all powerful, and obedience represents the most important virtue. Such an image of Ukraine was first projected by Kondraty Ryleev (1795–1826), a primary orchestrator and martyr of the Decembrist uprising. He was not Ukrainian himself; he had only spent some time there. Nevertheless, Ukraine became the major source of inspiration for his work. He composed romantic poetry about leaders of the Cossack uprising, and *Dumy* (1825), a propagandistic poem written in the style of Ukrainian folk poetry.[257] It is Ukraine's mission to teach Russia the meaning of freedom.

Ukrainian literature also wavers between these two visions. The first major work to be written in modern colloquial Ukrainian and not some variation of archaic Church Slavonic was the *Eneida* by Ivan Kotlyarevsky (printed in 1798). The *Eneida* presents a bucolic vision of Ukraine wrapped in a burlesque epic. Parodies of Virgil's *Aeneid* became quite fashionable in late eighteenth-century

---

257 See the selections translated (into Czech) in the anthology *Modří husaři: Z díla děkabristů* (Prague: Odeon, 1967), 102–110.

Europe from France to Saint Petersburg, and from Petersburg to Kotlyarevsky's home, Poltava.[258] Of all the parodies it was only Kotlyarevsky's *Eneida* which became a foundational work, a true *Aeneid* of its own national literature.

Discussing what he calls the "hollowness" of Ukrainian literature, the literary historian and well-known Ukrainian intellectual Dmytro Chyzhevsky (1894–1977) pauses to consider the problem of "Kolyarevskianism." By this he means the tendency in Ukrainian culture, present from the very beginning, to self-parody, to accept the burlesque-folkloristic kitsch forced upon it by its neighbors, depictions of "Ukrainianness" as hilariously self-indulgent and ahistorically plebian.[259]

Yet it is also possible to interpret this same "anomaly" as the exceptional advantage of Ukrainian literature. Sure, many literatures trace back to some profound foundational work at their point of origin. Jan Kollár's *Slávy dcera* (Daughter of Slava) serves as an example in the Czech case. On the other hand, most of these foundational works failed to capture the imagination of the reading public. Ukrainian literature has the good fortune to not have begun with profundity, but with laughter. A laughter that continued to stimulate a national literature and even today provides inspiration for new parodies— consider Yuri Andrukhovych, whose contemporary work manages to keep even a moderately educated (post)modern reader entertained.

The Romantic poet Taras Shevchenko (1814–1861) represents a more "sober" Ukrainian classic. One is hard pressed to find laughter in Shevchenko. This is understandable enough given his vision of Ukraine: once a land of freedom, yes, but a freedom which has

---

258   Cf. Mária Borbély-Bánki, "Aeneis-Travestien aus der Blütezeit der komischen Epen am Ende des 18. Jahrhunderts," in *Symposium Vergilianum,* (ed.) Tar Ibolya (Szeged, 1984): 127–136; cf. Martin C. Putna, "Vergilius: Učitel Evropy," *Publius Vegilius Maro: Aeneis* (Prague: Academia, 2011), 431–437.

259   Cf. Z. Rachůnková and F. Sokolová and R. Šišková (eds.), *Dmytro Čyževskyj: Osobnost a dílo.* Prague: Národní knihovna ČR—Slovanská knihovna, 2004.

been stolen. It is also understandable in light of the author's difficult life and the hardships he faced from the disgrace of hereditary serfdom to his brief sojourn among cultural elites followed by a grinding tour of various prisons and barracks. Shevchenko's poetry is full of sadness, nostalgic appeals to the country's past freedoms and the old Cossacks, and biblical-sounding lamentations and reproach toward the hated "Moscals." (It won't come as a surprise that these bitterly anti-Moscow verses did not find a place in Czech editions of Shevchenko during the Soviet era for fears that they would stir anti-Russian sentiment.)

Shevchenko formulated his critique in terms of a dichotomy between Ukraine-Rus and Muscovy, a dichotomy that was formulated in *Istorija Rusiv* and developed by his friend Kostomarov. According to his essay, "Two Russian Nations," Ukrainians differ from Great Russians not just by their separate geographical locations and distinct historical experiences, but above all by of their very different mentalities. Great Russia means imperialism, collectivism, and autocracy. Ukraine stands for freedom, individualism, and poetry.

It is true that Shevchenko also appealed to folklore, but his allusions are of an entirely different spirit: the self-stylization of the poet as an itinerate Cossack bard, a "kobzar," with his seldom joyous and usually pensive epic verses, the *dumy.* Even if Shevchenko recalls the memory of Kotlyarevsky as a pioneer in the cultivation of a living Ukrainian literary tradition, his elegies sound very different.

Both these basic visions of Ukrainian identity were brought together by an author who hailed from Ukraine and returned to it again and again as a theme in his work, who nonetheless chose to write in Russian and so became known not as Mykola Hohol but Nikolai Gogol (Scene 16). Paradoxically, he abandoned his mother tongue to win fame in the more "worldly" Russian—and in that language to sing the glory of his native Ukraine. Ukrainian cultural history attributes to Gogol an accordingly paradoxical status. Sometimes chided for having abandoned his homeland, sometimes praised for winning it recognition, scholars have devoted much space to discussing the author's complicated relationship to "Russianness" and "Ukrainianness."[260] Gogol had originally intended to win renown for Ukraine as a scholar. In 1834 he announced a plan to write a history of Ukraine, or Little Russia, as "a nation which has existed here and been active for four centuries independently of Russia."[261] As things turned out, his scholarly interests came to inform his literary prose.

Gogol depicted Ukraine as a rural idyll in his cycle *Evenings on a Farm near Dikanka* (1831–1832) as well as in several of his short stories from the collection *Mirgorod* (1835). A deeper, existential dimension underlies these "folkloric" writings, above all in the story "Viy," stories which mark the beginning of Russian Orthodox Romanticism. Gogol depicted "Ukrainian freedom" in his novella "Taras Bulba," also contained in the *Mirgorod* collection. Only, Gogol's "Taras Bulba" is no straightforward celebration of Ukraine, but is rather a deeply ambivalent text. The Cossacks who fight against Poles, Turks, and Tartars are described as independent, cheerful, proud, and courageous, but they can also be chaotic, cruel, and arbitrary. To get drunk and fight with swords—everything else bores them. Their life appears pointless and absurd: they fight and kill (and sometimes beat Jews!) because that's just what Cossacks do, absent any greater cause or purpose. And when they do feel the need to fight for a cause, they simply make one up. In this way, the whole of Taras' family perishes one at a time, and they do so for nothing at all.

With his talent for uncovering the darkness beneath the surface of things, Gogol also revealed the dark side of the Cossacks. Their freedom consists of arbitrariness, willfulness, caprice, and an

---

260 Cf. Josef Dohnal and Ivo Pospíšil (eds.), *N.V. Gogol: Bytí díla v prostoru a čase* (Brno: Tribun EU, 2010).
261 Ladislav Zadražil (ed.), *Záhadný Gogol* (Prague: Odeon, 1973), 91.

anarchistic "I do whatever I want." Gogol intended this self-satisfied description of martial, masculine anarchism to show the opposite of the constrained society in which he himself lived and suffered. At the same time, he became the unwitting prophet about the role that this arbitrary freedom would play in Ukraine's future.

In the generation of Shevchenko, Kostomarov, and Gogol it seemed that Ukrainian culture might take the path of development common to the other revivalist nations of central, southern, and eastern Europe. This sort of hopefulness came to an end just one generation later. During the latter half of the nineteenth century, the tsarist regime moved to liquidate traces of Ukrainian, Belarusian, and Polish culture from its territory. The impulse for this wave of repression was the Polish uprising of 1863, a rebellion in which Ukrainians and Belarusians also participated. Its deeper consequence was a far-reaching effort to russify the peoples of the entire Russian Empire. The printing of books in Ukrainian and Belarusian was forbidden in 1863, and in 1876 the Ukrainian and Belarusian language was banned in print and in schools.

Ukraine, however, again enjoyed an advantage which Belarus did not. There existed a "Ukraine beyond Ukraine," not as a diaspora, but an old Ukrainian settlement in Galicia and the Bukovina, both of which were territories belonging to Austria. While the second half of the nineteenth century witnessed a rolling back of liberties in Russia, in Austria it was a time of liberalization. Austria did not attempt to Germanize its citizens, and so Galicia and Bukovina became centers of Ukrainian cultural life. It was here that Ukrainian realism and modernism were developed in classic works by Ivan Franko, Olha Kobylyanska, and Vasyl Stefanyk. It was here, in Lviv, that the song *Shche ne vmerla Ukraina* (Ukraine has not yet died) was first played in 1864, later the anthem of independent Ukraine. The refrain makes reference to the Cossack myth, "and show that we brothers/ are of Cossack birth." At the same time, the hymn is a variation of the Polish anthem *Jeszcze Polska nie zginęła* (Poland is not yet lost). It was in Lviv that Mykhailo Hrushevsky settled to occupy the first chair in Ukrainian history and compose the greater part of his history of Ukraine-Rus.

These developments under the patronage of Austria could influence "greater" Ukraine after 1905 (at which point Belarusian cultural life also began to revive), fully only after the overthrow of the tsar in February 1917. Immediately thereafter, in March 1917, autonomy was declared in Kiev under the rule of the Central Soviet, and in November the Ukrainian People's Republic. In retrospect, this seems like a remarkably "European" project, the establishment of a democratic republic, the elite of which are Ukrainian scholars. The historian Hrushevsky became president, the young Dmytro Chyzhevsky belonged among the members of the Central Soviet. In March 1918, a People's Republic was declared in Belarus. Sadly, for both projects, high-minded ideals soon confronted the cold reality of an ongoing world war and the beginnings of civil war. And this represented the unkind fulfilment of Gogol's unintended prophecy about the dark side of Cossack freedom: Ukraine became the site of bloody peasant bunts, banditry, and partisan fighting. Anarchy was elevated to a quasi-state doctrine in the domains of ataman Nestor Makhno (1889–1934).

Bolshevik victory did not necessarily spell catastrophe for Ukrainian and Belarusian culture. To the contrary, like the other cultures of the Soviet Empire, Ukraine and Belarus enjoyed official state support in the 1920. All possible currents of contemporary art and literature could flourish there—so long as they did not stand in direct opposition to the government. A typical figure was the filmmaker Oleksander Dovzhenko (1894–1956), who reconfigured myths about Ukraine's "long history" (*Zvenyhora,* 1928) and her rural mentality (*Earth,* 1930) in distinctive ways, only later to gradually become a propagandist of the regime. Another representative figure is the poet and cultural philosopher Mykola Khvylovy (1893–1933), a devoted communist who occupied himself with historiosophic comparative cultural studies along the lines of Oswald Spengler, who propagated Ukrainian identity in the "anti-Moskal" spirit of the "bourgeois" scholars Kostomarov and Hrushevsky (see for example his pamphlet "Ukraine or Little Russia?" published in 1926).[262]

Khvylovy committed suicide in 1933. He did so amidst the horrific scenes of the Ukrainian Holodomor, a famine orchestrated by Stalin's functionaries to punish those peasants who resisted incorporation into the kolkhoz (collective farms). The millions of peasants who perished of hunger represent a cruel communist reversal of the myth about Ukraine's natural abundance and its gluttonous peasantry. Had Khvylovy not killed himself in 1933, it is quite likely that he would have died anyway in 1937, the year that Stalin ordered 80 percent of the Ukrainian and Belarusian elite be arrested and shot or sent to suffer in the Gulag.[263] The phrase "executed renaissance" has entered into the literary lexicon of these nations to designate this extirpation. Only few survived—and that at the price of becoming heralds of socialist realism, receiving official praise and consecration in the form of statues and street names.

Liquidation of the other Ukrainian and Belarusian elites occurred in 1939 when Stalin, fulfilling the terms of his agreement with Hitler, occupied the territory of western Ukraine and Belarus which between the wars had belonged to Poland. Other "cleansings" followed as when Stalin, now pursuing Hitler, reconquered the territory in 1944 and 1945. The Ukrainian army's desperate attempt to liberate its territory under the leadership of Stepan Bandera (1909–1959) again drew from the myth of the Cossack uprising, of Ukraine "against all," especially against all non-Ukrainian minorities in the country. This provided an excellent pretext for massive Soviet repression, also

---

262 Cf. Alexander Kratochvil, *Mykola Chvylovyj: Eine Studie zu Leben und Werk* (Munich: Verlag Otto Sagner, 2009).

263 Data according to Andrew Wilson, *The Ukrainians: Unexpected Nation* (New Haven: Yale University Press, 2000), 146.

"against all." The Greek Catholic Church belonged among the victims of the time and was forcibly merged with the Orthodox Church (Scene 14), though it continued on heroically in the underground.

Ukraine and Belarus appeared to be pacified, anchored firmly to the myth of eastern Slavic unity under the leadership of Moscow in the name of communist Orthodoxy. And yet! By the middle of the 1980s there had reappeared a civil, cultural, and religious movement aiming not only "far from communism," but "far from Moscow."

And again, the fates of the twin nations Ukraine and Belarus proved quite different. In Belarus, after a fragile attempt to create a civil society of the European type, the dictator Lukashenko forced his way into power and turned his country into something resembling a communist open-air museum. Ukraine, by contrast, managed to preserve a relatively open society, though with governments constantly alternating between pro-Moscow and pro-Europe orientations. Ukraine remained an unstable *okrai*, a margin between powers, while "the Belarusians continue to be the hobbits in the European forest."[264] Cultural and spiritual life continued to develop in both countries, quite freely in the case of Ukraine, less so in the case of Belarus. Each continued to work and rework myths of the national past.

Given the horrors of the twentieth century, not to speak of older historical traumas, Ukrainian literature is surprisingly vital and its best authors can even be characterized as downright cheerful. Literary criticism speaks of postmodernism, a Ukrainian version of magical realism, or even a "postcolonial" literature, by which we are to understand a literature freed from the cultural oppression of Moscow. This contemporary Ukrainian cheerfulness can draw from

---

264 Aleś Ancipienka and Valancin Akudovič (eds.), *Neznámé Bělorusko* (Prague: Dokořán—Člověk v tísni, 2005), 95.

a long national tradition going back to the burlesque of Kotlyarevsky and Gogol.[265]

The uncrowned king of contemporary Ukrainian literature, Yuri Andrukhovych (born 1960), draws from Kotlyarevsky's *Aeneid* together with traditional Ukrainian grudges directed toward Moscow in his novel *The Moscoviad* (1993). Moscow here appears as a tortured, dehumanizing, tyrannical space, a city one can only wish would collapse and give way to deep boreal forests. The novella *Recreations* (1992) is Andrukhovych's idiosyncratic homage to Gogol. In it, Ukrainian literati convene in the fictional city of Chortopol, a name recalling Gogol's obsession with demons (*chyort* in Russian), for some sort of carnivalesque celebration. The entourage includes all the archetypes and stereotypes drawn from the Ukrainian cultural tradition together with many other grotesque figures, ("Angels of God, Gypsies, Moors, Cossacks, Bears, Studiosi, Devils, Witches, Naiads, Prophets, the Basilian Fathers in brown cassocks, Jews, Pygmies [...]").[266] One of them asks his hair dresser to arrange a Cossack khokhol upon his head. Another character is named Khomsky, homage to the American linguist Chomsky whose parents happen to have been Ukrainian Jews. The nickname Khomsky, or Khoma, also refers to the hero of Gogol's "Viy." Only, unlike Gogol's Khoma Bruta, women do not take fright at his advances and are all too happy to jump into bed with him.

Andrukhovych and other contemporary intellectuals again confirm the basic features of Ruthenian/Ukrainian culture differentiating it from Muscovy/Great Russia. This culture is decidedly "horizontal," devoted to the description and contemplation of things this-worldly.

---

265 Cf. Rita Kindlerová, "Barevná hravost současné ukrajinské literatury," in Rita Kindlerová (ed.), *Expres Ukrajina: Antologie současné ukrajinské povídky* (Zlín: Kniha Zlín, 2008), 7–19; Cf. Tereza Chlaňová et al., *Putování současnou ukrajinskou literární krajinou: Prozaická tvorba představitelů tzv. "stanislavského fenoménu"* (Červený Kostelec: Pavel Mervart, 2010).
266 Yuri Andrukhovych, *Recreations*, trans. Marko Pavlyshyn (Edmonton and Toronto: Canadian Institute of Ukrainian Studies Press, 1998), 64.

This does not, however, mean it is without religion. The Kievan Baroque was woven into church life; the Greek Catholic Church played a key role in the formation of western Ukrainian identity; a part of the contemporary Ukrainian revival is the attempt to found an autocephalous Ukrainian Orthodox Church independent from the Moscow Patriarchate; Shevchenko read and paraphrased the Bible; and even Andrukhovych sometimes quotes from Church prayers, without ironic disparagement. In every instance, however, it concerns a religion directed to "the here and now," to human life and the everyday. Andrukhovych refers to the Bible at the burial of his father. This time indulging in irony, he maintains that "the amount of a church's embellishment carries more weight with the Ukrainian than any preaching from the soul."[267] Now without irony: The Great Russian tendency toward "verticality," toward mysticism and wide-ranging speculations about God, is foreign to the Ukrainian tradition. Perhaps only the non-academic philosopher-wanderer Hryhorii Skovoroda (1722–1794), a personality at the intersection of the Kievan Baroque and the Enlightenment, is normally labeled as a "mystic," although his "mysticism" consists rather in the attempt to anchor wisdom more deeply in practical life.[268]

Contemporary Belarusian literature is also "civil" as far as religious matters are concerned, but much less cheerful. Insofar as it knows humor, it is of the darker variety. Not least because Belarusian is a minority language. Lukashenko's regime prefers Russian and so does his mass media. To write in Belarusian is thus itself an act of opposition—and the gesture of a relatively small cultural elite. If one is to encounter Belarusian culture in Minsk, he must know precisely from which boulevard to turn into some back courtyard. In one such back courtyard sits the Belarusian PEN Club. In another, a gallery and book store with the name "Ў" (the "short U," the only

---

267 Jurij Andruchovyč and Andrzej Stasiuk, *Moje Evropa* (Olomouc: Periplum, 2009), 58.
268 Cf. Hryhorij Skovoroda, *Rozmluva o moudrosti* (Praha: Vyšehrad, 1983).

letter unique to the Belarusian Cyrillic alphabet) where one can find independent books and magazines. The souvenirs for sale here are typical of Belarusian black humor. A magnet shaped like the police van used to transport protestors, for example, carries the label "Welcome to Belarus."

This literature also works in an original way with what it has inherited from the past. In Belarus, the inheritance from the Soviet era is much more visible. This applies especially to the Soviet myth about Minsk. Destroyed in World War Two, the capital of Belarus was rebuilt during the 1950s as a modern urban space. No, this did not mean prefabricated housing blocks or the overbearing "gothic" skyscrapers which left their mark on Moscow's skyline (and, unfortunately, also on that of Warsaw and Prague's Dejvice neighborhood). It meant instead a program of antiquizing (neo-)neoclassicism. Minsk, too, was a "Potemkin village," its superb facades masking the totalitarian reality of its time (one of the columned palaces still houses the Belarusian KGB). Considered from a purely architectural point of view, however, the urbanistic design, wide boulevards, and plentiful green spaces lend the city an unexpected charm.

Minsk neoclassicism was made the subject of Belarus's most successful contemporary artwork. Artur Klinau (born 1965), chief editor of *pARTisan* magazine (a name ironically reflecting the Soviet ideological construct of Belarus as a "nation of partisans"), in 2006 assembled the literary artbook *Sun City of Dreams*. The name "Sun City" refers to the Renaissance utopia that Sovietism sometimes appealed to, a utopia reflected in the deliberately antiquizing style of Minsk. It is a work at once serious and ironic, like the city of Minsk itself is a work of beauty and horror.

If the modern Belarusian myth of Minsk is ambiguous, then the modern urban myth of Ukraine is unmistakably positive. It is the myth of Ukraine's belonging to Central Europe, to the multicultural Central European tradition of Lviv and Austrian Galicia, a clear contrast to the "Asiatic" steppe of the East and the endless expanse that stretches as far away as to the hated Moscow. In his essay "Central-East Revision" (2005), Andrukhovych discusses his love for ruins, the bygone era of Austria-Hungary, the "graveyard ruins" of communities that no longer exist there (the Jews, Germans, and Armenians), and the persistence of memory:

> I still remember the peculiar, round-shouldered men and women who cursed in their Galician dialect, remembered their Latin proverbs from gymnasium, and, in the time of Khrushchev and the Beatles, dressed as if they were on their way to greet the archduke Franz Ferdinand. How they managed to hold on to these old clothes—now, there's a question! In spite of all those purges, house searches, deportations, nationalizations.[269]

Yuri Andrukhovych writes in a tone similar to other intellectuals who offered Central Europe as an antidote to Moscow—Péter Esterházy, Václav Havel, or Czesław Miłosz. It is characteristic that, in the Czech version, was his essay published together with one by the Polish author Andrzej Stasiuk. And it is also characteristic that, so long as at international writers' forums continue to talk about Central Europe, Russian writers, even those unmistakably pro-Western, critical of the current regime, and democratic, people like Joseph Brodsky and Sergei Dovlatov, will continue to express their sincere lack of comprehension as to what all the fuss is about.[270]

And here is where the most important gulf separates the mentalities of Ruthenia-Ukraine-Belarus and Muscovy-Great Russia. The latter will never admit the sovereignty and independent existence of the former, never admit that they are not bound by "familial" "Slavic" ties, never admit that these peoples have the right to determine their own history and go wherever they choose.

---

[269] Jurij Andruchowycz and Andrzej Stasiuk, *Moje Evropa: Dwa eseje o Evropie zwanej Środkowa* (Wolowiec: Czarne, 2000), 10.

[270] Cf. Jiří Trávníček (ed.), *V kleštích dějin: Střední Evropa jako pojem a problém* (Brno: Host, 2009), 169–211.

Jewish Rus

YEAR:
1791 and 1795

PLACE:
Between the Baltic Sea and the Sea of Azov

EVENT:
Catherine the Great demarcates the boundaries
of Jewish Settlement

WORKS:
The Sermon on Law and Grace by the Metropolitan
Hilarion (before 1050); *The Protocols of the Elders
of Zion* (1903); *My Life* by Marc Chagall (1923);
The Red Cavalry by Isaac Babel (1926); *Russia
and Eastern Europe* by Bohdan Chudoba (1980)

When the writer and amateur historian Alexander Solzhenitsyn (Scene 19) attempted to describe the history of the Jews in Russia in his last—and most controversial—book, he gave it the title *Two Hundred Years Together* (2001). When the historian Vsevolod Vikhnovich attempted to describe the same topic from a different point of view (and to correct some of Solzhenitsyn's distortions), he gave his book the polemical title *Two Thousand Years Together* (2007). Both periodizations make sense historically. The beginning of the history of the Jews in Russia may be dated from the late eighteenth century when the majority of Ashkenazi Jews found themselves within the borders of Russia following Catherine the Great's occupation of eastern Poland. This "transfer of Jews to Russia" was completed with the Congress of Vienna, which ceded Poland's core to Russia—and all that without the Jews themselves having had to move anywhere.

On the other hand, Jewish settlement in what would later become Russian territory reaches much further back, history to the Greek colonies of Crimea where Jewish neighborhoods first appeared during the Hellenistic and Roman periods (Scene 1). It was precisely from these neighborhoods that ancient Christianity began to spread, as everywhere in the ancient Mediterranean. Kievan Rus, however, encountered Judaism in a different way than the rest of Europe. That is, it encountered Judaism not as a minority faith of an urban community, but rather as the official religion of the Khazar Kingdom whose Turkic-Tatar elite adopted Judaism in the same fashion as other elites in the history of Medieval states had adopted Christianity or Islam. The Khazars were present as participants in the famous "disputation of faiths" hosted by Prince Vladimir (Scene 4). The influence of the Khazars on Kievan Rus was apparently strong, especially early on, a fact reflected in the Kievan Metropolitan Hilarion's *Sermon on Law and Grace*. Its first part is a polemic with Judaism as the "religion of the Law," its second part affording rhetorical praise to Prince Vladimir, who is addressed in Khazar fashion as the "Khan" (Khagan).

Then, without a trace, the Kingdom of the Khazars vanished from the historical scene.[271] This sudden disappearance partially explains the attention shown to the Khazars in the modern period in works of the most diverse genres. The Serbian literary historian and post-modern author Milorad Pavić (1929–2009) created a grand literary mystification with his *Dictionary of the Khazars: A Lexicon Novel* (1984, English 1988), an alleged annotation to an alleged baroque manuscript describing a disputation of faith similar to that of Vladimir, but one which took place at the court of a Khazar Khan a century earlier on the occasion of a visit by Cyril and Methodius.

Other authors have taken the Khazar theme far more seriously, as something of fundamental concern to the fate of Russia and Europe. Lev Gumilev incorporated it into his speculations about the Eurasian ethnogenesis of Russia (Scene 5). The Czech Catholic historian (later more a historiosopher) Bohdan Chudoba (1909–1982), in later works such as *Rusia y el oriente de Europa* (Russia and Eastern Europe, 1980) and his historiosophical syntheses,[272] construed a theory according to which the Turkic-Tatar Khazars did not disappear, but were rather transformed into eastern Jews: the Ashkenazi. Ethnically speaking, they are not Jews at all. Due to this fateful biological foreignness, wrote Chudoba, they began to act against the interests of the Christian nations among whom they increasingly spread. The Khazars are associated with liberalism, atheism, Nazism, and Bolshevism. In this "Khazar hypothesis," Chudoba carefully differentiated between the concepts "Khazar" and "Jew" in order to arrive at an alternative concept which would draw all the negative connotations

---

271   Cf. Michal Téra, "Chazaři: Stručný životopis jedné zapomenuté říše," in *Kulturní, duchovní a etnické kořeny Ruska: Vlivy a souvislosti*, ed. Hanuš Nykl (Červený Kostelec: Pavel Mervart, 2006), 15–36.

272   Cf. Martin C. Putna, "Bohdan Chudoba: Česko-španělský katolický historiosof proti všem," in *Vím, v koho jsem uvěřil a jiné eseje*, by Bohdan Chudoba (Brno: CDK, 2009), 127–156.

normally associated with the anti-Semitic thinking of the extreme right (Catholic or Orthodox) but avoid the charge of anti-Semitism, unacceptable in European society after the Holocaust. In Chudoba's work one thus finds formulations such as: "the boy Tomáš, who was born in 1850 in Hodonín in the stinking tavern of the Khazar, i.e. actually Turkish, family Redlich [...] had nothing in common with Masaryk the coachman from Čejkovice."[273]

Before the rise of modern anti-Semitism, several centuries passed following the Khazar period during which the Jewish presence in Kievan and Muscovite Rus was minimal. Even if the speculations about the Jewish origins of the Novgorodian religious sect were well-founded, the so-called "Judaizers" would still represent only an isolated influence (Scene 8). The situation was different in Lithuanian Rus. The core of the Ashkenazi fled to Lithuania during waves of pogroms in Western Europe. The tolerant atmosphere of the Commonwealth made them feel welcome. Once there, the Jewish intellectual elite encountered the Russian-Lithuanian intellectual elite, and it isn't impossible that the reform and intellectual movements of the time were to some degree influenced by debates with the Jews. This seems especially plausible in the case of the radical Unitarian Symon Budny, or in the case of Skaryna's printings of the Old Testament (Scene 9). Given this (relative) level of peaceful coexistence, it is even more shocking that large parts of Lithuanian Rus were swept by waves of pogroms during Bohdan Khmelnytsky's uprising in the middle of the seventeenth century. Yet even this did not cause the majority of Ashkenazis to abandon the Commonwealth.[274]

When Catherine the Great took over "her" partition of the Commonweath, she demarcated a "Pale of Jewish Settlement" roughly along what had been the border separating Lithuania from Muscovite Rus. This was the eastern border beyond which Jews were

---

273 Bohdan Chudoba, "Do třetí války," manuscript, private archive of Eva Chudoba, Madrid.
274 Cf. Heiko Haumann, *Dějiny východních Židů* (Olomouc: Votobia, 1997).

not allowed to reside.[275] This "Pale of Settlement" would come to symbolize the inferior status of Jews in Russia. It was abolished by the Provisional Government after the fall of the tsarist regime in the spring of 1917. The transfer from a Polish to a Russian government was not otherwise accompanied by any fundamental change. In the spirit of her limited tolerance, Catherine left to the Jews a certain degree of autonomy (the *kahal*). Jewish cultural and spiritual history during the first half of the nineteenth century shared little with that of the rest of Russia, the Jews continued their own traditions and concerned themselves with their own problems.

The Jewish community dealt with its own ideological conflict during this period, its own "what is to be done?" This was a conflict between the Haskala (Judaism's version of the Enlightenment), traditional rabbinic Orthodoxy, and Hassidic mysticism. Hasidism, with its ecstatic piety and miracle-working rabbis, would later became the object of Romantic literary cults and even an opportunity for Jewish-Christian dialogue. Western readers began to take notice of "western Jewish" authors such as Martin Buber (who authored several studies from the beginning of the twentieth century and the *Tales of the Hasidim* in 1949) and Jiří Langer (*Nine Gates*, 1937). Yet by that time, what Buber and Langer were describing as its golden age, the influence of Hasidism was already beginning to wane and many educated Jews considered Hasidism the most backward and hopeless form of Jewish identity.

As Catherinian tolerance gave way to Nicholas and the spirit of Orthodox restoration (Scene 15), Jews were gradually integrated into the social structure of Russia. Of course, this happened against their will and in a humiliating fashion: the abolition of autonomy and all exemptions, the introduction of military obligations (but without the prospect of advancement to the higher ranks), and for a time even the forced separation of Jewish boys from their families

---

275 Cf. Martin Gilbert, *The Atlas of Jewish History* (New York: William Morrow and Co., 1993).

for "proper upbringing." The positive side effects of these actions began to appear with time. A part of Jewish youth acquired entry to the Russian universities and Russian culture. In the second half of the nineteenth century many hoped that Judaism might assert itself in Russia just as it had in Prussia, Austria, or Hungary, places where culture cannot be imagined without the Jewish presence.[276]

The actual course of events, however, would be completely different. With the influence of conservative, "restorationist" powers on the rise, the Russian state did not allow Jews to integrate fully, branding them instead with the inferior status of *inorodtsy* (allogenous, i.e. a "non-Russian" people). In response to their degrading status as eternal supplicants (and terrified by the periodically occurring pogroms), the Russian Jews sought alternative solutions to their identity conflict. One part favored an autonomous Jewish national culture. Their vehicle was at first Yiddish, which was raised to the status of a literary language and made impressive gains, finally achieving recognition globally with the work of Sholem Aleichem (1859–1916) and dozens of other authors.[277] Under the influence of Zionism, many writers later switched from Yiddish to Hebrew, which had the effect of strengthening the sense of belonging to a worldwide Jewish community and further weakening ties to Russia. This "re-Judaiziation" of a part of Russia's Jews, combined with waves of pogroms at the turn of the twentieth century, made it that much easier for some two million Jews to decide to leave Russia for America or Palestine. Those who left in time certainly had no idea that by doing so they were saving their own lives as well as that of their offspring.

From this exodus of the Jewish elite was born the phenomenon of the famous Russian Jew—more precisely, Jews from the former

---

276 Cf. András Geró et al., *Rakousko-uherská monarchie: Habsburská říše 1867–1918 slovem a obrazem* (Praha: Slovart, 2011).

277 Cf. Chine Shmeruk, *Dějiny literatury jidiš* (Olomouc: Votobia, 1996). The book is written from the Polish point of view but describes basically the same literary material.

Commonwealth, or the future Ukraine and Belarus. Among them belong artists of the Paris school. Marc Chagall and Ossip Zadkine from Vitebsk, Chaim Soutine from Smilavichy, Antoine Pevsner from Klimavichy. They include luminaries of American popular culture. The hitmaker Irving Berlin was born in Mogilev as Israel Beilin, the parents of the fashion designer Ralph Lauren came to America from Pinsk with the family name Lifshitz. They include Israeli politicians, Shimon Perez from Vishnyeva, Chaim Weizmann from Pinsk, and Menachem Begin from Brest.

They also include the famous tzadiks of Hasidism. One of the heroes in Buber's *Tales of the Hasidim* is "the Rebbe" Menachem Mendel from Vitebsk, who was responsible for bringing Hasidism to Palestine. The best known and most influential today (and the most controversial with respect to the messianic ambition of the seventh of the dynasty of tzadiks) is the Chabad movement, also called Lubavitch Hasidism, which originated in the village Lyubavichi (Yiddish Lyubavitsch) on what is today's Russian-Belorussian border. In his autobiography, *My Life* (written in French in 1923), Marc Chagall tells the story of how he met with the fifth Lubavitch Rebbe during the First World War to ask for advice about what he should do with his life and his spiritual heritage: "And to ask him if the Israelites are really the chosen people of God, as it says in the Bible. And to know, moreover, what he thought about Christ, whose pale face had been troubling me for a long time."[278] Disappointed, he describes the cold and formal atmosphere in which religious affairs were handled among those surrounding the famous tzadik: "My God! What sort of rabbi are you, Rabbi Schneerson!"[279]

To be sure, most of these luminaries of world culture, politics, and religion share little with Russia, Ukraine, or Belarus beyond their physical origin. This only confirms the idea that the Jews are

---

[278] Mark Chagall, *My Life* (New York: Orion Press, 1960), 128.
[279] Ibid., 129

at home all over the world, or, to say it with greater pathos, that the Jewish homeland is the world of the spirit. But there are exceptions. The most famous exception was the globetrotting Jew from Russia, or rather from Belarus, someone who never ceased to draw inspiration from his place of birth. This was Marc Chagall, born as Moisha Segal, an artist who spent his entire life painting his native Vitebsk. Chagall described in his autobiography, *My Life,* the trials and tribulations of a young Jew who had to travel to St. Petersburg to study painting, since the city lied beyond the "pale of settlement," he had to reside there semi-illegally. Once in France, he described Paris as "my other Vitebsk." He was an artist forced from the memory of his native city—until the 1980s, when his name was gradually resurrected and he was presented as the city's most famous son.[280]

Chagall wrote *My Life* in French. The stories of his wife Bella Chagall (1895–1944), *Burning Lights,* describe the same world of traditional Jewish communities in Russia from the distant, emotional, and aesthetic perspective of a young girl. She wrote in Yiddish. The works of both authors nevertheless belong to the treasury of Russian and Belarusian culture in the same way that Prague's German (Jewish) literature or the Hebrew poems of Jiří Langer belong to the culture of the Czechs.

Another part of the Jewish elite chose a different solution. These Jews decided to align themselves with Russian-language culture—but in this case with leftwing, revolutionary, anti-tsarist, and anti-clerical movements (Scene 18). This was one of the few places where Russified Jews were welcomed by a segment of the Russian public and regarded as a source of strength—but at the same time, they strengthened the party of restoration in its anti-Semitism. For members of the extreme right (called the Chernaya Sotnya, or Black Hundred, in Russia) and for more moderate Orthodox Russians, the

280 Cf. Arkadi Padlipski, *Vitebskie adresa Marka Shagala* (Vitebsk: Vitebski kraevedcheski fond imeni A. Sapunova, 2000).

figure of the Jew became equated with atheist and terrorist. A Jew, in other words, was someone who wanted to destroy Russia.[281]

From within these restorationist circles came a Russian book which immediately became famous all over the world. Yet this work is rarely counted among the Russian classics, though it certainly belongs to Russian literature just as do the tales of Sholem Aleichem or the memoirs of Marc Chagall—but in reverse tonality. The title of the book is *The Protocols of the Elders of Zion*. The text first appeared in the magazine *Znamya* in 1903 (it was published separately in 1905) and presented itself as a transcription from a meeting at the inaugural World Zionist Congress (which really did take place in Basel in 1897). The transcripts supposedly revealed the plan of world Jewry for global domination.

According to the *Protocols of the Elders of Zion,* preparations for global Jewish domination were already underway. Overturning religion and morality serves the interests of democracy, which is to say of anarchy. Having become sufficiently desperate, the peoples of the world will call for the rule of a firm hand—and then will come the time of the Jewish king. The language of the *Protocols* is succinct, aphoristic, tense, full of catchphrases. It is often forceful, sometimes naïve and unintentionally humorous. Its prose is however always striking and easy to remember:

> Political freedom is an idea but not a fact. This idea one must know how to apply whenever it appears necessary with this bait of an idea to attract the masses [...]. The despotism of Capital, which is entirely in our hands, reaches out to it a straw that the State, willy-nilly, must take hold of: if not—it goes to the bottom. [...] It is the bottomless rascality of the *goyim* peoples, who crawl on their bellies to force, but are merciless toward weakness, unsparing to faults and indulgent to crimes [...] it is

---

281   Cf. Zbyněk Vydra, *Židovská otázka v carském Rusku 1881–1906: Vláda, Židé a anti-semitismus* (Pardubice: Univerzita Pardubice, 2006).

those qualities which are aiding us to independence. [...] We shall further undermine artfully and deeply sources of production, by accustoming the workers to anarchy and to drunkenness. [...] We must offer resistance by a universal war.[282]

Historians eventually uncovered the true origin of this truly noteworthy Russian work. It was most likely written by the journalist Matvei Golovinski (1865–1920) at the behest of the chief of the Okhranka, the tsarist secret police, Pyotr Rachkovsky (1853–1910), in cooperation with anti-Semitic circles in France and drawing from older texts in the all-too popular conspiracy genre. From the perspective of literary history, it is interesting to compare the *Protocols* to another work of Russian literature, this one Russian in more than an ironic sense. This account of conspiratorial preparations for the creation of a totalitarian society in many ways parallels Dostoevsky's *Demons* (Scene 18), a novel which introduced the "revolutionaries" Verchovenski and Shigalev (who of course aren't Jews!). What's more, there were also the similar plans of Russia's real-life revolutionaries...[283]

The Protocols of the Elders of Zion had many more readers than did Dostoevsky's *Demons*. Tsar Nicholas II read the book. White Army officers read it while fighting against the Bolsheviks. Catholic reactionaries in western Europe read it. Anti-Semites without confessional affiliation, including Adolf Hitler, read it. Lovers of "conspiracy theories" everywhere continue to read it today. The book's enduring popularity surely rests on some psychological predisposition to such theories, but it is also a product of the pamphlet's literary qualities, making it a masterpiece in its boorish genre. It also harkens back to the equation of Jews with atheists and terrorists, an

---

282 *The Protocols of the Meetings of the Learned Elders of Zion,* trans. Victor E. Marsden (Chicago: The Patriotic Publishing Co., 1934), 143–4, 157, 167.
283 Cf. Janusz Tazbir, *Protokoly sionských mudrců: Pravda nebo podvrh?* (Olomouc: Votobia, 1996), 86–88.

equation having its positive equivalent in Uvarov's triad "orthodoxy, autocracy, and nationality," and an analogy in restorationist conceptions of other nations and confessions.

These prejudices would never have been so firmly rooted had it not been for the strong and powerful allegiance of many educated Russian Jews to parties of the extreme left and even to terrorist organizations. When Boris Savinkov (1879–1925), one of the most famous terrorists of the tsarist era, wrote *Memories of a Terrorist* (1909) during his Paris exile, almost all the names of his co-conspirators were Jewish. Savinkov pays no special attention to their Jewishness. He simply describes the everyday reality of his surroundings. Once the Bolsheviks took power in November 1917, there were suddenly so many Jews in the government, among officers of the Red Army, in organs of the Bolshevik Party, and in the leadership of new cultural circles that the dramatic changes undertaken by the communists appeared to many as a confirmation of the conspiracy described in the *Protocols of the Elders of Zion.* Jewish journalists in exile, such as the authors of the collection *Russia and the Jews* (1923), might have fought for the other side, professed a Russian-Jewish patriotism, and demanded atonement from their Bolshevized co-religionists— but they are just so many voices calling out into the desert.

Russia and the Jews thus found themselves trapped in a vicious circle. Russia under the old regime forced "its" Jews to Russify, but it never allowed them to become fully a part of Russian society (there are hardly any Jews present in nineteenth-century Russian art and culture). Many Russian Jews therefore turned against this regime and joined attempts to build a new Russia, a Russia they believed would be just and humane. What they in fact created was a regime which, next to the Nazis, was to be the most criminal and destructive social experiment of the twentieth century. It was a regime that, under Stalin, would devour many of its own. And their participation in that regime only served to encourage anti-Semites in their anti-Semitism.

The vicious circle continues in interpretations of this historical episode, for to speak of the Jewish part in the Bolshevik regime as a tragic historical occurrence risks giving implicit support to anti-Semitism (Solzhenitsyn's *Two Hundred Years Together*, which describes the phenomenon of Jewish Bolshevism in detail, often shifts from a description to a tone of reproach bordering on anti-Semitic). Yet to speak around the subject, to apologize for it, implicitly makes light of the Bolshevik regime and its monstrosity. And to ignore it completely means to sacrifice any deeper understanding of Russian and European history, of the Christian as well as Jewish spirit.[284]

Cultural history has the advantage over political science and the history of religious institutions in that it can exit this vicious circle; it can step away from grand concepts to concrete testimony as expressed in works of art. If nineteenth-century Russian culture was practically "without Jews," from the close of that century the Jewish presence began to grow. Among the first to assert himself was the painter of broody Russian nature scenes, Isaac Levitan (1860–1900). The poet Osip Mandelstam (1891–1938), too, who combined pictures of Petrograd with myths drawn from Russia's past in his neoclassicist poetry, without paying much regard to his Jewish identity. In the essay "Judaic Chaos" from the cycle *The Noise of Time* (1925), he does take time to reflect on his origins, on the complicated linguistic migration undertaken by his family between German, Yiddish, and Russian. After the Bolshevik revolution, Jewish presence in Russian culture increased by leaps and bounds. The individual fates, stories, and texts of Russian-Jewish artists reveals the multifaceted relationship between Russia and the Jews in a way that no general summary can.

---

284 The difficulty of working through such material and how quickly the scholar can find himself "on the edge" was experienced by Petr Bakalář in his book *Tabu v sociálních vědách* [Taboo in the social sciences] (Olomouc: Votobia: 2003).

We may turn once more to Marc Chagall. Although in principle an apolitical artist, he nevertheless at one point cooperated with Bolshevik authorities. Not long after the Bolsheviks had taken power, the new commissar for culture Anatoly Lunacharsky, who had known Chagall in Paris before the war, summoned the artist:

> But my knowledge of Marxism is confined to knowing that Marx was a Jew and that he had a long white beard. Now, I realized that, without a doubt, my art would not find favor with him.
> I said to Lunacharsky:
> "Above all, don't ask me why I painted blue or green and why a calf is visible in the cow's belly, etc. Anyway, let Marx, if he's so wise, come to life and explain it to you."[285]

Lunacharsky nonetheless dispatched Chagall to his hometown as the local cultural commissar. Chagall began his duties by calling together the local housepainters, informing them that they would now be painters of pictures. The biblically informed reader cannot but hear in this "transfiguration" an echo of Christ's words to the fisherman of Galilea, "follow me, and I will make you fishers of men" (Mt 4:19). That a Jew—and Bolshevik commissar—should rework New Testament passages is only an apparent paradox. Chagall in fact treated Christ as a Jew (consider his picture *White Crucifixion* from 1938, which depicts Christ's loincloth as a prayer shall!). And quasi-religious pathos inherently belongs to the rhetoric of revolution.

Chagall's engagement with the Bolsheviks was in the end brief and entirely platonic. Fortunately, he soon abandoned Russia for Paris. For others, like the expressionistic prose writer Isaac Babel (1894–1941), the clash between Jewish, Russian, and revolutionary identities continued as a life-long theme. Stories set in his native Odessa depicted the pre-revolutionary world of Jews in the "pale

285 Marc Chagall, *My Life*, 138.

of settlement," of people striving for social advancement through education and culture. The story "In the Basement" features the grotesque scene of a family dispute ("Cursing Bobka and me with Yiddish curses, he promised us that our eyes would fall out, that our children would begin to rot and decompose while yet in their mother's womb.").[286] The narrator, who has invited to his home a schoolmate from a wealthier and better integrated family ("He was pale, and he was looking around him. The locutions of Yiddish blasphemy were incomprehensible to him, but he was familiar with Russian cursing."[287]) seeks to distract his host by reciting a monologue from Shakespeare. That is the ambition, pathos, and bind of Jews in old Russia: Shakespeare recited in the basement of some poor Jews in Odessa.

Babel's fame of course rests in his *Red Cavalry* (1926), a cycle of quasi-journalistic short stories for which the author collected material during his time as a Cheka propagandist during the Red Army's campaign against Poland. The "Red Cavalry" travels through the territory of the Jewish Pale of Settlement, a territory where both Reds and Whites left their bloody footprints. Babel's expressionistic style draws from these places, from these footprints, juxtaposing harsh contrasts of dread and ecstasy, detailed cruelty and sweet dreams, the naturalistic grimace of death beside flashes of natural and human beauty. And so also—Jewishness and revolution.

The hero of the tale "Gedali" is a little old merchant from Zhitomir who survived the pogroms of the Whites, and asks painfully why revolution is violent:

> But the Pole shot, my gentle *pan*, because he was the counter-revolution: you shoot because you are the revolution. But the revolution—that is pleasure. [...] So who will tell Gedali where is the revolution and where is

286 Isaac Babel, *Red Cavalry and Other Stories* (New York: Penguin Books, 2005), 57.
287 Ibid., 57.

the counter-revolution? Once upon a time I studied the Talmud, I love the commentaries of Rashi and the books of Maimonides. [...] And so we all, we learned men, fall upon our faces and say aloud, "Woe to us, where is the sweet revolution? ... [...]

I too want the International of good men, I want each soul to be taken and registered and given first-grade rations. Here, soul, eat, please, and have from life your pleasure. The International, *panie* comrade, one does not know what to eat it with ...

"One eats it with gunpowder," I replied to the old man. "And seasons it with the finest blood ..."[288]

In a story titled "The Rebbe's Son," the spokesman of the Jewish-revolutionary symbiosis is not living at all, but rather a corpse, and the remains of this young revolutionary speak as follows:

Here everything was dumped together—the warrants of the agitator and the commemorative booklets of the Jewish poet. Portraits of Lenin and Maimonides lay side by side. Lenin's nodulous skull and the tarnished silk of the portraits of Maimonides. A strand of female hair had been placed in a book of the resolutions of the Sixth Party Congress, and in the margins of communist leaflets swarmed crooked ines of Ancient Hebrew verse. In a sad and meagre rain they fell on me—pages of the Song of Songs and revolver cartridges.[289]

The sadness of this story consists not only in mourning the death of a young boy. It also mourns the apparent end of that moment when it seemed possible to merge two identities. Bolshevik critics correctly understood that the true heroes of Babel's prose were not the "new men," the Russian soldiers of Bolshevik divisions (depicted throughout as vulgar primitives), but rather people who are unable to forsake

288   Ibid., 118.
289   Ibid., 226–227.

the familiar spiritual world of Judaism. Later, the Bolshevik regime would force its Jewish adherents to abandon everything that connected them to un-Bolshevistic, Jewish traditions. Stalin gradually murdered not only prominent Jewish communists—he also executed Jewish (to whatever extent) communist writers such as Babel, and of course the non-communist writers like Mandelstam as well.

The second half of the twentieth century brought yet another, not unrelated Russian-Jewish development: the "revolution against revolution," Russian Jews or Russians of Jewish origin participating in anti-Soviet political and artistic dissent. Just as Jews were strongly overrepresented among the first Bolsheviks, so too did they make up a disproportional part of dissidents. As an antidote to the litany of names of Jewish commissars and Cheka officers—beginning with Bronstein-Trotsky—so recited with such pleasure by anti-Semites, can serve an equally long list of personalities associated with samizdat or exile opposition culture: Eugenia Ginzburg (1906–1977), author of one of the first memoirs about the Gulag; Ginzburg's son Vassily Aksyonov (Scene 1); Vasily Grossman (1905–1964), who with the novel *Life and Fate* (posthumously in 1980) sought to create a modern parallel to *War and Peace*, leading protagonists through the horror of both kinds of concentration camp; Lev Kopelev (1912–1997), the literary historian and dissident depicted in Solzhenitsyn's novel *In the First Circle* (1968) as a Jew imprisoned by Stalin but still a firm believer in revolution; Alexander Galich (1919–1977), the "poet with a guitar," who sang his ironic songs of Stalin and the entire Stalinist regime; Boris Khazanov (born 1928), editor of the samizdat journal *Jews in the USSR*; Christian dissident theologians of Jewish origin Alexander Men, Anatoly Levitin-Krasnov (Scene 19) and others. Even three of the "Eight Brave Ones," individuals who protested the Soviet occupation of Czechoslovakia in August 1968, were Russian Jews. The writer and literary scholar Andrei Sinyavsky (1925–1997) forms a special chapter in the history of Russian-Jewish dissent. Turning the tradition of Russifying Jewish names on its head, he—not a Jew—chose for his samizdat texts the Jewish pseudonym Abram Terc—while his samizdat "co-conspirator" and fellow convict Yuli Daniel was even the son of an important Yiddish dramatist.

Many of those mentioned above came from communist families. As if wishing to resurrect their forefathers' messianic faith in a better future, a faith transformed by their more recent ancestors into a belief in Zionism or revolution, they now reached out for a vision of a more democratic future. And, like their distant and less-distant predecessors, they sacrificed everything for it. Such was the description given in the genre of biographical interview by Pavel Litvinov, grandson of the Bolshevik commissar for foreign affairs Maxim Litvinov, who was one of the "Eight Brave Ones," whose fates were distantly connected by this dramatic journey to Czech culture.[290] Some Russian communist Jews entered Czech culture directly—those who at some point in life chose to change their linguistic identity from Russian to Czech. Among the most remarkable literary testaments to this Russian-Jewish anabasis are the memoires of Stanislav Budín (1903–1979), titled *Jak to vlastně bylo* (How it actually was, published posthumously in 2007). Stanislav Budín was born Bentsyon Bať in Kamianets-Podilskyi, a town within Catherine the Great's "Pale of Settlement." Having grown up in Russian culture, he later left for Czechoslovakia, began to write in Czech and became an important communist journalist. He ended his life as a dissident and signatory of Charter 77. However, he never gave up his faith in revolution.

In the meantime, other Russian Jews turned to Zionism or returned to the faith of their fathers, Jewish Orthodoxy. Many of their Russian Orthodox fellow citizens in the meantime returned to their own "faith"—faith in anti-Semitism[291] (Scene 19 and Conclusion).

---

290 Cf. Adam Hradilek (ed.), *Za vaši i naši svobodu* (Prague: Torst – ÚSTR, 2010), 79–111.
291 Of the most recent literary works reflecting on the relationship between Judaism and Christianity in Russia, mention should be made of Ludmila Ulitskaya's *Daniel Stein, Interpreter: A Novel in Documents* (New York: Overlook Press, 2011).

Catholic Rus

YEAR:
1836

PLACE:
Saint Petersburg

EVENT:
Peter Chaadaev declares his sympathy for
Catholicism, for which he is declared insane

WORKS:
Dispute with the Latinists by Metropolitan Georgy
(before 1076); *Les Soirées de Saint Pétersbourg*
by Joseph de Maistre; *Philosophical Letters*
by Peter Chaadaev (from 1836); *Three Conversations*
by Vladimir Solovyov (1899–1900)

Rus cannot be understood without Catholicism. Though never a major influence, it was always present. It was present, above all, as the negative image of "the Other." In the beginning, Catholic clergy were allowed only a brief word at Prince Vladimir's "disputation of faith" in Kiev (Scene 4), but they did speak. In later phases, Catholicism was spoken of without the participation of Catholics. One spoke with the intention of highlighting that which divided. These discussions were initially led by Byzantines settled in Russia, for it was originally their quarrel with the "first" Rome, their negative image of Catholicism as heresy, "Latinism," "Papism." The *Dispute with the Latinists*, a polemical text by the Kievan metropolitan of Greek nationality Georgy (ruled probably 1065 to 1076), has been preserved in Church Slavonic. The text lists the various "heresies" of the Latinists, most of them concerned with details of ceremony or fasting from the use of unleavened bread during church services and the shaving beards to the terrible accusation that Catholics "eat pork fat from beneath the skin, which is unclean [...] they eat the meat of bears and donkeys [...] they eat from the same plates as dogs."[292] The unintentionally comical litany concludes with a malevolently distorted description of Catholic religious culture. For example, "they represent the likeness of saints in marble and on the tiling of the temple floor not at all to honor them, but rather to tread upon them with their feet."[293]

The Russians soon acquired this passion for anti-Catholicism and became "more Greek than the Greeks." With time, the emphasis on details of ceremony of course disappeared from Russian polemics; instead, the Russian Orthodox begin instead to fight amongst themselves about the ceremony (Scene 10). In principle, there remained only the central negative image of the pope as a demonic being who

---

292 Emilie Bláhová, Zoe Hauptová, and Václav Konzal (eds.), *Písemnictví ruského středověku od křtu Vladimíra Velikého po Dmitrije Donského* (Prague: Vyšehrad, 1989), 248–249.
293 Ibid., 249.

has usurped power over the church and the world. In the process, the pope was said not only to have upset the principle of collective decision making in council or *sobor*, but also to have asserted a political claim on Russia itself.

Unlike the nonsense about pork fat and bear meat, here there was an essential principle at stake. Russia's negative image of the papacy reflected a real ambition of popes in the late medieval and early modern periods. Consider the forged *Donatio Constatini* by which the Emperor Constantine was supposed to have ceded sovereignty over Rome and the western half of the Roman Empire to Pope Silvester. Consider the bull of Boniface VIII, *Unam sanctam* (1302), which elaborates on the "two swords" wielded by the pope, the swords of spiritual and worldly governance. The pope's claims were "modernized" at the First Vatican Council in 1870 with the declaration of papal infallibility, an act that confirmed negative perceptions of Catholicism in general and the pope in particular (and not just among Russian Orthodox).

In the Russian mental stereotype, Catholicism was reduced to the papacy. Catholicism was identified with the pope and his secular ambitions. This figure acquired in the Russian imagination all the traits of the Antichrist, the most dangerous adversary of Christ and the church. It is the Antichrist who is responsible for all evil in the world. Prince Myshkin, Dostoevsky's Christ-like hero in *The Idiot*, articulates a theory to the liberal "Petersburg" Russians according to which Catholicism can exist even under godless socialism: Catholicism begat Protestantism, Protestantism begat liberalism, and liberalism begat socialism. This, in the eyes of the liberals, confirmed Myshkin's "idiocy." In the eyes of the reader, however, it rather confirms Myshkin's Christ-like nature.[294] Criticism of the papacy in this way led to critique of the "modern," liberal, and secular

---

294 An analysis of Dostoevsky's concept of Catholicism, given of course from an extreme Catholic point of view, can be found in Alois Lang's *F.M. Dostoevsky* (Prague: Vyšehrad, 1946).

West. Similarly, Dostoevsky's legend of the Grand Inquisitor from *The Brothers Karamazov*, which describes Christ's encounter with the religious establishment in the form of the Antichrist, was at first understood in a simple way: Orthodoxy versus Catholicism, Christ verses the Antichrist! Dostoevsky again forcefully demonstrates something we already know! Further philosophical-theological reflection reveals that the traits of the Antichrist can also be acquired by the Orthodox Church. It reveals that interpretation of the story can be and indeed should be deeper.[295]

The Russian understanding of Roman Catholicism thus concentrated on all that which divided the two confessions. Everything that they have in common—the majority of church dogma, authoritative theological texts, saints, church structures, and common past—was passed over in silence. Protestantism, meanwhile, infinitely more distant and hostile to many of Orthodoxy's deeply rooted traditions (such as hierarchy, monasticism, the cult of the Virgin Mary, the veneration of saints and of images etc. etc.), received a more favorable treatment with emphasis falling on those few elements that potentially joined Orthodoxy and Protestantism in opposition to the Pope-Antichrist. These included especially the acceptance of communion under both kinds, the refusal of papal authority, and the secular role of the church generally. In the ruminations of Nikolai Danilevsky (Scene 16) and other Orthodox Romantics about the origin of the Bohemian Reformation there thus emerged the interpretation that Jan Hus and his followers wanted nothing more than to revive Orthodoxy. They didn't meet with much success at the time—but later notions of Slavic reciprocity in Bohemia would make up for that.

The readiness with which the Orthodox sought cooperation with the Protestants is itself testimony to how deeply rooted the archetype

295 See the selection of essays by K. Leontyev, V. Solovyov, V. Rozanov, N. Berdayev, S. Bulgakov and others in the collection *Velký inkvizitor* (Velehrad: Refugium Velehrad-Roma, 2000).

of Antichrist-Papist-Catholicism really was. There is probably no better explanation than the Jungian interpretation of Russian perceptions of the papacy as a "shadow", as the dark projection of the "light," of the universal, religiously sanctified authority of the tsar. In the mental world of "Muscovite" and "Petersburg" Rus it was he, and by no means the Moscow patriarch, who in fact played the role of pope, the "holder of both swords," the "deputy of Christ."[296]

Catholicism nevertheless appears in Russia "from within" as well. First as a simple demographic fact: thanks to Russia's territorial expansion, there were people in Russia who professed Catholicism, and that in the Russian language (a part of Ukrainians and Belarusians) as well as in other languages (Poles, Lithuanians). Second as an intellectual alternative, a way out from the troubles and traumas that had characterized Russia's spiritual development up to that point. It was an alternative sought out by some Russian intellectuals again and again.

The conjoining of Catholicism with a Russian-speaking population occurred outside of Moscow, in Lithuanian Rus and the wider territories of the Commonwealth. As in the Lithuanian-Polish dual state, the cultural influence of the Catholic West was strengthened (without it coming to the point of a direct, state-organized counter reformation!). Orthodox bishops of the western Russian eparchy, with the Kievan metropolitan Mikhail Rogoza (probably 1540 to 1599) in the lead, began to consider the establishment of a union with the Roman Catholic Church. They sent a message to Rome and in 1596, at the *sobor* of Brest in Lithuania, they festively declared the Union. There thus developed a church which continued to be "eastern" in form, its ceremony (with a few exceptions) remaining

296 On the secularization of the figure of the tsar, see Boris Uspensky "Tsar i Bog: Semioticheskie aspekty sakralizatsii monarkha v Rossii," in *Semiotika, istorii, semiotika kultury* (Moscow: Gnozis, 1994), 110–218.

"Orthodox" in structure and outward appearance, but subordinate to the pope.

The backers of this union assumed that a "small" union of a few eparchies would become the core of a future "great" union of the eastern and western churches. This was never to take place. The Orthodox looked upon the new "Uniate" or (imprecisely) "Greek Catholic Church" as an alliance of traitors and renegades. Roman Catholics for their part looked upon the "Greek Catholics" as a mere appendage, significant only as a lure for Orthodox believers. The nobility who entered into the union, however, often switched over to the more prestigious Latinate ceremony. As a result, the union remained little more than the despised faith of a few western Russian peasants.

An emblematic figure of the union in Lithuanian Rus was Josaphat Kuntsevych (1580–1623), the Uniate archbishop of Polotsk who was beaten to death in Vitebsk by his Orthodox opponents and beautified in 1643 as the first saint of the Greek Catholic rite. He was venerated as the patron of the hoped for (but never realized) expansion of the Union to the east. It was some compensation for sympathizers that Kuntsevych's main opponent, the Orthodox antibishop and intellectually more distinguished Meletii Smotrytsky (1578–1633), switched allegiance to the Union after Kuntsevych's death and became its advocate (Scene 14). Neither Kuntsevych nor Smotrytsky, nor any of their successors, ever developed in any detail this cultural union between Catholicism and Orthodoxy, between the West and the East.[297] The intellectual and artistic contributions of the Greek Catholic Church to Lithuanian Rus (and of its sister Uniate Church in Hungary, which developed from the Union of Uzhorod in 1646) remained rather modest.

---

297 Where a greater significance is attributed to them in modern Catholic hagiography, it has to do with projections into the past of much later developments in entirely different contexts. An example of this sort of pious retrospective glance is the book by Tateusz Zychowicz, *Josafat Kuncevič* (Prague: Zvon, 1995).

The significance of the church consists in something other than in elite production, however. It fostered a regional and, with time, national identity among those peoples at the border of Polish and Russian cultural spheres, it contributed to the formation of modern Ukrainian and Belarusian national identities. Neither in Ukraine nor in Belarus did it become a national church, for Orthodoxy remained important in both nations. But in both national cultures both the western (Greek) Catholic branch and the eastern Orthodox branch maintained themselves, sometimes competing, sometimes cooperated when national interests appeared more important than confessional interests.

This Catholic branch was of fundamental importance for Ukrainians. During the division of Poland, a part of the territory occupied by Ukrainians fell to Austria. While both Ukrainian culture and the Greek Catholic Church were always harshly oppressed in the Russian zone of occupation, Ukrainian national identity continued to develop in cooperation with Greek Catholic Church in the Austrian zone with Lviv as its center (Scene 12). Ukrainian and Belarusian Uniates in Russia were in the meantime confronted with subsequent waves of violent Orthodoxization. The Greek Catholic Church was first officially abolished in Russia in 1794 under the otherwise tolerant reign of Catherine the Great; it was last abolished in 1946 under Stalin. Throughout, Uniates demonstrated unbelievable perseverance in the face of persecution. In this, they showed that despite the Union's having been octroyed from above by the decisions of a few bishops, over the course of centuries the Greek Catholic Church had become a living and deeply rooted phenomenon that could not be simply thought away. If the Catholic Church canonized only one Russian-speaking martyr since the beginnings of the Union—from the history of the Union in the twentieth century it announced more of them, and it could have been many more still.

The church as a prop for national identity applied still more to Roman Catholicism in the part of Poland falling under Russian dominion. For centuries, Moscow and the Commonwealth had counted as equals. In 1610, Poland-Lithuania (and thus Lithuanian Rus!) temporarily occupied Moscow. Petersburg Rus "paid back" Poland on Moscow's behalf when, after the Napoleonic wars, it acquired the core of Poland including Warsaw.

Poland nearly perished. Nearly, but not quite. It was during the era of Polish division that the song which would later become the national anthem was born in exile, *Jeszcze Polska nie zginęła* (Poland has not yet perished). None of the Poles' nineteenth-century uprisings against Russia had proven successful, and amid the ensuing waves of repression the process of Russification only intensified. The greater part of Polish classical literature in the nineteenth century thus developed either in French exile or in the relatively free cultural environment of the Austrian partition with its centers in Cracow and Lviv.

Russian literature of a liberal persuasion sympathized with the Poles as fellow victims of the tsarist regime. Consider Herzen's memoirs *My Past and Thoughts* (Scene 18), in which the author encounters many a congenial Pole making the pilgrimage into exile, commenting that "for one badly concealed tear over Poland, for one boldly uttered word, there were years of exile, of the white strap, and sometimes even the fortress."[298] Orthodox romanticism, by contrast, confronted the Poles with laughter and contempt—see the arrogant episode from Dostoevsky's *Crime and Punishment* with the appearance of ridiculous "Polaks." Poles received the reputation of being the black sheep of the Slavic world, to use the words of Nikolai Danilevsky's programmatic volume *Russia and Europe* (Scene 16), the only nation of the coming "Pan-Slavic union" without a claim to a state of its own, for it is "not only not useful, but even harmful member of the Slavic family, which has betrayed common Slavic

---

298 Alexander Herzen, *My Past and Thoughts: The Memoirs of Alexander Herzen* (Berkeley: The University of California Press, 1973), 105.

ideals and tries to spread through violence and seduction the Catholic and aristocratic principle, anathema to the Slavic world, into the heart of Russia itself."[299]

By means of the annexation and contempt subsequently shown to them, Russians made the Poles into the merciless witnesses of their merciless empire. Ukrainians, Belarusians, Balts, and Fins were just in the process of fashioning themselves into modern nations, no one in the world knew of their literature. The Poles however stood out with a mature, cultured nation, with an educated elite in close contact with the elite of the rest of Europe. Polish "retribution" toward Moscow would thus take a cultural and artistic form.

As Orthodox romanticism was fashioning the messianic myth of Russia as the nation destined to redeem the world through Orthodox rule (Scene 16), Polish Catholic romanticism with Adam Mickiewicz (1798–1855) at its head was developing an even older "antimyth" of Poland as a messianic nation bound to redeem the world through its suffering. When a certain Russian historical painting celebrated the "building of a state" under Ivan the Terrible, the Polish historical painter Jan Matejko (1838–1893), who enjoyed a happier existence under Austrian rule, depicted the same epoch as a time of Russian terror and Polish glory. At a time when Russian Orthodox romantics celebrated the "simple piety of rural people," Eliza Orzeszkowa and other Polish realists were revealing the cruelty and superstition of the countryside (Scene 3). When the tsarist regime dispatched dissident Poles to Siberia, Wacław Sieroszewski (1858–1945) and other exiles painted for the regime a literary picture of Siberia that was truly unflattering. And when the Soviet regime later sent Poles to the Gulag, Gustaw Herling-Grudziński (1919–2000) published a testament to the Gulag in his memoirs *A World Apart* (1953). In a way, Danilevsky was correct when he complained that the Poles ruined pan-Slavic ambitions. By virtue of its entire historical experience

299 N.Y. Danilevsky, *Rossiya i Evropa* (Moscow: Kniga, 1990), 314.

as a great Slavic nation engaged in a struggle with Russia, Poland itself denied the very notion of a common Slavic destiny.[300]

Polish Catholicism, however, followed a route entirely different from that of Catholicism in Russia. It would not be until Solovyov that Mickiewicz's self-sacrificial messianism would be appreciated as an antidote to Russia's messianic triumphalism.[301] Catholicism could never represent a real alternative for Russia so long as it arrived by means of Polish mediation, which would be understood by the Russian elite to be the perfidious invasion of an ancient enemy. The Russian elite could only enter dialogue with Catholicism if it came from some other source, as if Poland did not exist.

The official Catholic missionaries to the heart of Muscovite Rus consisted mainly of Jesuits from the Bohemian lands—a country linguistically close but politically "neutral." Jiří David of Zdice left a valuable account of seventeenth-century Moscow—among other things, relating how the Jesuit mission was shut off in a ghetto for foreigners.[302] A more daring undertaking was that taken upon himself by the Croatian priest Juraj Križanić (1618–1683).

Križanić believed that the condition of the Slavs could only be significantly improved if they were to unify under the spiritual role of the Roman pope and the secular rule of the Russian tsar. He left in 1659 to gain a firsthand impression of the land which he expected to play the secular role in salvation. What he found, however, was disillusionment and a quick deportation to Siberia—not based on any concrete accusation, but mere suspicion. (Though it seems that the tsarist officers were not aware that they were dealing with a Catholic

---

300 Consider the split in nineteenth-century Czech culture between the pro-Polish and pro-Russian parties, cf. Marjan Szyjkowsky, *Polská účast v českém národním obrození,* 3 vols. (Prague: Slovanský ústav, 1931–1946).

301 Cf. Vladimir Solovyov, "Adam Mickiewicz," in *The Heart of Reality: Essays on Beauty, Love, and Ethics* (Notre Dame: University of Notre Dame Press, 2003).

302 Cf. Antonín Florovský, *Čeští jezuité na Rusi: Jezuité české provincie a slovanský východ* (Prague: Vyšehrad, 1941); cf. Jiří David ze Zdic, *Novodobý stav Velké Rusi neboli Moskevska* (Olomouc: Refugium Velehrad-Roma, 2008).

priest.) Križanić used his exile in Tobolsk to meet with other "dissidents," including the archpriest Avvakum (Scene 10), and to write down his pan-Slavic utopian vision. In a text titled *Grammatitchno iskaziniye ob ruskom jeziku* (Grammatical discourse on the Russian language, 1665), Križanić attempted to fashion a pan-Slavic language. Though he never accomplished anything of real use, his attempt represents one of the first efforts at comparative Slavic philology. In his *Politika ili Razgovor ob vladatelstvu* (Politics, or, a dialogue on government, 1663), Križanić described the ideal state which Russia should become. Russia was "just short" of possessing what it needed to fulfill its historical mission: a complete overhaul of its heretofore existing political order, of its economy, morals, church relations, and scholarship.[303]

Juraj Križanić thus foundered as a missionary from the very beginning. His sweeping utopian vision, however, represents one of the most distinctive works of the "Slavic Baroque," a cultural-religious conception which, for the first time, considered that nations speaking the same language—that is, Slavic—might also share a common historical fate. In the context of the time, this might consist in defeating the Turks (Križanić himself perished during the siege of Vienna…). In the various versions of the Slavic Baroque, the core of visions for unification is played by the southern Slavic space, or by Poland or Russia; and the role of common spiritual strength is played by either Catholicism or Orthodoxy.[304] Križanić thus presents us a very peculiar version in which Catholicism and Russia are connected. He was never to become a beloved figure among Orthodox slavophil romantics—but for all that he became a popular a figure in nineteenth-century Catholic unionism and twentieth-century Catholic neoromantic Russophilia (see Introduction).

303   Cf. Václav Huňáček, "Juraj Križanič," *Souvislosti*, no. 2 (1995): 40–46.
304   Rudo Brtán, *Barokový slavizmus: Porovnávacia štúdia z dejín slovanskej slovesnosti* (Liptovský Sv. Mikuláš: Tranoscius, 1939); Cf. Andreas Angyal, *Die slawische Barockwelt* (Leipzig: E.A. Seemann, 1961).

Catherinian tolerance showed its limits "from below" and "from within" toward the Uniates. Directed "outward," however, it demonstrated a surprising number of possibilities. When Pope Clement XIV abolished the Jesuit order in 1773, Catherine invited this elite guard of baroque Catholicism to Russia. Not to Catholicize Russia, of course, but to draw from the Jesuits' experience organizing schools. When revolution prevailed in France in 1789, Catherine invited members of the Catholic elite to Russia as exiles. And when Napoleon expelled Pope Pius VI from Rome in 1798, Catherine's son Paul I even extended Russia's invitation to the pope!

The pope did not come, true, but even without him Russia became a center of European, especially French-Catholic, restoration during the time of the French Revolution and the Napoleonic Wars. Russia—or more precisely St. Petersburg, since that is where the exiles landed and where they encountered a Europeanized (and passionately Francophone!) Russian elite. The most significant intellectual among the Catholic restorationists was the philosopher Joseph de Maistre (1753–1821). He was not an exile in the strict sense; from 1803 to 1817 he served in St. Petersburg as an envoy from the Kingdom of Savoy. In several writings, he polemicized with the French Revolution as well as with the Enlightenment, constructing the philosophical foundation for restoration from the idea of an absolutist Trinity: the absolute negation of social change after 1789, Catholicism with absolute rule by the pope, absolute government of kings as the one and only natural form of government. He presented his argumentation, however, in the "Enlightenment" style with a penchant for paradoxical formulations, plentiful sarcasm and wit, and a brilliant sense for polemic. The same means used by Voltarians against Catholicism in the name of Enlightenment before 1789 were used by Count de Maistre after the Revolution against the Enlightenment in the name of Catholicism.

The last of these works is situated in Petersburg: *Les Soirées de Saint-Pétersbourg* (The Saint Petersburg Dialogues, 1821). Three interlocutors—an autobiographical French duke and his two Russian friends—carry on a conversation during one of St. Petersburg's famously long summer nights, something to which de Maistre paid lyrical homage earlier than did Dostoevsky in his "White Nights" (1848). The topic of their discourse is the feasibility of providing rational proof of God's existence and of Providence. To his Russian friends, the French count insists that their cultural and religious roots share more in common than what makes them distinct:

> The Senator: In your quality as a Latin ...
> The Count: So whom do you call *Latin?* Be aware, I beg you, that in the matter of religion I am quite as Greek as you.
> The Senator: Let us go on then, my good friend, let us forget the joke, if you please.
> The Count: I am not joking a bit, I must assure you; was not the Apostle's creed written in Greek before it was written in Latin? Do not the *Greek creeds of Nicea and Constantinople*, and that of Athanasius contain my faith? [...] I ask you how it would be possible to be more Greek?
> The Senator: What you have just said gives me an idea that I believe just. If it were ever a question of a peace treaty between us, one could propose the *statu quo ante bellum*.[305]

To be sure, no "peace treaty" between Catholicism and the Russian elite emerges from de Maistre's writings. What does emerge, however, is the fact that Catholicism may be presented in a highly elite, modern, intellectually attractive, vibrant, and even provocative form—and that this form brings forth deep and paradoxical insights. Above all, that Catholicism can represent a serious intellectual alternative.[306]

305 Joseph de Maistre, *St Petersburg Dialogues, or, Conversations on the Temporal Government of Providence*, trans. Richard A. Lebrun (Montreal and Kingston: McGill-Queen's University Press, 1993), 123–124.
306 Cf. L.P. Karsavin, "Žozef de Mestr," *Voprosy filosofii* 3 (1989): 93–118.

Peter Chaadaev (1794–1856) was the first among Russian intellectuals to grasp this alternative, a man who as an officer in the Napoleonic wars experienced European culture in Paris and Rome as well as in Carlsbad. Chaadaev composed (characteristically in French) a series of letters in which he criticized the prevailing condition of Russian culture. He offered Catholicism as the leading spiritual power of European civilization as a starting-point for positive developments. Chaadaev's letters circulated for several years in manuscript form as a sort of samizdat. When the journal *Teleskop* then printed one of them in 1836, the regime went livid. It harshly intervened against the publishers of the journal and those associated with them. Chaadaev himself was neither imprisoned nor banished; he was declared mentally insane. After all, how else could one explain that such an intelligent man would regard Russian culture as inferior and encourage Catholicism to take its place? Chaadaev was thus the first among many Russian dissidents to be punished in such a "modern" and "scientific" way—that is, through the abuse of psychiatry. Those who demonstrated on Red Square in August 1968 together with the other opponents of the Soviet Regime who were later shut up into psychiatry wards (Scene 19) are all the spiritual offspring of Chaadaev.

The actual content of Chaadaev's letters is another matter. What was it about Catholicism that inspired him? To a certain extent, Chaadaev can be called a student of de Maistre—insofar as the rational, philosophical justification of faith is concerned, and insofar as the evaluation of Catholicism as a spiritual axis of European history is concerned.[307] In other respect, he represents de Maistre's counter opposite. For Chaadaev, Catholicism stands above all for the principle of progress: "That is why Christian people must always

307 About the other philosophical sources of Chaadaev's thought, see Dmitrij Čiževskij, "Petr Jakovlevič Čaadajev," in *Filosofické listy,* (ed.) P.Č. (Prague: Universum, 1947), 11–57.

advance."[308] The problem with Russia lies in its lack of historicity, in its stagnant fixation on an "atemporal" Byzantium:

> Glance over all the centuries through which we have lived, all the land which we cover, you will find not one endearing object of remembrance, not one venerable monument which might evoke powerfully bygone eras. [...] We proceeded to seek the moral code which was to constitute our education in miserable Byzantium, an object held in profound contempt by these peoples [...] We had nothing to do with the great work of the world.[309]

When then it comes to religion in the narrow sense of the word, Chaadaev does not at all speak as an advocate of restorationist, absolutist Catholicism a la Maistre, but instead as an enlightened deist-mystic, a freemason who turns away from (any kind of) ceremony and toward individual religious experience instead:

> When one finds in oneself beliefs which elevate the soul to the very source of all our certitude, yet which do not contradict but, rather, support popular beliefs; then, and only then, is it permissible to neglect external observance.[310]

The core of Christianity is ethics: "This fusion is the whole mission of Christianity. The truth is one: the kingdom of God, heaven on earth, all the promises in the Bible—all this is nothing but the prophecy and the work of the unification of all human thought in a unique thought; and this unique thought is the thought of God Himself, to put it another way, *the accomplished moral law.*"[311]

---

308 Peter Chaadaev, *Philosophical Works of Peter Chaadaev* (Dordrecht and Boston: Kluwer Academic Publishers, 1991), 80.
309 Ibid., 21, 25–26.
310 Ibid., 19.
311 Ibid., 101.

Chaadaev's Catholicism is thus specific. It is not a realistic, historical, ecclesiastical Catholicism. It is the negation of his experience with Russia and with hollow Orthodox ceremony. In this sense, Chaadaev is a "Catholic Romantic," close to the intellectuals and artists of western Europe who brought to Catholicism their dissatisfaction with the profane reality surrounding them. They interpreted Catholicism very much in their own way, and some of them chose their own paths while others continued along the path of "standard" church practice even to the point of merging with Catholic restoration.[312]

Such intellectual freedom did not exist in the hostile atmosphere of Russia, however, and the Catholic Church remained distant. Chaadaev therefore remained an isolated voice and did not find followers. As for the few members of Russia's aristocracy who converted to Catholicism during the nineteenth century, they did so during their stays in Catholic Europe, above all in Rome, which exerted a similarly magical influence on the Russian elite as it had on the elite from Protestant Europe and America. Among others, it was there that Gogol experienced the "Catholic temptation."[313]

One individual, however, played a key role as mediator: Ivan Gagarin (1814–1882), the descendent of an ancient princely dynasty harking back as far as the prince-founder Rurik (Scene 2), the Russian envoy to Paris and, from 1843, a member of the Jesuit order. After his conversion and theological training, Gagarin wrote broadly as a publicist in which he propagated the idea of Russian-Catholic unification, which to his mind represented not a betrayal of Russian national ideals but rather the opposite; to him, union represented the opportunity to accomplish Russia's global mission. At the core

312 Cf. Martin C. Putna, "Evropská katolická literatura," in *Česká katolická literatura v evropském kontextu* (Prague: Torst, 1998), 13–134.
313 Cf. Martin C. Putna, "Grand Tour jako téma evropské literary: Řím jako téma Grand Tour," in *Řecké nebe nad námi a antický košík: Studie ke druhému životu antiky v evropské kultuře* (Prague: Academia, 2006), 25–64.

of Gagarin's activities was the same idea that once stood at the core of Križanić's thinking. Gagarin's greatest service, however, was to publish the first comprehensive collection of Chaadaev's letters and, together with his own brochures, have them sent to Russia were they would go on to have a further impact.

The main character behind this impact was a man named Vladimir Solovyov (1853–1900). In his youth, this philosopher of religion passed through a materialist phase, after which he experienced a religious conversion. He considered himself a Slavophile and argued against western philosophy which was "merely" rationalist[314], though he later endeavored further in search of a consistent and comprehensive religious truth. In the end, he arrived at the same conviction as had Križanić, Chaadaev, and Gagarin: Russian Orthodoxy would not be "complete" until it joined with Rome. Solovyov did not understand Rome as the seat of the Antichrist, but instead as the "servant of Peter" there to assist in the unification of a universal church. Solovyov expressed this line of thinking in the book *Russia and the Universal Church* (1889), which, again following the lead of his predecessors, he wrote in French and published in Paris (in Russia the work was forbidden by the censors).

Solovyov voiced his final opinions on the subject in a Platonic dialogue, *Three Conversations* (1899–1900). In genre and the themes dealt with, the book resembles de Maistre's Petersburg *Soirées*. In Solovyov's *Conversations,* several friends discuss the possibility of understanding God through reason, they speak at length about history and providence, about Russia and Europe. The high point of the *Three Conversations* is a supplementary literary text, an anti-utopian apocrypha titled *Story of the Antichrist.* Solovyov's tale is based on themes from the biblical apocalypse: the declaration of

---

314   Cf. Jakub Kalenský, "Solovjovova kritika západní filosofie," in *Kulturní, duchovní a etnické kořeny Ruska: Vlivy a souvislosti,* (ed.) Hanuš Nykl (Červený Kostelec: Pavel Mervart, 2006), 155–172.

the Antichrist's arrival, the temptation of mankind, the beating and crucifixion of two "witnesses," and the Christ's second coming. Bridging the span between Solovyov and the apocalypse is the ancient Christian apocrypha about the end days and the Antichrist attributed to Hippolytus of Rome, which was already known in Kievan Rus (Scene 4), as well as other texts of the "antichrist genre" from the old traditions.

While the *Three Conversations* handled many themes considered controversial in Russia and Europe at the end of the nineteenth century, the *Story of the Antichrist* is a text set in the future. In prophetic stylization, Solovyov foretold a conflict between Asia and Europe, the rise of a United States of Europe, a secular civilization with individualistic remnants of religiosity—a constellation from which an ingenious politician would emerge to enthrall the masses with his talk of progressive humanity (among other things, he's a vegetarian and animal rights advocate!). This false savior would declare himself emperor of the world, though feel himself to be still something more. He would declare himself the new Christ, summon a general council in Jerusalem (capital of a renewed Jewish state!) and demand it to confirm him as the head of Christianity. Meanwhile, he would secure the support of individual religious groupings by promising to satisfy their longtime demands.

On this point, Solovyov's text is not free of sarcasm. To the Protestants, the Antichrist promises to support free inquiry about the Bible. To the Catholics, he vows to restore of papal authority over Rome. As for the Orthodox, he says:

today I have signed the statute and settled large sums of money on the world-museum of Christian archaeology in our glorious imperial city of Constantinople for the object of collecting, studying and preserving all relics of church antiquity, especially the Eastern. I ask you to elect tomorrow from among yourselves a committee to discuss with me the measures that must be taken in order to make the present manners, customs and ways of living as conformable as possible to the tradition and ordinances of the holy Orthodox Church.[315]

Russian Orthodoxy's obsession with Byzantine ceremony is thus equated with the obsessions of other confessions.

The text, however, suddenly shifts from bitter humor to apocalyptic pathos. The majorities of each confession succumb to the Antichrist's temptations. The leaders of those minorities who do not give in are led by men with names recalling the apostles and centers of religious culture: Pope Peter II, that is the "Petrine" Catholic tradition of ostensible unity, authority and continuity; the elder John, the "Johannine" Orthodox tradition of mystic contemplative inwardness; Professor Pauli, the "Pauline" Protestant tradition of biblical studies, ethics, and individual responsibility. Once Peter II and John have been killed, it is then left to Professor Pauli to direct what remains of the Christian flock away from the Antichrist. Once God has resurrected Peter and John as the "two witnesses" (Rev 11:3–12), it is Pope Peter to whom Pauli addresses the evangelical declaration, "I tell you that you are Peter" (Mt 16:18): "That was how the union of the churches took place on a dark night, in a high and solitary place."[316]

The message of Solovyov's *Story of the Antichrist* is thus not so much "Catholic" as it is "ecumenical."[317] Insofar as this was the message of Solovyov's entire corpus, it gives rise to questions about the message of Solovyov's life as well. According to the testimony of Nikolai Tolstoy (1867–1938), originally an Orthodox priest and later a convert to Catholicism, Solovyov declared his faith in a private chapel in Moscow in 1898 and thereby became a Catholic. He

---

315 Vladimir Solovyov, "A Short Story of Antichrist," trans. Natalie Duddington, *Cross Currents* 12, no. 3 (1962), 305.
316 Ibid., 310.
317 Cf. Ján Komorovský, *Solovjov a ekumenizmus* (Bratislava: Ústav pre vzťahy štátu a cirkví, 2000).

did not consider his conversation to mark a break with Orthodoxy, however. Instead, conversion represented for Solovyov a much more a personal step toward the longed-for "eschatological" ecumenism. Tolstoy published his testimony—though its authenticity was immediately doubted by Orthodox circles.[318]

To a certain extent, Solovyov's step continued along the lines of Chaadaev and Gagarin. Solovyov's "afterlife," however, was entirely different from theirs. While Chaadaev would be almost forgotten had it not been for the poems that Pushkin dedicated to him, and while Gagarin remained a "traitor" in Russian memory—both Catholics and Orthodox would declare themselves for Solovyov. He was recognized posthumously as a foundational figure and revered as a saint by a diminutive groups of Russian Catholics who, after the declaration of religious freedom in 1905, officially founded the Unified Russian Church (which would later be nearly extirpated by the communist regime, whose victims would include the priest Nikolai Tolstoy).[319] Meanwhile, however, Sergei Bulgakov, Pavel Florensky and other representatives of Orthodox theological reformism declared themselves for Solovyov, adopting and developing several of the religious thinker's key ideas such as Sophia, divine humanity, and *sobornost* (Scene 17). Solovyov thus won posthumous recognition and inspired both confessions.

Recollections by some of Solovyov's followers offer a glimpse into the chasm that separated visions of mystical unification entertained by a few elites and the reality of the church. When the symbolist poet Vyacheslav Ivanov (1866–1949) decided in 1926 during his exile in Rome to follow Solovyov's example by joining the Catholic Church without leaving Orthodoxy, the Vatican would not allow it. Ivanov's daughter remembers: "Whoever had converted to Catholicism

---

318 Nearly the whole of Tolstoy's testament is reprinted in Karel Jindřich, *Vladimír Sergejevič Solovjev: Jeho život a působení* (Prague: Vlast, ND), 270–275.
319 Cf. Dennis J. Dunn, *The Catholic Church and Russia: Popes, Patriarchs, Tsars and Commissars* (Burlington, 2003).

was required to give 'abjure'—renunciation of the church which he was leaving. The formula was the same for everyone—Protestants, Anglicans, Orthodox. [...] Such a condemnation was unacceptable to Vyacheslav: he believed in the One Holy Church, tragically torn between East and West. By means of its joining with the Catholic Church, or at least by virtue of his individual act, he renewed that union. Instead of the stereotyped formula laid out by the Vatican monsignors, he wished to recite a proclamation of faith composed by Vladimir Solovyov. Oh, the name said nothing to the ecclesiastical officials."[320] Once the bureaucracy finally yielded, Ivanov made his Catholic declaration of faith in the Cathedral of St. Peter at the altar of his patron, the Bohemian duke Wenceslas (Scene 4). To his friend, the Catholic literary critic Charles Du Bos (whose son-in-law would later become the Czech-Catholic writer Jan Čep), he reported: „When I was reciting the profession of faith (...) I felt truly Orthodox in the ful sense of the term."[321]

This story, too, seems to show that the line stretching from de Maistre to Chaadaev to Gagarin to Solovyov to Vyacheslav is a delicate one, an exclusive thread in the history of Russian spirituality that was neither connected to the real masses of Catholic Uniates in Ukraine and Belarus, nor part of the mainstream of Russian Orthodoxy, nor truly in touch with the existing Roman Catholicism. From second half of the twentieth century, however, the connections would become stronger. After the second Vatican Council, Catholic interest in the Christian East officially transformed from missionary unionism to "non-missionary" ecumenism, to a Solovyov-esque understanding of the eastern (Orthodox) and western (Roman Catholic) churches as forming a unity. Taken from the work of Vyacheslav Ivanov, the statement gained currency that the church must "breath from both lungs." It gained currency primarily thanks to the Czech

---

320 Lidiya Ivanova, *Vospominaniya: Kniga ob otse* (Moscow: RIK Kultura, 1992), 196.
321 Ibid., 197.

Jesuit active in Rome, Tomáš Špidlík, who in turn inspired the first "Slavic pope," and heir to the tradition of Polish Catholicism, Karel Wojtyła. Karel Wojtyła's speech about Vyacheslav Ivanov then used in 1987 as an epilogue to Ivanov's collected writings, published in Brussels by the exile publishing house for Russian Catholics, Zhizn s Bogom (which also published the writings of Orthodox dissent's most important theologian, Alexander Men, Scene 19).

Despite Rome's unofficial blessing and the cooperation of some intellectual circles within Russian Orthodoxy, "Catholic Rus" continued to exist more in the imagination than in fact, remaining an intellectual concept without mass support. Original Russian Catholicism, i.e. Uniatism, would continue to exist according to its own traditions in Ukraine and Belarus, not wanting anything to do with Russia. The future of "Catholic Rus" would thus depend on the development of Russian Orthodoxy and Roman Catholicism, how this one or the other would choose to formulate the values for which it stands.

The Orthodox Restoration

YEAR:
1782

PLACE:
The Neamț/Nyamets Monastery in the Principality
of Moldavia

EVENT:
Paisius Velichkovsky translates *Dobrotolubye*
as the "bible" for a revived piety

WORKS:
The Way of a Pilgrim (1870); *The Last Saint*
by Dmitri Merezhkovsky (1908); *The Brothers
Karamazov* by Fyodor Dostoevsky (1880)

The pivot toward Europe initiated by Peter and Catherine in the eighteenth century meant a sudden turn to the Enlightenment and secularization (Scene 11). Yet even in Europe religion had not disappeared. Those who wished to continue professing Christianity (or who wished to do so again) comprised a specific "Catholic milieu" in the framework of a "second confessionalization."[322] And from within this milieu there emerged a three-fold reaction to the Enlightenment. "Catholic reformism" stood for the attempt to forge a consensus between church and society, to orient the church toward the modern world and rid it of everything conditioned by history, ossified, and transmutable. "Catholic restoration," by contrast, insisted that all was well with the church, anything different in the world was bad, that the ideal would be a return to the premodern world of hierarchy and an alliance between the church and the authoritative state. Finally, "Catholic romanticism" as a movement arose not from the sphere of the church itself, but rather from artists and intellectuals. It represented the movement of those for whom the church was no longer at the center of life, for people who had grown up in a secular world but were drawn to the church precisely because it differed from the modern world. They were motivated by aesthetics, history, romantic nationalism, or by a sense of personal existential crisis.[323]

The development of Russia again mimicked that of Europe. This time however it was due above all to inner reasons, the need to come to terms with the rapid transition which was much more unexpected in Russia than in the countries of western Europe, the latter having worked their way to enlightenment and secularization along the gradual path of organic spiritual development. And again, European intellectual and artistic models influenced this phase of Russia's

322 Cf. Karl Gabriel, *Christentum zwischen Tradition und Postmoderne* (Freiburg: Herder, 1992).
323 These concepts of European cultural history were first applied in Bohemia by the German-language historian Eduard Winter, especially in the books *Josefinismus a jeho dějiny* (1943, 1945 in Czech) and *Bernard Bolzano a jeho kruh* (1932, 1935 in Czech).

development. Members of the Russian upper classes encountered these western models during travels to Europe. Russia and Europe were connected politically and intellectually as they had never been before. This was due particularly to Russia's engagement in the Napoleonic wars, when officers of the tsar's armies had experienced Vienna and Paris first hand—places where the transition from the Enlightenment to Romanticism and restoration was already underway.

The Russia of Tsar Alexander I was swept by a "anti-Enlightenment" wave which carried along with it an interest in Catholicism (Scene 14) and mystically-charged conceptions of German idealistic philosophy.[324] These contributed especially in giving rise to a specific "Orthodox milieu," groupings of people for whom questions of religion and religious practice were of utmost significance. Again, various answers were given to the question "what is to be done" in order that Orthodoxy again become the center of Russian society and culture. Again there arose an "Orthodox restoration" which longed to revive the pre-Petrine state of affairs and to adjust the modern world to better fit the church. An "Orthodox reformism" emerged, critical of the church's mistakes, hopeful of making it more appealing in the modern world. There also arose an "Orthodox romanticism" projecting its own, thoroughly modern, conception of the church into an idealized past. These three intellectual positions must not be understood as static and absolute, but instead as the points of a symbolic triangle. The spiritual culture of nineteenth-century Russia took place within the space of this triangle, amid the tension produced by a magnetic force projected from each of the three points.

The development of the Russian Orthodox milieu and of this Orthodox cultural triangle differed from the European model in

---

324 For a contextualized description of the Russian "anti-Enlightenment" see, for example, James Billington, *The Icon and the Axe: An Interpretive History of Russian Culture* (New York: Vintage Books, 1970), 269–358. Cf. Dmytro Čyževskyj, "Deutsche Mystik in Russland: Jakob Böhme in Russland," in Dmytro Čyževskyj (ed.), *Aus zwei Welten: Beiträge zur Geschichte der slavisch-westlichen literarischen Beziehungen* (The Hague – Berlin: Mouton, 1956), 179–219.

two important ways. First, because the turn toward secularization had been so rapid and unexpected, a much greater mental chasm separated the advocates of Europeanization (with formal bonds to Orthodoxy maintained) and secularization from "the others," from that great majority of society who continued to inhabit the mental universe of pre-Petrine Rus. This non-secularized, faithful, loyal mass would lend to its silent support to the Orthodox intellectual counter-current.

Second, while it is true that the Congress of Vienna stood behind restoration in Europe, its concerns were more political than religious. Religion was asked to provide its blessing, but secularization pushed its way through all the same. The governments of individual countries made little effort to stop its progress and sometime even directly supported it. The opposite was the case in Russia. There, state doctrine and official propaganda from Nicholas I. (ruled 1825–1855) to Nicholas II (ruled 1855–1881) lent unconditional support both to political and religious restoration. It supported restoration at home as well as in Europe. Alexander's armies liberated European nations from the yoke of Napoleonic imperialism; in 1848 and 1849 the armies of Nicholas I arrived to suffocate national revolutions and restore absolutism.

This is not to say that every intellectual who favored Christianity's revival in Russia automatically supported this Orthodox restoration "from above." The opposite was often the case. Orthodox romantics and reformists were no less suspicious of the regime than were liberals and revolutionaries. As Václav Černý stated concisely in his essayistic *The Development and Crimes of Pan-Slavism* (see Introduction), "the suspicion of Russian censors and their methods of bullying [...] was never in any way limited only to manifestations of democratic, revolutionary, and occidental thought; it applied to *any* manifestations of thought *whatsoever.*"[325] Nevertheless, the politics

---

[325] Václav Černý, *Vývoj a zločiny panslavismu* (Prague: Knihovna Václava Havla, 2011), 87.

of tsarism and the Orthodox milieu did share something fundamentally important—an aversion toward Europeanism, liberalism, and secularization.

If the "premodern" people give their implicit support to the Orthodox milieu "from below," then the politics of tsarism offered support "from above." In the spiritual culture of nineteenth-century Russia there thus existed yet another triangle: the people, the Tsar, and the Orthodox milieu. Here, our cultural history arrives at the infamous maxim formulated by the minister Sergei Uvarov: "autocracy, Orthodoxy, nationality" (see Introduction). While the Catholic culture in nineteenth-century Europe was rather a "counterculture" and its most important and influential figures (Joseph de Maistre, Félicité de Lamennais, Clemens Brentano, Leon Bloy, John Henry Newman etc.) remain in truth oppositional "counter-figures," in Russia the leading figures of the Orthodox milieu (Gogol, Dostoevsky, Solovyov, Berdyaev, etc.) were altogether typically Russian. In hindsight, it was the liberals who really belonged to the "counterculture" in Russia. As far as Russian revolutionaries are concerned, those who so unexpectedly seized power in 1917, the most remarkable thing about their mental universe, about the symbolism and the practice of their "new society," was precisely the passionately contradictory relation to religion (Scene 18).

All that would not appear in its entirety until the end of Russia's "long nineteenth century." At its beginning, the Orthodox restoration emerged inconspicuously from the Orthodox cultural milieu. It was born on the geographical periphery of Petersburg Rus and on the mental periphery of "Petersburg" culture in the era of Catherine the Great. The father-obstetrician of the restoration was Paisius Velichkovsky (1722–1794). A native of Ukrainian Poltava, dissatisfied with the overly "secular" instruction he received at Mohyl's College in Kiev, Paisius followed the advice of Kiev's monks and, in 1746, he set out to search for the source of spiritual life where Nilus Sorsky, Ivan Vyshensky, and others had searched before him—Greece and the sacred Mount Athos. After seventeen years on Athos, Paisius returned closer to Russia with the community he had formed in the skete (a smaller monastery) of St. Elias. He remained beyond Russia's borders, however, settling in Moldavia. At the invitation of Moldavian princes, he resided in the Dragomirna Monastery in the Bukovina region. After Austria annexed the Bukovina, Paisius moved a little further south to Moldavia "proper." His journey terminated at the monastery of Neamț, which together with the nearby Putna Monastery represented the center of Moldavian ecclesiastical life, a sort of Romanian version of the Czech monasteries Zbraslav or Břevnov. Church Slavonic had meanwhile remained the liturgical and cultural language of Romanian Orthodoxy. Paisius was therefore not a "foreigner" but instead a "bi-cultural" figure not unlike the Moldavian ducal family, the Cantemirs/Kantemirs, who were active in Russia in the opposite direction of secularization (Scene 11).

Paisius had unwittingly chosen an auspicious moment for his "journey to the source," for his trip to Mount Athos. The Greek Orthodox Church was at the time in the processes of overcoming its own crisis of the seventeenth century by means of its own return to the source, to its patristic and hesychastic past, to what the Romanian historian Nicolae Iorga has called "Byzantium after Byzantium."[326] The pillars of this "neo-Athosian" spirituality consisted of poverty and the absolute separation from the secular world, the hesychastic "Jesus prayer" recited according to the "mantric" tradition as the path toward inner enlightenment (Scene 7), and the cult of spiritual teachers called *startsy* (elders). Authoritative sources were found in the texts of Greek Christian antiquity and the Middle Ages. Paisius and his monks began to select and translate the most important texts. But when his fellow Athosian Nikodimos Hagorite (i.e. of the Holy Mountain, the traditional nickname of Athosian

---

[326] Cf. Nicolae Iorga, *Byzance après Byzance: Continuation de l'histoire de la vie byzantine* (Bucarest: Association Internationale d'Études du Sud-Est Européen, 1971).

monks) published a selection of Greek patristic texts and Byzantine authorities in 1782 in Venice, that traditional place of Greek and Slavic book printing, Paisius seized the compilations.

Nikodimos named his anthology the *Philokalia,* which literally means "love of beauty." With this title, he followed in the footsteps of two classics of Greek patristics, Basil the Great and Gregory of Nazianzus (Scene 4), who in turn had drawn from Origen, a teacher forgotten by Nikodimos's time but now considered the "classic of classics." Origen had first formulated some of Orthodoxy's central concepts and categories, many of which were later condemned by the same Orthodoxy as heretical. Basil and Gregory compiled the *Philokalia* sometime in the years 350 to 360, a time when they together lived the *bios theorétikos* (the contemplative life), a life outside of the social and ecclesiastical centers, a proto-monastic life spent in prayer and study. The future church patriarchs were at the time still young scholars who compiled the texts which they found to be most spiritually and intellectually interesting, both for their own pleasure and for the pleasure of those to come. Gregory later appended a short forward to a transcription of the *Philokalia* in which he described the text as a collection of "useful excerpts for the lovers of Logos" (eklogai chrésimoi tois filologois).[327]

Nikodimos's *Philokalia,* to the contrary, is an anthology of the entire tradition from Anthony the Hermit (4th century) to Gregory of Sinai and Gregory Palamas (14th century). Much of what has been said about the first *Philokalia* can nevertheless be said about the second as well. It also contains "excerpts," mostly short texts compiled from patristic writings as well as aphorisms and quotations which could be "useful" to those in search of spiritual or hesychastic enlightenment. Paisius and his assistants would later translate an abridged version of Nikodimos's *Philokalia* (in Church Slavonic and in Romanian). But they would name the work *Dobrotolublye,*

---

327 Cf. Martin C. Putna, *Órigenés z Alexandrie* (Prague: Torst, 2001), 63.

which means "love of the good." Their translation of *Philokalia* as *Dobrotolublye* was not inaccurate. The Greek *kallos*, which originally meant "beauty," had over time acquired the sense of "good." The monastic milieu exploited this ambiguity. For them, genuine beauty was necessarily good just as the genuinely good was necessarily beautiful—in a spiritual sense, of course.

But since Nikodimos's Greek *Philokalia* in Venice and Paisius's Church Slavonic *Dobrotolublye* in Moscow were published in print, both made their way to "the lovers of Logos/the Beautiful/the Good" beyond the monastery's walls. Paisius himself feared the consequences of giving this spiritual treasury to the "layman." Hesychastic mystical practice, he warned, is reserved for those,

> who not only have denied, but completely subdued their own will and judgment before that of their Fathers, their authentic and experienced instructors in the practice of prayer. [...] But now that the Book of the Fathers has been printed, not only monks but also all Christians will come to know [inner prayer]. I therefore worry and tremble with fear [...] because one who insists on beginning without spiritual guidance may surrender his own will to some deception or fraud."[328]

Paisius's fundamental importance consists precisely in having overcome this trepidation and opened the *Dobrotolublye* not only to the monks, but to the whole of Russian culture. The *Dobrotolublye* became a sort of second bible for the nineteenth-century Orthodox restoration. Or rather, its first bible. Reading the real Bible always seemed suspicious to the Orthodox, a sign of some covert sectarianism. This prejudice was described by Leskov in his bitter tale "Singlemind" about an ardent reader of the Bible who was ostracized by the church community. The *Dobrotolublye* gained popularity after

---

328 Cited in Karel Sládek et al., *O Filokalii: Kniha, hnutí, spiritualita* (Olomouc: Refugium Velehrad-Roma, 2013), 100.

being translated into modern Russian, and that in two separate versions prepared by two figures of the Orthodox restoration, each one of them representative in his own way: Ignatius Bryanchaninov (1807–1867) and Feofan Zatvornik (1815–1894). The Russian *startsy* (elders) of the nineteenth century stylized their spiritual guidance after this book, among them Bryanchaninov and Zatvornik, later canonized as saints. The *Dobrotolublye* was *the* book, the work carried in the rucksack the anonymous Russian wayfarer and author of *The Way of the Pilgrim* (released in its first version in 1870). This stylized autobiography describes the fate of a simple religious man, a layperson who dedicates his life to Logos, the Beautiful, and the Good. He travels among pilgrims through the lands of Rus, living by the mercy of others who are pious, praying the "Jesus prayer" without pause and following his own spiritual development.

The real authors were apparently "ordinary" clergy members. Regardless, the book won fame not just in Russia but across the entire world. It was translated into English (1931) and other languages as the prototypical description of Russian religiosity in its most attractive form—popular, emotional, naive, and straight from the heart. The pilgrim's statements about the practice of the Jesus prayer are echoed by the heroes of J.D. Salinger's *Franny and Zooey* (1961)— Salinger of course also drew inspiration from the Far East and its own vision of the spiritual journey and mantric prayer.[329] It is likely, however, that this sort of "supraconfessional" understanding of the *Dobrotlublye*'s message would have only confirmed Paisius Velichkovsky's fears.

What is it about the *Dobrotolublye* that has made the book so attractive to readers? So attractive that it became *the* book of the Russian Orthodox restoration and even a source of inspiration for

---

[329] Two editions of *The Way of a Pilgrim* have been released in Czech: one esoteric-yogic, *Poutník vypráví o své cestě k Bohu,* edited by Jiří Vacek (Prague: Orfeus, 1993), and the other Catholic philo-Orthodox, *Upřímná vyprávění poutníka svému duchovnímu otci* (Velehrad: Refugium Velehrad-Roma, 2001).

Americans seeking spiritual enlightenment? Any explanation must begin with the book's simplicity and functionality. According to the *Dobrotolublye,* the essence of piety consists neither in the proper execution of ceremony nor in theological learning (the more theologically demanding sections of the Greek *Philokalia* were left out of the Russian translation!) but rather in subjectively felt passion and everyday spiritual practice. The starting point of this religion is the immediate experience of the "religious person." Religious experience delivers the religious person from worldly ambition and suffering to the inner world of quietude and union with Jesus. No special education or contact with clerical structures is needed. It is available to everyone, but its most exalted member is the "simple religious person." The archetype of the "simple religious person" loves, invokes, and uses for his own purposes the disciplinary literature of the Orthodox (just like Catholic) restoration, whose *Pilgrim's Way* represents a masterpiece, as well as the Orthodox (just like Catholic) romanticism, thus intellectuals and artists who are themselves anything but "simple religious people"—though they would like to be or at least come close to being one. What's more, the personal dispositions of those "simple religious people"—their inner goodness, sincerity, and empathy—correspond exactly to the ideal of national character as defined by Romanticism. This isn't just any simple religious pilgrim—this is a specifically Russian pilgrim!

It would take a while before the pilgrimages of Orthodox restoration and Orthodox romanticism would meet at *Pilgrim's Way.* During the era of Alexander I, "Catherinian" Europeanism continued to blossom with its cult of antiquity, "masonic" spirituality, and enlightened playfulness combined with other European trends such as sentimentalism, the titanic, and the sharply subjective romanticism of Novalis and Byron. Alexander Pushkin inherited all of this and brought it to a peak. Yet Pushkin wrote during a time when crowds of pilgrims headed for the Sarov Monastery south of Nizhny Novgorod to hear Seraphim of Sarov (probably 1759–1833), the first of the *startsy* (wise elders) and, according to many church historians, one of the most important nineteenth-century Russian saints. Pushkin and Seraphin didn't know each other of course. Nor would they have found much to talk about. Seraphim's life experiences and interests were well beyond the horizon of the elitist, "worldly" culture of Pushkin and his circle, just as the life experiences and interests of Pushkin and his circle were beyond the horizon of Seraphim and his restorationist piety.[330]

The symbolist author and religious thinker Dmitry Merezhkovsky (1865–1941), in whose person Orthodox romanticism and reformism came into conflict, a man certain only of his objection to Orthodox restoration, turned Seraphim into the archetype of restorationist piety. Such piety focuses inward and exists contentedly beyond the world and its concerns: "He turned away and found salvation. He put a curse on this city and all the cities of the world as so many Babylons, as incarnations of the Beast, and he cursed all and alone he stood with God."[331] But that was exactly what the Christian in the modern age could not do: "What shall I do? Save myself or avoid all? I cannot put a curse on all, for God is in all. I cannot curse the holy old man, for, like all, God is in him, too, as He is in everyone. I want neither God without the world nor the world without God."[332] Merezhkovsky does not doubt that "Seraphim had a real power, one which, if unable to overcome the physical force, then enough to overcome the metaphysical force of the world; but he held it *for himself alone* and could not share it with others. In order to elevate himself *above* this world, he had to turn *from* this world—but to bring it to himself, to lift it up along with himself was something

---

330   Pushkin's irreverence continues to cause offence to this day, even to literary scholars who profess Orthodoxy, see Alexandr Pančenko, "Raný Puškin a ruské pravoslaví," in *Metamorfózy ruské kultury* (Červený kostelec, 2012), 299–318.
331   D.S. Merežkovskij, "Poslední svatý," in *Ne mír, ale meč* (Prague: Kvasnička a Hampl, 1928), 114.
332   Ibid., 114.

he could not do. [...] He was elevated, but the world fell, he is the higher, the lower is the world."[333]

Merezhkovsky named his bitter treatise about Seraphim, *The Last Saint* (1908). With this title, he made clear not only his endless desire to provoke but also the distance which separated him from Orthodox restoration. Yet this distance itself resulted from earlier encounters between Orthodox romanticism and restorationist piety. Alone the fact that Merezhkovsky had noticed Seraphim and felt it necessary to engage with him critically is testament to previous encounters which had left some hope for rapprochement between both cultures and churches.

The specific place where this rapprochement took place was another monastery, far from St. Petersburg and within reach of Moscow: the Optina Monastery west of Tula. The monastery was already old and nearly decrepit in the time of the Enlightenment, but it took on new life during the nineteenth century. The *startsy* of Optina— that is a Russian cultural phenomenon of the romantic-restorationist era. The first of the "*startsy* of Optina," Leonid (Lev) Nagolkin (1768–1841), reformed the monastery according to the monastic rules of Paisius Velichkovsky and attracted large numbers of humble pilgrims. The second of the *startsy*, Makary Ivanov (1788–1860), was by contrast a lover of Logos in its philological form and turned the monastery into a center for publishing. Ivanov prepared editions of the translational work of Paisius Velichkovsky and other translations of patristic and Byzantine classics. The third in order, Ambrose Grenkov (1812–1891), returned to the tradition of Leonid, to spiritual advising for the widest layers of society.[334] Intellectuals and artists did not come to Sarov—they came to Optina. The founder of Slavophilism, Ivan Kireyevsky (1806–1856), who spent a substantial portion of his family's wealth on Orthodox literature, cooperated

---

333 Ibid., 136.
334 Cf. Sergei Chetverikov, *Optina Pustyn* (Paris : YMCA Press, 1926).

with Makary. Tolstoy, Leontyev, Solovyov and Dostoevsky each made their journey to visit Amvrozy, a figure immortalized by Dostoevsky as the wise elder Zosima in *The Brothers Karamazov.*[335]

"Secular" intellectuals, however, were anything but the passive receptacles of spiritual advice handed down by the *startsy* of Optina or elsewhere. This is clear already in Dostoevsky's portrayal of Zosima-Amvrozy. The *starets* Zosima is true a living saint, a man of infinite wisdom and insight into the human soul, and above all into the darkness of the Karamazov family. In his own monastery, however, the elder held a rather ambiguous position, his informal authority annoying several fellow monks. Alyosha Karamazov, wanting to become a monk, was given the rather unexpected advice to leave the cloister and undertake a spiritual and social mission beyond its walls. For, as Zosima tells him, "of old from our midst came leaders of the people, and can they not come now as well? Our own humble and meek ones, fasters and keepers of silence will arise and go forth for a great deed. The salvation of Russia is from the people. And the Russian monastery was always with people."[336] And when the old Zosima dies, he breaks yet another "rule" of saintly comportment: his body wafts not the scent of a saint, but emits instead a quite foul stench. No wonder, then, that Dostoevsky's portrayal of Zosima was not at all to the liking of restorationist circles.

This doesn't concern *belles lettres* alone, however. Many writers, understood according to contemporary usage as a person called upon to express opinions about public questions across genres and fields of expertise, also attempted to contribute to restorationist religious literature. In this, too, they resembled many western thinkers who similarly "stepped aside," an act often interpreted as a form of intellectual humility, the submission of their own "willful" imagination

---

335 Cf. Leonard J. Stanton, *The Optina Pustyn Monastery in Russian Literary Imagination* (New York: Peter Lang International Academic Publishers, 1995).

336 Fyodor Dostoevsky, *The Brothers Karamazov* (New York: Farrar, Straus and Giroux, 1990), 308.

to the service of ecclesiastical truth. The most remarkable success in this respect was probably the German romantic Clemens Brentano (1778–1842), whose original corpus is of interest primarily to literary historians but whose self-denial in the role of the "recorder" of the visions of the nun Anna Catherine Emmerich are still read by Catholics nearly two centuries later.

Like their western counterparts, Russian intellectuals wanting to participate in this spiritual renewal sometimes allowed this intention to influence their literary works. This was the case with Dostoevsky in the portrait of the *starets* Zosima, and also in the philosophical passages of *The Brothers Karamazov*. Mostly, however, they step aside from strictly literary texts in the direction of religious journalism and polemics, as if wishing to carry on the literary stylization and spiritual gesturing of ecclesiastical scribes of pre-Petrine Rus.

The first to undertake this act of "stepping aside" was Nikolai Gogol. His *Meditations on the Divine Liturgy* (1845) related directly to patristic symbolism and the aesthetic interpretations of religious ceremony such as the *Mystagogic Catecheses* of Cyril of Jerusalem (Scene 4). His *Selected Passages from Correspondence with Friends* continued the Russian "epistolary" genre—ecclesiastical, political, and cultural meditations or polemics in the form of open letters (Scene 4). Fyodor Tyutchev (1803–1873), author of subtle spiritual poetry, similarly "stepped aside," writing (again, in French!) a series of religious-political treatises about Russia, revolution, and the papacy in which he defends the spiritual mission of Russia as a pillar of the traditional Christian order. Leo Tolstoy similarly turned toward the end of his life from fiction to the composition of religious treatises (Scene 17). It wasn't any different with Dostoevsky and his *The Diary of a Writer.* There is no doubt that the core of these writers' work consists in literary creation and their religious meditations are read rather because they represent the thought of important artists. Other visitors to the Optina Monastery such as Kireyevsky, Leontyev, and Solovyov, on the other hand, are first and foremost religious thinkers whose poetry and prose are read rather because they represent the literary work of important religious thinkers. And still other intellectuals who spent their entire lives dealing with questions of church and culture wrote about religion in a fashion characteristic of literature. Vasily Rozanov (Scene 17) succeeded in his religious meditation where Gogol had not—he was able to enter literary history through the genre.

Nevertheless, no unambiguous line can be drawn separating romanticism and restoration, not according to genre (that Gogol, for instance, would count as a "romantic" in *Mirgorod* and *Dead Souls* but as a "restorationist" in *Selected Correspondence with Friends*), nor according to the prevalence of literary or paraliterary works (that Dostoevsky was a "romantic", whereas Leontyev a "restorationist"). Nor can one draw the line according to how much this or that author reproduced church teachings in this or that text or how much he freely worked with his own speculations and imagination. One cannot do so for the simple reason that there exists no consensus on the matter. These authors even argued amongst themselves about who was "more Orthodox"—see Leontyev's attack on Dostoevsky.[337] And that the demand of restorationist religiosity to count these texts among exemplary restorationist readings and their authors into the standard clerical structure without further ado suited practically nothing and no one. Consider the consternation shown by the church structure toward Gogol's *Selected Passages from Correspondence with Friends* or toward Dostoevsky's portrayal of Amvrozy as Zosima. Consider the unwillingness of monks to leave Leontyev permanently in the Optina monastery as a fellow brother.[338]

It is necessary to come to terms with the fact that as soon as one moves from the "clearly" restorationist texts of the type *The Way of*

---

337 Cf. Hanuš Nykl, "Dostojevskij jako pravoslavný myslitel: Případ Leonťjevovy kritiky," in *Kulturní, duchovní a etnické kořeny Ruska: Tradice a alternativy,* (ed.) Marek Příhoda (Červený Kostelec, 2005), 109–137.

338 Cf. K.N. Leontyev: *Pro et contra* (Saint Petersburg: RCHGI, 1995).

a Pilgrim or the spiritual counseling of Bryanchaninov or Zatvornik to more demanding intellectual and artistic works, one most often encounters in nineteenth-century Russian culture an amalgamation of both romanticism and restoration. And the third point of the triangle enters this dynamic: the attempt on the part of numerous intellectuals to reform the church (Scene 17). Nor could it be any different. Not because Russian spirituality and literariness was so exceptional, but because the relationship between modern culture and the church is fundamentally awkward and contradictory. The blessed simplicity of the *Pilgrim* is available only to very, very simple pilgrims indeed.

Orthodox Romanticism and Pan-Slavism

YEAR:
1852

PLACE:
Moscow

EVENT:
Gogol burns his manuscripts in a fit of bad conscience

WORKS:
The Tale of Igor's Campaign (published in 1800);
"Viy," *Meditations on the Divine Liturgy,* and *Selected
Passages from Correspondence with Friends* by Nikolai
Gogol (1835, 1845, and 1847); *Russian Nights* by
Vladimir Odoevsky (1844); *The Appearance of Christ
Before the People* by Alexander Ivanov (1837–1857);
Sketches from a Hunter's Album by Ivan Turgenev
(1856); *Byzantinism and Slavdom* by Konstantin
Leontiev (1875); *The Reader of Dostoevsky* by Emil
Filla (1907); *Saint Sergius of Radonezh* by Boris
Zaytsev (1925); *The Summer of Our Lord* by Ivan
Shmelev (1933)

Romanticism, like Classicism was an European export to Petersburg Rus. The dominant interests of Romanticism—folk culture, the emotional life of the individual, art and the personality of the artist, and the revolt against tyranny[339]—have nothing in common with the domestic tradition of Muscovite culture, which disdains the individual, the people, and art while celebrating tyranny. Romanticism nonetheless found a way to connect with local traditions in Russia. Or more precisely, to interpret local traditions "romantically." The purest expression of individuality, of the exotic, of rebelliousness and revolt in this sense was certainly the poet Mikhail Lermontov (1814–1841) with his tales of pirates and demons and his romantically youthful death. Only one of the primary interests of Romanticism harmonized with local traditions from the very beginning: the nation. The conviction that Russia heeded a special calling to a global mission was deeply "Muscovite." Romanticism took hold of it completely.

For an example of the "imported" character of Russian Romanticism as well as of the role played by the idea of Russian messianism, one can point to a work by Vladimir Odoevsky (1803–1869), one of the "lesser" romantics of Pushkin's generation, with a characteristically romantic title, *Russian Nights* (1844). There is hardly anything "Russian" about this work, however, beyond the language in which it is composed and its St. Petersburg setting. *Russian Nights* is a small jewel of "German" romanticism, a variation on themes from Novalis and E.T.A. Hoffmann. A group of friends engage in nighttime discussions about the mysteries of knowledge and creativity, about the nature of musical affection and the relationship between reason and emotion. They tell each other spooky stories about cadavers, corpses, and madmen. The ideas that most excite these Russian intellectuals however come from Europe, from philosophers such as

339   Cf. Maarten Doorman, *Romantický řád* (Prague: Prostor, 2008); Cf. Václav Černý, *Soustavný přehled obecných dějin naší vzdělanosti,* vol. 4, *Pseudoklasicismus a preromantismus, romantismus, realismus* (Prague: Academia, 2009).

Friedrich Schelling or Thomas Malthus, artists like Giovanni Battista Piranesi or Ludwig van Beethoven. The company's host is given the Goethian nickname Faust. In the end, discussion eventually turns to the subject of Russia, and here the friends change their tone. They begin to reflect on the West, once a source of inspiration which has now become weak. The future belongs to a new nation, one that still possesses strong feelings and faith. Peter the Great wisely took over some things from the West which eventually took root in Russia. But no one back then had thought of exporting to the West the new energies from Russia: "Europe has called us Russians its *saviors!* [...] our duty is not only to *save the body,* but also to *save the soul* of Europe! [...] The nineteenth century belongs to Russia!"[340]

The "Russian" point of the "German" *Russian Nights* demonstrates how far "Petersburg" romantic nationalism had departed from "Muscovite" nationalism. The latter rested on religious arguments (Moscow is chosen because it is Orthodox), or on arguments that were historical, dynastic, and symbolic in nature (Moscow is chosen because it has taken over the mission of Rome, Constantinople, and Kiev through a process of *translatio imperii,* Scene 6). The racial aspect, i.e. Slavic ethnic and linguistic identity, hardly played a role in the Muscovite ideology. "Petersburg" nationalism, to the contrary, rested above all on racial arguments: Russia is chosen because it is Slavic; Slavs represent the "spirit of history" and are thus destined to fulfill their world-historical task of creating the perfect civilization.

In the meantime, Orthodoxy could be pushed to the background. This was the case with Odoevsky, who in this respect remained the heir to a free, supra-confessional, "Catherinian" spirituality fortified by the influence of German Romanticism. More typically, however, religion was part of the interpretation, though it played

---

340 Vladimir Odoevsky, *Russian Nights* (Evanston: University of Illinois Press, 1997), 210–11, 213.

a subservient role to arguments about race: Orthodoxy is righteous not just because its theology is correct, but more importantly because it represents the "natural" religion of the Slavs. Theological Orthodoxy, for whose sake tongues were cut off in Muscovite Rus, now seemed to be of little relevance. The remnants of pagan folk religiosity were enthusiastically embraced while Orthodoxy was celebrated as the "natural national religion." Seen from the perspective of romantic "racial" religiosity, this was not thought to diminish the truth of Russian Orthodoxy but rather to enhance it.

The work presented to the Russian public in 1800 as the most valuable monument to the Kievan era, *The Tale of Igor's Campaign,* fit perfectly with the spirit of romantic nationalism rooted in pagan and Christian elements. The text of *Igor's Campaign* was presented as surviving fragments from a medieval epic about the campaign of Kievan princes against nomadic tribes. And it enthralled the public. It was included in Russian textbooks and inspired artistic creations in the spirit of Russian romantic historicism (most famously the opera of Alexander Borodin, *Prince Igor,* which premiered posthumously in 1890).

At the same time, the text immediately gave rise to doubts about its authenticity. *The Tale of Igor's Campaign,* in fact, fits very well into the European tradition of pre-romantic and romantic forgery. Would-be medieval texts such as the "Celtic" *Poems of Ossian* (1760), with which *Igor's Campaign* was originally enthusiastically compared; the "ancient Czech" *Manuscripts of Dvůr Králové and Zelená hora* (1817–1818), which were enthusiastically compared to both the *Poems of Ossian* and *Igor's Campaign*; the "ancient Bulgarian" epic *Vede Slovena* (1874–1881); and the Russian falsifications of the twentieth century such as the *Book of Veles* (1957–1959).[341] Unlike

---

341 It is bewildering that the latest academic *Dictionary of Russian, Ukrainian, and Belarusian Authors* in the Czech Republic states in the corresponding entry that "the prevailing consensus in East and West today is to accept *Igor's Campaign* in the context of eastern Slavic medieval literature," and in the general introduction uses the questionable formulation the work is "taken

the English, Czech, and Bulgarian scholarship, which eventually admitted (often with sorrow) that the documents were fakes, mainstream Russian scholarship (and no small number of western Slavic scholars) still insist upon the veracity of Russian epic.[342]

It is difficult to imagine that this conflict will ever be resolved. No original manuscript has been found (and all the later manuscripts are clear forgeries). Nor is the defense of *Igor's Campaign* motivated by the search for objective truth, anyway. It is a question of national prestige. In this, Russian scholarship (unlike the English or the Czech) has continued in the tradition of "romantic science," a method which posits national prestige before the facts. The "Norman theory" (Scene 2) represents another example.[343] The passion with which adherents defend *Igor's Campaign,* together with the rejection of opponents as traitors and enemies of Rus, itself raises the greatest of doubts.

At least at the level of hypothesis one can accept the *Tale of Igor's Campaign* as an artistically splendid example of romantic religiosity, an idealized conception of an elemental paganism which endures in the midst of a nominally Christian society: nature animate, signs full of meaning, "Homeric" bards inspired by the spirit of prophecy, the references to Kievan princes as the heirs of ancient Slavic idols ("grandson of Veles," "grandsons of Stribog," "Korsun the Great," "the forces of Dazhbog"), heroes communicating with animals—and all of it in such a rich lyrical style unlike anything else in the older Russian literature:

The sun barred his way with darkness.
Night groaning at him awoke birds with the threat;
the howling of beasts rose up.

axiomatically as authentic." Of course, the same dictionary also presents *Book of Veles* as authentic. *Slovník ruských, ukrajinských a běloruských spisovatelů* (Prague: Libri, 2001), 30, 529.
342 Cf. Jiří Franěk, "Slovo o pluku Igorově aneb Ruské RKZ," *Souvislosti,* no. 2 (1995): 20–39.
343 Cf. Emanuel Rádl, *Romantická věda* (Prague: Laichter, 1918).

Div is aroused, he shrieks a command to the unknown land,
to the Volga, Pomorie, Posulie, Surozh and Korsun;
from the treetops he bids them take heed.
"And to you too, O idol of Tmutorokan!"[344]

All this was supposed to have taken place and been set into verse at the courts of Kievan princes two centuries after the baptism of Vladimir. From the standpoint of cultural history, this amounts to a powerful argument for dating *The Tale of Igor's Campaign* to the turn of the nineteenth century—and for the truly romantic ease with which "Orthodox Romanticism" integrated pagan themes into a vision of continuous natural piety in the emotions and intellect of the chosen nation.

The religious-cultural concept of Slavophilism was born of this romantic nationalism, this connection of Petersburg Rus to the local traditions of Moscow's historical-religious "choseness," with Orthodoxy providing what remained of paganism with the new "natural" religion of the Slavic race and Moscow the focal point of it all. Early Slavophiles such as the brothers Kireyevsky (Scene 15) were quite delirious as religious poets. Their followers in the second half of the nineteenth century, usually labeled "pan-Slavists" or "pan-Russianists," to the contrary, emphasized the "scientific" foundations of their opinions.[345] The final form of pan-Slavism found its expression in the writings of two "scholars," or rather ideological commentators: Danilevsky and Leontyev.

Nikolai Danilevsky (1822–1885) is the author of "just one" book, *Russia and Europe: The Slavic World's Political and Cultural Relations with the Germanic-Roman West* (1869). The first part of the

---

344 *On the Campaign of Igor: A Translation of the Slovo o polku Igoreve*, trans. J.A.V. Haney and Eric Dahl (1992), http://faculty.washington.edu/dwaugh/rus/texts/igorintr.htm, accessed February 15, 2017.
345 Cf. Radomír Vlček, *Ruský panslavismus: Realita a fikce* (Prague: Historický ústav AV ČR, 2002); Cf. Václav Černý, *Vývoj a zločiny panslavismu* (Prague: Knihovna Václava Havla, 2011).

book is organized in a scholarly fashion and formulates an inter-disciplinary theory of "cultural-historical types." These types range from the Egyptian to the "Germanic-Romanic," and the life cycle of each, says Danilevsky, has its own natural limits. Danilevsky describes these cultural-historical forms in analogy to nature, using the metaphor of youth, maturity, and old age. He likely found inspiration for doing so in the German historian Heinrich Rückert's *Lehrbuch der Weltgeschichte in der organischen Darstellung* (Primer of World History in Organic Description, 1857), which would later also inspire Oswald Spengler and his model of "cultural morphology", some even speculate that Spengler relied on Danilevsky.[346]

The second part of the book represents the practical application of theory, a new "scientific" justification for Russia and its imperial claims. Russia is not Europe! Russia must stand opposed to Europe! Europe, the "Germanic-Romanic West," he describes as "old" and "stagnant." The future belongs to the Slavs, and so the Slavs must defend their territory to strengthen their own "cultural-historical type." Although the "Germanic-Romanic" type has passed its peak of vitality and belongs to the past, it strongly resists stepping aside. Danilevsky therefore proposes an All-Slavic union encompassing its "natural borders," a union under Russian leadership to "save" the Slavs. It is worth noting that the boundaries of this proposed union correspond almost exactly to what would later become the borders of the Eastern Bloc under Soviet rule.

The novelist and journalist Konstantin Leontyev (1831–1891) drew from Danilevsky's theory of cultural-historical types in his essay "Byzantinism and Slavdom" (1875). Leontyev picked up where Danilevsky had left off. The approximate duration of each type's life-cycle he estimated at 1,200 years. For each type, he appraised

---

346 Cf. Martin C. Putna, "Zánik západu jakožto heslo, svědectví o době a kniha na průsečíku," in *Zánik Západu: Obrysy morfologie světových dějin,* by Oswald Spengler (Prague: Academy, 2010), 733–757.

its current phase of development. Leontyev considered democracy, egalitarianism, and liberalism symptoms of a type's aging, each of them contributing to the disintegration of society into a state of "elementary chaos." A new cultural-historical type was introduced, the Byzantine, making the contrast between Russia and Europe even more pronounced. According to Leontyev, Russia shares little with the other Slavic peoples, all of which are "infected" by Europeanianism (the liberal, westernized Czechs receive particularly spiteful condemnation!). Russia has more in common with the nations of the Near East and Asia, all of which share the "Byzantine" principle of strict social hierarchy. Russia should therefore ignore the West as much as possible and direct its attention to the south and east. "Byzantinism," an anti-liberal system, will save Russia—and together with it, those Slavs worth saving: "Three things with us are strong and powerful: Byzantine Orthodoxy, our native and unlimited autocracy, and perhaps also the peasant *mir*. [...] What I want to say is that our tsarism, so fruitful for us and full of salvation, took root under the influence of Orthodoxy, the influence of the Byzantine idea, Byzantine culture. Byzantine ideas and feelings united with half-wild Rus in a single body. [...] Byzantism gave us the strength to battle Poland, the Swedes, with France and Turkey. If we remain true to it, under its banner we shall naturally be able to withstand the pressure of the whole of international Europe should it attempt (after having exterminated in herself all that is noble) to prescribe to us the rot and stench of its new laws and pitiful earthly bliss and radical earthly misery!"[347]

The aggressive, arrogant, xenophobic, and authoritarian tone of Danilevsky and Leontyev's "racially scientific" justifications for Russian imperial claims reminds one less of Spengler than his wayward student, the Nazi theoretician Alfred Rosenberg (Scene 2). This entire concept of pan-Slavism played a deleterious role not only

347 Konstantin Leontyev, *Rossiya / Slavyanstvo* (Moscow: Iydatelstvo Respublika, 1996), 104.

in the sense that it became a central part of Russian imperialism's ideological apparatus (and its transformation under Putin's Rus, see Conclusion), but also because it led many intellectuals, politicians, and journalists (not only in the Balkans but also in Central Europe) to believe that if their country shared a linguistic and racial identity with Russia, then they were "naturally" bound to share also its political and cultural destiny. This belief moved many cultural elites in the region to turn away from Europe and become the un-witting—though often enough fully aware—accomplices of Russian (later, Soviet) imperialism. The Russophilism of Serbian or Bulgarian intellectuals during the romantic era was legitimate in the sense that it emphasized the enduring bonds of Orthodox religion and culture. In the case of Czech and Slovak romanticism, however, Russophilism meant a complete reversal of these nations' histories.[348] When Masaryk chose for his study about Russian spiritual history the same title as that used by Danilevsky before him, *The Spirit of Russia* (see Introduction), he did so to engage with the earlier author and return the meaning of Czech history back to the West, where it has always belonged.

The concept of pan-Slavism played an enormously important role in nineteenth-century Russian literature, painting, and music. Rather than Slavophilism, pan-Slavism, and pan-Russianism one can speak in a more value-neutral way of "Orthodox romanticism." In this lies Russia's one original and truly valuable contribution to world culture.

Nikolai Gogol (1809–1852) stands at the head of this gallery of Orthodox romantic classics. Pushkin is rather the "last" in a line of antiquiating poets of the early Petersburg era. He was the "first" among creators of a new literary Russian; he was a "Russian Goethe" or "Russian Dante." For subsequent Russian literature, Pushkin is quite simply *the* poet. But it is Gogol who represents the "first" writer

---

348 Cf. Rudolf Chmel, *Romantizmus v globalizme* (Bratislava: Kalligram, 2009).

to be at the same time a religious thinker at times resembling the Old Testament prophets or the holy fools of Muscovy.[349]

In Gogol's works one finds all the features that characterized romanticism in general and Orthodox romanticism specifically. The "Petersburg Tales" (in the *Arabesques* cycle, 1835–1836, and elsewhere), *The Government Inspector* (1836), and *Dead Souls* (1842–1846)— these all express a sense of estrangement from the modern, Europeanized Petersburg Rus which Gogol found cold, frightening, and preposterous. *Evenings on a Farm near Dikanka* (1831–1832) and *Mirgorod* (1835)—these represent a descent into ancient Rus, mysterious and premodern (the novel *Taras Bulba,* moreover, relates the co-creation of a Ukrainian identity idealized as the "Cossack nation," Scene 12). Religion belongs among the features characteristics of ancient Rus; pagan elements and "pagan" ghosts exist alongside Orthodox religious practice.

Gogol proceeded most deeply below the surface of folkloric stylization in the tale "Viy" contained in the collection *Mirgorod*. In this tale, a philosophy student named Khoma Brut, who represents rationality, light, and Christianity fatefully encounters the dark "pagan powers" represented by a living-dead girl, an entire chorus of demonic helpers, and that most awful, most ancient demon Viy. This latter figure, a sort of Tolkien "Balrog," is summoned to assist ordinary demons resist the power of Christian prayer. The location in which the conflict takes place is Christian, an Orthodox cathedral, but even in this holy site the anti-Christian powers prevail. It is hardly necessary to undertake a deep (psycho-) analysis to realize that the young philosopher's battle with demons represents his struggle with the demons of his own soul. It is a struggle against "romantic"

---

349 The sometimes contentious sometimes complementary relationship between the "Pushkin" and "Gogol" type of Russian artist is given literary treatment for example in the novel by Mark Kharitonov, *Den v fevrale* [A day in February] (Moscow, Sov. Pisatel, 1988)

irrationalism emerging from the depths below, beneath the façade of social conventions and ceremony:

> "Lift my eyelids, I can't see!" Viy said in a subterranean voice—and the entire host rushed to lift his eyelids.
> "Don't look!" some inner voice whispered to the philosopher. He could not help himself and looked.
> "There he is!" Viy cried and fixed an iron finger on him. And all that were there fell upon the philosopher. Breathless, he crashed to the ground and straightaway the spirit flew out of him in terror.[350]

Gogol has always taken second place to Dostoevsky. For while Dostoevsky is reputed to be the analyst of the human soul's demonic side, Gogol is considered "merely" a satirist, folklorist, and fantasist. But there is a more basic difference between the authors. Dostoevsky goes on at length about demons and spiritual depth. Gogol, on the other hand, shows it all directly. In this sense, Gogol is "more genuine" and "more poetic" than the endlessly philosophizing Dostoevsky.

At the same time, Gogol is the first among nineteenth-century Russian writers to engage seriously in philosophizing. After a certain period, the writer sets his literary pen aside to seize the role of religious moralist, one who feels himself called upon to prescribe Russia medicine for its spiritual ailments. Some passages of his *Selected Passages from Correspondence with Friends* (1847) are still of value as far as the evaluation of the period's literature is concerned. In some passages Gogol communicates the same thoughts as Dostoevsky using different words: Russia is called upon to lead a revival of world Christianity, but she must be revived first. In the passages where Gogol offers specific instructions for Russian society, when

---

350 Nikolai Gogol, "Viy," in *The Collected Tales of Nikolai Gogol* (New York: Vintage Books, 1999), 192.

emphasizing the important role played by governors (and their wives) in leading the social revival, when defending the preservation of serfdom as an ideal condition prescribed by the Bible itself, it is as if he were trying to deny himself and everything that he stands for. To deny his own "Khomabrutism" and offer his humble service to religious restoration.

In its conclusion, however, the *Meditations on Divine Liturgy* (1845) shows that Gogol-the-restorationist always gives way to Gogol-the-romantic. In the end, Gogol is concerned not with the "objective" character of dogma and ceremony but rather about their effect on the individual psyche of the modern "religious person":

> The effect of the Divine Liturgy is great. [...] If the worshiper follows every action reverently and diligently, his soul attains a high state, the commandments of Christ become possible for him, Christ's yoke becomes easy and His burden lights. After leaving the temple [...] he looks upon all men as his brothers.[351]

Selected Passages from Correspondence with Friends and *Meditations on the Divine Liturgy* did not bring forth any spiritual renewal of Russian society. What they did inaugurate was a dispute in Russian culture about Gogol. For if his work raises all the basic positions and themes of the Orthodox romanticism, then his personality still more suggestively embodies Orthodox romanticism together with all its possibilities and contradictions: Gogol's sensual "paganism," his intoxication with life (the themes of dance and food!), and even his nearly hysterical sentimentality; Gogol's "Catholic temptation" experienced in Rome (Scene 14); Gogol's feelings of regret, guilt, and rejection; and finally, Gogol's radical repentance which at the

---

351 Nikolai Gogol, *Meditations on the Divine Liturgy* (Jordanville, NY: Holy Trinity Publications, 2014), 93.

end of his life led him to burn several manuscripts, a self-imposed sacrifice and final exhaustion unto death.

What conclusions are we to draw about Russian culture and the Russian spirituality in light of these extreme alterations of life positions? In this lies the dispute about Gogol. A contemporary of the writer, the left-wing journalist Vissarion Belinsky (1811–1848), described Gogol's turn to religion to be an unhappy mistake. The symbolist Dmitri Merezhkovsky (Scene 15), in his Gogolian study in the book *Sick Russia* (1910), interpreted Gogol's life as a struggle between "the white" and "the black," between the pleasures of life, on the one hand, and religion (mis-)understood as the denial of life, on the other. The most demonic figure in Gogol's life, his own "Viy," was said to be his confessor, father Matvey Konstantinovsky, who evoked feelings of guilt and set the writer in the direction of that destructive final "penance." Gogol thus acted correctly in seeking the "white" Christ—but he became confused when he thought himself to have found it in the "black" monk Matvey.

The exile literary critic Konstantin Mochulsky (1892–1950) offered a completely contrary interpretation in his book *Gogol's Spiritual Path* (1934). Gogol, it is true, appears naively utopian in his *Selected Passages from Correspondence with Friends*, but his journey during those final penitent years was one of spiritual enlightenment. Father Matvey does not deserve the harsh judgment of Merezhkovsky, for he led Gogol to humility. It was sickness that killed Gogol, not the advice of father Matvey. Another exile, the historian of theology Georges Florovsky, labeled Gogol's celebrated conversion to the church a misunderstanding. For Gogol, according to Florovsky, psychologized Christ and Christianity in an intolerably "un-Orthodox" manner, and in this he was rather the heir to German romantic idealism and pietism than to authentic Orthodox tradition.[352] Nor did

---

[352] Cf. Georges Florovsky, *The Ways of Russian Theology* (Belmont, Mass: Nordland Pub. Co., 1979).

the church comprehend Gogol's epic significance. In his monograph *The Sexual Labyrinth of Nikolai Gogol* (1976), the American Slavic scholar Simon Karlinsky offers yet another solution—psychoanalysis in the narrow Freudian sense of the word. The apparently insolvable conflicts in Gogol's life and work supposedly resulted from chaos and privation in the writer's erotic life.

Surely, not even Karlinsky would deny the character which Mochulsky attributes to Gogol's place in Russian literature:

> With his hysteria and "holy madness," [Gogol] destroyed the harmony of classicism and upset aesthetic balance, that miracle which had been achieved by Pushkin. From Gogol proceeds all the "nocturnal awareness" of our literature: Tolstoy's nihilism, Dostoevsky's gulf, the revolt of Rozanov. The "daytime" of literature, Pushkin's gold-woven tapestry was thrown off. Gogol is the first "sick man" of our literature, its first martyr.[353]

Gogol is thus the first. Immediately beside him stood his friend, the painter Alexander Ivanov (1806–1858). Ivanov, however, didn't consider himself to be a "mere" painter any more than Gogol felt himself to be a "mere" writer. Ivanov wrote utopian tracts on the rise of Russia as the world's leading spiritual power, he described the tsar (yes, Nicholas specifically!) as the new Messiah and maintained that there should stand beside the tsar-Messiah a Russian spiritual artist, someone who would paint images from the history of Christianity and paganism (!) in the new Moscow Cathedral of Christ the Savior (See Conclusion) and thereby transform it into the center of world spirituality. This artist, of course, was to be Ivanov himself.[354]

The greater part of Ivanov's oeuvre was inspired by classical Italy and antique mythology: idyllic, academic (in places cold) and, in

---

353 Konstantin Mochulsky, *Duchovnyi put Gogolya* (Paris: YMCA Press, 1934), 86.
354 Dmytro Čyževskyj, "Die Utopie des Malers A.A. Ivanov," in *Aus zwei Welten: Beiträge zur Geschichte der slavisch-westlichen literarischen Beziehungen* (Berlin: Mouton, 1956), 291–307.

terms of themes, not at all Russian. Ivanov thus stood at the end of a line of Russian painters enchanted by their sojourns in Italy (Orest Kiprensky, Karl Bryullov, and others), a period forming the most optimistic section of the Tretyakov Gallery's collection of Russian art. This work forms a counterpoint in the fine arts to the literary classicism from Derzhavin to Pushkin, that "gold-woven tapestry." And just as Pushkin stood at the end of a line of poets, so did Ivanov stand at the end of a line of painters. Only, after all the Apollos, Hyacinths, and idyllic Italian landscapes, Ivanov decided to create a work of art that would not only be an artistic statement, but above all a religious one—a work that would bring forth a spiritual revival in Russia and throughout the world.

This was to be the picture *The Appearance of Christ Before the People,* which Ivanov worked on for twenty years (1837–1857). Gogol devoted an enthusiastic chapter of his *Selected Passages from Correspondence with Friends* to the picture. The completed work occupies an entire wall at the Tretyakov Gallery. John the Baptist preaches on the bank of the river Jordan, people undress before entering the water and they shake with cold in awareness of sin. Pharisees give voice to their doubts, but the faces of those baptizes are nevertheless ecstatic with joy. Christ arrives to the crowd quite alone. He approaches from a distance, he is small and many viewers will not notice him—and yet it is around him that the picture revolves. His profile is the only one not depicted in academic-realist style, but stylize archaically so that the Czech viewer might be reminded of Jan Zrzavý's other-worldly depiction of Christ.

From Ivanov's sketches and his comments in correspondence with Gogol, it is clear that his aim was not just to squeeze as many psychological types as possible onto a single canvas. The picture is rich in complicated symbolism. Its major theme is the cleansing effect of beauty, thus the acceptance of the human body transformed and relieved of its sinfulness. This represents one of Gogol's major themes and one of major traumas experienced by his heroes, and not just Khom Bruta from "Viy." It is also one of Orthodox Romanticism's major themes, one that resonated with Dostoevsky and Solovyov: how does one distinguish between demonic beauty leading to damnation and spiritual beauty leading to God? Does the question concern quite simply the distinction between the experience of the beauty of the world and the body and spiritual beauty of the liturgy (remember the aesthetic experience of the church service, the "heavenly beauty" which according to Nestor led Prince Vladimir to receive Orthodoxy; Scene 4)? Or does it concern a rather more circuitous and complicated boundary line that can and should contain the beauty of both the world and of the body?

But what does it matter when the picture itself is cold and academic like Ivanov's other canvases? Or more exactly, coldly academic and at the same time convulsive, as if the artist were trying to join antique classicist style and religious ecstasy. Critics reacted to the painting with ambivalence. No religious revival followed. Orthodox romanticism left its mark through the works of Gogol, Dostoevsky, and Solovyov—in painting, the same evangelical exaltation fell flat.

In the wake of Ivanov's ruined project, the ongoing problem of how beauty should relate to spirituality continued to surface, but differently than Ivanov or Gogol would have wished. For centuries it was only ecclesiastical artwork that existed, above all the transpersonal and atemporal canon of iconography.[355] Recall how Archbishop Avvakum raged at the onset of realism, at a Christ who "looks like a German, fat and potbellied" (Scene 10). Russian spiritual culture only knew the body humbled and shrouded. Nudity could only be thought of as naked disgrace and torment, or in the form of the ostracized holy fool. Then came Petrine Europeanization, and with it, for many artists, the experience of Italy and "southern," "antique" nudity. As artists leisurely painted landscapes and mythological

355 Cf. Fyodor Buslayev, "Obshchiye ponatiya o russkoy ikonopisi," in *O literature* (Moscow: Khudozhestvennaya literatura, 1990), 349–414.

nudes in Italy, Ivanov and Gogol grappled with the problem of reconciling the sensual beauty of paganism with Russian piety. Ivanov's painting was to be the solution. But instead of solving the problem, it only called attention to it. This is not a problem for Orthodox romanticism alone, by the way. It represents a central question for all art that wishes to be both religious and modern.

The development of Russian painting after Ivanov featured renewed attempts to depict Christ. These, however, would all take place in the context of the social-critical realism of the "peredvizhniki" who sometimes worked with religious themes but usually only to push them in a different direction. In these works, Christ enters not so much as a triumphant victor but rather as a silent sufferer. Vasily Perov (1834–1882) paints *Christ in the Garden of Gethsemane* with his face lying on the ground and on his head a crown of thorns. Ivan Kramskoy (1837–1887) paints Christ as he sits in the desert and meditates.

Russian painters were more successful when, like their literary colleagues, they depicted subjects that were not directly religious, theological, or hagiographic, but focused instead on the "simple religious person" of contemporary Russia. This was true of Surikov's *Boiarynia Morozova* mentioned above (Scene 10) and the *Easter Procession in the District of Kursk* by Ilya Repin (1844–1930). These artists did not depict Christ directly, but for that his presence is felt more strongly through the presence of individual human beings. And that is the case even when, or especially when, the pictures smack of bitter anticlerical satire as in Perov's *Tea Drinking in Mytishchi* (1862), a painting showing the figure of a paunchy bishop sipping tea as his servant pushes away a disabled beggar and child. The biblical reader and reader of fairy tales and apocrypha cannot help but think of Christ's presence precisely in the figures of the poor, the outcast, and the needy (Mt 25). Christ is evoked in yet another way through the portraits artists paint of themselves and of intellectuals from the circles of Orthodox romanticism and reformism. This was the case with Repin's portraits of Tolstoy and Solovyov, or Nesterov's double portrait of Sergei Bulgakov and Pavel Florensky (Scene 17). The philosopher Vasily Rozanov aptly describes Nesterov, and in fact the whole of this new religious painting: "Nesterov does not paint an icon, that is not his affair. [...] His task is not to depict 'God' but only 'how man arrives to God.' Prayer, but not that to which it is directed."[356]

It is even possible to approach, "through pictures," the author who stands as the indisputable head of Russian Orthodox romanticism, Fyodor Dostoevsky (1821–1881). Too much has already been written about Dostoevsky, both in Russia (see for all the collection of philosophical-theological interpretations *Legends of the Great Inquisitor from the Brothers Karamazov*[357]) and in the West. At the same time, Dostoevsky was one of the last to be accepted among nineteenth-century Russian classics because he seemed the most incomprehensible. It was only with a turn in European cultural modernism at the turn of the twentieth century, tired of classicist descriptive realism and longing to plunge into the depths of human consciousness and unconsciousness, that his work was accepted and made into the object of a literary cult. In Dostoevsky, many thought they had found the quintessence of Russian art and Russian mentality.

As the archetypes of "Russian soul," Dostoevsky's heroes are in Europe seen as being deeply anchored in Christianity. They are quiet saints, unknown to the outside world: the prostitute Sonya Marmeladova from *Crime and Punishment* (1866) who reads about the resurrection of Lazarus (an event central to Orthodox liturgy and depicted on every iconostasis); the priest Myshkin, the impoverished, sickened, and, because of his superhuman goodness, ridiculed hero of *The Idiot* (1868–1869); or the young Alyosha from *The Brothers Karamazov* (1880) who submissively argues with his

356 Vasilij Rozanov, *Svět ve světle "ruské ideje,"* (Prague: OIKOYMENH, 1999), 209.
357 Cf. *Velký inkvizitor* (Velehrad: Refugium Velehrad-Roma, 2000).

brother over the existence of God and would like to become a monk himself, but is dispatched to evangelize to the outside world by the unusual spiritual father Zosima (Scene 15).

Dostoevsky's heroes of another lineage are also considered to be archetypal "Russian souls." These are the pessimists, nihilists, atheists, suicides, and men or women in despair like Raskolnikov in *Crime and Punishment,* Ippolit in *The Idiot,* and Ivan Karamazov. As the Czech literary critic Václav Černý observes, however, "in these characters Dostoevsky embodies the Occident, the corrupted, rationalistic, individualistic and de-Christianized West of Satan!"[358] The dichotomy of "holy Russia" and "Russia-in-damnation," Russia remaining true to its Orthodox traditions and Russia yielding to the destructive influence of the West, forms the simple foundation of Dostoevsky's ideological constructions. But no one would dedicate such careful study to the corpus if these constructions were not buried so deeply and ambiguously in texts that are otherwise extraordinarily suggestive. What remained a bare ideological outline with Ivanov became art in the hands of Dostoevsky.

Dostoevsky became the symbolic center of Russia and Christianity. His prose was elevated to the status of sacred text to be consulted and interpreted in relation to every social, artistic, and personal problem or crisis. All the better reason to approach Dostoevsky "through pictures." Not through a picture of Dostoevsky himself, however, but *The Reader of Dostoevsky* painted by the Czech Cubist Emil Filla in 1907, at the peak of Europe's first "Dostoevsky craze." A collapsed figure with a pallid appearance sits in an armchair, his features not unlike those of Dostoevsky himself. A crucifix hangs on the wall and the silhouette of a Cathedral can be seen through the window. On the table lies a book with a clearly legible name "Dostoevsky" written on it—and a glass. Water or vodka? We can't know what exactly the reader is thinking about. We can be certain,

---

[358] Václav Černý, *André Gide* (Prague: Triáda, 2002), 133.

however, that he is struggling with the question of salvation. And, like a true romantic, he is left to solve this question on his own.

Dostoevsky isn't the only one to have incorporated the romantic dichotomy of Russian spirituality into literary texts. A literary figure considered to be of equal stature is Leo Tolstoy—but his religious exploration belongs rather to "Orthodox reformism," or to that part of it which reaches for an alternative religiosity. As if lost behind the figures of Dostoevsky and Tolstoy are several other authors who spent less time theorizing about religion and instead told stories about "religious man."

Nikolai Leskov is an author unjustly relegated to secondary status. Leskov depicted the upper echelons of Russia's clergy with sarcasm, but for that wrote with great affection about pious eccentrics and saints hidden among the people, be they the biblical readers in "Singlemind" (Scene 15), Old Believers in love with iconography (Scene 10), or paradoxical saint-heroes adopted from the stories of Byzantium (Scene 7). In Leskov's mostly amiable corpus one also finds prose with an explicitly pan-Slavic message, albeit in Leskov's characteristically good-natured version—consider the tale "Alexandrite" about a Czech gem-cutter who weeps bitterly over the death of the Russian tsar.

Another author unjustly taking second place is Konstantin Leontyev. Leontyev not only founded the romantic-restorationist theory "Byzantinism," which was to save the Slavs from Europe, he also penned charming lyrical prose about the life of Greeks and other Christians living on the territory of the Turkish empire, a place where the author resided for some time (including on the sacred Mount Athos!). The Greek-Slavic Orthodox Balkans are for Leontyev a sort of "blissful South", an idealized "second homeland," a role Italy played for Gogol and others. Only, what a shame that from his love for this "second homeland" Leontyev deduced such monstrous political theories...

Another underappreciated author is Ivan Turgenev (1818–1883), usually held to be a "mere" lyrical depicter of aristocratic dwellings and unrequited love. Turgenev was not a "religious" author but a political liberal and "Westernizer." A number of passages in his prose nonetheless display a deep affection for the "religious person" of the popular milieu. One of his most moving pieces appears in his *Sketches from a Hunter's Album* (1856), a story titled "Living Relic." The story is often translated as "the living corpse," (e.g. in Czech as "Živá nebožka"), but this is to misunderstand of the meaning of the Church Slavonic term *moshchy*. Moshchy are not "the deceased," but rather the remains of the deceased—physical remnants of a saint which, according to Orthodox legend, do not decay and may be a source of miracles. A "living relic" is what the narrator calls the rural girl whom he encounters when wandering through the Russian countryside. Illness has confined her to bed, yet neither does she despair nor does not deplore her fate. She instead accepts it with humility and Christian love; without speeches or dramatic gestures she is transformed into a "living sacrifice."[359] In this sense she resembles the saint-martyr type of the Medieval Christina Mirabilis portrayed in Czech literature by the Catholic (neo)romantic Julius Zeyer, or the modern Anna Catherine Emmerich whose visions were reworked into literature by the German Catholic romantic Clemens Brentano.

Like her more famous counterparts, Turgenev's quietly suffering Lukeria is consoled by a vision of Christ-the-groom:

> And, behold! Over the very top of the ears [of corn] there came gliding very quickly towards me, not Vassya, but Christ Himself! And how I knew it was Christ I can't say; they don't paint Him like that—only it was He! No beard, tall, young, all in white, only His belt was golden; and He held

---

359 Cf. N.F. Budanova, "Rasskaz Turgeneva Zhivye moshchi I pravoslavnaya tradicia," *Russkaya literatura*, no. 1 (1995) : 188–194.

out His hand to me. "Fear not," said He; "My bride adorned, follow Me; you shall lead the choral dance in the heavenly kingdom, and sing the songs of Paradise." And how I clung to His hand! My dog at once followed at my heels... [...] Then only I understood that that dog was my illness, and that in the heavenly kingdom there was no place for it."[360]

Lukeria remains a poignant figure in Russian literature. Unlike the hidden saints in Dostoevsky, she lacks the element of hysteria, which makes her more sympathetic. She thereby confirms that even in the modern world Christ may be faithfully depicted through the description of "religious people" and their visions.

The Bolshevik seizure of power brought an end to the whole of this old religious world. But for all that it was cultivated in the cultural memory. Thanks to that, Orthodox romanticism didn't wither away at the outset of modernism but to the contrary gained new impulse for life. Thus would it endure the entirety of the twentieth century in Russian exile culture, "Russia beyond Russia." Of course, in the recollections of exiles, "sacred Rus" was freed from its inner contradiction, of the idiosyncratic tension in the style of Dostoevsky. In memory, "sacred Rus" would continue to exist as an idyll.

This is to be seen, for example, in the work of Ivan Shmelyov. When he published his account of Bolshevik violence (Scene 1), he described the spiritual beauty of a vanished world. Far better than in his novels, Shmelyov evoked this world in two volumes of "Pictures of Ancient Rus," *Leto Gospodne* (The summer of the Lord, 1933) and *Bogomole* (Pilgrimage, 1935). History doesn't exist in these works. Time is circular, constantly repeating the cycle of the ecclesiastical calendar. The young narrator awakens each day with joy because there is almost always some religious holiday. The old carpenter Gorkin, embodiment of the religious Russian people, the

360 Ivan Turgenev, *Sketches from a Hunter's Album* (NC: Seven Treasures Publication, 2008), 219.

"voice of God" and "living tradition," explains the significance of each holiday and its rituals to the young man.

This sort of fold theology flawlessly combines Christianity with folklore (Gorkin explains why apples are consecrated in September—because Adam committed his sin through biting an apple), with the cycle of fieldwork, nature, and transparent paganism (divination from the "Ring of Solomon", prayer to "mother Earth" and so on), and with that which at celebrations of countless holidays plays a role no less important than the liturgy—that is, food. The description of food and its liturgical-apocryphal significance takes up a significant part of the book:

> What is the number of our Saviors? You know nothing at all. We have three. The first is the Honey Savior, who carries the cross. That means he can tap honey, the honeybees do not become angry, and the queen is done already. The second Savior, the one coming up tomorrow, the Savior Transformation, the one who sprinkles apples. And why? Look, Adam sinned with Eve, the snake is a cheat, that waas a sin. But Christ climbed up to the heal and then blessed it. [...] And the third Savior is the Nut.[361]

The narrator doesn't distance himself from this understanding of Christianity. He finds himself in a never-ending circle of contentedness, protected against the incursion of history. What more could one wish for? Everything radiates beauty: the peasants work, petty conflicts among the inhabitants are settled with the declaration, "we are all sinners, after all," and "sacred Rus" surrounds us with its icons, candles, banners, the domes of Moscow's cathedrals, and excellent pierogi. This is heaven on earth! Shmelyov's work strikes a careful balance between poignancy and kitsch, bringing to the mind of the Czech reader that romantic work one hundred years

361 Ivan Šmeljov, *Sočiněnija II* (Chudožestvennaja literatura, 1989), 250.

earlier, but one similarly evocative of the bygone world of the author's happy childhood: Božena Němcová's *The Grandmother.*

Boris Zaytsev (1881–1972) was another Parisian exile who inserted into his evocation of "sacred Rus" an interpretation of what exactly he thought "Russian holiness" meant. In the biography *Saint Sergius of Radonezh,* (1925) the medieval monk from Mongolian Muscovy (Scene 5) is constantly confronted with another monk, Francis Assisi, a man close to Sergius and Zaytsev (the theme of liberation through poverty!) but also quite different. Francis was a man of ecstasy, a provocateur of holy willfulness who upset social norms, whereas Sergius in Zaytsev's portrayal is holy precisely because of his ordinariness: he is neither eloquent nor gifted, neither is he obstinate (when his parents forbid his becoming a monk, he obeys) nor does he come into conflict with the church hierarchy. But for all that he teaches simple things like the importance of truth, forthrightness, manliness, work, and faith—nothing more is necessary. For Zaytsev, Sergius of Radonezh demonstrates that Russian holiness need not imply iurodstvo, "Dostoevskianism," delirium, and hysteria. Sergius's is a "saintliness of the North," a saintliness without visions, a moderate saintliness which is restrained, humble, and measured—and thanks to that capable of shaping to culture and values.

To be sure, one can discuss the contrast between Dostoevsky and Zaytsev, between paroxysm versus cool "northern piety." What one cannot do, however, is forget that both instances concerned the romantic projection of "sacred Rus" onto modern art. And that this tension within Orthodox romanticism is itself quintessentially "romantic."

Scene 17

Orthodox Reformism

YEAR:
1882

PLACE:
Yasnaya Polyana

EVENT:
Leo Tolstoy stops confessing and begins preaching

WORKS:
A Confession and *What I Believe* by Leo Tolstoy (1879–1882 and 1884); *Solitaria* and *The Apocalypse of Our Time* by Vasily Rozanov (1913 and 1918); *Anathema* by Alexander Kuprin (1913); *The Pillar and Ground of the Truth* by Pavel Florensky (1914); "Under the Sign of our Time" by Maria Skobtsova (1941); *Self-Knowledge: An Essay in Autobiography* by Nicolas Berdyaev (1949)

Every church undergoes periods of reform, efforts to rectify its religious, ethical, and intellectual condition. Reformers often react to the critical impulses coming from outside. They attempt to understand the relevance of these objections and advocate ways in which the church might learn and change. For the Roman Catholic Church of the eighteenth century, the Catholic Enlightenment represented a reaction to the skeptical and anticlerical Enlightenment. Catholic modernism at the end of the nineteenth century was a reaction to positivism and the overall modernization of European society. The second Vatican council was a reaction to social change following the Second World War.[362]

The Orthodox Church is often seen as static, conservative, carrying over religious forms inherited from Byzantium. The ideal of permanence can be understood as Orthodoxy's greatest asset (as it was understood in an extreme form by Leontyev, the advocate of "Byzantinism," Scene 16) or the cause of its decline (as understood in an equally extreme form by Chaadaev, Scene 14). Upon closer inspection, the history of Orthodoxy is full of attempts to reform. Only, these efforts at reform are usually less conspicuous than their Catholic counterparts. The efforts of Orthodox activists in Lithuanian Rus to improve the catastrophic state of religious scholarship was a first attempt, one motivated by the cultural dominance of Lithuanian Catholicism (Scene 9). A second attempt was made by the Bogoliubtsy, whose activities paradoxically led to a conflict over religious ceremony (Scene 10). A certain impulse to reform was also provided by the modernizing policies of Peter the Great, an effort supported by part of the clergy, though this resulted primarily in the bureaucratization of church structure (Scene 11).

Any parallel to the "big" reforms of Catholicism as direct reactions to the Enlightenment (which, in the end, Peter and Catherine brought to Russia) was long absent. Reactions to enlightenment

---

362 Cf. Claus Arnold, *Kleine Geschichte des Modernismus* (Freiburg in Breisgau: Herder, 2007).

secularization were either restorationist (a return to Byzantine traditions, Scene 15) or romantic (Orthodoxy in the service of anti-modernism, Scene 16). Seraphim of Sarov, Gogol, and Dostoevsky each in his own way pointed away from modernity toward the ideal of permanence. Only toward the close of the nineteenth century does one notice the effort to open the church to modern intellectual trends. This is the meaning of "Orthodox reformism" in the narrow sense of the word. The turn of the twentieth century is often characterized as a "religious renascence." But this is a very broad term expressing the diverse manifestations of educated elites' interest in religion as well as the revival of church structures themselves. "Orthodox reformism" makes up only one current within this broad "religious renaissance," a current that cannot always be separated from its romantic and restorationist counterparts. It is therefore necessary to understand its specificity. In contrast to Orthodox romanticism and restoration, with Orthodox reformism one encounters a consistent, if diversely formulated, demand: the church, yes, but in a different way than before.

The radical prologue to Orthodox reformism and to the whole of the religious renaissance at the turn of the century was the project to modernize Christianity born in the head of Leo Tolstoy (1828–1910). During the second half of the nineteenth century Tolstoy was not only among the most revered writers at home, he was also the best known Russian writer abroad. This status as a global celebrity, however, was also the starting point of Tolstoy's existential crisis. He described this crisis in a work titled *A Confession* (written 1879–1882). Overwhelmed by a sense of human futility, Tolstoy drew from the Old Testament *Ecclesiastes* as well as from themes taken from the life of Buddha, known in old Rus under the cover of the lives of saints Barlaam and Josephat (Scene 4). On the edge of suicide, Tolstoy found salvation by turning away from his own life and looking elsewhere. He perceived that the common people lived in conditions infinitely worse than the wealth and fame he knew, yet they did not commit suicide. They endure because they believe in God. He now looked toward a God in whom earlier he could not believe because the church did not present it in a credible way. Now he found God's existence to be self-evident and obvious, confirmed by an inner-experience which requires no proof. Characteristically, this didn't happen at church, but during a springtime walk through the forest.

Up to this point, Tolstoy's *Confession* might as well be fiction, a typical story told by a romantic Orthodox (or Catholic) convert. But what matters is what arrived together with Tolstoy's newfound faith. Tolstoy initially sought a place for himself in the ecclesiastical order as lived by the simple people:

> Together with this meaning rooted in the faith of the people, there was much that was inextricably bound to the non-sectarian people among whom I lived, which revolted me and which I found incomprehensible: the sacraments, the church services, the fasts, the bowing before relics and icons. The people could not separate one thing from another, and neither could I. However strange I found much of what went on in the people's faith, I accepted all of it, attended services, prayed morning and evening, fasted, received communion, and for the first time my reason did not oppose anything. The very thing I had formerly found impossible now provoked no opposition.[363]

Only, it didn't take long until the writer's intellect rebelled against his faith. Tolstoy then turned to the theological axiom about the church as a community united in reciprocal love, in whose name one must accept the whole of what the community believes. During this phase, Tolstoy employed nearly the same formula used by European and especially Czech Catholic writers—the "community of the living, the dead, and the unborn"[364]:

363 Leo Tolstoy, *A Confession and Other Religious Writings* (New York: Penguin Books, 1987), 67.
364 On the genesis of the concept, see Martin C. Putna, *Česká katolická literatura v kontextech* (Prague: Torst, 2010), 1175.

In fulfilling the church rituals I subdued my reason and submitted myself to a tradition shared by all mankind. I united myself with my ancestor and loved ones, with my father and mother, and grandfather and grandmother. They and all who came before them had believed and lived, and they had brought me into the world. And I joined those millions of the common people, whom I respected.[365]

Tolstoy could not hold out for long in this position. The more he occupied himself with Orthodoxy, the more he became aware of its weaknesses: its fixation on ceremony and a premodern conception of the world; its claim to theological exclusivity, no more capable of demonstration than the identical claim made by other churches. Tolstoy then stepped away from the Orthodox Church completely and set out to theologize on his own. He adopted the method of the reformers, "sola scriptura" and his own (modern) intellect, to read the Gospels for himself. He gradually came to formulate his own understanding of Christianity, which he described in the treatise *What I Believe* (1884). Neither dogma nor ceremony plays any role in this Christianity, which is about ethics and nothing besides—the radical ethics of "nonresistance to evil" (Mt 5:39) and principled separation from the sinful structure of the state and from materialistic society. To follow Christ is to follow the ethic of his Sermon on the Mount, that is all. So that this ethic may be understood correctly, Tolstoy undertook his own translation of the four Gospels, *The Gospel in Brief* (1891–1894).

Several of Tolstoy's enthusiastic followers founded a religious movement they called "Tolstoyism," similar in part to certain European and American Protestant sects and in part resembling Russian rationalist sects (Scene 10). Through the mediation of Tolstoy's personal physician, a Slovak named Dušan Makovický (1866–1921), and Tolstoy's former secretary, Valentin Bulgakov (1886–1966), living in

---

365 Leo Tolstoy, *A Confession*, 69.

Prague in exile, the movement attracted followers and wide popularity in Czech and Slovak culture, influencing for example the thought of the Christian pacifist Přemysl Pitter. It is of no less significance to the history of literature that Tolstoy gave voice to his religious crisis, his discovery of faith, and his idiosyncratic reading of the Gospels in the characters that inhabit his later fiction—the recapitulation of a wasted live in the tale "The Death of Ivan Ilyich" (1886), the conversion of the nobleman Nekhlyudov in the novel *Resurrection* (1899), or the radical journey to humility and solitude of the title character in the posthumous short story, "Father Sergius" (1912).

By this time Tolstoy had clearly ceased to be an "Orthodox modernist" in the strict sense. He was excommunicated from the Orthodox Church and prosecuted with a public ban. In the story "Anathema" from 1913, the writer Alexander Kuprin (1870–1938) describes a deacon whose duty it is to pronounce the ecclesiastical anathema at a church service. One day he finds Tolstoy's name on the list of those to be condemned, someone whose stories had given him such joy and tranquility, and he decides to rebel.[366] Though only fiction, the story shows the contradictory nature of Tolstoy's place in spiritual history. Yes, he was officially excommunicated from Orthodoxy. And yes, his groupings of followers were few and scattered. But his authority as a critic of religious and social conditions remains huge, and as an example of a "secular" intellectual who found faith and discussed theological questions in an effort to revive religion in modern society, Tolstoy continues to inspire many.

The "Tolstoy type" appeared among the Russian elites at the turn of the twentieth century in a multitude of sub-types. All of them shared the opinion that contemporary Orthodox religiosity was inadequate for modern man. Their opinions diverged, however, on the question of how far religious reform should be taken and what

366 An English translation can be found in Alexander Kuprin *The Duel and Selected Stories* (New York: New American Library, 1961)

direction reform should follow. Nicolas Berdyaev (1873–1948), who emerged from these surroundings to become a philosopher known around the world, reflected on the religiously excited atmosphere in his *Self-Knowledge: An Essay in Autobiography* (published posthumously in 1949).

To this atmosphere belonged the Religious-Philosophical Society in Memory of Vladimir Solovyov. Two prominent members of the Society were the "theologians of Sophia," Sergius Bulgakov and Pavel Florensky. To it belonged meetings organized in the "tower," the poet Vyacheslav Ivanov's Petersburg apartment (Scene 14), where the relationship between Christianity and antiquity was discussed, and where somebody came up with the idea to organize a sort of "Dionysian mysterium," an idea which never quite caught on. To it also belonged meetings in another Petersburg apartment, that of Dmitri Merezhkovsky (Scene 15), where participants discussed the relationship between Christianity and the body. A part of it were the number of Russian intellectuals, among themes the "Crimean" Maximilian Voloshin (Scene 1) or the writer Andrei Bely (1880–1934), and the anthroposophy of Rudolf Steiner seeking to enrich Christianity with elements of the occult, Hinduism, and Buddhism. To it belonged the revival of Russian freemasonry (Scene 11). To it belonged shades of neo-paganism, which to its devotees and followers of Nicholas Roerich meant to penetrate the lower layers of Christian culture (Scene 3).

More vividly than anything else, Berdyaev recollected the debates that took place between intellectuals and folk religious dissidents in a Moscow tavern:

> A great number of the many religious factions were present—the "Immortals" (*bessmertniki*), the most interesting of all the sects, Baptists and Evangelicals of all stripes: left Schismatics, Doukhobors, underground Khlysts, Tolstoians. [...] More than anything else, I was struck by the sectarians' informal manner of speech—powerful, colorful, metaphorical.

The intellectual's way of talking is bland and abstract in comparison. [...] There was a mystical tension to it all, a complicated and deeply religious thinking, a passionate search for the truth. [...] The Tolstoians were of little interest. An Orthodox missionary, tasked with uncovering and refuting the arguments of the sectarians, made the most complicated impression. He crossed himself according to the Orthodox custom and was leapt upon by the crowd even when saying something sensible. Of course, I found all this repugnant.[367]

For intellectuals in search of spiritual grounding, official Orthodoxy thus only inspired distrust. Yet the greater part of those who comprised this very passionate and very chaotic religious search—people undergoing the twists and turns of alternative religiosity from Nietzscheanism through anthroposophy and neo-paganism to the search for a "Third Testament" (a key term for the speculations of Merezhkovsky[368])—sooner or later returned to Orthodoxy. Of course, this wasn't the return of "prodigal sons" who, having abandoned all that they had come to think and to know "in the world," now accepted Orthodoxy as handed down from church authorities. It was rather the return of mature thinkers and creators who now brought their intellectual and existential experiences to Orthodoxy.

Vasily Rozanov (1856–1919) serves as an example. In his deliberations, this idiosyncratic and independent thinker freely associated fragments in a fashion reminiscent of the fragmentism of Novalis and German Romantics and, further back, to the history of antiquity and Marcus Aurelius' *Meditations*. For this form, for his furiousness and apocalyptic sentiment, for his restless love of the church, Rozanov reminded Czech Catholicism of the analogical fragmentism of the French-Catholic fury of Léon Bloy (Scene 7),

367 Nikolaj Berďajev, *Vlastní životopis* (Olomouc: Refugium Velehrad-Roma), 241.
368 Cf. Radomír Vlček, *Rusky panslavismus: Realita a fikce* (Prague: Historický ústav AV ČR, 2002); cf. Václav Černý, *Vývoj a zločiny panslavismu* (Prague: Knihovna Václava Havla, 2011).

for which Rozanov was ranked among the major authors of the translation agenda of Josef Florian's Czech Catholic publishing in Stará Říše.[369]

Rozanov was a bitter critic of Orthodoxy in the form that he knew it. He reproaches the church for its lack of interest in the real world and its obsession with ceremony. Among the subjects which Orthodoxy failed most miserably to address were questions of sexuality and the family. Orthodoxy constantly stressed monasticism and celibacy, called "whole mindedness" (tselomudriya) in Church Slavonic, at the expense of increasing fertility and the family size. For that reason, Rozanov admired observant Jews with their sense for combining religion and the family (though he hated Jews insofar as they relate to revolution). The infertility of historical Christianity was blamed on the fact that those in charge of church affairs were themselves sterile and without passion, cold and spiritually dead people. In his literary excitement, Rozanov was even moved to issue the intentionally shocking "blasphemy" that even "Christ planted no tree, he didn't even cultivate a plot of grass; he is completely lacking in 'worldly vitality'; he is neither *seed* nor *egg* [...] Christ is, in essence, a non-being—little more than a mere phantasm or a shadow which, by way of some miracle, was briefly cast upon this earth."[370]

One finds in *Solitaria, The Apocalypse of Our Time* and other collections of Rozanov's fragments beside exclamations about the church's failures other exclamations about how the church is the natural mediator for family life and the nation, as well as regret about the things he had earlier written about the church:

Regarding the goodness of our clergy: oh, how I have sullied them already! *Those who have known me* [...], though they "repudiated my ideas" and

369   Cf. Libuše Heczková, "Rozanov a ti druzí: Rozhovor s Andrejem Stankovičem," *Volné sdružení českých rusistů* 8 (1992): 65–67.
370   Vasilij Rozanov, *Apokalypsa naší doby* (Prague: Torst, 1996), 109.

fought against them verbally and in print, *they have always liked me.* So I turned to the Church (at the end of 1911), to that alone which *warms the earth,* to the *last warmth* of this world... [...] A person who *believes* is greater than any philosopher, any poet, greater than the victor or the tribune. "He who prays" will rise victorious above all, the Saints will prevail over the world. I am going to the Church! I am going! I am going![371]

The Bolshevik seizure of power only strengthened Rozanov in his apocalyptic temperament. It led him to consider the failure of the Orthodox Church in the life of the nation: just look at how quickly the masses turned away from it (Scene 17)! At the same time, the Bolshevik grab for power and the church's disintegration led him to identify himself more closely with church institutions: Rozanov spent the remainder of his life in the center of Russian Orthodoxy, in the Trinity Lavra of St. Sergius. It was here that he received the sacraments from Pavel Florensky and it was here that he was buried.

Even in this last phase, Rozanov remained an ecclesiastical "amateur." Other representatives of the "religious revival" went further: they entered the church structures to act directly toward Orthodoxy's revival from within. These are however "Orthodox modernists" in the narrowest sense of the word, the identical twins of the Catholic modernists in western and central Europe. In distinction to their western twins, however, the Orthodox modernists were to a surprising extent successful in their efforts.

Two intellectuals who exerted the strongest influence in this process had received a secular education first, and only then (a thing most unusual in Russia!) studied theology to receive the priesthood. These two intellectuals together founded the Religious-Philosophical Society in Memory of Vladimir Solovyov, and Solovyov's concepts of "Sophia," "Godmanhood," and "sobornost" play key roles in their thought. These are the two intellectuals who Mikhail Nesterov

---

371   Ibid., 83–84.

(1862–1942) depicted on a double portrait in 1917. In the picture, Florensky wears the priest's robe. Bulgakov would acquire his one year later.

Pavel Florensky (1882–1937) was a mathematician and physicist by training. In contrast to Rozanov's fragments, Florensky attempted to summarize his theological thought into a "summa," *The Pillar and Ground of the Truth* (1914). The "summa" declares its goal to be nothing other than to justify the Orthodox conception of ecclesiality, the truth, and the world. While providing this justification, however, the work moves quite freely and "non-academically" between genres. It sometimes engages with the classical theological method, i.e. comparisons of biblical and patristic authorities. Sometimes, however, the author adopts the methods of formal logic (here one notices the author's secular education!) and sometimes he switches over to lyrical descriptions of mystical experiences in autumnal nature.

At the same time, the author's main definitions are lyrical and mystical rather than conceptually precise. What is the being or principle Sophia which according to Solovyov's teaching represents the form of God's manifestation leading man to a higher spiritual synthesis, to "Godmanhood"? Sophia is ecclesia, Sophia is beauty, "Sophia is creation, Sophia is consciousness, Sophia is humanity." [372] And what is "ecclesiality," that quality which connects man to the church, to truth, and to God?

> Ecclesiality is the name we give that haven that calms the heart, the place where the demands of reason are humbled and thinking gives way to a great serenity. [...] I repeat: the impossibility of defining Orthodox ecclesiality is the best possible evidence of its vitality. [...] The *concept* of ecclesiality does not exist; ecclesiality itself exists. For every member

---

[372] Cf. Pavel Florenskij, *Sloup a opora pravdy* (Velehrad and Olomouc: Refugium, 2003), 304.

of the Church, ecclesiastical life is the most concrete, most tangible thing he knows.[373]

These references to "indefinability" and "inconceivability" do not mean that Florensky is unable to be precise when he wants to—just look at his excursuses into logic. What they mean is that Florensky seeks to establish a new style of Orthodox theologizing, a new style as different from the scholastic dryness of Catholicism as from the earlier and no less dry paraphrasing of patristic authorities so common among the "scholasticism" of Orthodoxy. It difference was to consist in a certain "pliability" of style, although at the same time in a much higher level of cultivation, greater literary and scholarly value than the usual restorationist literature of spiritual guidance. The text of *The Pillar and Ground of the Truth* did not become the "summa" of a new theology.[374] Instead, it became a model of a new approach, that "soft" Orthodox style of writing which reinterprets the old theologoumena (the dogmata, the sacraments, the liturgy) in a new, philosophizing, and lyrical manner.[375]

An example of this enormously influential reworking of an "old" subject is Florensky's book *Iconostasis* (1922, published posthumously in exile in 1972). Florensky offers in it a complex and even interdisciplinary interpretation of Orthodox reverence for icons. The icon he describes as the boundary between the visible and invisible worlds. It is a means toward suprasensory recognition, a mystical experience for the one who paints the icon as well as for the one who looks at it. The "premodern" technique, its lack of shadow, shading,

---

373   Ibid., 28–30.
374   Cf. Hanuš Nykl, "Záhadný artefakt stříbrného věku (Sloup a opora pravdy Pavla Florenského)," in *Kulturní, duchovní a etnické kořeny Ruska: Vlivy a souvislosti,* ed. Hanuš Nykl (Červený Kostelec: Pavel Mervart, 2006), 189–212.
375   Cf. Zdeněk Neubauer, "O tvrdém a měkkém stylu ve filosofii," in *Smysl a svět* (Prague: Nadace Vize 97, 2001), 41–82.

and hue, its clear and unbroken fields of color, all of this represents a spiritual "metaphysics of light."

The second man of the pair, an economist by training, was Sergius Bulgakov (1871–1944), who in a similar fashion devoted his life to the teaching of Sophia. Bulgakov gradually built an entire system of Orthodox dogmata around the theme. He composed his first sophiological book, *Unfading Light,* still under the name of Sergei Bulgakov, independent philosopher. It appeared in 1917, a year before the author was ordained a priest to become Father Sergius. Bulgakov did not form the "mature" sophiological system, however, until his exile in Paris where he held the position of professor of dogmatics and dean of the Russian Orthodox theological institute. The system consists of a "little trilogy" (*The Burning Bush*—Mariology, *The Friend of the Bridegroom*—instruction about John the Baptist and *Jacob's Ladder*—angelology) and a "big trilogy" (*The Lamb of God*—Christology, *The Comforter*—pneumatology, and *Bride of the Lamb*—ecclesiology). Alongside the two trilogies must also be included the study of iconology, *Icons and the Name of God,* the polemic with the papacy, *Peter and John,* an attempt at a "theological linguistics," *Philosophy of the Name,* and several other texts. In all the subjects, the crux of interpretation is to explain how the principle of Sophia brings together the divine with the human, the high with the low. This principle plays its greatest role in Christology and Maryology because Christ and the Mother of God are the primary forms in which Sophia is made manifest. At the same time, Sophia appears just about everywhere in just about everything. "The Divine Ousia, like Sophia, is precisely the All-unity that is the life of God and that lives in God by the whole of Divine reality […] Likewise, God is Sophia; Sophia is Divine. She is God in His self-revelation, *Deus revelatus.*"[376]

376 Sergius Bulgakov, *The Lamb of God* (Grand Rapids, Mich.: William. B. Eerdmans, 2008), 102.

But where did Sophia, this great dame of Florensky and Bulgakov's philosophical ideology, come from? Both men adopted her from Vladimir Solovyov, who wrote about Sophia as a personal mystical experience through which were sublimated feelings of Platonic love toward specific women.[377] From Solovyov the trail leads back to an older cultural history, above all to Novalis who in just this way identified his beloved Sophie von Kühn with the divine Sophia. Going even further back, the trail leads to the sixteenth-century German mystic Jakob Böhm and from him still further back to the Jewish Kabbalah and then to "more Orthodox" sources. In the Bible, namely, Sophia appears in Old Testament texts about divine wisdom (chokhma) and glory (shekhina). Attempts have been made to provide a precise "genealogy of Sophia," tracing the development of Sophia from the Scripture through Kabbalah up to Solovyov.[378] There also exist "supraconfessional" compendiums of sophiological thinking setting Russian Sophialogy into its broader context.[379] Then there is the dispute as to whether or not Bulgakov's understanding of Sophia is truly compatible with the dogmata of traditional Orthodoxy, a dispute in which Bulgakov is labeled a heretic by representatives of conservative Orthodoxy.[380] Of greatest importance for cultural history is the fact alone that modernist Orthodox theologians worked with this sort of "supraconfessional" theologoumena; Sophia, as a "pliable" theologoumenon, made possible an new imaginative and poetic way of theologizing.

---

377   Cf. Karel Sládek, *Vladimír Solovjov: Mystik a prorok* (Olomouc: Refugium Velehrad-Roma, 2009).
378   Cf. Gennidi Eykalovich, "Rodoslovnaya Sofii," *Novyi zhurnal* 164 (1986): 196–229 and *Novyi zhurnal* 165 (1986): 307–335.
379   Cf. Thomas Schipflinger, *Sophia—Maria: Eine ganzheitliche Vision der Schöpfung* (München and Zürich: Verlag Neue Stadt, 1988)
380   See Bulgakov's defense in the "white book" Sergius Bulgakov, *O Sofii, Predmudrosti Bozhie* (Paris: YMCA Press, 1935); cf. Martin C. Putna, "Sofia, Sofie, (my všichni) sofiologové," in *My poslední křesťané* (Prague: Torst, 1999), 219–256.

Florensky and Bulgakov together represent the peak of Orthodox reformism at the turn of the twentieth century. Both, however, belonged to a much wider movement striving for the inner rejuvenation and modernization of the Orthodox Church. During the last phase of the tsarist regime, the church was made present to the public through such odious figures as the Ober-Procurator of the Most Holy Synot Konstantin Pobedonostsev (1827–1907) and the cunning "miracle worker" Grigori Rasputin (1869–1916). The latter famously manipulated bishops as his puppets and enjoyed the unconditional support of the last tsar Nicholas II and the tsarina Alexandra Fyodorovna. Several enlightened members of the clergy, for example the Petersburg metropolitan Anthony Vadkovsky (1846–1912), nonetheless strove to reconcile the church and modern society. Social developments also testify to the need for modernization of the church. The 1905 revolution was unsuccessful, nevertheless it introduced an easing of social and cultural restraints in Russian society, including a law guaranteeing religious freedom. For Russian Orthodoxy this meant the abolition of its monopoly on public religious practice; for Old Believers and other religious dissidents it meant legalization. By point of fact it introduced freedom for all.

All the currents pushing for inner-ecclesiastical reform demanded the same: Council! Council! They argued for the necessity of summoning an all-Russian synod—the first since 1666!—to scrutinize the direction in which the church was headed in the modern age. Committees were summoned to prepare for the meeting, but prime minister Stolypin put an end to the proceedings in 1907.[381] The synod was not to meet until after the tsar's overthrow in the spring of 1917. As a first step toward inner consolidation, the church selected a patriarch, the first since Peter the Great's abolition of the patriarchate

---

381 Cf. James W. Cunningham, *A Vanguished Hope: The Movement for Church Renewal in Russia, 1905–1906* (Crestwood, NY.: St. Vladimir's Seminary Press, 1981).

in 1721. Patriarch Tichon was chosen from the three candidates on November 5, 1917—two days before the Bolshevik seizure of power.

The history of Orthodox reformism doesn't end with the Bolshevik seizure of power. The modernizing movement did, however, stand before a fork-in-the-road, a choice to be confronted by reformism and the entire church: a choice between staying at home and leaving for exile. For those who chose to stay at home, a second choice had to be made between open opposite to the new regime, along with all the consequences that entailed, and reaching some sort of agreement that might make possible the further modernization of the church (the latter option did not seem so futile at the beginning, Scene 18).

It only took a few years before it became clear that the second choice was an illusion – and the first choice was in fact the option between life in exile or death at home. Fortunately for the culture of Orthodoxy, the regime preferred at first to force inconvenient intellectuals into exile; only later would they make the decision to liquidate them systematically. Pavel Florensky and countless others would perish in the Gulag, specifically on the Solovetsky Islands. An extraordinary variety of theologians, on the other hand, would gather in exile, in "Russia beyond Russia."

In Paris they assembled at the St. Sergius Orthodox Theological Institute located on the rue Crimen. Priests received training at the institute for service in all the lands of the Russian diaspora. It also offered space for many religious thinkers who found themselves in exile. The first academic year at the institute began already in the fall of 1926. The level of instruction there surpassed that of similar schools in tsarist Russia, for here the task was not to produce dog-matically flawless bishops but to encourage the development of true theological thinking. The institute became the first Orthodox school not to shun scientific methods and to question credulous legends and pious forgeries so abundant in premodern religiosity.

Possibly thanks to this fact, Sergius Bulgakov long served as the institute's director. Bulgakov gathered around himself other professors who were at one religious thinkers and scientists of European standards – and who for the most part, like Bulgakov, came from leftist or liberal backgrounds and only later turned to religion. The books they wrote there represent some of the most basic works of Russian spiritual history's various disciplines. George Fedotov was the first to apply culturalogical methods to the study of the Russian sainthood and later to the entire "history of the Russian religious spirit" (Scene 3). Vasily Zenkovsky (1881–1962) produced the first synthetic monograph on the disputes surrounding Orthodox ceremony (Scene 10) and the history of Russian religious thinking. Boris Vyshevlavtsev (1877–1954) created a complex Orthodox anthropology, integrating modern streams of Jungian deep psychology in his work *The Ethics of Transfigured Eros* (1931). Konstantin Mochulsky interpreted personalities and works of classic Russian literature from a religious perspective (Scene 16).[382]

This wide variety of activity was supplemented by religious personalities active beyond the institute itself. Foremost among them was Nicolas Berdyaev, too independent a thinker to join a religious institute, but he did cooperate with French Catholic intellectuals, especially those around Jacques Maritain. Thanks not only to Maritain's recommendation, Berdyaev became the most important Russian thinker in interwar Europe. It was through Berdyaev's books that the West came to know philosophical interpretations of Dostoevsky, Russian Slavophilism, and the Russian Revolution. Another independent personality was Maria Skobtsova, known simply as "Mother Maria" (1891–1945), a poet and former left-wing activist who entered a religious order while in exile, but who soon decided that this old religious form need be changed in light of the new age. Following the example of Catholic Action, Skobtsova founded Orthodox Action and helped the poor and Jews during the war – actions

---

[382] For a collection of portraits of these thinkers see Nikolai Poltoratsky (ed.), *Russkaya religiozno-filosofskaya mysl XX veka* (University of Pittsburgh, Slavic Series no. 2, 1975)

which landed her in a concentration camp by the war's end. After her remained a reputation of saintliness, collections of rather apocalyptic poetry poems, and considerations about how the current crisis of Christianity might help it return to its roots:

> Our godless—not just unchristian—epoch, our materialistic and nihilistic age is, when seen from a certain perspective, also a deeply Christian age. It is an age tasked with revealing and upholding in the world a Christian secret, the secret of the Apocalypse. Evidence for this is not to be found in the development of some new Christian teaching or the advancement of the ecumenical movement or the successes of missionary work. Proof, rather, is in the substance of the epoch itself, its trajectory toward decline, its bareness. […] An epoch when mankind is standing at the base of the cross, an epoch when mankind sighs from his suffering, when the image of God is demeaned in every human soul, is beaten, spit upon, and crucified—is that not a deeply Christian age?[383]

Skobtsova's essay, "Under the Sign of Our Time," was written in 1941, a year when her apocalyptic tone well suited the situation–and not just the situation of the Russian community in Paris. It is now clear that the new global Christian era that she had envisioned did not take place. However, the theological and philosophical production of the Russian intellectuals in Paris, precisely at that "apocalyptic" moment in exile, comprises the most enduring contribution of Russian Orthodoxy to the modern world. For everything that comes to mind when many Europeans in search of spiritual alternatives think of Orthodoxy—the theology of icons, reflections on the liturgy, "soborny" (collective) ecclesiology, the "anthropology of the heart"; all that which from the romanticizing point of view is held to be the enduring spiritual core of Orthodoxy; the artifacts of Medieval

---

383 Matka Marie, "Ve znamení zániku," in *U řek babylonských: Antologie ruské emigrační poezie,* Martin C. Putna and Miluše Zadražilová (eds.) (Prague: Torst, 1995), 303–304.

Orthodox culture in the fine arts and in literature which receive such admiration today; the popularized philo-Orthodoxy which is intentionally atemporalized, idealized, and styled as "the Russian idea"[384]—all of this was the offspring of Orthodox reformism at the turn of the century, a movement which reached its peak at St. Sergius's Institute in Paris. In exile—and in freedom. In an atmosphere of freedom unknown in Russia itself.[385]

384 Cf. the title and idealized, celebratory presentation in the book of Tomáš Špidlík, *Ruská idea: Jiný pohled na člověka* (Velehrad: Refugium Velehrad-Roma, 1996).
385 Cf. Ivana Noble et al., *The Ways of Orthodox Theology in the West* (Crestwood, NY: St. Vladimir's Seminary Press, 2015).

Revolutionary Rus and the Piety of the Godless

1881

Saint Petersburg

Terrorists from the organization Narodnaya Volya
assassinate Tsar Alexander II

My Past and Thoughts by Alexander Herzen (1852–1870);
Demons by Fyodor Dostoevsky (1871–1872); *Vekhi*
by Sergius Bulgakov and others (1909); *The Twelve*
by Alexander Blok (1918)

Among nineteenth-century Russian tsars, only one had the courage to initiate liberalizing reforms, including the abolition of serfdom: Alexander II (ruled 1855–1881). And among nineteenth-century Russian tsars, only one died by assassination: unfortunately, also Alexander II. After several of unsuccessful attempts, in 1881 the organization Narodnaya Volya (The People's Will) tossed a bomb in Saint Petersburg and hit their target. The assassination brought an end to reforms, a wave of pogroms (though there were no Jews in the group of attackers), and established an enduring association in the mind of the Russian public between the concepts of revolution and terrorism. A work of art was commissioned on the site of the attack to commemorate the assassination, the cathedral Tserkov Spasa na Krovi (Savior on the Spilled Blood) on the banks of the Petersburg canals. The cathedral certainly counts among St. Petersburg's less becoming structures; the pompous variation on Moscow's Saint Basil's Cathedral sticks out like a sore thumb among the classicist surroundings of St. Petersburg. It is as if Moscow wanted to "subdue" its too European rival.

An entirely different artistic work began to be published ten years earlier, one inspired by a different murder: that of a member of a similar revolutionary-terrorist group. The murder took time, the fame of Dostoevsky's *Demons* (1871–1872) endures, and attempts to match it with other artistic productions (such as the filmed version by Andrzej Wajda from 1985) do not end.

Dostoevsky portrayed Russian revolutionaries and leftists as a gang of psychopaths, malcontents, criminals, and suicidal maniacs who want to destroy the world's traditional order but who, for the time being, are able only to destroy themselves and their closest surroundings. Pyotr Verkhovensky is an inexhaustible organizer of intrigues and crimes. Stavrogin is the group's ideological leader, considered by the others a Messiah proclaiming the new religion of nihilism—but Stavrogin himself seems unmoved. Shigalyev is a pitiful cripple who develops a scheme to organize the world on the principle of absolute freedom, a freedom to be attained through absolute terror. It is likely that *The Protocols of the Elders of Zion* drew inspiration from this anti-utopia (Scene 13). Kirillov is delirious, wishing to kill himself so he can prove that God does not exist and, therefore, all is permitted:

> But I will proclaim self-will, it is my duty to believe that I do not believe. I will begin and end and open the door. And save. [...] The attribute of my divinity is—Self-will! That is all by which I can show in the main point my new fearsome freedom. [...] It is I who will necessarily kill myself in order to begin and prove it.[386]

The working-class member of this terrible band of "liberators of mankind" is Shatov, who in the end tries to break away from the group. At the very moment when he would like to begin his new life, however, he is murdered by his companions—Stavrogin and Verkhovensky maintain that communal murder is the best means of binding the collective.

Perhaps even more bitter than this depiction of a communal murder is Dostoevsky's portrait of the old gentleman Stepan Verkhovensky, a cultivated liberal of European stature, a "leftist intellectual" with "good intentions" who over coffee chatters on (half in French) about revolution—then he wonders as his more activist progeny take his words literally. Stepan Verkhovensky is in a sense the most culpable of the party, for he sets the young "demons" on their path of evil. At the same time, it is Verkhovensky alone whom the author affords a moving portrayal *in articulo mortis*. For it is Verkhovensky who calls the demons by name and requests that the Gospel According to Luke be read upon his deathbed. It is the passage about devils driven from the possessed into a herd of pigs (L 8:32–37). He interprets the passage as a prophecy about Russia:

---

386 Fyodor Dostoevsky, *Demons* (New York: Vintage Books, 1995), 619.

It's all the sores, all the miasmas, all the uncleanness, all the big and little demons accumulated in our great and dear sick man, in our Russia, for centuries, for centuries! [...] We will rush, insane and raging, from the cliff down into the sea, and all be drowned, and good riddance to us, because that's the most we're in it for. But the sick man will be healed and "sit at the feet of Jesus".[387]

Dostoevsky was understood for a century to come as more than just a Russian writer—he was considered to be a religious thinker and prophet. Insofar as we take this "prophetic discourse" seriously, Dostoevsky was indeed a prophet when warning about the destructive side revolutionary fervor. Following the Bolshevik seizure of power, Russia and its surrounding territories were transformed into a hell that neither Dostoevsky nor any of his contemporaries could have imagined. The writer showed himself to be a poor prophet, however, when he declared that Russia would eventually turn to pure Christianity and thereby regain its full health. This poor prophecy was doomed from the very start since it resulted from a poor analysis. Dostoevsky committed a grave error when he opposed "Christianity as Russian" to "revolution as un-Russian."

First, revolutionary fervor and criticism of the tsar and the servile Orthodox Church belong inseparably to the spiritual history of Russia. Dostoevsky's bitter caricature of the revolutionary demons and their naive, westernizing progenitor effaced what had always been the stick wielded by the state against critics of Russia, of its brutish conditions, its autocracy, its claim to "choseness," and its proud ignorance—the idea of Moscow as the Third Rome. This critical tradition goes back as far as the Russian Middle Ages with the dispute between Prince Kurbsky and Ivan the Terrible. Surely, nobody can consider Kurbsky an "agent of the West" (Scene 6 and 9). From Kurbsky the line leads to Radishchev, Novikov, and other

387   Ibid., 655.

enlightened critics of serfdom and censorship under Catherine the Great (Scene 11), then further on to Ryleev (Scene 12) and the Decembrists. Pushkin should be included, for he too was disgusted by the omnipotence of a dull tsarist machinery and he expected nothing positive to come from the Orthodox Church. This Pushkin was celebrated by Dostoevsky in his ecstatic "Pushkin Speech" (1880) as the representative of an all-embracing Russian national character. According to Dostoevsky, Pushkin showed that:

> to be a true Russian does indeed mean to aspire finally to reconcile the contradictions of Europe, to find resolution of European yearning in our pan-human and all-uniting Russian soul, to include within our soul by brotherly love all our brethren. At last it may be that Russia pronounces the final Word of the great general harmony, of the final brotherly communion of all nations in accordance with the law of the gospel of Christ![388]

This line leads to the "young Dostoevsky," the Dostoevsky who received a death sentence for attending a reading circle. The rage felt by the "demons" in *Demons* is also the rage felt by "old Dostoevsky" toward the "young Dostoevsky." Rarely in literature does rage as depicted by an author equal the seething fury that the author holds toward an image in which he no longer wishes to recognize himself. And further on, the line leads to the journalist Alexander Herzen (1812–1870), who from his refuge in Paris, London, and Geneva perceptively analyzed Russian social relations at a time when free discussion was nearly impossible at home. In his memoirs *My Past and Thoughts* (1852–1870), Herzen portrays himself as a social liberal who had parted ways with religiosity as understood by the church; who bitterly derides the Orthodox Church for assisting in state repression; who also scoffs at popular religious pilgrimages,

---

[388] Fyodor Dostoyevsky, *The Diary of a Writer* (New York: C. Scribner's Sons, 1949), 250.

the veneration of relics, and the "inviolable" rules of fasting; who can no longer stand the illusory promises of Slavophilism; a man who, for all that, nevertheless admits that "at all ages and under various circumstances I have gone back to reading the Gospel, and every time its words have brought peace and meekness to my soul."[389]

This line leads to other liberals and "Westernizers" such as the young Leo Tolstoy (Scene 17), Goncharov (Scene 2) and Turgenev (Scene 16) who inserted social criticism into their literature, insofar as that was possible, and would have liked to lead Russia gradually down the standard European path, had they only been given the chance to do so. There remained only three-quarters of a year following the dethronement of Tsar Nicholas II in 1917, and that was in the middle of the World War. Who can blame them for not having accomplished more?

And yes, one branch of the same line leads to the radical leftists, to the "revolutionary democrats" of Vissarion Belinsky's generation (Scene 16): the Narodniks, Narododovoltsy, terrorists, Marxists, SRs (Social Revolutionaries), Mensheviks (moderate Social Democrats), and finally to the Bolsheviks. To them who overthrew the fragile liberal government in November 1917 and made the country into a hell much worse than the tsarist regime. Only, to insist that this line of succession was necessary and unavoidable, that Herzen, Radishchev, or even Prince Kurbsky prepared the way for Bolshevism—that would be like insisting that Jesus Christ paved the way for the reign of Dostoevsky's Grand Inquisitor.[390]

Secondly, the relationship between the Russian Revolution and Russian Christianity is neither so simple nor as straightforwardly antagonistic as Dostoevsky and similarly minded Orthodox romantics and restorationists would have it. On the contrary, the history

389 Alexander Herzen, *My Past and Thoughts: The Memoirs of Alexander Herzen* (Berkeley: The University of California Press, 1982).

390 Cf. Jiří Hanuš and Radomír Vlček (eds.), *Interpreting the Russian Revolution* (Brno: CDK, 2008).

is full of overlaps and interconnections often forgotten in the shadow of the great Bolshevik persecution, connections of which Dostoevsky's contemporaries were fully aware. It is no exaggeration to claim that the Russian Revolution was in fact a product of Russian Christianity.

There existed, for example, the tradition of maintaining contacts between the Russian Left and Old Believers or other religious dissidents. As part of their "going to the people" campaign, the Narodniks went first to the non-Orthodox community. These people were often better educated than the common Orthodox peasantry and they could read the Bible; they were often at odds with the state and the official church, which made them more susceptible to conversion—from faith in the Kingdom of God to faith in the Revolution. Though neither the Old Believers nor other "sectarians" gave mass support to the revolution, in the early years of Bolshevik rule there were still attempts to use them in this way. Efforts to this end were made especially by Vladimir Bonch-Bruyevich (1873–1955), a close collaborator of Lenin who concentrated on the Dukhobors, sometimes living among them himself.[391]

There were also attempts to combine Christianity and socialism in church surroundings. More than anything else, these represented so many reactions to the social crisis facing Russia at the turn of the century. At the same time, they also drew from the venerable tradition of reading the Gospel in a socially critical spirit. Consider the parable about the wealthy young man leading to the parable about the "camel through the eye of a needle" (Mt 19:16–26), or the one about the rich man and Lazarus (L 16:19–31), or any number of other assertions opposed to wealth and property. This sort of reading is strongly present in the patristic literature, especially with John Chrysostom, who was known and read in Kievan Rus (Scene 4).

---

391 Cf. Alexander Etkind, *Internal Colonization: Russia's Imperial Experience* (Cambridge, UK: Polity Press, 2012), 194–213.

Social themes in older Russian sermons also drew authority from the Bible and patristic literature. In the West, Catholic reformism and liberal Protestantism gave rise to strong currents of the Christian Left: intellectual and artistic, theoretical-utopian and practical-political, moderate and radical. Personalities such as Félicité de Lamennais, Charles Péguy, or Dorothy Day and a wide spectrum of associations, organizations, and parties belonged to these currents. In Russia, too, there developed Christian unions and associations—efforts to "socialize" Christianity or "baptize" socialism. All these undertakings were brief and chaotic. They nevertheless lent expression to the deeply held belief that the church would not accomplish its mission so long as it continued to defend the existing social order and did not intervene decisively on behalf of the oppressed.

This sentiment found expression in a poem by Alexander Blok (Scene 20), "The Twelve" (1918), which describes the journey of twelve revolutionaries through a Russia submerged in chaos. One finds hardly a reference to religion in the poem itself, though the number "twelve" in the title should signal to the reader of the Bible that something more is hidden here. Then at the end of the poem, this "something more" suddenly shows itself:

Forward as a haughty host they tread.
A starved mongrel shambles in the rear.
Bearing high the banner, bloody red,
That He holds in hands no bullets sear—
Hidden as the flaying snow veils veer,
Lightly walking on the wind, as though
He Himself were diamonded snow,
With mist-white roses garlanded:
Jesus Christ is marching at their head.[392]

392 Vyacheslav Zavalishin, *Early Soviet Writers* (New York: Frederick A. Praeger Publishers, 1958), 8.

The understanding of revolutionary faith as a new secular religion marks another aspect of the ambivalent relationship between Christianity and revolution. In this analogy, the bearer of revolution, European-educated and leftist "intelligentsia," comprise a secular monastic order.[393]

This quasi-religious understanding of revolution and the intelligentsia was described in a sharply critical spirit by Nikolai Berdyaev, Sergius Bulgakov, and other contributors to the 1909 volume of *Vekhi* ("milestones" or "signposts," though the title is usually left untranslated). Berdyaev in his contribution distinguished between the truth of philosophy and the pseudo-truth of intelligence—the lofty Church Slavonic *istina* was used to designate the former and the more civil *truth* to designate the latter. He reproached the intelligentsia, stating that "this falsely directed love of man, it turned out, destroyed the love of God."[394] Similarly, Bulgakov in his piece contrasted Christian selflessness (using the old ecclesiastical term *podvizhnichestvo*) with the "heroism" of the intellect, the latter a mere imitation of Christian selflessness. Form, pathos, asceticism, suffering—all of these things might be similar, but their meanings are quite different since the latter places man-the-hero in the position of the Messiah: "The hero puts himself in the role of Providence, and by this spiritual usurpation he assigns himself a responsibility greater than he can bear and tasks that are beyond the reach of men."[395] Semyon Frank (1877–1950) analyzed this same "nihilistic moralism," describing the "classic member of the Russian intelligentsia" as "a militant monk professing the nihilistic religion of earthly well-being."[396]

393   Cf. Richard Pipes, "The Intelligentsia Versus the State," in *Russia under the Old Regime* (New York: Penguin Books, 1995), 249–280.
394   Marshall S. Shatz and Judith E. Zimmerman (eds.), *Vekhi: Landmarks* (London and New York: Routledge, 1994), 6.
395   Ibid., 34.
396   Ibid.,151.

Berdyaev, Bulgakov, Frank, and others knew well of what they spoke; they themselves had formerly been Marxists. The *Vekhi* collection represents a collection of repentance. As Tolstoy and other Russian penitents before them, they also shifted quickly from the mode of confession to that of sermon. In many respects, their analysis is apposite. The Bolshevik takeover confirmed their worst fears about the further development of Russian left-wing intellect. That is why they convened in 1918 for a new collection called *Iz glubiny* ("from the depths"), a volume in which they reflected on the recent catastrophe and their new fears. After a few years most of them met once again, this time aboard the "philosophy steamer," a ship used by the governing leftist intelligentsia to expel oppositional intellectuals to the West. In doing so, they spared their lives, lives which would thenceforth be dedicated to further analyses.[397]

These analyses left out one important "detail," however. It was a fact which led ever more Russian youth down the "road of the intelligentsia" to revolution and Bolshevism: the intransigence of the tsarist regime, its refusal to reform, and the unwillingness of the official Orthodox Church to address the social question. It was this intransigence that Vasily Rozanov (Scene 17) expressed not through analysis but by aphorism:

In what does *the secret* of this judgment over the Church consist, whence this *wrath and rage,* this wild clamor of Apocalypse. [...] We find ourselves at once in our own era—the impotence of Christianity, its inability to give human life, this "earthly life" its due order. [...] Everyone has suddenly forgotten about Christianity because *it is no longer there to help them.* It has saved them neither from war nor from hunger. It sings and just sings.[398]

397   Cf. Lesley Chamberlain, *Lenin's Private War: The Voyage of the Philosophy Steamer and the Exile of the Intelligentsia* (New York: St. Martin's Press, 2007).
398   Vasilij Rozanov, *Apokalypsa naší doby* (Prague: Torst, 1996), 107.

For the religious, the Bolshevik seizure of power evoked mostly feelings of dread and expectations of the apocalypse. There nevertheless were some among the Orthodox reformers who had earlier considered the possibility of merging Christianity and socialism. Now they hoped that the new regime, once it "settled down", would give the church a chance at inner revival. There thus arose an organization in 1922 calling itself the Living Church. The Living Church is usually evaluated negatively in church history, often described as an association of Bolshevik collaborators whose goal was to undermine the authority of Patriarch Tikhon and the legitimate church structure (Scene 19). At its beginning, however, the core of the Living Church consisted of people who hailed from reformist circles and felt themselves to be undertaking a difficult but potentially successful "narrow road" between opposition and collaboration.

What a cruel mistake this in fact was would soon become apparent. Bolshevism showed itself not to be straightforwardly "demonic" and anti-clerical, it transformed itself into an ambivalent secular religion by adopting the form of Orthodox religious culture: the five-point star and/or the hammer and sickle as the cross; the Bolshevik party as the church; all-party congresses as synods; fallen revolutionaries as martyrs and their portraits as icons; the May Day parades and other processions; the "success of the Soviet leaders" as the miracles of Russian saints; the vision of Communism as a the coming of the Kingdom of God; all sorts of "leftist" and "rightist" deviations within the party as so many "heresies" and "sects" within the church; and, as a "sancta sanctorum," as the grave of God, the eternal seat of the eternally living Messiah—the remains of Lenin in the wall of the Kremlin.[399]

These "anti-Christian" imitations of Christian forms have already received sufficient attention from the political scientists and

---

[399] Cf. Alexandr Pančenko, "Osmý div světa," in *Metamorfózy ruské kultury* (Červený Kostelec: Pavel Mervart, 2012), 319–338.

cultural analysts; they have been condemned in literature and made the objects of postmodern irony (see Conclusion).[400] For the image of Russia in world culture, they became as notorious in the twentieth century as the work of Dostoevsky. Of course, the fact that this new secular religion and its symbols became so deeply rooted in in Russian culture only testifies to the deep rootedness of the Christian symbols that came before them.

---

400   Cf. Mikhail Epshtein, *Vera i obraz: Religioznoe bessoznatelnoe v russkoi kulture 20-go veka* (Tenafly, NJ: Ermitazh Publishers, 1994); Cf. Boris Groys, *Gesamtkunstwerk Stalin: Rozpolcená kultura v Sovětském svazu* (Prague: AVU, 2010)

Soviet Rus and the Renewal of the Orthodox Trinity

YEAR:
1972

PLACE:
Moscow

EVENT:
Solzhenitsyn calls for the Patriarch of Moscow
to repent

WORKS:
The End of Our Time by Nicolas Berdyaev (1924);
The Inextinguishable Lamp by Boris Shiryaev (1954);
The Gulag Archipelago and "Repentance and
Self-Limitation as Categories of National Life"
by Alexandr Solzhenitsyn (1973 and 1974); *The Place
of the Skull* by Chingiz Aitmatov (1986); "Why Don't
We Do It in the Road" by Volodymyr Dibrova (1991);
"Russophobia" by Igor Shafarevich (1981–1989)

The spiritual history of the Soviet era may be summarized in a single sentence: Communism persecuted Christianity, and Christianity tried to survive. All the books devoted to the history of the church in twentieth-century Russia—academic and essayistic, Russian and non-Russian—are but explications of this sentence. They back it up with numerous facts; descriptions of Bolshevik campaigns of church oppression;[401] lists of tortured, or "merely" imprisoned, clergy and Christian activists;[402] biographies of the important figures of church resistance against the regime, beginning with Patriarch Tikhon and the theologian Pavel Florensky;[403] survivor testimonies; analyses of official anti-religious propaganda; visual evidence of church cupolas having been demolished or of churches transformed into "museums of atheism"; and so on and so forth.

Such evidence is brutal and emotionally forceful. It gives rise to feelings of deep and sincere respect toward those who were tortured and those who were brave enough to resist. This respect, however, does not preclude the necessity of adopting a more complex lens than the simple dualism of "the persecuted versus the persecutors." To understand Russian spiritual history during this period it is necessary to observe it from the perspective of spiritual and intellectual developments in modern society.

Contemporaries themselves attempted this sort of deep reflection, of course. Nicolas Berdyaev (Scene 16) experienced the first wave of anti-church repression in Russia: the confiscation of church property, the abolition of religious schools and monasteries, the internment of Patriarch Tikhon Bellavin (1865–1925), the murder of priests and monks, the demonstrative destruction of sacred relics,

---

401 One example to stand for the rest: Andrzej Grajewski, *Rosja i krzyż: Z dziejów Kościoła prawosławnego w ZSRR* (Katowice: Gość Niedzielny, 1991).

402 Cf. A. Ya. Razumov (ed.), *Leningradskii martirolog 1937–1938* (St. Petersburg: Rossiiskaya natsionalnaya biblioteka, 1995).

403 Cf. Andronik Trubachov, *Obo mne ne pechaltes: Zhizneopisanie svyashchennika Pavla Florenskogo* (Moscow: Izdatelskii sovet Russkoi pravoslavnoi tserkvi, 2007).

the establishment of the so-called Living Church as a means of undermining the patriarchate's authority. The metropolitan of St. Petersburg, Vasily Kazansky (b. 1873), was executed in August 1922. Berdyaev did not remain to experience what followed. In September 1922, Berdyaev and others were shipped out of Russia aboard the "Philosophy steamer." The first years of his exile he devoted to an analysis of what had taken place during the first Five Year Plan, reflecting on what this portended for Russia, for Europe, and for Christianity. In one of the books upon which Berdyaev's fame rests, *The End of Our Time* (also known as *The New Middle Ages*), the author shifts now and again from a mode of analysis to one of prognosis (or, put biblically, of prophecy):

> The Church loses numbers, but for that increases in quality. Christianity again demands of its true believers the ability to sacrifice. And this ability to sacrifice has appeared precisely in the revolutionary elements. The greater part of Russian Orthodox priests remained true to the holy truth, defended Orthodoxy heroically, bravely faced the gallows. Christians have demonstrated their ability to die. Outwardly, the Russian Orthodox Church appears broken. Inwardly, however, she has recovered and been revitalized. [...] The intelligentsia, for entire centuries hostile to the faith and proclaiming atheism, in the end tending toward revolution, has now returned to religion. That is a new development. And in Russia itself this return to religion is in no way reactionary, it is unconnected with any plans for restauration and the desire to return to lost yesterdays. The Russian people have undergone a spiritual experience, they have changed their relationship to earthly affairs.[404]

A new epoch was to arise from the renewal of faith, an epoch which Berdyaev designated, in a positive sense, "a new Middle Ages." Berdyaev was correct that Bolshevism could not completely uproot

---

404 Nikolai Berďajev, *Nový středověk* (Červený Kostelec: Pavel Mervart, 2004), 99.

Christianity in Russia, and that with time a renewal of faith would take place precisely among the "intelligentsia." The actual form of this renewal, however, and the values that the (re)converts understood by Christianity, was to create anything but the new, collective, "organic" epoch that Berdyaev had envisioned.

There would be no "new Middle Ages" befitting the daydreams of the freshly exiled Berdyaev (in fact, he would later repudiate this ideal, returning instead to the idea which was originally central to his thinking—an understanding of individual spiritual freedom as the highest value). There would be no "sacred Rus," no modern iteration of the older model (a model which had anyway only existed in the idealized projections of nineteenth-century romantics and restorationists.) Together with the renewed Russian Orthodoxy of the twentieth century were also awakened older, pre-revolutionary currents, conflicts, and contradictions—differing opinions about what Christianity means in the modern world. It wasn't just "faith itself" that was revived. Orthodox romanticism, Orthodox reformism, and Orthodox restoration also returned. Russian spiritual history of the Soviet era was not only shaped by the external conflict between the atheistic regime and religious milieu; it was also formed by the inner dynamic of relations within this Orthodox "trinity."

The endurance and renewal of religious communities also formed a complicated triangular relationship. Exile, dissent, and the gray zone comprise the peaks of this triangle. Exile, "Russia beyond Russia," was materially difficult but spiritually easy—because one was free. In exile, church life and religious thought could develop in every possible direction. Disputes about ecclesiastical jurisdiction paradoxically contributed to this freedom. One section of the exile Orthodox Church continued to recognize the canonical authority of the Moscow patriarchate. Another group chose "exile in exile" by professing adherence directly to Constantinople. Yet a third grouping chose to found an independent Russian Orthodox Church abroad. Though this trichotomy made ecclesiastical life rather difficult, it did generally correspond to the real divisions within the religious thinking of exiles: the pro-Moscow "left"; the reformist and liberal "middle" with its center in Paris (Scene 17); and a conservative, restorationist "right" with its center in Serbian Sremski Karlovci.

Not just the pro-Moscow branch, but the entire "Russia beyond Russia" remained informed about religious and social developments in the homeland. New exiles constantly arrived (sometimes in waves resulting from new political upheavals, sometimes individually), some exiles returned (again, in waves and individually), and texts circulated back and forth. Manuscripts were smuggled out and printed texts were smuggled in. The act of carrying these texts has played a large role in twentieth-century literature. Berdyaev, for example, figures in the tale "Why Don't We Do It in the Road" (1991), written by the Ukrainian author Volodymyr Dibrova (*1951). The story's narrator is carrying handwritten excerpts from Berdyaev's book about Dostoevsky when he is stopped and searched by the police. What would happen if they find the papers with quotations from "a book about Dostoevsky in which the word 'God' was written with a capital letter."[405] The hero manages to make his way to a toilet in the police station and save himself—by destroying his valuable notes: "I stand above the hole, release a stream, crumble the piece of paper, cross myself (Come on!) and watch Berdyaev together with Dostoevsky follow their course and disappear into oblivion. — Jesus Christ, thank you very much!"[406]

Dibrova's tale bitterly describes everyday experience in the era of dissent and samizdat. This could only have happened after Stalin's regime of terror had given way to the relatively "softer" regime of Khrushchev and Brezhnev.[407] One finds records of individuals and small

405 Volodymyr Dibrova, "The Beatles' Songbook: Why Don't We Do It in the Road," *Agni* no. 29–30 (1990), 256.
406 Ibid., 266.
407 Cf. Irina Alpatova et al. (eds.), *Drugoe iskusstvo : Moskva 1956–1988* (Moscow : Galart, 2005).

groups becoming active from the middle of the 1950s, including Orthodox activists. Orthodox dissidents wrote letters to local offices protesting wrongs done to the church or complaining of its current unhappy condition. They founded civic, academic, and political organizations to defend the faith and Orthodox culture. They produced type-written books, editions, and periodicals. It was then that the poet Nikolai Glazkov (1919–1979) thought up the word *samsebyaizdat,* a shorthand neologism for *samostoyatelnoe izdatelstvo* (independent publisher, an ironic take on the official term *gosizdat* (*gosudarstvennoe izdatelstvo,* the state publisher).[408] In the version "samizdat," the word caught on and became one of the few Russian words with unambiguously positive associations to have entered the modern global vocabulary—less salubrious but equally successful words include "vodka," "tsar," and "pogrom."

It didn't take more than a few years before the editors and organizers of these samizdat editions and dissident groups were arrested and sentenced by the state (the sentences now limited to "just" a few years at internment camps). Sometimes, however, "alternative" methods were also used to break and eliminate dissidents. In 1980, for example, the popular priest Dmitri Dudko (1922–2004) was forced to "repent" his "anti-Soviet activities" on television. He would repent this forced repentance, though the tremendous authority he once enjoyed among Orthodox dissidents would never return.[409] Others were forced to emigrate. All of this together forms the remarkable history of Russian Orthodox dissent; like Russian Catholicism, a "thin" chapter in the history of Russian spirituality (Scene 14).[410] While Orthodox dissidents received the constant

408 Compare with the entry "samizdat" in Wolfgang Kasack, *Slovník ruské literatury 20. století* (Prague: Votobia, 2000).
409 Dudko was later made into a literary character by Lyudmila Ulitskaya in her novel *The Big Green Tent* (2010, in English 2015), which describes the atmosphere of dissent in Russia.
410 Compare this with the modern Anglo-Saxon historiography of Russian church history, in which the narrative centers around Orthodox dissent: Jane Ellis, *The Russian Orthodox Church: A Contemporary History* (Bloomington: Indiana University Press, 1986).

attention of the communist authorities, they were also able to use the freedom enjoyed by writers of samizdat to write whatever they wanted. The world of Orthodox dissent brought together the entire spectrum of opinions and viewpoints from left to right, from Orthodox reformism to extreme forms of Orthodox restoration.

Orthodox reformists naturally cooperated with secular dissidents (and many among the latter eventually returned to Orthodoxy).[411] Dissidents of Jewish origin together with those from communist families protested the occupation of Czechoslovakia in August 1968 (Scene 13)—Natalya Gorbanevskaya (1936–2013), author of spiritual poetry, and other Orthodox dissidents also joined the protest.[412] Orthodox restorationists more often stood to the side, continuing the tradition of *Demons* and *Vekhy* (Scene 18) of accusing Russian liberals (whose spiritual heirs were the secular dissidents) of complicity in the crimes of Bolshevism. Pressure from the regime nevertheless pushed them all together to share in the solidarity of "the aggrieved and humiliated," a situation like Charter 77 in Czechoslovakia. This solidarity, however, lasted only up to the moment of the regime's collapse.

One can use the term "gray zone" to designate the third form of the Russian religious milieu. The term was introduced by the sociologist Jiřina Šiklová to describe the situation in Czechoslovakia. It describes that part of society and culture which stood "between" dissent and collaboration during normalization. Hence the metaphor "gray". The gray zone formally adopts the rules and conventions of a given regime, but from within it struggles for the greatest possible space for social and creative activity which, in spirit, are independent of the regime's ideology.[413]

---

411 Cf. Philip Boobbyer, *Conscience, Dissent and Reform in Soviet Russia* (New York: Routledge, 2005).

412 Cf. Adam Hradilek (ed.), *Za vaši i naši svobodu* (Prague: Torst, 2010).

413 Jiřina Šiklová, "The Gray Zone and the Future of Dissent in Czechoslovakia," *Social Research* 57, no. 2 (Summer 1990): 347–63. In her article, Šiklová calls attention to the fact that the term was earlier used by others in samizdat.

The "gray zone" of Orthodoxy in Russia was specific in that it included two "sub-zones": the ecclesiastical and the cultural. On the one side was the official church hierarchy, nearly wiped out by Stalin at the end of the 1930s, whose surviving members the dictator resuscitated as a formal structure with a patriarch in 1943 to assist in mobilizing manpower in the Second World War. Bishop Sergius Stragorodsky (1867–1944) was named patriarch, a man who had previously demonstrated his willingness to compromise the church and cooperate with the regime. Other patriarchs and metropolitans followed in the spirit of Stragorodsky. They treaded lightly in the narrow space permitted them, always prepared to demonstrate their loyalty to the regime and almost always ready to help the regime repress Orthodox dissident. They defended their actions by claiming that compromise was the price to be paid for maintaining a basic church structure and the functions of ecclesiastical life such as church services and the naming of parish ordinations. Orthodox dissidents repeatedly objected that the extent of the compromise was excessive, accusing those in the gray zone of being nothing other than collaborators who in fact harmed the church. The most important text in this genre was *Velikopostnoe pismo Vserossiiskomu Patriarkhu Pimenu* (A Lenten Letter to Pimen, Patriarch of All Russia), published in 1972 by the most widely known among Orthodox dissidents, Alexander Solzhenitsyn (1918–2008).

Solzhenitsyn was already a dissident at the time when he composed the reproachful letter to the patriarch. His literary career, however, had begun in the gray zone as part of the second "sub-zone"; he belonged to those artists who published their works in the official cultural forums, but who pressed the boundaries of official culture by inserting "unofficial" themes and opinions. For "Soviet artists" it was certainly not possible to speak openly about religion, especially not about religion in modern "Soviet society." It was possible to speak however about older periods of national history, as was done for example by Andrei Tarkovsky in his film *Andrei Rublev,* and in this way to focus on older religious culture (Scene 5). It was possible to highlight religious gestures and symbols as examples of patriotism during the time of the Napoleonic wars, as was done by Sergei Bondarchuk (1920–1994) in the filming of Tolstoy's *War and Peace* (1965–1967).

One could also write about old Russian art and thereby call attention to the phenomenon of iconography. That was the lifelong subject of Vladimir Soloukhin (1924–1997), a writer who became an expert on icons before turning to other artifacts of older Russian cultural history, including religious artifacts. In his text *Poseshchenie Zvanki* (A visit to Zvanka, 1975), Soloukhin describes the sad state of the lands that had once belonged to Derzhavin and launched into philosophizing about the poet's ode *God* (Scene 11), attempting to "modernize" Derzhavin's terminology—indicating, for example, that where Derzhavin writes "spirit" we should understand "consciousness."[414] In 1980 he composed an essay about the similarly unhappy visit to Optina Pustyna (Scene 15), *Vremya sobirat kamni* (A Time to Gather Stones).

A similar refuge was found in the academic sphere in such "distant" disciplines such as medieval literature, the history of medieval art, or Byzantine studies. These are subjects where the religious dimension and religious artifacts are hardly to be avoided. Alexander Panchenko (1937–2002) addressed the phenomenon of iurodivye under the cover of an analysis of "the world of folk laughter," Sergei Averintsev (1937–2004) wrote about ancient Christian folk poetry in a work ostensibly dedicated to "the poetics of early Byzantine literature"—only later did he begin to publish his broadly conceived essays about the philosophical dimensions of Orthodox religious culture.[415]

---

414 Cf. Vladimir Soloukhin, *Pisma iz Russkogo muzeya* (Moscow: Molodaya gvardiya, 1990), 243.
415 See also the extensive dictionary of Christian culture, *Khristianstvo,* published under the editorship of Averintsev between 1993 and 1994.

It was also possible to write about the traditional village, its way of life and the importance of family connections, and about the preservation of landscape and memory. Those comprise the subjects of books such as *Farewell to Matyora* (1976) by Valentin Rasputin (*1937), the leading figure of the "derevenshchik" school, or "village literature," a movement similar to the French regionalists or the Czech ruralists.[416] Solzhenitsyn's tales "A Day in the Life of Ivan Denisovich" (1962) and "Matryona's Place" (1963) were understood at the time as manifestations of the same tendency, portrayals of "the simple Russian people" as models of quiet perseverance and spiritual immensity. That religious moral principles underlay this perseverance and immensity, that was to be understood by the reader more from the subtext than from the text itself.

The risks involved in inhabiting this borderline position are clear. Some artists and scholars persisted in the "gray zone," even from within the ranks of official artistic organizations and the Communist Party. Others, like Solzhenitsyn, to the contrary became dissidents and yet others found themselves in exile. While dissidents and exiles were free to express themselves as they wished, those in the gray zone paid for their relative comfort and material advantages with limits imposed upon what they could express and how they could express it.

One might certainly wonder how spokesmen for the Orthodox Church could at the same time be functionaries of the Communist Party. This was the curious logic of the gray zone. On the one hand, during the later phase of the Soviet regime, membership in the Communist Party and other official organizations meant nothing more than an outward demonstration of formal loyalty, much like membership in the Orthodox Church under the Old Regime. On the

---

416 Cf. Norbert Mecklenburg, *Erzählte Provinz: Regionalismus und Moderne im Roman* (Königstein/Ts.: Athäneum Verlag, 1986); Martin C. Putna, "Regionalismus a ruralismus," in *Česká katolická literatura v kontextech* (Prague: Torst, 2010), 137–144.

other hand, Russian communists and the Russian Orthodox easily found a common theme—the theme of Russia's "choseness."

The peak and point of exhaustion of the "poetics of the gray zone" was a novel by Chingiz Aitmatov (1928–2008), *The Place of the Skull* (also known as *The Scaffold*, 1986). Aitmatov was Kyrgyz by origin, and so counted as one of the "fraternal Soviet peoples" who had made a career in Russian as *the* literary Kyrgyz (not so unlike Gogol in Russia as *the* literary "Little Russian"). Aitmatov specialized in the portrayal of typical Kyrgyz scenes and characters, above all sheepherders and other "rural people." In this regard, Aitmatov resembles the Russian "village writers." Traditional Kyrgyz lifestyle provides the framework for *Place of the Skull*. Built into it, however, is also the confrontation of purely modern problems (drug production and plundering of the landscape) and the theme of the search for God. The novel's central figure, Avdi Kallistratov, is a former seminarian, an unorthodox religious thinker, and a pure Christian character who finds himself confronted by a cruel group of cynical goons who torture him. In the end, he is crucified.

It isn't at all difficult to locate in Aitmatov's novels models taken from Russian classical literature. The Christian youth whose purity and spiritual depth evoke only the incomprehension of his profane surroundings—that is precisely prince Myshkin from Dostoevsky's *Idiot*. Avdi's confrontation with the dogmatic seminarian who sees the essence of religion in conformity and discipline—that is precisely the discourse between Christ and the Grand Inquisitor from *The Brothers Karamazov*. Avdi's delirious enthusiasm for Jesuits and his thoroughly un-Orthodox conversation with Pilate—that is precisely the "apocrypha" from Mikhail Bulgakov's (1891–1940) *The Master and Margarita* (1928–1940), a novel which had been long forbidden but by Aitmatov's time was widely familiar and respected as the Russian predecessor to magical realism. Avdi's musings, which are supposed to represent a deep and original connection of religious traditions to the programmatic "un-dogmatic-ness" of modern man, are often rather pseudo-deep: "If history can come up with a new central figure on the horizon of faith, the figure of a contemporary God with a new conception of the divine that is relevant to the needs of today's world, then there is hope that faith still might be worth something."[417]

Ignoring for a moment this and other awkward passages from the novel; ignoring for a moment the effort with which Aitmatov sought new subject matter (all said and done, his most convincing pages are those naturalistic "Kyrgyz" descriptions of goatherds and wolves) or how much he wished to ride and the emerging wave of public interest in religion—in its time, *The Country of the Skull* represented an extraordinarily controversial social event. A writer who was himself a communist functionary (and, what's more, whose nation traditionally belonged to the Muslim world) wrote a novel in which the main hero reveals himself a Christian in life and death, and in which Christ himself makes a personal appearance, albeit in a dream-like apocryphal context. The journal *Voprosy literatury* dedicated much space in its 1987 volume to a discussion of Aitmanov's novel: "Is this permitted?" or "Is this forbidden?" These questions would lose their significance in only a few years (and Aitmatov would lose much of his glamor) because religion would lose its taboo status. Aitmatov's novel is important not because it contributed in any major way to the art of the novel, to say nothing of offering original religious insights, but because it shifted the boundary of the permissible in the direction which would lead to that final abolition of political taboos—the collapse of the communist regime and, with it, of the entire gray zone.

Parallel to the external trinity of forms (exile—dissent—the gray zone) there also developed an internal trinity of spiritual currents (romanticism-reformism-restoration).

---

417 Chingiz Aitmatov, *The Place of the Skull,* trans. Natasha Ward (Boston: International Academy of Sciences, Industry, Education & Arts, 2000), 64.

The turn of the gray zone's writers and directors to idealized pre-modern periods, rural life-styles, and ancient art clearly belonged to the wider context of Orthodox romanticism, to the heritage of writers like Melnikov-Pechersky, Leskov, and Shmelyov (Scene 16). At the same time, Orthodox romanticism received a new powerful theme during the period of communist rule, a theme handed to it from the regime itself. This was the theme of suffering, a suffering that destroys the body but it purifies the soul and strengthens faith.

Thousands of exiles of the first generation left in the spirit of such suffering, people who had experienced the crimes of the red terror directly after the Bolsheviks seized power. The theme "purification through suffering" gained its ultimate form, however, in the texts of those who witnessed the growing system of concentration camps called the Gulag. The term "Gulag" is of course most closely associated with the name Alexander Solzhenitsyn, the writer who chose the term for the title of his first attempt at a systematic—photographic and spiritual—history, *The Gulag Archipelago* (1973). The word "Gulag" (an abbreviation of *glavnoe upravlenie lagerei*—"Chief Directorate of Camps") continues to be used even in the most recent historical works, works which of course bring a much more complicated perspective to the Gulag than did Solzhenitsyn in his role as a dissident and amateur historian. The word continues to be used simply because it is immediately understood the world over.[418]

Solzhenitsyn, however, drew from an existing tradition, from a "Solzhenitsyn before Solzhenitsyn." Boris Shiryaev (1889–1959) may be considered his immediate forerunner, a writer who got out of Russia during the German advance during the Second World War and published several books of uneven quality in the West. Only one of his works is significant for the period under discussion, the collection *Inextinguishable Lamp* (1954) about the Solovetsky Islands.

---

418 Cf. Anne Applebaum, *Gulag: A History* (New York: Doubleday, 2003).

The Solovetsky Islands carry double significance in Russian history. They are the site of one of Russia's most famous medieval monasteries, but also of a labor camp located on the abolished monastery's grounds. The book *Inextinguishable Lamp* attempts to show that the contradiction between these two functions is only apparent. For Shiryaev, the Solovetsky Islands represent the continuity of resistance and of the Russian religious tradition. This continuity encompasses the saintly founders Zosim and Savvatiy who sought salvation not only in prayer but above all through physical labor; the uprising of the Solovetsky monks against the enforced reform of church ceremony in the seventeenth century, seven years when the monastery was turned into a fortress and when most of the monks perished during the siege of the monastery by the tsar's army (Scene 10); the Bolshevik prison camp, heir both to Zosim's salvation through the cultivation of the north as well as to the inner resistance against the Cheka army of evil. When Solzhenitsyn received news that he would be sent to the Solovetsky labor camp, the painter Nesterov (Scene 17) "whispered: don't worry! It's for the best. One is close to Christ there."[419]

Fragments of an older religious culture (great wooden crosses, the remains of temples), everywhere present on the islands, became a part of the new inhabitants' life, stones in the foundation of the religious revival which began on the Solovetsky Islands. The suffering experienced there represented a journey toward the restoration of "sacred Rus." Among the prisoners Shiryaev found a gallery of "modern day saints": martyrs who had suffered; priests who held their office in secret; prostitutes who befriended the priests and suffered alongside them; "peasant tsars" who had stood up to the Bolshevik government, turning their villages into little independent states, leaders who continued to command the respect of fellow prisoners.

---

419 Boris Širjajev, *Věčné světlo: Solovecké ostrovy v epoše GULAGu* (Červený Kostelec: Pavel Mervart, 2011), 259.

Solovetsky was a place where new myths were born, and Shiryaev consciously helped lift these myths into existence.

One of the most powerful images to come from Shiryaev's horrifying and consoling vision of Solovetsky, one that truly ties into the themes of nineteenth-century Orthodox romanticism, is that of the "muzhik Christ" (peasant Christ). The image is of a wooden cross with the carved figure of Christ's body, a figure that does not resemble canonical depictions:

> This is something else entirely. Have a look at those muscles. And the small eyes, even a little slanted. And those clumps of lightly tangled facial hair... That's just some poor guy from some village in the foothills or marshes. Were he to put on some ragged, country robe and a satchel over his shoulder—and wander along all sorts of trails through snow drifts... Where to? Where to? To his kingdom. To that place which is not of this world.[420]

In the context of the entire Gulag system, the Solovetsky Islands come across as a rather spiritually exclusive environment, a place where it was relatively easy to find this sort of solace. In *The Gulag Archipelago* Solzhenitsyn attempted to describe the entire "profane" system—and yet he, too, emphasized solace. Not just on the historically sacred Solovetsky Islands, but anywhere where one could find spiritual awakening:

> Your soul, which formerly was dry, now ripens from suffering. [...] Gradually it was disclosed to me that the line separating good and evil passes not through states, nor between classes, nor between political parties either—but right through every human heart [...] Since then I have come to understand the truth of all the religions of the world: They struggle with the *evil inside a human being* (inside every human

420 Ibid., 259.

being). [...] And since that time I have come to understand the falsehood of all the revolutions in history: They destroy only *those carriers* of evil contemporary with them (and also fail, out of haste, to discriminate the carriers of good as well). And they then take to themselves as their heritage the actual evil itself, magnified still more. [...] And that is why I turn back to the years of my imprisonment and say, sometimes to the astonishment of those about me: *"Bless you, prison,* for having been in my life!"**421**

As if having become aware of the precariousness of this escalating point of view, the author of this most pathos ridden passage in *The Gulag Archipelago* suddenly threw in the parenthetical comment: "And from beyond the grave come replies: It is very well for you to say that—when you came out of it alive!"**422** This self-denigrating line is itself a silent reply to criticisms coming from survivors of other labor camps across the world and accusations that Solzhenitsyn's descriptions are overly idealized.

The *Kolym Tales* by Varlam Shalamov (1907–1982) serves as an anecdote to the sometimes-histrionic Solzhenitsyn. Shalamov wrote the stories between 1954 to 1973. They were published in exile in 1978, but Solzhenitsyn and a few others had read typewritten copies before then. Shalamov, drawing from his own experience, described circles of hell much more severe than those depicted by Solzhenitsyn, and his stories of naked suffering reveal something quite different. At a certain point, physical suffering does not bring spiritual clarity but only unambiguous evil, without religion and without culture. Shalamov describes with bitterness and irony prisoners who attempt to salvage something from their religion or art. At a place like Kolym one thinks only of survival. Said one prisoner: "Envy,

421 Alexandr Solzhenitsyn, *The Gulag Archipelago Abridged* (New York: HarperCollins, 2007), 309, 312–313.
422 Ibid., 313.

like all our feelings, had been dulled and weakened by hunger. We lacked the strength to experience emotions."[423]

Yet even this, in its own way, represents a sort of spiritual testament—testimony to the limits of Orthodox romanticism.

In the end, it wasn't the reserved Shalamov (who described himself as "just a writer") who gained recognition as *the* witness of the Gulag. That was Solzhenitsyn. It was Solzhenitsyn who combined testimony from the Gulag with moral sermonizing. He was compared to Tolstoy and Dostoevsky as a story-teller and preacher (Tolstoy is mentioned by name also in the passage about the blessed prisoners). And like Tolstoy and Dostoevsky, Solzhenitsyn later turned away from prose to the composition of religious-philosophical-historical treatises in which he tried to answer the question, "what is to be done."[424] Of course, in exile after 1974, Solzhenitsyn no longer answered this question with the communist regime in mind (for him it was clear that the regime would sooner or later collapse). The question became instead, "what is to be done" once the regime falls? Which direction will Russia take?

Russia—not the Soviet Union. In "Rebuilding Russia" Solzhenitsyn called for the dissolution of the Soviet Bloc and the Soviet Union itself, he demanded the "release" of all the nations whose rights Russia had trampled upon, and he called for the renunciation of territorial expansion. Russia, he said, should concentrate on its own inner transformation. Voluntary self-limitation and the rejection of hatred were to be key to this transformation—of nation and of the individual. This theme formed the core of the essay "The Gulag Archipelago and Repentance and Self-Limitation as Categories of National Life," which Solzhenitsyn placed at the head of *Iz-pod glyb* (From Under the Rubble, 1974), a collection whose title referenced

---

423 Varlam Shalamov, *Kolyma Tales* (New York: Penguin Books, 1994), 80.

424 Cf. Niels C. Nielson, Jr. *Solzhenitsyn's Religion* (Nashville and New York: Thomas Nelson Inc., 1975).

the "counterrevolutionary" tradition of compendium *Vekhi* and *From the Depths* (Scene 18). The passion of Solzhenitsyn's rhetoric recalls not just that of Dostoevsky, Gogol, and others of Orthodox romanticism, it also reminds one of older Russian preachers and their patristic predecessors with John Chrysostom in the lead:

> For half a century now we have acted on the conviction that the *guilty* ones were the tsarist establishment, the bourgeois patriots, social democrats, White Guards, priests, émigrés, subversives [...]—anyone and everyone except you and me! Obviously it was *they*, not we, who had to reform. [...] But who, if not we ourselves, constitutes *society*? This realm of darkness, of falsehood, of brute force, of justice denied and distrust of the good, this slimy swamp was formed by *us*, and no one else.[425]

At the same time, Solzhenitsyn explicitly distanced himself from the unreflective nationalism standing behind claims of Russian exceptionalism and superiority:

> An even harsher, colder point of view, or rather current of opinion, has become discernible of late. Stripped to essential, but not distorted, it goes like this: the Russian people is the noblest in the world; its ancient and its modern history are alike unblemished; tsarism and Bolshevism are equally irreproachable [...]
>
> Their general name for all this is "the Russian idea." (A more precise name for this trend would be "National Bolshevism.")
>
> "We are Russians, what rapture," cried Suvorov. "And how fraught with danger to the soul," added F. Stepun after our revolutionary experiences. [...]
>
> We ought to get used to the idea that no people is eternally great or eternally noble [...] that the greatness of a people is to be sought not

---

425 Alexander Solzhenitsyn, "Repentance and Self-Limitation as Categories of National Life," in *From Under the Rubble* (Washington D.C.: Regnery Gateway, 1981), 117–118.

in the blare of trumpets—physical might is purchased at a spiritual price beyond our means—but in the level of its *inner* development, in the breadth of soul (fortunately one of nature's gifts to us), in unarmed moral steadfastness (in which the Czechs and Slovaks recently gave Europe a lesson.[426]

The romanticism of the gray zone culminated in Aitmatov's novel; Solzhenitsyn's essay represents the culmination of romanticism in dissent and exile. If Aitmatov's novel preceded the dissolution of the gray zone into the mainstream, then Solzhenitsyn's essay precipitated the eventual convergence of dissent Orthodox romanticism and Orthodox restoration.

In the meantime, restoration went its own way. In exile, it was represented above all by the Russian Orthodox Church abroad, seated in Yugoslavia between the wars and later moving to the United States. The exile church sought nothing less than the most severe restorationist measures—a return to autocracy and the monopoly of the Orthodox Church—before November and, even more aggressively, before February 1917. Other groups gathered around it: monarchists, officers, Cossacks, ultraconservatives, and anti-Semites. All of them rallied in the fight against so-called "Judeo-Bolshevism" (Scene 13).

A much nobler and more cultivated version of restoration was represented by a shift in the Orthodox theology of exile. The first exile generation dedicated to reform gathered around Sergius Bulgakov—with time, the lead of these groups were taken by traditionalists and theologians of the second generation such as Pavel Jevdokimov (1901–1970), Vladimir Lossky (1903–1958), Alexander Shmemann (1921–1983), and others who considered it the role of

---

426 Ibid., 120.

exile Orthodoxy to remain pure and faithful to the patristic tradition.[427] While it is true that this new Orthodox theology chose to close the door to further development and innovation, it nonetheless remained academically relevant. It appealed to a western audience and did not succumb to excessive fundamentalism, anti-intellectualism, chauvinism, or anti-Semitism.

Unfortunately, the same cannot be said for many factions of dissent at home, which to the contrary became passionately involved in these sorts of excess, considering them to be a part of the nation's spiritual tradition. The samizdat journal *Veche*, which appeared in the first half of the 1970s, may stand for the rest. Another, somewhat more sophisticated grouping acquired greater influence when Alexander Solzhenitsyn lent to it his support and reputation.

It was Solzhenitsyn himself who invited these people to cooperate in his collection *Iz-pod glyb*, and he thereby implicitly lent them his authority. The group's most exceptional figure was Igor Shafarevich (*1923), an internationally known mathematician and Orthodox dissident. In his contribution for *Iz-pod glyb* titled "Does Russia Have a Future?", Shafarevich took fright at the Russian nation's apparent deterioration. In that work, he didn't pretend to know who was responsible. For that, readers had to wait for his text "Russophobia" from the early 1980s (it was published in Russia in 1989). Shafarevich pointed to the "small nation" nestled within the great nation, a small nation which he accused of possessing an existential hatred toward the great nation, wishing to disintegrate and destroy it from within. This small nation carries within itself an inexorable drive for world domination.

---

427 The role of mediator between this new generation of exile theologians and the older theology of restorationist orientation was played by the personality and work of Bulgakov's contemporary and opponent Georges Florovsky, who in polemics with Bulgakov declared the necessity of turning away from all western (especially German idealist) influences and for a "renewed patristic style," cf. Georges Florovsky, *The Ways of Russian Theology*, vol. 2 (Belmont, Mass.: Nordland Pub. Co., 1979).

Which "small nation" could he possibly have in mind? Why, the Jews of course! In literature, Jews such as Isaac Babel and the songwriter Alexander Galich demonstrated their hatred for Russia. In contemporary dissent and literary science blame fell on Andrei Sinavsky (Shafarevich did not know, or did not want to know, that Sinavsky used a Jewish pseudonym as a provocation). In politics, Judeo-Bolshevism was set upon Russia's destruction. The murder of the last tsar and his family was no usual act of terror—it was Jewish ritual murder! Thus spake Shafarevich...

What's worse, the subjects discussed by Shafarevich, the deterioration of the Russian people and the unwholesome role of the Jews in modern Russian history, were taken up by Solzhenitsyn himself in the 1990s. Like Wittgenstein, in whose case historians have distinguished between a "Wittgenstein I" and a "Wittgenstein II," one can speak also of a "Solzhenitsyn I" and "Solzhenitsyn II." The first belongs to romanticism, the second to restoration. The thinking of Solzhenitsyn II involves thinking about "the after," i.e. after the fall of communism.

Finally, Orthodox reformism also played a role in the religious milieu during the communist era. At first glance, Orthodox reformism might seem to be "third in line" to the other currents. The communist regime however presented a certain impulse for attempts at reform. For Russia, after all, communism meant not just terror but also the comprehensive modernization of society. Communism thus provided an impetus to question Orthodox religious culture, to ask if some things should not be changed. Not only to accommodate the regime, but also to address the needs of the "new religious man" who was growing up in this oppressive regime and wished to return to the faith.

A foundational figure of Orthodox reformism from within the context of dissent was also a central figure for Orthodox dissent as a whole: Anatoly Levitin-Krasnov (1915–1991). Originally ordained a priest of the Living Church, he later returned to the regular church structure, though designating himself a "Christian socialist." A theologically far more exceptional figure in that direction, however, was Alexander Men (1935–2000). Like Dudko of the older generation, Men was a priest whose parish attracted converts and members from intellectual circles. For that he faced the harassment of the church as well as communist authorities and faced endless transfers to other parts of the country.

Men, sought after as a catechist and preacher, based his ideas on a wide theological basis. According to his understanding, Orthodoxy was by no means as an exclusive religion "against all," but rather one step in the religious development of mankind, a development that would gradually mature into a recognition of the truth. Men in this way continued the work of Vladimir Solovyov (Scene 14). This is also seen in his understanding of Christianity as spontaneously ecumenical, in his writings about the religious development of mankind (six volumes, 1970–1983), about Jesus Christ (Mens most important work, *Syn chelovechesky*–The Son of Man, 1969), or in his writings on the liturgy (published in exile not by one of the Orthodox publishing houses, but, like Vyacheslav Ivanov, by the Russian-Catholic publisher in Brussel, Zhyzn s Bogem).

Men's thinking about the liturgy, however, included a practical aspect. He certainly did not share the "Avvakumian" conception of the ceremony as unchanging. Nor did he share the "Vladimirian" conviction that the most important part of the ceremony was the experience of mystical beauty. Men thus attempted a (very moderate!) reform of Orthodox ceremony to make it more intelligible and to bring it closer to the modern believer unversed in Byzantine symbolism and unwilling to settle for the sensual-aesthetic experience of the ceremony. The most remarkable element of Men's reforms was probably the revision of the ceremonial language, Church Slavonic, to correspond more closely to modern spoken Russian.[428] Alexander

---

428 Cf. Yves Hamant, *Alexandr Meň: Kristův svědek pro dnešní Rusko* (Kostelní Vydří: Karmelitánské nakladatelství, 2003). A selection of Men's works have also appeared in Czech: Alexandr Meň: *Rozbít led: Křesťan ve společnosti* (Prague: Triáda, 2004).

Men together with his friends and parishioners thus undertook a step in Russian Orthodoxy analogous with that taken in Roman Catholicism by the Second Vatican Council: to create an ecumenically open theology as well as liturgy of greater relevance to modern believers.

Alexander Men was murdered in the fall of 1990, thus shortly before the definitive end of the Soviet empire. The perpetrators of the murder were never identified. If we are to consider Aitmatov's *The Country of My Skull* the symbolic finale of the gray zone's romanticism, and Solzhenitsyn's essay about penitence the endpoint of romanticism in dissent—then we may regard as the unquestionable turning point of modern Orthodox restoration the domestic publication of Shafarevich's "Russophobia" and the murder of Alexander Men, a priest of Jewish origin who was revered as a saint by his followers.

The question was the "whence and whither"—where would the turning point lead?

CONCLUSION

New Struggles Over Old Rus

In Russia, Ukraine, Belarus, and across the entire territory of the former empire, the present begins with the collapse of communist regimes at the end of the 1980s. The carapace of the old order cracked, and out emerged something which was new—again, one is tempted to adopt Spengler's notion of pseudomorphosis (Scene 4). The carapace cracked; it happened officially in 1991 with the fall of the Soviet Union. As far as the spiritual history of the period is concerned, however, the central question is rather how something old appeared amidst the new—those old Russes which have alternated throughout history and throughout the pages of this book.

The "new" was itself in large part the return of the "something older," something pre-communist, and hence something Christian. In 1987, official Soviet journals debated the character of Jesus in Aitmatov's *The Place of the Skull*. In 1988, under the regime's benevolent patronage, a sobor of the Russian Orthodox Church was summoned in the Trinity Lavra of St. Sergius. The gathering marked the millennium of Christianity in Russia by canonizing figures of historical and cultural significance, not just from across centuries but also from across spiritual traditions: Andrei Rublev and Dmitry Donskoy from Mongolian-Muscovite Rus (Scene 5); Maxim the Greek from Moscow's spiritual counter-culture (Scene 7); Xenia of Saint Petersburg from the Petersburg era (Scene 11); representing the Orthodox restauration (Scene 15) were Ignatius Bryanchaninov, Theophan Zatvornik, and Ambrose Grenkov of Optina, the spiritual father of many writers, and through his presence Orthodox romanticism (Scene 16) was included at least by proxy. And in 1989 the magazine *Novy Mir* printed that most anti-regime book by any of the anti-regime authors—Solzhenitsyn's *The Gulag Archipelago*

(Scene 19). With that, the gradual process of dismantling the censorship of religious thought reached its highpoint.

All the spiritual traditions of all the old Russes returned to public discourse: the Orthodox reformist tradition of Alexander Men's disciples and ultrarestorationist circles reading the *Protocols of the Elders of Zion* and Shafarevich's *Russophobia*; traditions of the Old Believers; the Russian-Catholic; the Uniate or Greek-Catholic; the Protestant; the Zionist; the Islamic; the Buddhist; the esoteric; the nonorthodox Marxist; the nonorthodox atheist; the "anti-Muscovite" Ukrainian and Belarusian traditions; not to mention traditions of the non-Slavic nations, all of them wanting out of the empire.[429]

Postmodern literature provided an artistic response to the "great opening" that took place at the turn of the 1990s. Postmodernism treats all traditions as so many "texts" to be quoted, combined, or parodied according to whim or artistic intent.[430] The novel *Marina's Thirtieth Love* by the Moscow conceptualist Vladimir Sorokin (*1955) may be regarded as the period's emblematic work. Though composed in 1982–1984, deep in the years of samizdat, the book did not appear in print until 1995—but when it did, it seemed to have been written specifically for the new era. The novel successively paraphrases each of twentieth-century Russia's grand ideological "ways of speaking," or discourses: Orthodox romanticism and its discourse of conversion; the civil-heroic discourse of dissent; the nebulous rambling of esoteric discourse (in which concepts from the work of Nicholas Roerich make an appearance, Scene 3); and the dull, dehumanized rhetoric of the communist regime. All the discourses, however, are reduced to a shared plane of "nothing but discourse" by being incorporated into sexualized and obdurately

---

429 Cf. Matti Kotiranta, ed., *Religious Transition in Russia* (Helsinki: Kikimora Publications, 2000).

430 Cf. Hana Řehulková, "Postsovětská postmoderna: Sorokin, Akunin, Pelevin," *Host* 30, no. 4 (2014): 41–43.

(pseudo-)pornographic descriptions of the heroine's experiences. Harsh parody is reserved for effusive Russian patriotism, in which Rus herself is worshipped as the central deity:

> "'Rus…'" whispered Marina and suddenly understood something that was of immense significance for her.
> "BUT NOT THAT RUS, NOT THAT ONE!!!" the critical voice continues. "HEAVENLY RUS!"
> Her palm began to pale and turn blue, the outlines of rivers, mountains, and lakes contracted and expanded, gradually filling up the entire sky, and shined through the aperture of limply clenched fingers, inside flared a blinding white star: Moscow! The star transformed into a cross and there sounded from somewhere beneath the firmament the dense, deep bass of the protodeacon of Volkhov:
> Alexander full of glooooory,
> Who since tender youth has Christ adooooored,
> And the lightest of his burdens diiid receeeiiive
> And by many miracles God has celebrated yoooou.
> Prey for the salvation of ouuur soooooouls![431]

This mystical apparition, surprising Marina in her dreams after an evening of revelry, instructs her about her duty to fight on behalf of Rus, a Rus suffering through a process of spiritual rebirth in the Gulag. "Alexander full of glory"—that's none other than Alexander Solzhenitsyn…

Sorokin's work is harsh, "blasphemous," and, to many readers, scandalous. It indicates the "zero point" that had been reached by Russia in the 1990s, a situation of openness, true religious freedom, and cultural and political choice—something hitherto unknown in Russian society. It signals a "window of opportunity" in which anything was possible.

---

431 Vladimir Sorokin, *Třicátá Marinina láska* (Prague: Český spisovatel, 1995), 171.

In theory, at least.

In practice, the situation provided artists and intellectuals an opportunity to discuss anything, to put everything into word and image—but it also forced them to confront the fact that the non-elite public cared less and less. It provided the church with all its venerable traditions an opportunity to confront a new world of diverse opinions and competing viewpoints—and once again to pose the old question, what to do about it? Whether to proceed down the path of reform, or to push for restoration and home for the arrival of a new romanticism? It also represented an opportunity for democratic politicians to realize how weak "western" political culture—with its political parties, elections, programs, and arguments—truly was in Russia. And not least, it provided power-holders from the communist regime an opportunity to demonstrate their ability to adapt to new conditions.

A new current emerged with the openness of the 1990s, one that grabbed hold of government and society during the 2000s by combining in a distinctive way discourses that until recently had seemed incompatible. This was no longer the non-binding, literary game of Sorokin, however; it was a game of politics and power. In this game, Orthodoxy in its conservative, Muscovite-restorationist form (Scene 6) combined with post-communist structures and other ideological trends: the Eurasianist appeal to Moscow's Asiatic roots in the tradition of Lev Gumilev (Scene 5), the esoteric invocation of Russia's pagan antiquity in the spirit of Nicholas Roerich (Scene 3), the anti-Semitic exorcizing of Jewishness and all other marks of "alterity" (Scene 13), the pan-Slavic excoriation of a decadent Europe along the lines of Danilevsky and Leontiev (Scene 16), but also the Orthodox-romantic celebration of spiritual transformation and a return to Christ offered by the Gulag in the manner of Alexander Solzhenitsyn (Scene 19). Even Shiryaev's theme of continuity between the two historical guises of Solovetsky was connected to this structure—though with an appalling shift of emphasis. Zakhar Prilepin (*1975), quite the distinctive author, member of the National Bolshevik Party, and Putin's opponent on the right, set his novel *Obitel'* (Abode, 2014) on the premise that the monastery and the labor camp were both in fact positive—positive because they were "ours," because they were Russian...

What do all these trends have in common? Rus, of course—that same Rus that appeared to Sorokin's Marina in her sleep. Each one will to set aside differences in the common interest—in the interest of Russian nationalism; of dislodging "western" liberalism and democratic openness; of again constructing society along authoritarian lines and creating a Russian imperium that would be respected, and feared, abroad.[432] Today, in the early twenty-first century, this alliance is headed by Vladimir Putin, longtime agent of the KGB, and by the Moscow Patriarch Kirill Gundyaev, a long-time collaborator of the same secret service. Gathered around them are not only the practitioners of power, but also the theoreticians of this new nationalism. The political scientist Alexandr Dugin (*1962), for example, continues to develop the old idea of Eurasianism in a sharply anti-European spirit.

We can turn again to the work of Vladimir Sorokin for an artistic reflection on this unexpected alliance, this time to his novel *Day of the Oprichnik* (2006). The word "oprichnik" in the title is historical and refers to Ivan the Terrible's corps of servants, the *oprichniki,* gendarmes or political police who terrorized society and stood above the law (Scene 6). But the story is not set in the past; it takes place in the future, the year 2028. A new tsar rules over Russia and the world is again divided by an iron curtain. The plot concerns an "ordinary day" in the life of a modern oprichnik for whom murder, torture, and rape all belong to a day's normal routine as much as do the rituals of Orthodoxy or the ideological blathering about the spiritual significance of the absurd cruelty:

---

432 Cf. Peter J. Duncan, *Russian Messianism: Third Rome, Revolution, Communism and After* (London: Routledge, 2000).

Now you, my dear Enochs, you're wondering, why was the Wall built, why are we fenced off, why did we burn our foreign passports, [...] why were intelligent machines changed to Cyrillic? To increase profits? To maintain order? For entertainment? For home and hearth? [...] Now you see, my dearest Enochs, that's not what it was for. It was so the Christian faith would be preserved like a chaste treasure, you get it? For only we, the Orthodox, have preserved the church as Christ's body on earth.[433]

The reference to "an ordinary day" in Sorokin's anti-utopia, moreover, bitterly parodies yet another classic work: Solzhenitsyn's *A Day in the Life of Ivan Denisovich*, the description of a single "ordinary day" of a prisoner in the Gulag. Solzhenitsyn is not only a literary giant standing somewhere on the horizon of "celestial Rus," he himself actively engaged in current debates and questions. Here, however, we are dealing with a different Solzhenitsyn. This Solzhenitsyn attempts in his history of Russian-Jewish relations, *Two Hundred Years Together* (Scene 13), to absolve Rus from accusations of anti-Semitism by emphasizing the Jewish contribution to the revolution.[434] It is this other Solzhenitsyn who, in his cycle of novels *The Red Wheel* (*Krasnoje koleso*, 1971–1991), attempts to understand the causes of the Russian revolution and the Bolshevik putsch. He constructs something like an iconostasis of Russian society from dozens of heroes drawn from every walk of life. Though so deeply mired in the breadth of motifs and events that the novel eventually unravels in his hands, he nevertheless manages clearly to communicate the main point of his analysis: democracy was introduced too quickly and, as a result, was too weak to maintain itself and to guide society. Russian democracy consequently entered a deep crisis. Rather than

---

433 Vladimir Sorokin, *Day of the Oprichnik,* trans. Jamey Gambrell (New York: Farrar, Straus and Giroux, 2011).
434 Regarding the complicated evolution of Solzhenitsyn's earlier stance on the Russia-Jewish question, see Martin C. Putna, "Alexandr Solženicyn a Židé," *Světová literatura* 38, no. 5 (1992): 72–77.

the automatic introduction of electoral democracy and party politics, what was needed was a moderately authoritarian government, enlightened administrators capable of guiding the country toward democracy while preserving Russian identity.

In *The Red Wheel* Solzhenitsyn points to one person who might have led such a transition—Peter Stolypin (1862–1911), who became prime minister in 1906 after the revolution. Unfortunately, Stolypin was murdered by the Jewish revolutionary Dmitri Bogrov (1887–1911). The anti-Semitic undertone of the analysis cannot be missed. Shortly before his death, Solzhenitsyn revealed who he considered to be the "new Stolypin," a person who would lead Russia from the infirmities of a democratic order which the country had carelessly stumbled into after the fall of communism, just like after the fall of tsarism. The man he pointed to was Vladimir Putin. Solzhenitsyn thus made possible his own insertion into the iconostasis of the new regime—deeply disappointing those who saw in him an uncompromising defender of human freedom; providing bitter satisfaction to those who, since his *Harvard Lectures* in the 1970s, had warned about the limits of Solzhenitsyn's defense of freedom;[435] and giving sweet satisfaction to western Christian conservatives and ultraconservatives on the Right who welcomed him as a comrade-in-arms in introducing authoritarian systems into the West.[436]

Putin's cunning and unscrupulous rise to power, his steady expurgation of democracy, and alliances with the Orthodox hierarchy and conservative nationalist intellectuals has already been the

435 Cf. John B. Dunlop, Richard S. Haugh, and Michael Nicholson, eds., *Solzhenitsyn in Exile: Critical Essays and Documentary Materials* (Stanford: Hoover Institution Press, 1985)
436 Compare, for example, with books by leading figures of the Christian conservative scene in the U.S.: Edward E. Ericson, Jr, *Solzhenitsyn and the Modern World* (Washington, DC: Regnery Gateway, 1993); Cf. Joseph Pearce, *Solzhenitsyn: A Soul in Exile* (Grand Rapids: Baker Books, 1999); Cf. Daniel J. Mahoney, *Aleksandr Solzhenitsyn: The Ascent from Ideology* (Lanham, MD: Rowman & Littlefield, 2001).

object of analysis.[437] Putin's machinery of power and propaganda has enveloped Russia in an atmosphere of neo-Soviet timelessness that has often proven well suited to rulers of his type. This timelessness differs from that of the late-Soviet period in one important respect: it manages to secure consumption. Moscow under Putin is not the Moscow of the Brezhnev era. High-speed rail lines lead from the Sheremetyevo Airport to downtown. There are shops and restaurants, bookstores and nightclubs to the heart's content. Some shopkeepers and waiters have even learned to smile at their guests. One can find any title from any literary genre—if it is not available at the store, it can be ordered online. There are newly renovated Orthodox churches with well-attended services. For a church which is loyal to the state and receives privileges from the state "satisfies religious needs," or put differently, it provides spiritual consumption.[438] Among these superficial shifts toward western norms belong other conveniences; visitors to the Tretyakov Gallery, for example, are no longer required to wear plastic bags over their shoes.

But then there are the words uttered by Satan to Jesus in the desert, confronting him with all the riches of the world, words interpreted anew by Dostoevsky in *The Brothers Karamazov* and Solovjov in *The Legend of the Antichrist*: "All these I shall give to you, if you will prostrate yourself and worship me" (Mt 4.9). I'll give you the advantages of a western lifestyle (if you can afford it, but that's your problem) if you remain loyal to me, the almighty tsar—just don't demand real freedom and democracy.

Of course, some have organized resistance to the restoration of the authoritarian regime. The less this is possible through politics, the more emphasis must fall on the cultural and the spiritual. This has often been the case in Russian history, as in the letters of Kurbsky to

---

437 Cf. Edward Lucas, *Nová studená válka aneb Jak Kreml ohrožuje Rusko i Západ* (Prague: Mladá fronta, 2008).
438 Irina Papkova, *The Orthodox Church and Russian Politics* (Oxford: Oxford University Press, 2011).

Ivan the Terrible (Scene 6), Radishchev's *Journey from Petersburg to Moscow* (Scene 11), and Solzhenitsyn's *Gulag Archipelago.*

As far as culture is concerned, the methods of today's regime differ ostensibly from those of the past. Today one can write books about whomever and whatever one wants. But that is because Putin's regime recognizes that books matter much less than they did in the time of Radishchev or Solzhenitsyn. Because it recognizes that mass media, rapid newsfeeds, and images are of much greater significance. In its attempt to control public space, Putin's regime is just as uncompromising as the tsars and Soviets were before it. Authors are usually left alive, although journalists sometimes mysteriously disappear. The publishers of books are usually left alive, but free radio is controlled and in general repressed, to say nothing about television. One may speak relatively freely about the past, but not about the present.

It is in this context that one must understand the phenomenon of Pussy Riot. Formed in 2011, the group organized several political happenings wearing their colorful balaclavas. But they became most famous for a short anti-Putin concert in the Cathedral of Christ the Savior, a performance immediately halted by the cathedral's security. A gigantic structure on the bank of the Moscow River, the Cathedral of Christ the Savior was not a randomly chosen location. The building forms one of the most central visual symbols of the restoration of a "sacred Rus." It is not a vestige of the Middle Ages, but a romantic, historicizing restoration project of the late nineteenth century (consecrated in 1882). Demolished in 1931 during one of Stalin's the anti-religious campaigns, the cathedral was rebuilt after the regime's fall. It was there, in 2000, that the Romanovs were canonized, an extremely controversial event at the time. While it is true that the Bolsheviks murdered Nicholas and his wife, it is also true that their incompetence and ruinous mistakes (blind faith in Rasputin!) drove Russia to the edge of catastrophe and prepared the ground for the Bolshevik seizure of power. Before that, in 1981, the tsar's family had been canonized in exile by the Restoration Russian Orthodox Church Abroad as a sign of opposition to the communist regime. Now they were being canonized as "passion bearers"—the same category to which belong the sainted Kievan princes Boris and Gleb (Scene 4)—an ostentatious act of national consensus and under the sign of an imperial lineage that stretches from the tsars to the Bolsheviks to the current regime of Vladimir Putin.

At a time when Putin was suppressing peaceful demonstrations, the group Pussy Riot stood in the cathedral and sang the "Punk Prayer":

Virgin Mary, Mother of God, banish Putin, banish Putin,
Virgin Mary, Mother of God, banish him, we pray thee!

Congregations genuflect,
Black robes brag gilt epaulettes,
Freedom's phantom's gone to heaven,
Gay Pride's chained and in detention.
KGB's chief saint descends
To guide the punks to prison vans.

Don't upset His Saintship, ladies,
Stick to making love and babies.
Crap, crap, this godliness crap!
crap, crap, this holiness crap!

Virgin Mary, Mother of God.
Be a feminist, we pray thee,
Be a feminist, we pray thee.

Bless our festering bastard-boss.
Let black cars parade the Cross.
The Missionary's in class for cash.
Meet him there, and pay his stash.

Patriarch Gundy believes in Putin.
Better believe in God, you vermin!
Fight for rights, forget the rite —
Join our protest, Holy Virgin.[439]

Immediately arrested and subsequently sentenced, Pussy Riot united world opinion but divided opinion at home. Supporters abroad organized concerts on their behalf. European ambassadors engaged in discussions about the affair with Russian metropolitans over dinner. Groups of activists continued their mission, spreading the "punk prayer" across Russia. "Virgin Mary, Mother of God, banish Putin!" Some recite the line under their breath before icons of the Virgin Mary, others scream it out loud—and know that the police will come for them just as they had come for Pussy Riot.

What is at stake here? The whole affair is certainly about more than musical taste. The aim is not to make the "punk prayers" performed in balaclavas part of the Orthodox service. Pussy Riot represents a struggle over public space, a debate about the legitimacy of political protest by means of cultural action and the deeper significance of actions and counter-actions. Sympathizers place Pussy Riot's performance into the context of a democratic movement which, lacking "standard" means, must reach for "non-standard" means of political engagement. Their opponents, headed by patriarch Kirill Gundyaev (nicknamed "Gund'aj," rendered as "Gundy" in the translation above), characterize the protest as a criminal attack on an Orthodox cathedral, something which does sometimes occur in Russia, and thereby mobilize simple believers "in the defense of Orthodoxy."

But there is a deeper cultural background to the controversy: Pussy Riot's performance falls into the Orthodox tradition of iurodstvo, or

---

439 "Pussy Riot's Punk Prayer is pure protest poetry," Carol Rumen's Poem of the Week, *The Guardian,* August 20, 2012, http://www.theguardian.com/books/2012/aug/20/pussy-riot-punk -prayer-lyrics, accessed February 16, 2017.

holy foolery (Scene 7). The "old" iurodstvo became absorbed into the system of "canonical" church practices long ago, reduced to its exterior markers and in this way robbed of its original provocativeness. In its place, however, there has arisen new, "non-canonical" iurodstvo, one less attached to ecclesiastical surroundings but nevertheless fulfilling the traditional function of religious provocation, a moral warning in grotesque form. Pussy Riot's colorful balaclavas are today's equivalent to the chains of Basil the Blessed.

Pussy Riot's performance at the Cathedral of Christ the Savior and many other cultural and political actions in today's Russia immediately recall another venerable phenomenon of Russian religious culture: the longing for martyrdom, the cult of bearing pain, the intentional incitement of situations that carry fatal consequents, and events leading directly to a violent death. When considering Pussy Riot's mini-concert, concluded by arrest; the vociferous prayers of their sympathizers, brought to the same end; the activists going to Red Square with white anti-Putin ribbons; the whole of this culture of flash protests which must in advance count on police repression and possible prosecution, one remembers the Old Believers of the seventeenth century (Scene 10) who similarly stood defenseless against the combined machinery of the church and threw themselves into ruin by ostentatiously crossing themselves in the forbidden, "anti-state," "heretical" manner—with two fingers instead of three. One cannot help but recall the Decembrists standing on Senate Square in December 1825, waiting to be apprehended and subsequently hanged or at least expelled to Siberia. And one cannot help but remember the "eight brave ones" of August 1968 who stood in Red Square with banners protesting the Soviet occupation of Czechoslovakia, each one of them knowing that every minute of protest could be met by a year of imprisonment.[440]

---

440 Cf. Adam Hradilek, ed., *Za vaši i naši svobodu* (Prague: Torst, 2010).

To be sure, one must recognize a substantial difference between holy fools and Old Believers, on the one side, and the Decembrists, "Eight Brave Ones," or today's anti-Putin demonstrators, on the other. When westerners living in a secular age think of the former, the "religious fanatics," they can only shake their heads uncomprehendingly. The civil activists of the latter group, however, receive applause and even support. But from the perspective of mentality and style of protest, these groups all have something in common. Each inspires admiration for their sacrifice, a level of sacrifice no longer common in the West. On the other hand, they also raise the painful question as to when, and if, there will ever emerge strategies in Russia beyond this tradition of self-destruction, strategies of opposition truly capable of overthrowing the power of authoritarianism. Whatever the case may be, Russia at the beginning of the twenty-first century is witnessing the latest scene in an ancient struggle between two competing notions of patriotism and the sacred.

Still another ancient rivalry persists in Russia today—that between "eastern" Russia and "western" Russia, the latter historically embodied in Galician Rus, Novgorod Rus, and Lithuanian Rus. "Western" Russia has long abandoned its claim to the name of Russia. It is now called Ukraine. Ukraine, which developed as an independent state in 1991, long wavered between a European and a Russian orientation. A large section of the political and economic elite is tied to Russia. Yet two revolutionary waves have already attempted to turn Ukraine toward Europe: the "Orange Revolution" of 2004 and the "Maidan" of 2013. In distinction to Russian conditions, these revolutions received support not merely from a small intellectual elite, but from the overwhelming part of the population; it received significant support from the churches as well, at least from the Greek Catholic church in western Ukraine and the Ukrainian Orthodox church, having torn itself away from the Moscow patriarchate.

In the end, the "Orange Revolution" succumbed to the contentiousness of its democratic leaders and to Russian economic pressure.

The "Maidan," so far, has been more successful—and that's why it awakens such ferocity in Vladimir Putin. That is why Putin occupied Crimea (Scene 1), the symbolic cradle of Rus. That is why he seeks to remove the Russian-speaking eastern region from Ukraine. That is why he propagandistically portrays the Ukrainian movement for independence as "fascists," as followers of Stepan Bandera (Scene 12).

Currently, the West is not considering the role of Ukraine with sufficient gravity. In his book *The Clash of Civilizations* (1996), Samuel Huntington assigns Ukraine along with Belarus to the sphere of "Orthodox" civilization. Accordingly, it is best that they stick together and the West resist the urge to intervene. But Ukraine represents a fundamentally weak link in Huntington's thesis. Ukraine is more than just Ukraine. Ukraine is (fellow) heir to the European state known as Kievan Rus, heir to Galician Rus and Lithuanian Rus. Indirectly, Ukraine is also heir to Novgorod Rus and to all "western" Russia, demonstrating that "Russianness" need not be wed to Uvarov's triad of "orthodoxy, autocracy, and nationality," that "Russianness" can contribute positively to the cultural currents of Europe.

Truly, Ukraine is more than just Ukraine. Ukraine today represents the hope of neighboring Belarus; it provides a haven for democratically-minded exiles from Putin's Russia who are constructing in Ukraine a new, alternative "Russia beyond Russia." Ukraine represents a very distant hope even for Russia itself.

BIBLIOGRAPHY

1/ Cited sources

(In the case of works not previously translated, original translations have
been prepared for the present volume.)

Afanasyev, Alexander, *Erotic Tales of Old Russia* (Berkeley: Berkeley
Slavic Specialties, 1988).
Goethe, Johann Wolfgang von, *Wilhelm Meister's Apprenticeship and
Travels,* trans. by Thomas Carlyle (London: Chapman and Hall, 1907).
Aitmatov, Chingiz, *The Place of the Skull,* trans. Natasha Ward (Boston:
International Academy of Sciences, Industry, Education & Arts, 2000).
Andruchovyč, Jurij, and Stasiuk, Andrzej, *Moje Evropa* (Olomouc:
Periplum, 2009).
Andrukhovych, Yuri, *Recreations,* trans. Marko Pavlyshyn (Edmonton
and Toronto: Canadian Institute of Ukrainian Studies Press, 1998).
Babel, Isaac, *Red Cavalry and Other Stories* (New York: Penguin Books,
2005).
Berďajev, Nikolaj, *Nový středověk* (Červený Kostelec: Pavel Mervart,
2004).
Berďajev, Nikolaj, *Vlastní životopis* (Olomouc: Refugium Velehrad-Roma,
2005).
Bláhová, Emilie et al. (eds.), *Byzantské legendy* (Prague: Vyšehrad, 1980).
Bláhová, Emilie, Hauptová, Zoe, and Václav Konzal (eds.), *Písemnictví
ruského středověku od křtu Vladimíra Velikého po Dmitrije Donského*
(Prague: Vyšehrad, 1989).
Blok, Alexander, "The Scythians," trans. Guilbert Guerney, in
*An Anthology of Russian Literature in the Soviet Period: From Gorki
to Pasternak* (New York: Random House, 1960), 27–29.
Bulgakov, Sergius, *O Sofii, Predmudrosti Bozhie* (Paris: YMCA Press,
1935).
Bulgakov, Sergius, *The Lamb of God* (Grand Rapids, Mich.: William.
B. Eerdmans, 2008).
Bunin, Ivan, *Cursed Days: A Diary of Revolution* (Chicago: Ivan R. Dee,
1998).

Chaadaev, Peter, *Philosophical Works of Peter Chaadaev* (Dordrecht and Boston: Kluwer Academic Publishers, 1991).

Chagall, Mark, *My Life* (New York: Orion Press, 1960).

Chudoba, Bohdan, *Vím, v koho jsem uvěřil a jiné eseje* (Brno: CDK, 2009).

Chudoba, Bohdan, "Do třetí války," manuscript, private archive of Eva Chudoba, Madrid.

Danilevsky, N.Y., *Rossiya i Evropa* (Moscow: Kniga, 1990).

Derzhavin, Gavrila, "God," trans. John Bowring, *Specimens of the Russian Poets* (London, 1821).

Dostoyevsky, Fyodor, *The Diary of a Writer* (New York: C. Scribner's Sons, 1949).

Dostoevsky, Fyodor, *Demons* (New York: Vintage Books, 1995).

Dostoyevsky, Fyodor, *The Brothers Karamazov* (New York: Penguin Books, 2003).

Fedotov, George, *Stikhi dukhovnye: Russkaia narodnaia vera po dukhovym stikham* (Paris: YMCA Press 1935).

Fedotov, G.P., *The Russian Religious Mind*, vol. 1–2 (Cambridge: Harvard University Press, 1966).

Florenskij, Pavel, *Sloup a opora pravdy* (Velehrad and Olomouc: Refugium, 2003).

Gogol, Nikolai, *The Collected Tales of Nikolai Gogol* (New York: Vintage Books, 1999).

Gogol, Nikolai, *Meditations on the Divine Liturgy* (Jordanville, NY: Holy Trinity Publications, 2014).

Goncharov, Ivan A., *Oblomov*, trans. David Magarshack (New York: Penguin Books, 2005).

Havlíček-Borovský, Karel, *Básnické dílo* (Prague: Orbis, 1951).

Herodian, *History of the Roman Empire from the Death of Marcus Aurelius to the Accession of Gordian III.* (Berkeley: University of California Press, 1961).

Herodotus, *The Histories*.

Herzen, Alexander, *My Past and Thoughts: The Memoirs of Alexander Herzen* (New York: A. Knopf, 1973).

Herzen, Alexander, *My Past and Thoughts: The Memoirs of Alexander Herzen* (Berkeley: The University of California Press, 1982).

Hodrová, Daniela (ed.), *Smích a běs: Staroruské hagiografické příběhy* (Prague: Odeon, 1988).

Hradilek, Adam (ed.), *Za vaši i naši svobodu* (Prague: Torst – ÚSTR, 2010).

Ilek, Bohuslav (ed.), *Život protopopa Avvakuma* (Prague: Odeon, 1975).

Ivanova, Lidiya, *Vospominaniya: Kniga ob otse* (Moscow: RIK Kultura, 1992).

Karamzin, Nikolai, *Obrazy z dějin říše ruské*, vol. 2 (Prague: Odeon, 1975).

Kharitonov, Mark, *Den v fevrale* [(Moscow, Sov. Pisatel, 1988).

Kindlerová, Rita (ed.), *Expres Ukrajina: Antologie současné ukrajinské povídky* (Zlín: Kniha Zlín, 2008).

Knazhnin, Jakov, *Vadim Novgorodski* (Moscow: Tipografiya Mamontova, 1914).

Kollár, Jan, *Slávy dcera: Báseň lyricko-epická v pěti zpěvích*, with commentary by Martin C. Putna (Prague: Academia, 2014).

Kuprin, Alexander, *The Duel and Selected Stories* (New York: New American Library, 1961).

Lichačov, Dmitrij, and Pančenko, Alexandr (eds.) *Smích staré Rusi*, ed. (Prague: Odeon, 1984).

The Life of the Archpriest Avvakum by Himself, trans. Jane Harrison and Hope Mirrlees (Hamden, Conn.: Archon Books, 1963).

Leskov, Nikolai, "An Iron Will," in *Five Tales*, trans. Michael Shotton (London: Angel Books, 1984).

Maistre, Joseph de, *St Petersburg Dialogues, or, Conversations on the Temporal Government of Providence*, trans. Richard A. Lebrun (Montreal and Kingston: McGill-Queen's University Press, 1993).

Mathauserová, Světla (ed.), *Povídky ze staré Rusi* (Prague: Odeon, 1984).

Merežkovskij, D.S., "Poslední svatý," in *Ne mír, ale meč* (Prague: Kvasnička a Hampl, 1928).

Morávková, Alena (ed.), *Děti stepní Hellady: Pražská škola ukrajinských emigrantských básníků* (Prague: Česká koordinační rada Společnosti přátel národů východu, 2001).

Nestor, *The Russian Primary Chronicle*, Laurentian text, trans. and ed. Samuel H. Cross and Olgerd P. Sherbowitz-Wetzor (Cambridge, MA: The Mediaeval Academy of America, 1953).

Odoevsky, Vladimir, *Russian Nights* (Evanston: University of Illinois Press, 1997).

On the Campaign of Igor: A Translation of the Slovo o polku Igoreve, trans. J.A.V. Haney and Eric Dahl (1992), http://faculty.washington .edu/dwaugh/rus/texts/igorintr.htm, accessed February 15, 2017.

Orzeszkowa, Eliza, *Vědma* (Prague: SNKLU, 1961).

The Protocols of the Meetings of the Learned Elders of Zion, trans. Victor E. Marsden (Chicago: The Patriotic Publishing Co., 1934).

Pushkin, Alexander, *Boris Godunov and Other Dramatic Works* (Oxford: Oxford University Press, 2009).

Pushkin, Alexander, "Who Knows the Land?" trans. Adrian Room, in *The Complete Works of Alexander Pushkin*, vol. 2, *Lyric Poems: 1820–1826* (Norfolk: Milner, 2000).

"Pussy Riot's Punk Prayer is pure protest poetry," Carol Rumen's Poem of the Week, *The Guardian*, August 20, 2012, http://www.theguardian.com/books/2012/aug/20/pussy-riot-punk-prayer-lyrics, accessed February 16, 2017.

Putna, Martin C., and Zadražilová, Miluše (eds.) *U řek babylonských: Antologie ruské emigrační poezie* (Prague: Torst, 1995).

Putování k Mongolům (Prague: SNKLU, 1964).

Radishchev, Aleksandr Nikolaevich, *A Journey from St. Petersburg to Moscow*, trans. Leo Wiener (Cambridge: Harvard University Press, 1958).

Rozanov, Vasilij, *Apokalypsa naší doby* (Prague: Torst, 1996).

Rozanov, Vasilij, *Svět ve světle "ruské ideje,"* (Prague: OIKOYMENH, 1999).

Shalamov, Varlam, *Kolyma Tales* (New York: Penguin Books, 1994).

The Secret History of the Mongols: A Mongolian Epic Chronicle of the Thirteenth Century, trans. Igor de Rachewiltz, vol. 1 (Leiden and Boston: Brill's Inner Asian Library, 2004).

Ševčenko, Taras, *Bílé mraky, černá mračna* (Prague: Československý spisovatel, 1977).

Sinitsyna, N.V., *Tretii Rim: istoki i evoliutsiia russkoi srednevekovoi kontseptsii, XV–XVII vv* (Moscow: Izdavatelstvo Indrik, 1998).

Skalová, Hana, *Tři zpěvy staroruské* (Prague: SNKHLU, 1955).

Šmeljov, Ivan, *Sočiněnija II* (Chudožestvennaja literatura, 1989).

Soloukhin, Vladimir, *Pisma iz Russkogo muzeya* (Moscow: Molodaya gvardiya, 1990).

Solovyov, Vladimir, "A Short Story of Antichrist," trans. Natalie Duddington, *Cross Currents* 12, no. 3 (1962).

Solovyov, Vladimir, "Adam Mickiewicz," in *The Heart of Reality: Essays on Beauty, Love, and Ethics* (Notre Dame: University of Notre Dame Press, 2003).

Solovyov, Vladimir, "Pan-Mongolism," in *From the Ends to the Beginning: A Bilingual Anthology of Russian Verse*, ed. Ilya Kutik and Andrew Wachtel (Evanston, IL: Dept. of Slavic Languages and Literatures, viewed May 27, 2016), www.russianpoetry.net.

Solovyov, V. et al. (K. Leontyev, V. Rozanov, N. Berdayev, S. Bulgakov and others), *Velký inkvizitor* (Velehrad: Refugium Velehrad-Roma, 2000).

Solzhenitsyn, Alexandr, *The Gulag Archipelago Abridged* (New York: HarperCollins, 2007).

Sorokin, Vladimir, *Třicátá Marinina láska* (Prague: Český spisovatel, 1995).

Sorokin, Vladimir, *Day of the Oprichnik*, trans. Jamey Gambrell (New York: Farrar, Straus and Giroux, 2011).

"Stich o Golubiné knize," *Souvislosti* 1 (1994): 57–58.

Suetonius, *The Twelve Caesars* (New York: Penguin, 2007).

Tacitus, *The Annals of Imperial Rome* (New York: Penguin, 1956).

Tolstoy, Leo, *A Confession and Other Religious Writings* (New York: Penguin Books, 1987).

Turgenev, Ivan, *Sketches from a Hunter's Album* (NC: Seven Treasures Publication, 2008).

Ulitskaya, Lyudmila, *The Big Green Tent* (New York: Farrar, Straus and Giroux, 2015).

Upřímná vyprávění poutníka svému duchovnímu otci (Velehrad: Refugium Velehrad-Roma, 2001).

Vacek, Jiří (ed.), *Poutník vypráví o své cestě k Bohu* (Prague: Orfeus, 1993).

Vymazal, František (ed.), *Ruská poezije* (Brno: Matice moravská 1874).

Zábrana, Jan, *Celý život: Výbor z deníků 1948–1984* (Prague: Torst, 2001).

2/ Specialist Literature and Annotated Primary Source Editions

Akinčyc, Stanislav, *Zlatý věk Běloruska* (Pardubice: Světlana Vránová, 2013).

Alexeev, A.I. (ed.), *Nil Sorskyi v kulture i knizhnosti drevnei Rusi*, (St. Petersburg: Rossiyskaya natsionalnaya biblioteka, 2008).

Alpatova, Irina et al. (eds.), *Drugoe iskusstvo: Moskva 1956–1988* (Moscow: Galart, 2005).

Altrichter, Michal, *Velehrad: filologoi versus filosofoi* (Olomouc: Refugium Velehrad-Roma, 2005).

Ancipienka, Aleś, and Akudovič, Valancin (eds.), *Neznámé Bělorusko* (Prague: Dokořán—Člověk v tísni, 2005).

Angyal, Andreas, *Die slawische Barockwelt* (Leipzig: E.A. Seemann, 1961).

Anichkov, Evgeny Vasil'evich, *Zapadnyye literatury i slavyanstvo* (Prague: Plamya, 1926).

Applebaum, Anne, *Gulag: A History* (New York: Doubleday, 2003).

Arendt, Hannah, *The Origins of Totalitarianism* (New York: Harcourt, Brace & World, 1966).

Arnold, Claus, *Kleine Geschichte des Modernismus* (Freiburg in Breisgau: Herder, 2007).

Averintsev, Sergei, *Poetika rannevizantiyskoy literatury* (Moscow: Nauka, 1977).

Bakalář, Petr, *Tabu v sociálních vědách* (Olomouc: Votobia: 2003).

Běloševská, Ljobov, and Sládek, Zdeněk (eds.), *Karel Kramář: Studie a dokumenty* (Prague: Slovanský ústav, 2003).

Billington, James, *The Icon and the Axe: An Interpretive History of Russian Culture* (New York: Vintage Books, 1970).

Boček, Pavel, *Stát a církev v Rusku na přelomu 15. a 16. století* (Brno: Masarykova univerzita, 1995).

Boobbyer, Philip, *Conscience, Dissent and Reform in Soviet Russia* (New York: Routledge, 2005).

Borbély-Bánki, Mária, "Aeneis-Travestien aus der Blütezeit der komischen Epen am Ende des 18. Jahrhunderts," in *Symposium Vergilianum*, (ed.) Tar Ibolya (Szeged, 1984): 127-136.

Bouzek, Jan, and Hošek, Radislav, *Antické Černomoří* (Prague: Svoboda, 1978).

Brodsky, Yuri, *Solovki: Dvadcat' let Osobogo Naznacheniya* (Moscow: Rosspen, 2002).

Brtáň, Rudo, *Barokový slavizmus: Porovnávacia štúdia z dejín slovanskej slovesnosti* (Liptovský Sv. Mikuláš: Tranoscius, 1939).

Budanova, N.F., "Rasskaz Turgeneva Zhivye moshchi I pravoslavnaya tradicia," *Russkaya literature*, no. 1 (1995): 188–194.

Budovnic, I.U., *Russkaia publicistika XVI. Veka* (Moscow and Leningrad: Izdatelstvo Akademii nauk SSSR, 1947).

Buslayev, Fyodor, "Obshchiye ponatiya o russkoy ikonopisi," in
O literature (Moscow: Khudozhestvennaya literatura, 1990), 349–414.

Bylinin, V.K., and Odesski, M.P. (eds.), *Ekaterina II. Sochinenia*
(Moscow: Sovremennik, 1990).

Černý, Václav, *André Gide* (Prague: Triáda, 2002).

Černý, Václav, *Soustavný přehled obecných dějin naší vzdělanosti*, vol. 4,
Pseudoklasicismus a preromantismus, romantismus, realismus (Prague:
Academia, 2009).

Černý, Václav, *Vývoj a zločiny panslavismu* (Prague: Václav Havel Library,
2011).

Chamberlain, Lesley, *Lenin's Private War: The Voyage of the Philosophy
Steamer and the Exile of the Intelligentsia* (New York: St. Martin's
Press, 2007).

Chetverikov, Sergei, *Optina Pustyn* (Paris: YMCA Press, 1926).

Chilandarec, Sáva, *Kniha o Svaté hoře Athonské* (Prague: Matice česká,
1911).

Chlaňová, Tereza et al., *Putování současnou ukrajinskou literární krajinou:
Prozaická tvorba představitelů tzv. "stanislavského fenoménu"* (Červený
Kostelec: Pavel Mervart, 2010).

Chmel, Rudolf, *Romantizmus v globalizme* (Bratislava: Kalligram, 2009).

Čiževskij, Dmitrij, "Petr Jakovlevič Čaadajev," in *Filosofické listy*,
(ed.) P.Č. (Prague: Universum, 1947), 11–57.

Čiževskij, Dmitrij et al., *Literárny barok* (Bratislava: Vydavateľstvo SAV,
1971).

Conybeare, Frederick C., *Russian Dissenters* (Cambridge: Harvard
University Press, 1921).

Chupin, G.T., *Predystoriya i istoriya Kievskoy Rusi, Ukrainy i Kryma*
(Kharkov: Litera Nova, 2010).

Cunningham, James W., *A Vanguished Hope: The Movement for Church
Renewal in Russia, 1905–1906* (Crestwood, NY.: St. Vladimir's
Seminary Press, 1981).

Čyževskyj, Dmytro (ed.), *Aus zwei Welten: Beiträge zur Geschichte der
slavisch-westlichen literarischen Beziehungen* (The Hague – Berlin:
Mouton, 1956).

David ze Zdic, Jiří, *Novodobý stav Velké Rusi neboli Moskevska*
(Olomouc: Refugium Velehrad-Roma, 2008).

David-Fox, Michael, *Showcasing the Great Experiment: Cultural Diplomacy and Western Visitors to the Soviet Union, 1921-1941* (Oxford: Oxford University Press, 2012).

Denissoff, Élie, *Maxime le Grec et l'Occident* (Paris: Université de Louvain, 1943).

Dohnal, Josef, and Pospíšil, Ivo (eds.), *N.V. Gogol: Bytí díla v prostoru a čase* (Brno: Tribun EU, 2010).

Doorman, Maarten, *Romantický řád* (Prague: Prostor, 2008).

Duncan, Peter J., *Russian Messianism: Third Rome, Revolution, Communism and After* (London: Routledge, 2000).

Dunlop, John B., Haugh, Richard S., and Nicholson, Michael, (eds.), *Solzhenitsyn in Exile: Critical Essays and Documentary Materials* (Stanford: Hoover Institution Press, 1985).

Dunn, Dennis J., *The Catholic Church and Russia: Popes, Patriarchs, Tsars and Commissars* (Burlington, 2003).

Dus, Jan A. et al. (eds.), *Novozákonní apokryfy*, 3 vols (Prague: Vyšehrad, 2001-2007).

Dvorník, František, *The Idea of Apostolicity in Byzantium and the Legend of the Apostle Andrew* (Cambridge: Harvard University Press, 1958).

Dvorník, František (ed.), *Konstantinos Porfyrogennetos: "De Administrando imperio"* (London: Athlone Press, 1962).

Dvorník, František, *Zrod střední a východní Evropy: Mezi Byzancí a Římem* (Prague: Prostor, 1999).

Ellis, Jane, *The Russian Orthodox Church: A Contemporary History* (Bloomington: Indiana University Press, 1986).

Ekonomtsev, Ioann, "Isikhazm i vozrozhdenie (Isikhazm i problema tvorchestva)," in *Pravoslavie, Vizantiya, Rossiya*, vol. 2 (Lewiston, NY: Edwin Mellen Press, 1999), 177–206.

Epshtein, Mikhail, *Vera i obraz: Religioznoe bessoznatelnoe v russkoi kulture 20-go veka* (Tenafly, NJ: Ermitazh Publishers, 1994).

Eramin, I.P. (ed.), *Ivan Vyshenskii: Sochineniia* (Moscow: Izd-vo Akademii nauk SSSR, 1955).

Erben, K.J., *Slovanské bájesloví* (Prague: Etnologický ústav a Slovanský ústav AV ČR, 2009).

Ericson, Edward E., Jr, *Solzhenitsyn and the Modern World* (Washington, DC: Regnery Gateway, 1993).

Etkind, Alexander, *Internal Colonization: Russia's Imperial Experience* (Cambridge, UK: Polity Press, 2011).

Eusebius, *The History of the Church from Christ to Constantine*, trans. G.A. Williamson (New York: Penguin Books, 1965).

Eykalovich, Gennidi, "Rodoslovnaya Sofii," *Novyi zhurnal* 164 (1986): 196–229 and *Novyi zhurnal* 165 (1986): 307–335.

Fadeeva, T.M., *Krym v sakral'nom prostranstve: Istorija, simvoly, legendy* (Simferopol': Biznes-Inform, 2000).

Faggionato, Raffaela, *A Rosicrucian Utopia in Eighteenth-Century Russia: The Masonic Circle of N.I. Novikov* (Dordrecht: Springer, 2005).

Florovsky, A.V., *Chekhi i vostochnie Slavyane: Ocherki po istorii cheshsko-russkikh otnoshenii (X–XVIII) vek* (Prague: Slovanský ústav, 1935).

Florovsky, George, *Puti russkogo bogosloviya* (Paris: YMCA Press, 1988).

Florovsky, Georges, *The Ways of Russian Theology* (Belmont, Mass: Nordland Pub. Co., 1979).

Florovský, Antonín, *Čeští jezuité na Rusi: Jezuité české provincie a slovanský východ* (Prague: Vyšehrad, 1941).

Francev, Vladimir Andrejevič, *Cesta J. Dobrovského a hraběte J. Šternberka do Ruska v letech 1792-1793* (Prague: Unie, 1923).

Jiří Franěk, "Slovo o pluku Igorově aneb Ruské RKZ," *Souvislosti* 2 (1995): 20–39.

Frazer, James George, *The Golden Bough: A Study in Magic and Religion* (New York: St. Martin's Press, 1990).

Frček, Jan, *Zádonština: Staroruský žalozpěv o boji Rusů s Tatary r. 1380: Rozprava literárně dějepisná* (Prague: Slovanský ústav-Orbis, 1948).

Gabriel, Karl, *Christentum zwischen Tradition und Postmoderne* (Freiburg: Herder, 1992).

Geró, András et al., *Rakousko-uherská monarchie: Habsburská říše 1867-1918 slovem a obrazem* (Praha: Slovart, 2011).

Giardina, Andrea, and Vauchez, André, *Il mito di Roma: da Carlo Magno a Mussolini.* (Rome: Editori Laterza, 2000.).

Gilbert, Martin, *The Atlas of Jewish History* (New York: William Morrow and Co., 1993).

Goldberg, Aleksandr L., "Tri 'poslaniia Filofeia': (opyt tekstologicheskogo analiza)," *Trudy Otdela drevnerusskoi literatury* 23 (1974), 68–97.

Golenishchev-Kutuzov, Ilya Nikolaevich, *Gumanizm u vostochnykh slavian: Ukraina i Belorussia* (Moscow, Izdatelstvo Akademii nauk SSSR, 1963).

Grajewski, Andrzej, *Rosja i krzyż: Z dziejów Kościoła prawosławnego w ZSRR* (Katowice: Gość Niedzielny, 1991).

Grasshoff, Helmut, *Antioch Dmitrievič Kantemir und Westeuropa* (Berlin: Academie Verlag, 1966).

Grekov, B.D., *Kyjevská Rus* (Prague: Nakladatelství ČSAV, 1953).

Groys, Boris, *Gesamtkunstwerk Stalin: Rozpolcená kultura v Sovětském svazu* (Prague: AVU, 2010).

Gurevič, Aron, *Nebe, peklo, svět* (Jihočany: H&H, 1996).

Hamant, Yves, *Alexandr Meň: Kristův svědek pro dnešní Rusko* (Kostelní Vydří: Karmelitánské nakladatelství, 2003).

Hanuš, Jiří, and Vlček, Radomír (eds.), *Interpreting the Russian Revolution* (Brno: CDK, 2008).

Haumann, Heiko, *Dějiny východních Židů* (Olomouc: Votobia, 1997).

Hauptová, Zoe, and Bechyňová, Věnceslava (eds.), *Zlatý věk bulharského písemnictví* (Prague: Vyšehrad, 1982).

Heczková, Libuše, "Rozanov a ti druzí: Rozhovor s Andrejem Stankovičem," *Volné sdružení českých rusistů* 8 (1992): 65–67.

Holeček, Josef, *Rusko-české kapitoly* (Prague: privately printed, 1891).

Huizinga, Johan, *The Autumn of the Middle Ages* (Chicago: University of Chicago Press, 1996).

Hultsch, Anne, *Ein Russe in der Tschechoslowakei: Leben und Werk des Publizisten Valerij S. Vilinskij, 1901-1955* (Köln: Böhlau, 2011).

Huňáček, Václav, "Juraj Križanič," *Souvislosti* 2 (1995): 40–46.

Iorga, Nicolae, *Byzance après Byzance: Continuation de l'histoire de la vie byzantine* (Bucarest: Association Internationale d'Études du Sud-Est Européen, 1971).

Ivanov, Sergey, *Holy Fools in Byzantium and Beyond*, trans. Simon Franklin (Oxford: Oxford University Press, 2006).

Ivanov, Sergej A., *Byzantské misie aneb Je možné udělat z barbara křesťana?* (Červený Kostelec: Pavel Mervart, 2012).

Ivanov, V.V., and Toporov, V.N., *Slavyanskie jazykovye modeliruyushchuhe senuitucheskie sistemy* (Moscow: Nauka, 1965).

Ivanova, Alena, and Tuček, Jan (eds.), *Cesty k národnímu obrození: Běloruský a český model* (Prague: UK FHS, 2006).

Jindřich, Karel, *Vladimír Sergejevič Solovjev: Jeho život a působení* (Prague: Vlast, ND).

Jordanes, *The Gothic History of Jordanes*, trans. Charles C. Mierow (Princeton: Princeton University Press, 1915).

Kabanova, Marija Sammut, "Imperskiie motivy v tekste Stepennoi knigi tsarskogo radoslovia," in *Prolínání slovanských prostředí*, Marcel

Černý, Kateřina Kedron, Marek Příhoda (eds.) (Červený Kostelec –
Prague: Pavel Mervart, 2012), 31–39.
Kalandra, Záviš, *České pohanství* (Prague: František Borový, 1947).
Kalenský, Jakub, "Solovjovova kritika západní filosofie," in *Kulturní,
duchovní a etnické kořeny Ruska: Vlivy a souvislosti*, (ed.) Hanuš Nykl
(Červený Kostelec: Pavel Mervart, 2006), 15572.
Kandert, Josef, *Náboženské systémy: Člověk náboženský a jak mu
porozumět*. (Prague: Grada, 2010).
Karlinsky, Simon, and Appel, Alfred Jr. (eds.), *The Bitter Air of Exile:
Russian Writers in the West, 1922–1972* (Berkeley: University of
California Press, 1977).
Karsavin, L.P., "Žozef de Mestr," *Voprosy filosofii* 3 (1989): 93–118.
Kasack, Wolfgang, *Slovník ruské literatury 20. století* (Prague: Votobia,
2000).
Kasianov, Georgiy, and Ther, Philipp (eds.), *A Laboratory of
Transnational History: Ukraine and Recent Ukrainian Historiography*
(Budapest: CEU Press, 2009).
Kazakova, Natalia A., and Lure, Yakov S., *Antifeodalnye ereticheskie
dvizheniya na Rusi XIV-nachala XVI veka* (Moscow: Izd-vo Akademii
nauk SSSR, 1955).
Keenan, Edward L., *The Kurbskii-Groznyi Apocrypha: The Seventeenth-
Century genesis of the "Correspondence" Attributed to Prince A.M.
Kurbskii and Tsar Ivan IV*. (Cambridge: Harvard University Press,
1971).
Klein, Joachim, *Russkaya literatura v XVIII veke* (Moscow: Indrik, 2010).
Kocourek, Katya, *Čechoslovakista Rudolf Medek: Politický životopis*
(Prague: Mladá fronta, 2011).
Komendová, Jitka, "Haličsko-volyňské knížectví a jeho letopis,"
in *Haličsko-volyňský letopis* (Prague: Argo, 2010).
Komorovský, Ján, *Solovjov a ekumenizmus* (Bratislava: Ústav pre vzťahy
štátu a cirkví, 2000).
Konstam, Angus, *The Historical Atlas of the Viking World* (New York:
Checkmark Books, 2002).
Kotiranta, Matti (ed.), *Religious Transition in Russia* (Helsinki: Kikimora
Publications, 2000).
Králík, Oldřich, *Historická skutečnost a postupná mytizace mongolského
vpádu na Moravu roku 1241: Příspěvek k ideologii předbřeznové Moravy*
(Olomouc: Socialistická akademie, 1969).

Kratochvil, Alexander, *Mykola Chvylovyj: Eine Studie zu Leben und Werk* (Munich: Verlag Otto Sagner, 2009).

Krivochéine, Basile, "Asketické a theologické učení sv. Řehoře Palamy," *Orthodox revue* 2 (1998): 8–47.

Kroupa, Jiří, *Školy dějin umění: Metodologie dějin umění* (Brno: Masarykova univerzita, 2007).

Kubínová, Kateřina, *Imitatio Romae: Karel IV. a Řím* (Prague: Artefactum, 2006).

Kudělka, Milan, *O pojetí slavistiky: Vývoj představ o jejím předmětu a podstatě* (Prague: Academia, 1984).

Kyas, Vladimír, *Česká bible v dějinách národního písemnictví* (Prague: Vyšehrad, 1997).

Lang, Alois, *F.M. Dostoevsky* (Prague: Vyšehrad, 1946).

Lazarev, Viktor, *Svět Andreje Rubleva* (Prague: Vyšehrad, 1981).

Le Goff, Jacques, *La civilisation de l'Occident médiéval* (Paris: Grand Livre du Mois, 1964).

Lebedeva, I.N. (ed.), *Povest' o Varlaame i Ioasafe* (Leningrad: Nauka, 1985).

Leontyev, K.N., *Pro et contra* (Saint Petersburg: RCHGI, 1995).

Leontyev, Konstantin, *Rossiya I Slavyanstvo* (Moscow: Iydatelstvo Respublika, 1996).

Lev Gumilev–pro et contra (Saint Petersburg: Nauchno-obrazovatelnoe kulturologicheskoe obshchestvo, 2012).

Levitt, Marcus C. (ed.), *Eros and Pornography in Russian Culture* (Moscow: Ladomir Publishers, 1999).

Lichačov, Dmitrij, *Člověk v literatuře staré Rusi* (Prague: Odeon, 1974).

Lotman, Yuri M., "The Poetics of Everyday Behavior in Eighteenth-Century Russian Culture," trans. Andrea Beesing, in *The Semiotics of Everyday Russian Cultural History*, edited by Alexander D. Nakhimovsky and Alice Stone Nakhimovsky, (Ithaca, NY: Cornell University Press), 67–94.

Lucas, Edward, *Nová studená válka aneb Jak Kreml ohrožuje Rusko i Západ* (Prague: Mladá fronta, 2008).

Lupanova, Marina E., *Krymskaya problema v politike Ekateriny II* (Riazan: RVAI, 2006).

Lurje, Ja. S., *Pověsť o Drakule* (Moscow-Leningrad: Izdatelstvo Nauka, 1964).

Lurje, Ja. S., *Russkije sovremenniki Vozrožděnija: Knigopisets Jefrosin i d'jak Fjodor Kuritsyn* (Leningrad: Izdatelstvo Nauka, 1988).

Machátová, Ludmila, "Cesta Jana Jeruzalémského do Jeruzaléma a zpět: K otázce protorenesance v novgorodském písemnictví," in *Prolínání slovanských prostředí*, ed. Marcel Černý, Kateřina Kedron, Marek Příhoda (Červený Kostelec and Prague: Pavel Mervart, 2012), 119–125.

Macůrek, Josef, *Dějiny východních Slovanů*, 1–3 (Prague: Melantrich, 1947).

Magocsi, Paul Robert, *Ukraine: A Historical Atlas* (Toronto: University of Toronto Press, 1985).

Maiello, Giuseppe, *Vampyrismus v kulturních dějinách Evropy* (Prague: NLN, 2004).

Magid, Sergei, "Lev Gumilev, předposlední eurazijec" *Souvislosti* 2 (1994): 70–80.

Mahoney, Daniel J., *Aleksandr Solzhenitsyn: The Ascent from Ideology* (Lanham, MD: Rowman & Littlefield, 2001).

Makarov, A.G., and Makarova, S.E. (eds.), *Malorossija, Novorossija, Krym: Istoricheskij i etnograficheskij ocherk* (Moscow: Airo-XXI, 2006).

Malanjuk, Jevhen, "Varjažská balada," in *Děti stepní Hellady: Pražská škola ukrajinských emigrantských básníků*, edited by Alena Morávková (Prague: Česká koordinační rada Společnosti přátel národů východu, 2001), 38.

Mathauserová, Světla, *O Vasiliji Zlatovlasém, kralevici české země* (Prague: Vyšehrad, 1982).

Mathauserová, Světlana, *Cestami staletí: Systémové vztahy v dějinách ruské literatury* (Prague: Univerzita Karlova, 1988).

Matya, Natalia Nikolaievna, *Ivan Groznyj: Istorizm i lichnost pravitelia v otechestvennom iskusstve XIX–XX věka* (Sankt Peterburg: Aleteja, 2010).

Mecklenburg, Norbert, *Erzählte Provinz: Regionalismus und Moderne im Roman* (Königstein/Ts.: Athäneum Verlag, 1986).

Miljukov, Pavel, *Obrazy z dějin ruské vzdělanosti III* (Prague: Laichter, 1910).

Mochulsky, Konstantin, *Duchovnyi put Gogolya* (Paris: YMCA Press, 1934).

Molnár, Amedeo, *Valdenští: Evropský rozměr jejich vzdoru* (Prague: Kalich, 1991).

Moravová, Magdalena (ed.), *Bájné plavby do jiných světů* (Prague: Argo, 2010).

Morozov, A.A., "Emblematika barokko v literature i iskusstve petrovskogo vremeni," in *Problemy literaturnogo razvitia v Rossii pervoi treti vosemnadtsatogo veka*, ed. G.P. Makogonnenko (Moscow: AN SSSR, 1974): 184–226.

Němec, Ludvík, *Francis Dvorník: Mistr historické syntézy* (Olomouc: Refugium Velehrad-Roma, 2013).

Neubauer, Zdeněk, "O tvrdém a měkkém stylu ve filosofii," in *Smysl a svět* (Prague: Nadace Vize 97, 2001), 41-82.

Nichik, Valeria, *Feofan Prokopovich* (Moscow: Mysl, 1977).

Nielson, Niels C., Jr. *Solzhenitsyn's Religion* (Nashville–New York: Thomas Nelson, 1975).

Noble, Ivana et al., *Cesty pravoslavné teologie ve 20. století na Západ* (Brno: CDK, 2012).

Noble, Ivana et al., *The Ways of Orthodox Theology in the West* (Crestwood, NY: St. Vladimir's Seminary Press, 2015).

Novák, Pravomil et al., *Sborník 70 let nakladatelství Vyšehrad* (Prague: Vyšehrad, 2004).

Nykl, Hanuš, *Náboženství v ruské kultuře* (Červený Kostelec: Pavel Mervart, 2013).

Okariňskij, Volodomir, "Formuvaňňa polskogo narodoljubnogo ukrainofilstva, jak nonkonformistskoj sociokulturnoi tečii," in *Slovanský svět: Známý či neznámý?* Kateřina Kedroň and Marek Příhoda (eds.) (Červený Kostelec: Pavel Mervart, 2013), 157–166.

Ostretsov, Viktor, *Masonstvo, kulutra i russkaia istoriia* (Moscow: Kraft, 2007).

Padlipski, Arkadi, *Vitebskie adresa Marka Shagala* (Vitebsk: Vitebski kraevedcheski fond imeni A. Sapunova, 2000).

Pančenko, Alexandr, "Bojarka Morozovová: Symbol a osobnost," in *Metamorfózy ruské kultury*, ed. Alexandr Pančenko, Michal Řoutil et al. (Červený Kostelec: Pavel Mervart, 2012), 129–142.

Pančenko, Alexandr, "Raný Puškin a ruské pravoslaví," in *Metamorfózy ruské kultury* (Červený kostelec, 2012), 299–318.

Papkova, Irina, *The Orthodox Church and Russian Politics* (Oxford: Oxford University Press, 2011).

Parolek, Radegast, and Honzík, Jiří, *Ruská klasická literatura* (Prague: Svoboda, 1977).

Patier, Dominique, "Přišel svatý Prokop z ruské kolonie u Cařihradu?" *Souvislosti*, no. 2 (2007): 178–191.

Pearce, Joseph, *Solzhenitsyn: A Soul in Exile* (Grand Rapids: Baker Books, 1999).

Petschar, Hans, *Altösterreich: Menchen, Länder und Völker der Habsburger-Monarchie* (Vienna: Brandstätter, 2011).

Philaret (Voznesensky), *Tysyacheletiye kreshcheniya Rusi* (Moscow: Moscow Patriarchate, 1988).

Pipes, Richard, *Russia under the Old Regime* (New York: Scribner, 1974).

Poltoratsky, Nikolai (ed.), *Russkaya religiozno-filosofskaya mysl XX veka* (University of Pittsburgh, Slavic Series 2, 1975).

Procopius, *History of the Wars, Volume V: Books 7.36-8. (Gothic War)*, trans. H.B. Dewing, Loeb Classical Library 217 (Cambridge: Harvard University Press, 1928).

Pryakhin, Yu. D., *Greki v istorii Rossii, XVIII-XIX vekov: Istoricheskie ocherki* (Sankt-Peterburg: Aleteyya, 2008).

Příhoda, Marek (ed.), *Kulturní, duchovní a etnické kořeny Ruska: Tradice a alternativy*, (Červený Kostelec: Pavel Mervart, 2005).

Příhoda, Marek, "Vyprávění o pádu Novgorodu: Pojmy traduce, vláda, dědičná země" in *"Rýžoviště zlata a doly drahokamů...": Sborník pro Václava Hrnka*, ed. Věra Lendělová and Michal Řoutil (Červený Kostelec: Pavel Mervart, 2006), 317–334.

Prokhorov, Gelian M., "Poslaniia Nila Sorskogo," *Trudy Otdela drevnerusskoy literatury* 29 (1974), 125–143.

Proskurina, Vera, *Mify imperii: Literatura i vlast' v epokhu Ekateriny II.* (Moscow: Novoe literaturnoe obozrenie, 2006).

Putna, Martin C., *Česká katolická literatura 1848-1918 v evropském kontextu* (Prague: Torst, 1998).

Putna, Martin C., *Řecké nebe nad námi a antický košík: Studie ke druhému životu antiky v evropské kultuře* (Prague: Academia, 2006).

Putna, Martin C., "Bohdan Chudoba: Česko-španělský katolický historiosof proti všem," in *Vím, v koho jsem uvěřil a jiné eseje*, by Bohdan Chudoba (Brno: CDK, 2009), 127–156.

Putna, Martin C., *Obrazy z kulturních dějin americké religiozity* (Prague: Vyšehrad, 2010).

Putna, Martin C., *Česká katolická literatura 1918-1945 v kontextech* (Prague: Torst, 2010).

Putna, Martin C., *Česká katolická literatura 1945–1989 v kontextech* (Prague: Torst, 2017).

Putna, Martin C., "Vergilius: Učitel Evropy," *Publius Vegilius Maro: Aeneis* (Prague: Academia, 2011).

Racek, Jan, *Ruská hudba od nejstarších dob po VŘSR* (Prague: SNKLHU, 1953).

Rádl, Emanuel, *Romantická věda* (Prague: Laichter, 1918).

Rachůnková, Z., and Sokolová, F., and Šišková, R. (eds.), *Dmytro Čyževskyj: Osobnost a dílo*. Prague: Národní knihovna ČR—Slovanská knihovna, 2004.

Razumov, A. Ya. (ed.), *Leningradskii martirolog 1937–1938* (St. Petersburg: Rossiiskaya natsionalnaya biblioteka, 1995).

Řehulková, Hana, "Postsovětská postmoderna: Sorokin, Akunin, Pelevin," *Host* 30, 4 (2014): 41–43.

Reichel, Peter, *Der schöne Schein des Dritten Reiches: Faszination und Gewalt des Faschismus* (Munich: Hanser, 1991).

Reichertová, Květa et al., *Sázava, památník staroslověnské kultury v Čechách* (Prague: Odeon, 1988).

Roerich, Nicholas, *Altai-Himalaya: A Travel Diary* (New York: Frederick A. Stokes Company, 1929).

Roerich, Nicholas, *Vrata v budushchee: Esse, rasskazy, ocherki* (Moscow: Eksmo, 2010).

Rogov, A. I., Bláhová, Emilie, and Konzal, Václav (eds.), *Staroslověnské legendy českého původu* (Prague: Vyšehrad, 1976).

Rosenberg, Alfred, *Der Mythus des 20. Jahrhunderts* (München: Hoheneichen Verlag, 1943).

Runciman, Steven, *The Fall of Constantinople 1453* (Cambridge: Cambridge University Press, 1965).

Runciman, Steven, *The Great Church in Captivity: A Study of the Patriarchate of Constantinople from the Eve of the Turkish Conquest to the Greek War of Independence* (Cambridge: University of Cambridge Press, 1968).

Ryazanovsky, Fyodor Alekseevich, *Demonologia v drevnerusskoi literature* (Leipzig: Reprint Zentralantiquariat der DDR, 1974) (originally, Moscow: Pechatnaja A.I. Snegirevoj, 1915).

Rybakov, Boris, *Jazychestvo drevnei Rusi* (Moscow: Nauka, 1987).

Rybina, Elena A., *Novgorod i Ganza* (Moscow: Rukopisnye pamjatniki Drevnej Rusi, 2009).

Said, Edward, *Orientalism* (New York: Vintage Books, 1994).

Sasse, Gwendolyn, *The Crimea Question: Identity, Transition, and Conflict* (Cambridge: Harvard University Press, 2007).

Schipflinger, Thomas, *Sophia–Maria: Eine ganzheitliche Vision der Schöpfung* (München–Zürich: Verlag Neue Stadt, 1988).

Sedelnikov, A.D., "Ocherki katolicheskogo vliyaniya v Novgorode v kontse XV – nachale XVI vekov," *Doklady Akademii nauk SSSR* 5, no. 1 (Leningrad: AN SSSR, 1929).

Serczyk, Władisław, *Ivan Hrozný: car vší Rusi a stvořitel samoděržaví* (Prague: Lidové noviny, 2004).

Serman, I.Z., "Literaturno-esteticheskie interesy i literaturnaya politika Petra I.," in *Problemy literaturnogo razvitia v Rossii pervoi treti vosemnadtsatogo veka*, ed. G.P. Makogonnenko (Moscow: AN SSSR, 1974): 9–49.

Shaposhnikova, L.V. (ed.), *Muzei imeni Rerikha* (Moscow: Mezhdunarodnyi Tsentr Rerikhov, 2006).

Shatz, Marshall S., and Zimmerman, Judith E. (eds.), *Vekhi: Landmarks* (London–New York: Routledge, 1994).

Shklyar, I.V., "Formirovanie mirovozzrejia Antiokha Kantemira," in *XVIII vek, sbornik 5* (Moscow–Leningrad: Izdatelstvo AN SSSR, 1962), 129–152.

Shmeruk, Chine, *Dějiny literatury jidiš* (Olomouc: Votobia, 1996).

Siažik, Michal, "Charakteristické rysy bezpopovecké eschatologie," in *"Rýžoviště zlata a doly drahokamů…": Sborník pro Václava Huňáčka*, ed. Věra Lendělová and Michal Řoutil (Červený Kostelec: Pavel Mervart, 2006), 209–222.

Šiklová, Jiřina, "The Gray Zone and the Future of Dissent in Czechoslovakia," *Social Research* 57, 2 (1990): 347–63.

Sinicyna, N.V., *Odysea Maxima Řeka* (Červený Kostelec, 2013).

Širjajev, Boris, *Věčné světlo: Solovecké ostrovy v epoše GULAGu* (Červený Kostelec: Pavel Mervart, 2011).

Skalová, Hana (ed.), *Listy Ivana Hrozného* (Prague: SNKLHU, 1957).

Skovoroda, Hryhorij, *Rozmluva o moudrosti* (Praha: Vyšehrad, 1983).

Sládek, Karel, *Vladimír Solovjov: Mystik a prorok* (Olomouc: Refugium Velehrad-Roma, 2009).

Sládek, Karel et al., *O Filokalii: Kniha, hnutí, spiritualita* (Olomouc: Refugium Velehrad-Roma, 2013).

Sobková, Helena, *Kateřina Zaháňská* (Litomyšl and Prague: Paseka, 2007).

Sokolová, Františka (ed.), *Francisko Skoryna v díle českých slavistů* (Prague: Národní knihovna-Slovanská knihovna, 1992).

Soušek, Zdeněk (ed.), *Knihy tajemství a moudrosti: Mimobiblické židovské spisy*, 3 vols. (Prague: Vyšehrad, 1998–2013).

Solzhenitsyn, Alexander, "Repentance and Self-Limitation as Categories of National Life," in *From Under the Rubble* (Washington D.C.: Regnery Gateway, 1981), 117–118.

Spencer, Terence, *Fair Greece, Sad Relic: Literary Philhellenism from Shakespeare to Byron* (Athens: Denise Harvey & Company (1986).

Spengler, Oswald, *The Decline of the West*, trans. Charles F. Atkinson (New York: A. Knopf, 1992).

Špidlík, Tomáš, *Ruská idea: Jiný pohled na člověka* (Velehrad: Refugium Velehrad-Roma, 1996).

Špidlík, Tomáš, *Spiritualita křesťanského Východu* (Olomouc: Refugium Velehrad-Roma, 2002).

Stanton, Leonard J., *The Optina Pustyn Monastery in Russian Literary Imagination* (New York: Peter Lang International Academic Publishers, 1995).

Stellner, František, and Soběhart, Radek, "Rusko jako hrozba? Vytváření negativního obrazu Ruska u české veřejnosti v letech 1848–1849" in *19. století v nás: Modely, instituce a reprezentace, které přetrvaly*, ed. Milan Řepa (Prague: Historický ústav, 2008).

Stennik, Ju. V., "Pravoslavie i masonstvo v Rossii XVIII veka," *Russkaya literatura* 1 (1995): 76–92.

Stravinsky, Igor, *Chronicle of My Life* (London: V. Gollancz, 1936).

Švec, Luboš, Macura, Vladimír, and Štol, Pavel, *Dějiny pobaltských zemí* (Prague: Nakladatelství Lidové noviny, 1996).

Szyjkowsky, Marjan, *Polská účast v českém národním obrození*, 3 vols (Prague: Slovanský ústav, 1931–1946).

Tazbir, Janusz, *Protokoly sionských mudrců: Pravda nebo podvrh?* (Olomouc: Votobia, 1996).

Téra, Michal, "Chazaři: Stručný životopis jedné zapomenuté říše," in *Kulturní, duchovní a etnické kořeny Ruska: Vlivy a souvislosti*, ed. Hanuš Nykl (Červený Kostelec: Pavel Mervart, 2006), 15–36.

Téra, Michal, *Perun: Bůh hromovládce* (Červený Kostelec: Pavel Mervart, 2009).

Trávníček, Jiří (ed.), *V kleštích dějin: Střední Evropa jako pojem a problém* (Brno: Host, 2009).

Trubachov, Andronik, *Obo mne ne pechaltes: Zhizneopisanie svyashchennika Pavla Florenskogo* (Moscow: Izdatelskii sovet Russkoi pravoslavnoi tserkvi, 2007).

Tschižewskij, Dmitrij, *Geschichte der altrussischen Literatur: Kiever Epoche* (Frankfurt a.M.: V. Klostermann, 1948).

Tschižewskij, Dmitrij, *A History of Ukrainian Literature: From the 11th to the End of the 19th Century* (Littleton, Colo.: Ukrainian Academic Press, 1975).

Trepavlov, V.V., *"Belyi tsar": Obraz monarkha i predstavlenie o poddanstve u narodov Rossii XV–XVII veka* (Moscow: Vostochnaia literatura, 2007).

Třeštík, Dušan, *Mýty kmene Čechů: Tři studie ke "starým pověstem českým"* (Prague: NLN, 2003).

Ulitskaya, Ludmila, *Daniel Stein, Interpreter: A Novel in Documents* (New York: Overlook Press, 2011).

Uspensky, Boris A., "Schism and Cultural Conflict in the Seventeenth Century," in *Seeking God: The Recovery of Religious Identity in Orthodox Russia, Ukraine and Georgia*, ed. Stephen K. Batalden (DeKalb: Northern Illinois University Press, 1993), 110–127.

Uspensky, Boris, "Tsar i Bog: Semioticheskie aspekty sakralizatsii monarkha v Rossii," in *Semiotika, istorii, semiotika kultury* (Moscow: Gnozis, 1994), 110–218.

Valerov, A. V., *Novgorod i Pskov: Ocherki Politicheskoi Istorii Severo-Zapadnoi Rusi XI–XIV Vekov* (St. Petersburg: Aleteiia, 2004).

Váňa, Zdeněk, *Svět slovanských bohů a démonů* (Prague: Panorama, 1990).

Vašica, Josef, *Literární památky epochy velkomoravské* (Prague: Vyšehrad, 1996).

Veber, Václav (ed.), *Ruská a ukrajinská emigrace v ČSR v letech 1918–1945* (Prague: Karolinum, 1996).

Vershinina, I. Ya., *Rannie balety Stravinskogo* (Moscow: Nauka, 1967).

Veselovskij, A. N., *Razyskanija v oblasti russkich duchovnych stichov*, vols I–XXIV (Saint Petersburg: Imperatorskoj Akad. Nauk, 1879-1891).

Viskovatá, Janina, *Ruské motivy v tvorbě Julia Zeyera* (Prague: Slovanský ústav, 1932).

Vlček, Radomír, *Ruský panslavismus: Realita a fikce* (Prague: Historický ústav AV ČR, 2002).

Voloshin, Maximilian, *Istoriia moei dushi* (Moscow: Agraf, 1999).

Voráček, Emil, *Eurasijství v ruském politickém myšlení: Osudy jednoho z porevolučních ideových směrů ruské meziválečné emigrace.* (Prague: Set out, 2004).

Vydra, Zbyněk, *Židovská otázka v carském Rusku 1881-1906: Vláda, Židé a anti-semitismus* (Pardubice: Univerzita Pardubice, 2006).

Weinlick, John R., *Hrabě Zinzendorf* (Prague: Stefanos, 2000).

Werner, Michael, and Zimmermann, Bénédicte, "Beyond Comparison: Histoire Croisée and the Challenge of Reflexivity," *History and Theory* 45, no. 1 (February 2006): 30–50.

Wilson, Andrew, *The Ukrainians: Unexpected Nation* (New Haven: Yale University Press, 2000).

Winter, Eduard, *Bernard Bolzano a jeho kruh* (Brno: Akord, 1935).

Winter, Eduard, *Josefinismus a jeho dějiny* (Prague: Jelínek, 1945).

Yakovenko, Natalia, "Choice of Name versus Choice of Path: The Names of Ukrainian Territories from the Late Sixteenth to the Late Seventeenth Century," in Georgiy Kasianov and Philipp Ther (eds.),*A Laboratory of Translational History: Ukraine and Recent Ukrainian Historiography*, (Budapest: CEU Press, 2009), 117–148.

Zadražil, Ladislav (ed.), *Záhadný Gogol* (Prague: Odeon, 1973).

Zástěrová, Bohumila et al., *Dějiny Byzance* (Prague: Academia, 1992).

Zavalishin, Vyacheslav, *Early Soviet Writers* (New York: Frederick A. Praeger Publishers, 1958).

Zenkovsky, Serge, *Russkoje staroobriadchestvo: Dukhovnye dvizheniia XVII veka* (Munich: Wilhelm Fink Verlag, 1970).

Zilynskyj, Bohdan, "Mychajlo Hruševsky and His Relations to Bohemia and to the Czech Scholarship," *Acta Universitatis Carolinae–Studia Territorialia* 1, no. 2 (2001): 185–200.

Ziolkowski, Margaret (ed.), *Tale of Boiarynia Morozova: A Seventeenth-Century Religious Life* (Lanham, Md.: Lexington Books).

Zychowicz, Tateusz, *Josefat Kuncevič* (Prague: Zvon, 1995).

3/ Author's Works on Russia and Related Themes

(In chronological order, excludes translations and journalism)

Putna, Martin C., "Apollón a Dionýsos u Vjačeslava Ivanova," *Volné sdružení českých rusistů* 1991, 7, 46–49.

Putna, Martin C., "Duchovní profil Alexandra Solženicyna," *Souvislosti* 2 (1991), 4, 59–63.

Putna, Martin C., "Alexandr Solženicyn a Židé," *Světová literatura* 38, 5 (1992): 72–77.

Putna, Martin C., "Staromladé bloudění. Z duchovně-politických dějin emigrace – Berďajev, Karsavin a porevoluční hnutí," *Volné sdružení českých rusistů* 1993, 9, 59–61.

Putna, Martin C., and Zadražilová, Miluše, *Rusko mimo Rusko: Dějiny a kultura ruské emigrace 1917-1991*, 2 vols (Brno: Petrov, 1993–1994).

Putna, Martin C., and Zadražilová, Miluše (eds.), *U řek babylonských: Antologie ruské emigrační poezie* (Prague: Torst, 1995).

Putna, Martin C., "Stichy duchovní aneb Dokumenty ruské lidové religiozity a Georgij Fedotov", *Souvislosti* 6 (1995), 1, 49–56.

Putna, Martin C., "Svatá hora Athos ruskýma a českýma očima," *Souvislosti* 7 (1996), 1, 87–101.

Putna, Martin C., "Dějiny ducha staré Rusi in brevissimo," *Světová literatura* 41 (1996), 1, 126–175.

Putna, Martin C., "Sofia, Sofie, (my všichni) sofiologové," in Martin C. Putna, *My poslední křesťané* (Prague: Torst, 1999), 219–256.

Putna, Martin C., "Řecká křesťanská literatura a české národní obrození," *Teologický sborník* 6 (2000), 4, 63–76.

Putna, Martin C., *Órigenés z Alexandrie* (Prague: Torst, 2001).

Putna, Martin C. (ed.), *Karel VI Schwarzenberg: Torzo díla* (Prague: Torst, 2007).

Putna, Martin C., "Zánik západu jakožto heslo, svědectví o době a kniha na průsečíku," in Oswald Spengler: *Zánik Západu: Obrysy morfologie světových dějin* (Prague: Academia, 2010), 733–757.

Putna, Martin C., "Překlad a výklad Slávy dcery z panslavistického mýtu do kulturní historie", in Kollár, Jan, *Slávy dcera: Báseň lyricko-epická v pěti zpěvích*, with commentary by Martin C. Putna (Prague: Academia, 2014).

INDEX

The index contains names of historical persons (including those of disputed historical authenticity), but not purely literary characters or mythological beings.

The **Václav Havel Series** aims to honor and extend the intellectual legacy of the dissident, playwright, philosopher, and president whose name it proudly bears. Prepared with Ivan M. Havel, and other personalities and institutions closely associated with Václav Havel, such as the Václav Havel Library and Forum 2000, the series focuses on modern thought and the contemporary world – encompassing history, politics, art, architecture, and ethics. While the works often concern the Central European experience, the series – like Havel himself – focuses on issues that affect humanity across the globe.

Published titles

Jiří Přibáň, *The Defence of Constitutionalism: The Czech Question in Postnational Europe*

Matěj Spurný, *Making the Most of Tomorrow: A Laboratory of Socialist Modernity in Czechoslovakia*

Jacques Rossi, *Fragmented Lives: Chronicles of the Gulag*

Jiří Přibáň & Karel Hvížďala, *In Quest of History: On Czech Statehood and Identity*

Miroslav Petříček, *Philosophy en noir: Rethinking Philosophy after the Holocaust*

Petr Roubal, *Spartakiads: The Politics of Physical Culture in Communist Czechoslovakia*

Josef Šafařík, *Letters to Melin: A Discourse on Science and Progress*

Martin C. Putna, *Rus – Ukraine – Russia: Scenes from the Cultural History of Russian Religiosity*

Forthcoming

Olivier Mongin, *The Urban Condition: The City in a Globalizing World*

Jan Sokol, *Power, Money, Law*

Ivan M. Havel et al., *Letters from Olga*